If Not Empire,
What?

A Survey of the Bible

Praise for *If Not Empire, What?*
***

"It turns out there is an alternative to empire. Read this book for instructions for resisting the presumption that empire is inevitable."
—Stanley Hauerwas, Gilbert T. Rove Professor Emeritus of Divinity and Law, Duke University.

"Friesen and Stoner's book is a very helpful tool for beginners to start the process of engaging the real struggles that take place in the Bible between the people of God and 'empire.' So many pay little attention to the worlds that generated those texts and such an introduction is vitally necessary. Their enthusiasm is infectious! I hope it will inspire a new generation to take up the joyous discipline of authentic entry into the narratives that make up our biblical inheritance."
—Wes Howard-Brook, author, *"Come Out, My People!" God's Call Out of Empire in the Bible and Beyond;* instructor of Theology and Religious Studies, Seattle University.

"This book shows how giving careful attention to scripture inspires a counter-cultural vision of Christian faithfulness. Examining the Bible book-by-book, Friesen and Stoner illuminate the many ways the biblical story, in diverse cultural settings throughout its long history, consistently challenges dominant narratives of greed, violence and power. The sheer number of passages examined here is impressive and helpful. Even more important is seeing firsthand the Bible's capacity to unmask the false promises of empire in our day. I hope many congregations will take the opportunity to learn from and with this resource."
—Jewel Gingerich Longenecker, Associate Dean for Leadership Education, Anabaptist Mennonite Biblical Seminary.

"Our way of life is an endgame and we must be about embodying alternatives. This book seeks to resource that task by nurturing biblical literacy. The authors refer to it as a 'book written by laypersons for laypersons,' but the truth is, we are *all* laypersons when it comes to resisting and transforming the imperial values and structures that inhabit and surround us. That is why reading scripture together with eyes wide open to our world is so urgent, and this project so welcome."
—Ched Myers, author, *Binding the Strong Man: A Political Reading of Mark's Story,* Founder of Bartimaeus Cooperative Ministries.

"For far too long, Christians have remained blissfully ignorant of how much the Bible is a text about *resisting*—not kowtowing—to empire. It's time for a clear and accessible book that will help overcome the ignorance. With this book, we have just what we need. Friesen and Stoner unveil the actual message of the Bible—turn from Babylon and toward the Lamb—and give us tools that will empower a Bible-like resistance today."
—Ted Grimsrud, Professor of Theology and Peace Studies, Eastern Mennonite University.

"*If Not Empire, What?* can help any teacher, preacher or discussion group leader quickly spot the significance of empire and its alternative in any part of the Bible. And it can help any group daring to wrestle with the authors' pressing question: what does it mean to form a society now that is just, liberating and sustainable?"
—Dorcas Miller Lehman, Campus Pastor and Guidance Counselor, Lancaster Mennonite High School

"Friesen and Stoner offer this gift to the global church. Written unapologetically from within the belly of empire, they proclaim the vision of another Empire— God's Empire functioning through the agency of the church. They wrestle with the rough texts and present a coherent, fresh and popular reading of the Bible, from Genesis to Revelation. Its simplicity amplifies the profound academic integrity that undergirds their telling of God's story. It is a resource for every teacher and preacher. It can serve as a consultant in every effort to take the Bible seriously as we engage our own worlds of inequality, oppression and the insidious violence of empires that pervade our lives."
—Robert J. Suderman, Secretary of the Peace Commission of Mennonite World Conference.

"We need to dive into the Bible and understand the empire in which Jesus lived and how he interacted with it. Then, we need to consider what it means to follow the revolutionary Jesus today. Stoner and Friesen have written a manifesto to the church, an invitation to join a holy uprising. It is about turning the world upside-down so that the last are first and the first are last, the mighty are cast from their thrones and the lowly are lifted up. What are we waiting for?"
—Shane Claiborne, author, activist and founder of The Simple Way community.

If Not Empire, What?

A Survey of the Bible

Berry Friesen
John K. Stoner

www.bible-and-empire.net
CreateSpace
December 2014

International Standard Book Number: 978-0692344781
For Library of Congress information, contact the authors.

Bible quotations unless otherwise noted are taken from the
New Revised Standard Version (NRSV), copyright 1989,
Division of Christian Education of the National Council of the Churches of Christ
in the United States of America.

Cover design by Judith Rempel Smucker.

For information or to correspond with the authors,
send email to **info@bible-and-empire.net**

Bound or electronic copies of this book may be obtained from
www.amazon.com. The entire content also is available in PDF format
reader at **www.bible-and-empire.net**. For the sake of concordance with
our PDF edition, the page numbering in this book begins with the title page.

Published in cooperation with
CreateSpace, DBA On-Demand Publishing, LLC
December 2014

***

Naboth owned a vineyard beside the palace grounds;
the king asked to buy it.
Naboth refused, saying, "This land is my ancestral inheritance;
YHWH would not want me to sell my heritage."

This angered the king.
Not only had Naboth refused to sell, he had invoked his god as his reason.
The king's wife told him to cheer up.
"You're king of Israel," she said. "I'll get you Naboth's vineyard."

The queen approached the leaders of Naboth's town.
"The nation is under threat," she confided;
"the king's security staff suspect Naboth.
He must be killed without involving the king."

The town's leaders convened an official inquiry
and summoned Naboth to appear.
Two witnesses accused him of disloyalty to god-and-the-king.
So the townspeople killed Naboth with stones.

When the queen heard Naboth was dead, she said to the king:
"Remember that guy who wouldn't sell his vineyard?
Apparently he died and his property is available."
So the king took possession of Naboth's vineyard.

Then Elijah the Tishbite heard the word of YHWH, saying:
"Go to Naboth's vineyard;
there you will find the king, who has taken it for himself.
Confront him about his violence and his greed."

Authors' paraphrase of 1 Kings 21:1–19

Table of Contents

Preface 7

PART I: The Worldview of Biblical Writers 11
1.   A Particular God 13
2.   The Voice of YHWH 19
3.   A Heavenless Faith 22
4.   The Story of a People 25
5.   A Pilgrimage of Nations 29
6.   Resistance to Empire 33
7.   A Good Society 39

PART II: The First Testament Writings 43
8.   In the Beginning 46
9.   A Subversive God 55
10. Life Beyond the Empire (Part A) 71
11. Possessing the Land (or not) 89
12. Israel Like the Nations 99
13. Speaking Inconvenient Truth 124
14. Finding YHWH in Babylon 151
15. Collaboration with the Empire 168
16. Beyond State, Tribe or Ritual 185
17. Living Wisely (Part A) 201
18. Despair, Praise, Exultation 212

PART III: The Second Testament Writings 217
19. Who is this Man Called Jesus? 219
20. Jesus, One with YHWH 239
21. A New Political Community 248
22. Life Beyond the Empire (Part B) 268
23. Living Wisely (Part B) 319
24. Steadfast Resistance and Faithful Witness 324
25. So What? 336

PART IV. Praying Biblical Texts 341

Bibliography 347

Discussion Questions: 42, 88, 149, 200, 216, 246, 267, 322, 339

Book Finder: Number refers to page where discussion begins.

First Testament

Genesis 1–11	46	Ecclesiastes	201
Genesis 12–50	55	Song of Solomon	207
Exodus 1–15	56	Isaiah 1–39	132
Exodus 16–40	72	Isaiah 40–55	161
Leviticus	77	Isaiah 56–66	187
Numbers	80	Jeremiah	142
Deuteronomy	84	Lamentations	212
Joshua	90	Ezekiel	152
Judges	92	Daniel 1–6	157
Ruth	190	Daniel 7–12	197
1 Samuel 1–12	96	Hosea	129
1 Samuel 13–31	103	Joel	194
2 Samuel	103	Amos	128
1 Kings 1–10	103	Obadiah	127
1 Kings 11–22	108	Jonah	192
2 Kings	108	Micah	135
1 Chronicles	122	Nahum	139
2 Chronicles	123	Habakkuk	140
Ezra	170	Zephaniah	137
Nehemiah	178	Haggai	172
Esther	165	Zechariah 1–8	173
Job	203	Zechariah 9–14	196
Psalms	213	Malachi	182
Proverbs	208		

Second Testament

Matthew, Mark, Luke	219	1 Timothy	314
John	239	2 Timothy	297
Acts of the Apostles	248	Titus	315
Romans	289	Philemon	282
1 Corinthians	274	Hebrews	303
2 Corinthians	287	James	319
Galatians	270	1 Peter	311
Ephesians	299	2 Peter	317
Philippians	293	1, 2, 3 John	307
Colossians	283	Jude	306
1 Thessalonians	273	Revelation to John	324
2 Thessalonians	309		

***

As authors, we are simply asking people to read the Bible
the way it was written—as a collection of arguments
about life, love and power.
Especially, we ask people to pay attention to the big argument,
whether God created the world to work by the imperial paradigm
of domination and homicidal power or by
the peasant-and-commoner vision of compassion and community.

***

Preface

Most people simply want "a life:" loving relationships, satisfying work, a creative outlet and occasional encounters with the spiritual dimension of the cosmos. They do not want to bother with the empire, its devices and deceptions. Life is too sweet, too fragile, too short to waste on such matters. Or so it seems, at least in our corner, the United States of America (USA).

Yet trends within our era require us to pay attention to where the empire is taking us. We live in natural environments with shrinking space for habitation, in market economies that consume our future while giving back less and less, and in political entities that treat everyday people as somehow suspect. War, deception and arrangements that enrich the few at the expense of the many have become routine. The policies of the empire drive these trends, even while its leaders claim to be our salvation.

And so we must deal with the empire and its way of running the world; ignoring it is no longer an option. We can give ourselves to the imperial project and try our best to swim toward the top of its destructive tide, or we can accommodate part of it while maintaining a foothold in another reality. Or we can join the resistance and create an alternative.

By "empire" we mean a system of coordinated control that enriches itself through overwhelming socio-economic and military power at the global level. An empire justifies its violence and greed by morally powerful stories about evil and by potent myths and religious beliefs related to divine purpose and the tragic complexity of life. It portrays itself as the primary source of security and peace in the world.

The biblical saga introduces another understanding of power for organizing human life, one that operates by truth-telling and compassion, forgiveness and opportunities to try again, empowerment at the base and varied ways of coping with the challenges of living. Jesus called this multi-voiced, nonviolent yet pro-active approach the kingdom, or empire, of God.

The story of Jesus and his message of the kingdom of God has been, for good and ill, the most influential story of human history. It illuminates the story of YHWH, the god of the Hebrew people (throughout—though not exclusively—we use this name YHWH, which signifies a refusal to be named, and "god" as a generic term signifying a being or thing that is worshipped). But this story is not nearly as religious as that description makes it seem. As it turns out, Jesus and his god are all about saving the world (John 3:17), not metaphysically or by miraculous intervention in human affairs, but through communities of people whose ways of living on Earth are just, liberating and sustainable. The process of finding and following those ways of living is what we mean by "political."

In our time, such communities challenge three commonly-held assumptions that are leading us toward the destruction of human life on Earth. The first is that marketplace indicators are virtually laws of nature, like gravity. The second is that of all available options, an imperial arrangement of power is the best way to organize the world and avoid chaos. The third is that life for individuals after death is what is really important; life on Earth is only of passing significance.

The Bible speaks to these assumptions in a variety of voices and not all agree with one another. Yet on balance, the biblical message subverts these three assumptions. It insists the market must serve humanity, not we the market. It rejects the claim that the violence and domination of the empire lead to a just, liberating and sustainable life. It promises not immortality in heaven or hell for each individual, but hope for resurrection after death to a renewed Earth.

In short, this book is for those who have been disillusioned by the empire's way of running the world and are curious about what insights the Bible may contain on how to think about, organize and act collectively to restore a just and sustainable life on Earth.

Part I introduces the theology and worldview of the biblical writers. Some of their assumptions were very different from those religious people hold today. To understand and appreciate what they wrote, we need to bring their assumptions back into play. Parts II and III provide surveys of the Hebrew and Christian texts. We provide a bit of context and highlight passages relevant to the question of how we organize ourselves politically. Part IV consists of prayers found in the biblical texts. Prayer is the voice of humanity's deepest hopes and spiritual life. These texts are offered as an aid to our understanding of what we have been given in the biblical texts and what is possible in human communication with the divine.

This book is written for at least two audiences. The first is the Millennial Generation—those who will give leadership to the world as the deadly consequences of the current empire become too clear, too horrendous to ignore. In our effort to write a text relevant to their challenge, we have neither assumed biblical faith nor attempted to persuade readers to embrace such a faith. Instead, we have simply tried to highlight texts that are relevant to the task of forming a political community outside the ideology of empire.

Second, we write for Christians, especially those who have just about given up trying to make sense of the moral offenses and intellectual contradictions they find in the Bible.

For both audiences, we write as lay-followers of Jesus who have read and studied the Bible within Mennonite congregations. Our desire is the recovery of the faith of Jesus of Nazareth. In the various christianities of our world today, the character and content of Jesus' faith has been distorted and domesticated. How this has come to pass is a tragic and troubling story that we do not attempt to tell or critique here. Instead, we want to facilitate a fresh encounter with Jesus, the man who proclaimed and embodied the kingdom of God, a political path that undermined and delegitimized the claims of empire.

Our work together as authors grew out of our collaboration in 1040 for Peace, an action group calling for conscientious reflection on the fact that we are supporting imperialism and war through payment of the federal income tax. Resistance to that tax—or any other act of resistance to the empire—can only be sustained if rooted in a larger, positive vision. This book reflects our attempt to describe that vision as found in the Bible. John took the lead in drafting chapters 19, 23 and 24; Berry took the lead in drafting the other chapters.

We survey each text included in the Protestant Bible, including those that say little about political community or ways of organizing society. This approach yields fewer words on the teachings of Jesus than they deserve, but provides an introduction to the broad and varied scope of the Bible's concerns and positions Jesus' teachings within the tradition out of which they came. Though we touch on all the biblical texts, we do not claim to have discussed all the significant themes of those texts. Instead, we focus on how each speaks to the political dimensions of life: the framing of public issues, how collective action is organized, what purposes and tactics are judged to be legitimate and how power is exercised. These were core questions for biblical authors, just as they are for politically engaged people in our time.

Each of the authors listed in the Bibliography has contributed to our understanding of the Bible's discussion of public life. Through comments on drafts of our text, others have contributed to our writing: Kathleen Kern, Dorcas Lehman, Sue Swartz, Wes Bergen, Norman Lowry, Peder Wiegner, Jacob Lester, Jordan Luther, Jacob Landis and Myron Schrag. Our wives, Janet Stoner and Sharon Friesen, have been our most frequent discussion partners. Margaret High has edited our writing; Dennis Rivers has coordinated the publication process. We thank one and all.

We urge you to find at least one discussion partner to join you in reading this book. The discussions you have together, and the collective actions you join because of your tentative conclusions, will contribute to the political alternative we need to create. To aid your process of discussion and searching, we offer discussion questions throughout this text, the first of which you might want to see now on page 42.

PART I:
The Worldview of Biblical Authors

In the Bible we find the oldest writings most of us will ever read. Although there is much controversy about how old the oldest texts are, many scholars agree that some of the texts were written nearly 3,000 years ago (soon after 1,000 BCE). It is difficult for contemporary readers to make sense of writings and stories that old. To ease the difficulty a bit, this opening section discusses seven aspects of the biblical worldview that are likely to be different from the reader's worldview.

Of course, it is presumptuous to speak of "the biblical worldview" as if it were one thing. Among the scores of authors who contributed to the Bible, there were significant differences in how they perceived the world to work. Nevertheless, there is value in identifying some of the assumptions many of them shared with one another, but perhaps not with us. By naming those here at the start, we improve the reader's chances for translating what s/he reads into relevant content.

Much of the controversy related to biblical history relates to which stories are legend and which are historically accurate. Many people of faith believe all the stories from the beginning of Genesis are "truly historical." Other believers (as well as skeptics) see myths, allegories and legends in the Bible and describe a story as historically accurate only when it is corroborated by evidence from outside the text. Using this latter approach, stories further back than the Israelite kings who reigned 2,850 years ago (around 850 BCE) are likely legends or allegories communicating important understandings or ideas rather than histories describing actual people and events.

However one views this, it is important to recognize that ancient texts are themselves historical documents and evidence of something valuable, even if not historical accuracy. This does not mean we must take them at face value, but it does ask us to regard them with respect. At least some of what those ancient writers said may be useful to us.

Discussion questions related to Part I are found on page 42.

The biblical story, focused as it is on one particular group of people, features various individuals and events displayed against the backdrop of empire. Following is a partial list of important events along with their approximate date of occurrence and an identification of the dominant empire at the time. The period covered by this list (900 BCE to 96 CE) is nearly 1,000 years.

Event	Date	Empire
Two kingdoms (Ephraim & Judah) in Canaan	900	---
Ephraim under King Jehu becomes vassal state	830	Assyria
Judah under King Ahaz becomes vassal state	733	Assyria
Ephraim invaded; northmost provinces annexed	732	Assyria
Samaria destroyed; Ephraim's existence ends	722	Assyria
Towns of Judah destroyed; siege of Jerusalem	701	Assyria
Babylon destroys Nineveh; Josiah king of Judah	612	Babylon
Nebuchadnezzar's army destroys Jerusalem	586	Babylon
Jews exiled to Babylon are authorized to return	538	Persia
Second temple in Jerusalem dedicated	516	Persia
Emperor gives Ezra ecclesial and civil authority	457	Persia
Alexander the Great annexes Palestine	332	Greece
Seleucids defeat Ptolemies, control Palestine	200	Greece
Maccabees expel Greeks; Hasmonean era starts	165	Greece
Pompey annexes Palestine	63	Rome
Jesus of Nazareth born	4-3	Rome
Jesus of Nazareth executed for sedition	30	Rome
Jerusalem council on Gentile believers	50	Rome
Paul of Tarsus executed, probably for sedition	65	Rome
Jerusalem and the second temple destroyed	70	Rome
Persecution of Christians by Emperor Domitian	89-96	Rome

1. A Particular God

It is difficult to have a conversation about "god" because that word means different things to different people. When talking about god, how can we be sure we mean the same thing?

In conversation, we might say god is love, god is merciful, god is powerful. If we share that much and understand those words similarly, then the conversation gets a little easier. Though differences in how we express our understandings of god will almost certainly persist, we are apt to quickly agree that it does not make sense to argue about them. As people frequently say, "We're all guessing."

Usually in such conversations, people assume there is just one god. This assumption has been a bedrock teaching of the three great religions we in the West know best. Judaism is generally credited with being the first monotheistic religion in human history. Christianity follows that line of teaching, but complicates matters by insisting this god encompasses three persons: Father, Son and Holy Spirit. Islam is strictly monotheistic.

Our conversations about god could be illustrated by the story of the blind men and the elephant. Each describes the part he experiences. The man touching the legs says the elephant is like a tree, the man touching its side says it resembles a rough wall, and the man holding the tail says it reminds him of a rope. But of course, it's all the same elephant.

This understanding—that there is only one god who is ill-defined and described in different ways by different people—fits nicely with the ideology of empire. An empire seeks to position itself as "the one" experienced in various ways by various people, but whose unified power benefits everyone. Its goals of domination are more likely to encounter resistance in a world where there are various gods whose differences generate different worldviews, imaginative alternatives for organizing the world, and resistance to empire and its unitary ways. (For a fuller discussion of empire, see chapter 6.)

Mark Van Steenwyck elaborates another aspect of the potential synergy between empire's ideology and our ideas about god. "Imperialism is about ordering creation," he writes. "It is about obedience. It is about mastery." An empire finds it useful for society to imagine a god that acts in such a manner. "He is distant, floating high above the world, refusing to be dirtied by it. He is the supreme hierarch, the ruler of all." [1]   Van Steenwyck suggests we instead think of god "as a creative, feral spring from which our own lives pour. We encounter this God in the wild places where life is unfettered. We encounter this God when we name and let go (repent) of those structures that trammel life and subjugate people and the land." [2]

With this background in mind, we are ready to identify two ways biblical writers thought about god that are different from the ways we are likely to think about god.

First, during biblical times, each group of people or locality had its own god or gods. As people moved from place to place, it was understood that they came under the authority of different gods. These were not similar versions of the same divine being; they were very different one from the other, thus accounting for big differences in human cultures. Some required human sacrifices, some did not. Some rewarded this behavior and some that.

The god worshipped by the Hebrew people is introduced to readers by stories of human encounters with the divine. This god told a Chaldean man named Abram (later Abraham) to leave his father's house at the headwaters of the River Euphrates and "go to the land that I will show you." An Egyptian named Moses met this same god in a burning bush out in the wilderness where it told Moses: "I have observed the misery of my people who are in Egypt . . . and I have come down to deliver them from the Egyptians, and to bring them up out of that land to a good and broad land, a land flowing with milk and honey" (Ex. 3:7–8). In both of these formative encounters, this god first identified with a particular place: Canaan. This is entirely consistent with the ancient worldview.

Moses said he needed to give the Hebrew people a name for the god in whose authority he made demands of the Pharaoh. The god answered, "I am who I am." In Hebrew, this enigmatic answer was

---

[1]   Van Steenwyck, *The Unkingdom of God,* 115.
[2]   Ibid., 119.

rendered by the name YHWH. It is the name we use throughout our discussion of First Testament texts to refer to the god of Abraham and Moses. YHWH is also the god of Jesus. In our discussion of Second Testament texts, we will occasionally use "YHWH" and occasionally "God," which is the translation of the term used in the original Greek manuscripts.

The notion that there is only one god developed over time. The early writings reflected the view that though there were many gods, the Israelites had been called by and had covenanted with a particular god, YHWH, who did things differently than the others. Thus, Psalm 16 tells us YHWH does not desire "drink offerings of blood" and that those who choose another god "multiply their sorrows" (Ps. 16:4). Other psalms speak in a similar vein. "There is none like you among the gods, O Lord, nor are there any works like yours" (Ps. 86:8). "For I know that the LORD is great; our LORD is above all gods" (Ps. 135:5). "I give thanks, O LORD, with my whole heart; before the gods I sing your praise" (Ps. 138:1).

Later writings insist there is only one god: "I am the first and I am the last; besides me there is no god" (Isa. 44:6). Other so-called gods were "like scarecrows in a cucumber field" (Jer. 10:5), hunks of mulberry wood overlaid with gold and set on a pedestal (Isa. 40:19–20). "It cannot move from its place. If one cries out to it, it does not answer or save anyone from trouble" (Isa. 46:7).

Still, even when mocking other gods, biblical writers did not dismiss their power entirely. Even idols made of mulberry wood have a surprising capacity to shape people who worship them:

> The idols of the nations are silver and gold, the work of human hands. They have mouths, but they do not speak; they have eyes, but they do not see; they have ears, but they do not hear; and there is no breath in their mouths. Those who make them and all who trust in them *shall become like them.* (Ps. 135:18, emphasis added)

This tendency for us to resemble what we worship may have prompted Paul, the Second Testament author, to nuance his assertion that "there is no God but one" with the acknowledgement that on Earth, there are in fact "many gods and many lords" (1 Cor. 8:5). "For our struggle is not [only] against the enemies of blood and flesh, but against the rulers, against the authorities, against the cosmic powers of this present darkness, against the spiritual forces of evil in the heavenly places" (Eph. 6:12).

Thus, in contrast to many of us, biblical writers did not assume all peoples are worshipping the same god known by different names. In their view, it always was necessary to ask, "What is the name of the god you worship, and what does this god ask of you?"

Biblical writers made a second assumption very different from ours: when describing YHWH, they did not start by identifying attractive traits and values and then attributing those to YHWH. Instead, they reported historical events in which the Hebrew people had experienced a surprising and remarkable turn of events in which they sensed YHWH had been present. Then they reflected on what those events said about this god's character.

As Israel's history continued, many events occurred that were understood to display the character of YHWH. Some revealed YHWH to be a mighty warrior. When Pharaoh's army was swamped and drowned in its pursuit of the Israelite people across the Red Sea, the prophet Miriam sang: "Sing to the LORD, for he has triumphed gloriously; horse and rider he has thrown into the sea" (Ex. 15:21). Some revealed YHWH to be a passionate being who hated evil and became angry when the Hebrew people worshipped other gods: "For [YHWH] your God is a devouring fire, a jealous God" (Deut. 4:24). Other events revealed YHWH's concern for individuals who had been marginalized by the disappointments of life: "YHWH gives the barren woman a home, making her the joyous mother of children" (Ps. 113:9).

As we read how authors understood YHWH to be part of particular events, it should not surprise us that some interpretations flatly contradict others. One of the most dramatic examples of this is the Assyrian Empire's invasion of Judah, which **Isaiah** portrays as ending in YHWH's victorious deliverance and **Micah** as ending in disastrous judgment. There are many differences in perspective, especially between the defenders of Israel's Davidic dynasty and the prophets who sharply criticized its attempt to be like other nations. Indeed, a case can be made that biblical texts provide multiple versions of YHWH. This difficulty is inescapable with a theology and worldview like the Hebrews, which insisted YHWH is revealed primarily through the unfolding of history.

What is most important to understand here at the beginning is that for biblical writers, YHWH defines and discloses him/herself through specific people and events. *YHWH is not a god we create out of mulberry wood or through philosophical thought.* This assumption carries throughout the Bible and reaches its climax in the Second Testament where "by close attention to Jesus himself we are invited to discover, perhaps for the first time, just who the creator and covenant God was and is all along." [3] Sylvia Keesmaat and Brian Walsh put it this way: "From a biblical perspective, truth is not a correspondence between ideas and facts. Truth is embodied in a person." [4]

Admittedly, some accounts of biblical writers are myths or legends. In such stories, it is much easier to portray YHWH as acting decisively and dramatically than in stories tethered to historical fact. So it is important for the reader of the Bible to hold this question in her/his mind: am I reading an historical account or a myth/legend? Often, we cannot be sure, but the exercise makes us more careful about the conclusions we reach.

Finally, as is obvious by now, biblical writers understood YHWH's "strong hand and outstretched arm" (Ps. 136:12) to be exercised from time to time in harsh punishment. In their view, divine punishment was not the arbitrary decision of a capricious being; *instead, it was the natural and inevitable consequence of wrong-doing.* When the judicial system became corrupted and the economic system rigged to help the rich get richer, then the cohesion and resourcefulness of society, as well as the resilience and virtue of its leaders, decline. Within life's relentless competition, deeply dysfunctional societies do not survive for long. When collapse or defeat occurs, modern observers will discuss it in terms of government policies, political leadership and economics. In contrast, biblical writers used language of divine punishment because the fallen society *had failed to comprehend how the world works.*

---

[3]   Borg & Wright, *The Meaning of Jesus,* 214-215.
[4]   Keesmaat and Walsh, *Colossians Remixed: Subverting the Empire,* 130.

"Whoever sows injustice will reap calamity" (Prov. 22:8); this is the biblical worldview. Paul used a similar metaphor to describe the natural consequences of our actions: "You reap whatever you sow. If you sow to your own flesh, you will reap corruption from the flesh; but it you sow to [YHWH], you will reap eternal life" (Gal. 6:8).

As we encounter these assumptions in the biblical texts, it is important to respect them enough to hear them out. This is no place for condescension; in some matters, we modern empiricists may be more primitive than the biblical writers.

Can we agree each culture is a power that conveys in myriad ways the "truth" of its version of history and its ideology? Can we agree that in some partial yet shared sense, we as individuals conform to an image—a collage of assumptions and attributes—our culture holds before us? If so, then is it such a stretch to say each culture has its own god, which people of that culture are inclined to worship? That even today many gods seek to rule Earth and its peoples? That they are not all ultimately the same god? That we must choose among them, not on the basis of abstractions, but on the basis of *what they ask of us and what they do in the world*?

If we can go that far, then we are ready to consider YHWH, the god of the Israelites, the god in whom Jesus of Nazareth put his faith and trust.

The Hebrews got to know their God by experiences, not by principals.

The framework is empire, Jesus used Kingdom but today empire is more understand

2. The Voice of YHWH

Frequently in the First Testament and occasionally in the Second, the authors quote YHWH. This is a problem for most readers because we are highly suspicious of human voices that claim to speak for the divine. In some settings, making that claim is evidence of mental illness.

Of course, we can describe YHWH's voice in the text as a literary device that enabled authors to elevate the authority of their words. At one level this is an accurate description of what was going on; authors who wrote in the name of YHWH got more attention than those who simply said, "In my opinion. . . ." But many Christians take the matter to another level; they believe that when we see "God said" in the text, we are about to read the actual words of YHWH, who inspired human authors to write them.

Each way of understanding "God said" has its place and sometimes both can be true, but not always. For example, chapter 28 in the book of **Jeremiah** famously tells about two prophets, Hananiah and Jeremiah, each of whom attempted to elevate the importance of what he said by claiming to speak for YHWH. The problem was that they disagreed: Hananiah said that a group of Jews exiled to Babylon would be allowed to return to Jerusalem after only two years, while Jeremiah said release would not happen until seventy years had passed. With time, the Israelite people learned that Jeremiah had been closer to the mark. Thus, he is remembered as having spoken the words of YHWH, not Hananiah.

Did Jeremiah get lucky or did YHWH inspire him to say what he did? That question cannot be answered head-on. In the end, how we regard "God said" will depend in part on whether or not we believe YHWH and humans communicate. Biblical writers obviously thought they did, but no one can offer scientific proof one way or the other.

The point of this chapter is to invite readers to hear YHWH's voice in the text *as the testimony of the author*. This third way of "hearing" the text does not preclude viewing "God said" as a literary device, nor does it preclude viewing what follows as YHWH's inspired words. But it helps reframe the matter in a way that gives the reader a reprieve from the inner debate about how to regard god-statements in the text. This reprieve gives the reader a better opportunity to "hear" what the text has to say.

What do we mean by "testimony of the author?" Perhaps an illustration will help.

As children, the authors of this book attended churches that had frequent testimony meetings. These were gatherings where the format was open and anyone could stand and speak briefly from personal experience about his or her metaphorical "walk with God." Generally, people would speak for several minutes about an issue in their lives: a land purchase, a dispute with a neighbor, a health issue, a change in assignment at work, or a business failure. Often, they would end their testimonies by asking listeners to pray that they would make the "right" decisions, "feel a clear sense of God's direction" or "receive the strength to endure."

Somewhere in the course of these testimonies, it was very common for speakers to say something such as this: "As I was praying about this, god told me . . ." Those audacious words seemed very natural in that setting and not at all a sign of mental illness.

What is particularly interesting was how our parents discussed those testimonies after the meeting was over. Some testimonies moved them deeply, and they took seriously the possibility that YHWH had been speaking to the entire congregation through the voice of the individual who had testified. But they seemed to regard other testimonies with skepticism. As children, we could not account for the difference.

Looking back now, we realize they were evaluating what they had heard within the context of what they had learned about YHWH, their personal experiences in life, what they knew of the character and intentions of the person speaking, and what they felt during the moments the testimony was being given. They absolutely believed the wisdom of YHWH could be communicated by the human voice, but they also knew of the human tendency to claim YHWH's voice for selfish purposes. So along with others in the congregation, they carried the responsibility of discerning which it was.

Assembling the Bible involved a similar discernment process over many years. When someone stood up and claimed YHWH had said something, the first listeners had to make a judgment, as did the scribes who later wrote those words on parchment, as did the readers of those parchments in subsequent years. Over time, these various judgments revealed a consensus view about whether or not YHWH had truly spoken through that particular human being. If yes, then the speaker's claim of "God said" was included in the Bible.

Each contemporary reader of the Bible continues that process of discernment. While the biblical text has been set for over 1,500 years, we can add our voices to those who regard a particular "God said" passage as truly the voice of YHWH. For followers of Jesus, his way of using the biblical text is given special authority. But as a first step, as one is getting acquainted with the Bible, the task is simply to read and "listen" to the author's testimony, including his impression of what YHWH said. Evaluation can come a bit later.

The voice of God could be called the word of God, not just scriptures. It is not confined to written scriptures John Stoner, See Sept '15 The Mennonite

3. A Heavenless Faith

The First Testament does not anticipate another life after this one. It describes "heaven" as YHWH's "habitation" (Deut. 26:15) and "dwelling place" (I Kings 8:30), but it never speaks of humans enjoying a second life there.

This is important because it tells us that even if we are convinced death marks the end of individual consciousness, *we still may be people of biblical faith.* Conversely, so long as we make biblical faith dependent on a belief in an afterlife, we are likely to be confused about what biblical faith is all about.

Yes, most of the Second Testament looks forward to another life after we die. Jesus spoke of "the resurrection of the righteous" (Luke 14:14). His followers were convinced YHWH had resurrected Jesus from the dead; Peter spoke of it in his first sermon in **Acts**. And Paul wrote extensively about the resurrection: "For the trumpet will sound and the dead will be raised imperishable, and we will be changed" (I Cor. 15:52).

The teaching of the resurrection certainly expanded the array of rewards for biblical faith. Unfortunately, for many religious people, this expansion became the point of it all. The eternal pay-off, in other words, is so attractive that it has eclipsed everything else. To put the matter crassly, if by being religious one can transform death into the gateway to eternal bliss in a place better than Earth, then being religious is a no-brainer.

If we understand that biblical faith existed before there was an expectation of life after death, then we have a chance of becoming people of faith in our time. Thus, as we read the First Testament, we ask: Why did some of the Israelites bother to commit themselves and their living to YHWH? Why didn't they instead assimilate to the empires around them?

In brief, here is how the First Testament speaks of death. When Abraham died, he "was gathered to his people" (Gen. 25:8). The same phrase was used to describe the deaths of Ishmael, Isaac and Moses; it seems to have meant they had passed into the same status as their ancestors. A woman of Tekoa described death another way: "We must all die; we are like water spilled on the ground, which cannot be gathered up"

(2 Sam. 14:14). The author of **Ecclesiastes** put it this way: "For the fate of humans and the fate of animals is the same; as one dies, so dies the other. They all have the same breath, and humans have no advantage over animals; for all is vanity. All go to one place; all are from the dust and all turn to dust again" (Eccl. 3:1–20).

First Testament texts often associate death with Sheol, a place of silent darkness. "The dead do not praise [YHWH], nor do any that go down into silence" (Ps. 5:17). In his famous prayer to be spared from death, King Hezekiah voiced this sentiment: "For Sheol cannot thank you, death cannot praise you; those who go down to the Pit cannot hope for your faithfulness. The living, the living, they thank you, as I do this day" (Isa. 38:18–19).

This mixture of unvarnished realism and faith is perhaps best captured by a psalm:

> [Our] days are like grass; we flourish like a flower of the field, the wind passes over and [we] are gone, and [our] place knows [us] no more. But the steadfast love of [YHWH] is from everlasting to everlasting on those who fear him, and his righteousness to children's children to those who keep his covenant and remember to do his commandments. Ps. 103:15–18

Certainly Hebrew people of faith thought of the future. But generally, their expectations were fixed on community aspirations, not individual identities. Many texts speak of the generations to come and of the everlasting covenant of YHWH. "Great is [YHWH] and greatly to be praised; his greatness is unsearchable. One generation shall laud your works to another, and shall declare your mighty acts" (Ps. 145:3–4). They understood these "works" of YHWH would occur in the material world, not some metaphysical realm.

Some texts used the concept of memory to describe the fate of individual identities. The lament of Psalm 88 speaks despairingly of "those forsaken among the dead . . . those whom [YHWH] remembers no more" (Ps. 88:5). Other psalms rejoice in how the wicked are forgotten: "The face of [YHWH] is against evildoers, to cut off the remembrance of them from the earth" (Ps. 34:16). "The wicked perish . . . they vanish—

like the smoke they vanish away" (Ps. 37:20). On the other hand, among the blessings of the righteous is that "they will be remembered [by YHWH] forever" (Ps. 112:6).

Daniel, the last-written text of the First Testament (about 165 BCE), speaks clearly of a resurrection of the dead: "Many of those who sleep in the dust of the earth shall awake, some to everlasting life and some to shame and everlasting contempt" (Dan. 12:2). The **Wisdom of Solomon,** a text included in non-Protestant versions of the Bible, speaks in similar terms: "The souls of the just are in God's hands . . . their departure was reckoned as defeat, and their going from us as disaster. But they are at peace . . . they have a sure hope of immortality" (Wisd. 3:1–4).

During the time of Jesus, a belief in the resurrection of the righteous had become common, especially among the Pharisees. Paul, the Pharisee who became a follower of Jesus as the Messiah after being convinced YHWH had raised him from the dead, reflected this view. He understood the promise of YHWH to include eternal life for individuals "who by patiently doing good seek for glory and honor and immortality" (Rom. 2:7). Yet even within the Second Testament, we do not find a uniform understanding of the matter. Thus, in **The Gospel of John,** "eternal life" is a qualitative change in our first life, not a chronological extension of the first into a second in the way Paul described.

Because the emphasis on a rewarding afterlife is strong in the writings of some Second Testament authors, it is tempting to regard the heavenless faith of the First Testament as somehow inferior. Yet that would be a mistake. *Biblical faith is about how YHWH is saving Earth and its inhabitants from destructive paths and dead ends.* Yes, it has a metaphysical element, but it also is resolutely historical and political. If we think biblical faith is about heaven, we are missing the main point.

First Testament is not inferior in terms of authentic faith

4. The Story of a People

If the Bible is not about getting to heaven, what is it about? As we said in the Preface, it is first and foremost about YHWH, god of the Hebrews. It also is accurate to say the Bible is a partial history of the people initially known as the Hebrews, then as the Israelites and still later as the Jews.

Why should Gentiles pay close attention to this history of the Jews? One reason is that so many of the writings describe the hard realities of life under the heel of empire. Such texts can inform and inspire our own responses to empire.

The covenant YHWH made with Abraham offers a second reason: in his descendants, "all the families of the earth shall be blessed" (Gen. 12:2). In other words, YHWH's relationship with the Israelites was intended to benefit *all* of Earth's people. When we read the Bible, we are reading accounts of how this one group lived out its role as midwife to YHWH's promise to bless the Earth and save it from destruction.

Throughout the history recounted in the Bible, various individuals played dynamic and pivotal roles in shaping Israelite identity and setting the direction of the Jewish people. But with the exception of Jesus in the Second Testament, these were supporting roles in the biblical drama; YHWH, Israel as a group and the social movement that followed Jesus' death played the lead roles.

If the purpose of YHWH were to sort out which individuals are going to heaven and which are not, then this way of telling the story would not make sense. But the purpose of YHWH is to save Earth through the formation of a community whose way of living is just, liberating and sustainable. Thus, it makes sense for the Bible to focus on a specific group of people whose communal life attempted (at least some of the time) to fulfill that purpose.

This approach to "blessing the world" reflects a particular worldview and anthropology: cultures and their gods, not individuals, create social reality. How we as individuals perceive the world to work (the possibilities we imagine, the meaning we give to words such as "love"

[handwritten note:] Biblical writers — We got to have a group — Hebrews, then Christians?

and "justice," our response to violence and coercion, our attitudes toward strangers and outsiders, our understanding of economics) is shaped by the group with which we identify.

Because groups and their gods construct social reality, and because YHWH intends for that reality to be just, liberating and sustainable, the Bible focuses on the transformation of a group to lead the way by example.   In the next chapter we will look at how this is meant to benefit the wider world.

Some readers will be uncomfortable with our claim that biblical writers often identified "the empire" as the problem that animated their writing. The desire to secure one's advantage, get one's way and dominate others resides in each human heart. Sin is the universal human experience, so why speak so much about the empire?

Indeed, most biblical writers seem to have been fully convinced of human selfishness. Yet in their view, the problem is not that the human heart is completely and unalterably depraved, but rather that it is perpetually divided and plagued by mixed intentions. Indeed, that is how we understand this well-known verse: "The heart is devious above all else; it is perverse—who can understand it" (Jer. 17:21)?

So while perceiving each human being to be divided in his/her commitment to what is good, most biblical authors also seemed to have been fully convinced of the human capacity to live in a righteous and peaceful manner according to YHWH's intention.   In the biblical worldview, this certainly entails individual choice and commitment, but *what is even more decisive is the god one worships and the resulting social milieu in which one lives.* Only a worldview and community animated by YHWH will enable the multitudes (not just a few heroic individuals) to *see* what is good and for many to embrace it.

Thus, the biblical focus is not the metaphysical redemption of the autonomous individual, but a righteous and just society oriented toward the true god. For this to happen, we need to be liberated from false gods and deceitful realities and embedded in life-giving social structures, what Paul called "a new creation" (Gal. 6:15). Only then will humanity's positive capacity fully flower.

We see this worldview displayed most dramatically in the story of Hebrew slaves liberated by YHWH from bondage to the Egyptian Empire and shaped into a new political community by their experiences in the wilderness and their covenant with YHWH at Sinai. For biblical writers, this story is a parable of human existence; *it describes who we are, who YHWH is, and how the world is saved.* The path to salvation first entails breaking our physical and mental bondage to empire and then leads to participation in a new political community that reshapes our desires, intentions and actions.

Before ending this chapter, it is important to say a bit more about how this book's description of divine salvation differs from the popular Christian view. The specific difference is in how Jesus' life and death is understood. We understand it to be an extension and expansion of First Testament's prophetic project of liberating people from the empire, forging an alternative political community, and inviting all people to join the worship of YHWH though a life of justice and peace. In contrast, popular Christianity understands Jesus to have made a decisive shift away from the First Testament emphasis on human history and saving Earth, and toward metaphysical reconciliation with god and eternity in heaven.

These are very different understandings of the Bible. Especially in Part III of this book, we encourage readers to keep this distinction in mind.

Also before closing this chapter, we need to acknowledge how complicated it is to make connections between the people who carried the biblical story along and contemporary people-groups. Many simply draw a line from the ancient Hebrews to today's Jews. There is an element of truth in this, but it also is profoundly misleading.

First, such an approach fails to recognize how over time, the great majority of Abraham's descendants—Ishmael, Esau and most of those who comprised the Northern Kingdom of Israel—dropped out of the biblical storyline. The small minority who lived in the Southern Kingdom of Israel (Judah) carried the story of Abraham for 200 years longer, but eventually most of them also were excluded by Ezra's emphasis on purity at the start of the second temple era. Thus, only a tiny portion of Abraham's descendants are part of the biblical story to its end.

Second, it fails to recognize that over thousands of years in one of Earth's most war-wracked regions, the genetic seed of Abraham (and of Jacob) can be found in many people who we today do not think of as Jews because they became Muslims, Christians or converts to some other religion.

Third, it misses how the focus of the biblical narrative broadened in the Second Testament to include Gentiles who gave their allegiance to a Jewish Messiah, but did not fully adopt Jewish religious practices. These Gentiles lacked a genetic link to Abraham but worshiped YHWH, the god first revealed to Abraham.

Fourth, it misses what happened hundreds of years after the biblical period when the prophet Muhammad affirmed his allegiance to YHWH, the god of Abraham. Thus, followers of Islam also have a strong connection to the biblical narrative.

In summary, when we imagine contemporary people who are the "seed of Abraham," we must include along with today's Jews those who bear a genetic connection to the ancient Semites, but not a contemporary Jewish identity (Palestinians are an example) and those who do not have a Semitic genetic heritage, but claim allegiance to Abraham's god. And when we wish to identify *the people of YHWH* in today's world, we must start with the identity of YHWH, not a confusing welter of ancestral claims related to men and women who may have lived thousands of years ago.

5. A Pilgrimage of Nations

So how do the blessings of YHWH get shared with the rest of us? This question brings us deep into biblical assumptions about how the world works.

Because the Bible is a religious book that portrays YHWH as active in historical events, it is tempting to fall back on the childhood assumption that YHWH uses magical power to "do stuff" in the world. The Bible recounts many events that seem to fit that assumption.

We read, for example, that Moses struck the Red Sea with his staff and YHWH divided the waters, enabling the Hebrew people to pass through on dry land (Ex. 14:21–22). During Israel's battle with the Amorites, Joshua spoke to YHWH and "the sun stood still, and the moon stopped, until [Israel] took vengeance on their enemies" (Josh. 10:12–13). Elijah prayed and YHWH sent fire down from the skies to consume Elijah's sacrifice, thus humiliating the prophets of the rival god, Baal (1 Kings 18:38). When the army of the Assyrian Empire surrounded Jerusalem, King Hezekiah prayed to YHWH and "that very night the angel of the LORD set out and struck down 185,000 in the camp of the Assyrians; when morning dawned, they were all dead" (2 Kings 19:35). After executing James, the disciple of Jesus, King Herod arrested Peter in order to execute him too. As Peter, bound with two chains, slept between two soldiers, "an angel of the Lord appeared and a light shone in the cell. [The angel] tapped Peter on the side and woke him, saying 'Get up quickly.' And the chains fells off his wrists" (Acts 12:7).

Most important of all, after the Roman Empire killed Jesus, YHWH raised him back to life.

Descriptions of these events and others like them are important; we need to engage each of them seriously and on its own terms. Some reflect exaggeration and the legend-making that often occurs when events are passed along orally for centuries and finally published in written form long after they occurred. Some reflect the writer's impatience with *how* something happened; he primarily wanted to say it was YHWH who prompted natural events to occur. Others reflect the writer's confidence that there is no "natural" explanation; only a supernatural cause provides an explanation.

However we regard remarkable events, their seemingly magical character can distort our understanding of the Bible by causing us to miss the everyday method YHWH is portrayed to use. That everyday method is the influence of those who live their lives according to YHWH's ways.

Finding this everyday method in the biblical texts starts with a basic assumption: we as people constantly imitate each other's desires and actions. That we copy each other's "successful" actions is very obvious, but it goes deeper than that: for good or ill, *we subconsciously desire what others desire.* This mechanism is wired into our brains and operates at a subconscious level. Indeed, we can see it in children well before they reach their first birthdays. Often it leads to envy, rivalry, competition, even violence, *but it also can lead in the other direction towards cooperation, kindness and forgiveness* (see Rom. 5:15–21).

The biblical stories of Eve and Adam and of Abel and Cain demonstrate this dynamic, as do many of the stories of people responding to Jesus.

When we project this dynamic on the screen of larger society, we use words such as "reputation" or "witness" to describe how the mechanism works. A society's way of life, mores and aspirations are on display for all to see, and people from other societies pay attention. For example, people from all over the world want to immigrate to the USA because they perceive it to be a land of economic opportunity. Similarly, we are fascinated by how the poor Cuban society achieves excellent public health and near universal literacy and by how Iranian society maintains its coherence and emphasis on the arts despite the hostile punishments of the empire. This "fascination" is a power in and of itself.

Biblical writers were keenly aware of this; most often, they expressed it in terms of YHWH's reputation. Thus, the **Psalms** repeatedly plead with YHWH to "lead me in the right paths" (Ps. 23:3), "pardon my guilt" (Ps. 25:11), "lead me and guide me" (Ps. 31:3), "help us" (Ps. 79:9), "act on my behalf" (Ps. 109:21), and "preserve my life" (Ps. 143:11) *"for YHWH's name sake"* (emphasis added).

In his farewell address as a prophet, Samuel chided the Israelite people for their insistence on having a king. Yet he also comforted them: "For [YHWH] will not cast away his people, for his great name's sake" (1 Sam. 12:22). Later, the prophet Isaiah quoted YHWH to the same effect: "For my name's sake I defer my anger, for the sake of my praise I restrain it for you" (Isa. 48:9). Jesus' phrasing was a bit different, but the idea was the same: "Let your light shine before others so that they may see your good works and give glory to your Father in heaven" (Matt. 5:16).

What we see in these texts is the assumption that life includes intense competition among competing worldviews, each explaining how the world works. Within that competition, our imitation of others often drives us toward conformity with traits and behaviors that are undesirable, but it also can work in the reverse direction and beckon toward the ways of peace. Humanity has not been totally corrupted by sin; *we can be drawn by our own desires to the light*, to YHWH's way of living on Earth.

But for this to happen among "all the peoples of the earth," YHWH's way of living has to be made visible, even prominent, so that others can observe, experience, desire and embrace it. It cannot remain the private possession of one ethnic group, one culture or a collection of individuals. And so in the **Gospel of John**, we find Jesus saying to Nicodemus, "Just as Moses lifted up the serpent in the wilderness, so must the Son of Man be lifted up" (John 3:14). And we find him saying on another occasion, "No one after lighting a lamp puts it under the bushel basket, but on a lampstand and it gives light to all in the house" (Matt. 5:14–15).

Thus, Abraham staked his tent in Canaan at the bottle neck of the great trade routes of his era. Jeremiah, Ezekiel, John the Baptist, Peter and Paul lived and engaged people day after day in public places. Jesus spent his adult life in the public eye and died after he was "lifted up" on a hilltop and made into a horrific spectacle people still talk about today. The first messianic believers regularly met in the temple, the public space where Jesus had carried out his most outrageous direct action against civil authority.

More than any other text in the Bible, the book of **Isaiah** makes this logic explicit. "In days to come, the mountain of [YHWH's] house shall be established as the highest of the mountains, and shall be raised above the hills; all the nations shall stream to it. Many peoples shall come and say, 'Come, let us go up to the mountain of [YHWH], to the house of [YHWH]; that he may teach us his ways and that we may walk in his paths'" (Isa. 2:2-3).

This pilgrimage of the nations to YHWH's mountain is the context for Jesus' proclamation of the empire of YHWH. By calling his Jewish community back to YHWH's way, Jesus tried to reenergize a light he knew would fascinate and attract all peoples. Most attractive of all would be Israel's nonviolence. The book of **Isaiah** had anticipated this: "(YHWH) shall judge between the nations and shall arbitrate for many peoples; they shall beat their swords into plowshares and their spears into pruning hooks; nation shall not lift up sword against nation, neither shall they learn war any more" (Isa. 2:4).

Jesus embodied nonviolence all the way to the point of death and it fascinates still. But did the pilgrimage of nations occur? Did peace break out among the peoples? Yes, said Peter in his first public sermons after the miraculous events of Pentecost unleashed an unprecedented spirit of cooperation and sharing among the diverse followers of Jesus. Yes, said leaders of the second century church as they observed that people who had once killed one another because of differences in culture or creed now lived together in peace.

How does truth establish its reign upon Earth? How does it win the hearts of people? The Biblical authors did not assume truth—YHWH's truth—would only be handed down from on high. They did not assume people would adopt a different worldview and change their ways of living simply because of miraculous occurrences or because someone claimed YHWH said they should. Instead, they recognized that YHWH's truth had to take on flesh and blood within history as men and women lived in public ways that others observed, experienced and desired because those ways embodied peace, nurtured community and prepared the way for justice.

This is the everyday way in which Earth is saved. In between occasional supernatural signs and wonders that none of us can explain, this is how YHWH's blessings are shared with all the peoples of Earth.

6. Resistance to Empire

While some who read this book have experienced the terrors of the reigning empire and yearn for its demise, most will likely hold the view that despite its many failures and errors, today's empire makes the world a safer and more prosperous place. We are better off with this empire, in other words, than without it.

In contrast, many biblical writers viewed the empires of their times as enemies of YHWH. Theologically, this hostility makes sense. An empire is god-like in its ability to create reality by defining how the world works and what changes are possible. In many ways this is a false reality, yet the empire's deceit is so massive, so overwhelming, that usual accountability mechanisms cease to function. Alternative ways of living, of organizing human activity and solving problems, are marginalized and stigmatized as threats to peace and prosperity. The empire may be hurtling toward the abyss, but its range of options is perceived to encompass all of the reasonable choices. This is what empire is and what empire does, *no matter how lofty its ideals and how sincere its leaders.*

Only YHWH can save us; this is the leading biblical worldview. YHWH's salvation comes to us in many shapes and forms, but always includes communities that resist the empire by living an alternative. *This is how YHWH saves the world.*

Keesmaat and Walsh provide our definition of empire: "systematic centralizations of power . . . secured by structures of socio-economic and military control. They are religiously legitimated by powerful myths that are rooted in foundational assumptions, and they are sustained by a proliferation of imperial images that captivate the imagination of the population." [5]

In addition to the military and related security and intelligence apparatus of the USA, the current empire includes the parallel capacities of allied governments; international financial institutions; and global networks of private entities (business enterprises, media and entertainment outlets, think tanks, NGOs, charitable foundations, even human rights

---

[5]   Ibid., 31.

groups). Together, they create the reality that enriches and empowers elite members of these reinforcing structures and institutions.

Many call global dominance "hegemony" when it does not look like the empires of the past. Ancient empires were led by a single leader who exercised control of subordinate nations through imperial viceroys. This contrasts with current arrangements within the empire: dominant nations change leaders every few years via popular elections and those leaders often engage in highly publicized debates with the executives of subordinate nations. This apparent lack of operational authority over weaker nations causes some to consider the term "empire" outmoded, even if the leader of a subordinate nation holds office largely at the will of the dominant nation.

While some will debate whether "empire" or "global hegemony" better describes the current global reality, it is important to recognize how the tools of domination have evolved. In addition to control of global financial institutions, the current imperial configuration of power maintains constant satellite visual surveillance of every part of the globe and constantly monitors digital communications worldwide. It maintains the capacity for intensive combat operations out of nearly 1,000 global bases; circles rivals with missile batteries and nuclear weapons; maintains an overwhelming firepower advantage in space, in the air, on and under the seas and on the ground; and conducts covert military operations in over 100 countries each year. *Most perniciously, through covert intelligence, private contractors, mercenaries, proxies who function as "terrorists" and organized crime networks, it can anonymously kill, destroy and disrupt in ways that prompt common people around the globe to desire the empire's protection.* It is god-like in its knowledge, scope and reach.

Nations that do not toe the line drawn by today's empire are stigmatized as "rogue states," punished in the terms of trade and targeted by destabilizing internal violence and/or external attack. The list of those disrupted includes Cuba, Vietnam, Chile, Nicaragua, North Korea, Iran, Serbia, Afghanistan, Iraq, Myanmar, Sudan, Libya, Syria, Ukraine and Venezuela. Russia is a recent addition to the list.

Yet the current empire has little interest in exercising executive operational authority over subordinate nations. Instead it pursues three goals: the uninterrupted flow of economic benefits from those nations to individuals and institutions (most of which are in private hands); disruption of all efforts by subordinate nations to assemble the capacity to defend themselves; and stigmatization and marginalization of any competing worldview.

Keesmaat and Walsh provide perspective:

> Empires project a sense of all-embracing normality. Not only do empires want us to think that reality is totally composed of the structures, symbols and systems that have been imperially constructed, they also want us to believe that the future holds no more than a heightened realization of imperial hopes and dreams . . . If all the maps are provided by the empire, if all the reality we can see is what the empire has constructed as reality for us, then our *praxis* will never be creative, and it will never be subversive to that empire.[6]

Some readers will be uncomfortable identifying the USA as the leader of an empire. For some, this discomfort arises out of fondness for the current arrangements of power and wealth in the world. For others, the discomfort arises from experience with forms of domination and control that are not part of the USA-led empire, but reflect the same worldview and aspirations. As authors, we heartily agree that biblical writings challenge the imperial worldview across the board, not just when manifest in a functioning empire. Yet honesty requires us to name the reigning empire, even while acknowledging that others are eager to take its place.

John Dominic Crossan starts from the premise that although some cultures do not seek to dominate through force, every *civilization* does exactly that. "My point is . . . that to resist empire-as-such we must know what we are up against. It is something inherent in civilization itself. Non-imperial civilization is something yet to be seen upon earth." [7] Yet Crossan insists a non-imperial civilization is possible, a conviction for which he finds support in Jesus of Nazareth and the Apostle Paul. And he

---

[6]   Ibid., 155-156.

[7]   Crossan, *God and Empire*, 36.

describes the urgency of finding a non-imperial way forward in the starkest of terms: "The future of everything we have accomplished since our intelligence evolved will depend on the wisdom of our action over the next few years." [8]

We do not mean to suggest that all biblical writers agreed on how to relate to the empire. Some advocated resistance, some collaboration in one form or another, still others that the Israelite people achieve empire for themselves. Occasionally this debate was very visible and intense; at other times, it faded into the background. Though the viewpoints on empire vary within the Bible, "many [texts] strive to resist imperial rule while inevitably making accommodation to it." [9] Implicitly, such texts reject the view most in North America and Europe still accept: that on balance, the empire reduces the frequency of violence, improves security and creates the conditions in which people can thrive.

In part, the Bible's anti-empire perspective was rooted in the oppressive circumstances in which Israel found itself. Scribes in the Northern Kingdom of Israel (Ephraim) wrote **Exodus** during an era when the Assyrian Empire emerged as a serious threat to their tiny nation. Scribes in the Southern Kingdom (Judah) had the same threat in mind a couple of hundred years later as they wrote their history of the kings. The prophets Amos, Hosea, Micah, Habakkuk and Isaiah spoke during this period and often referenced Assyria.

Later, another empire, Babylon, attacked the Southern Kingdom (Judah), carried off its most skilled people and eventually destroyed Jerusalem. The prophet Jeremiah spoke in Jerusalem while it was under siege. During the decades of forced exile, **Ezekiel** and the second part of **Isaiah** were written.

A portion of the exiled Jews eventually returned to Jerusalem and the surrounding areas. The institutions they and their descendants built functioned under the authority and direction of a third empire, the Persians. During this complicated time of renewed hope within the

---

[8]   Ibid., 47.

[9]   Horsley, *In the Shadow of Empire: Reclaiming the Bible as a History of Faithful Resistance,* 177.

parameters of imperial collaboration, scribes assembled **Genesis, Leviticus** and **Numbers** and wrote the **Chronicles, Ezra** and **Nehemiah**.

Under the leadership of Alexander the Great, the Greek Empire followed the Persians to ascendency. While the Jews in Palestine found a way to accommodate Greek rule that emanated from Egypt (the Ptolemy dynasty), they suffered horribly under Greek rule from Syria (the Seleucid dynasty), which assumed control around 200 BCE. **Joel** and **Daniel** were written during the Seleucid era.

The Maccabean revolt against the Greek empire restored a measure of Jewish autonomy, including control of the temple in Jerusalem. Then after a century of partial self-rule, a fifth empire (Rome) took control. Its brutal reign included the execution of Jesus for sedition. About thirty-six years after Jesus' death, a Zealot-led revolt fed by anti-tax protests evicted the Roman military from Jerusalem. The First Jewish-Roman War followed. The decisive event in the war was the Roman siege of Jerusalem. That ordeal continued for seven months before the Romans breached the walls, destroyed nearly all of the buildings of the city and enslaved the survivors.

Paul wrote his letters during a fifteen-year period just before this war began. Several of his letters were written from Roman jail cells. The last book of the Second Testament, **The Revelation to John,** was written on the island of Patmos by a man exiled there by the Roman emperor, Domitian.

While not all biblical authors wrote under duress, all worked within a tradition that wanted to live outside imperial control. It is a perspective we badly need today as we seek a sustainable way of living on Earth beyond the failed "solutions" on offer from the empire of our time.

Brutality and terror reflect the spirit of empire and are among its most important tools. Because empires so dominate the arena of violence and are so unaccountable to usual limits, we will not find one that does not employ brutality and terror to impose its will. This raw reality can easily get lost in a short discussion like this, particularly if we become absorbed in the distinctions between empire, hegemony and the routine exercise of sovereign power by the typical nation-state.

Consider, for example, this quote from an Assyrian emperor:

> I built a wall before the great gates of the city; I flayed the chief men of the rebels, and I covered the wall with their skins. Some of them were enclosed alive in the bricks of the wall, some of them were crucified on stakes along the wall; I caused a great multitude of them to be flayed in my presence, and I covered the wall with their skins. I gathered together the heads in the form of crowns, and their pierced bodies in the form of garlands. [10]

Or accounts of how Greek king Antiochus Epiphanes roasted Jews alive in large frying pans because they refused to eat pork. Or reports of Roman stadium crowds cheering as wild animals tore Christians limb from limb.

The empire of today also employs terror and brutality, albeit with more sophisticated weapons and behind veils of humanitarian necessity and deception. Arguably, the incineration of Japanese civilians in Tokyo, Hiroshima and Nagasaki for political ends was terrorism. Even if one does not accept that view, there is ample evidence of terrorism in the 500,000 premature deaths of Iraqi children caused by the harsh sanctions of the late 1990s, or in the many killings of civilians through "counter-terrorism" initiatives conducted by imperial forces and their proxies in Vietnam, El Salvador, Guatemala, Honduras, Kosovo, Afghanistan, Iraq, Pakistan, Yemen and Somalia. The use of torture post-9/11 has been portrayed as an aberration, but it was already standard practice during the USA invasion of the Philippines a century earlier and it occurs through proxies and at "dark sites" yet today. The fomenting of violence between Sunni and Shia in Iraq and the use of snipers to murder indiscriminately in order to tip popular protests in Libya, Syria and Ukraine into armed violence and civil war—these reveal how today's empire uses terror and brutality to pursue its goals.

We dare not forget any of this, deny it ever happened, or deny it happens still.

---

[10]   *Bible History Online,* www.bible-history.com/destruction_of_israel/destruction_of_israel_assyrians.html

7. A Good Society

Would we choose to live in a society committed to ethical outcomes related to the distribution of income or the stability of the family? Or would we avoid such a society because it is likely to be rigid, authoritarian and riven by conflict?

Biblical writers were passionate supporters of the "ethical outcomes" approach to society. Indeed, many of them went beyond making "value judgments" about what was "good" or "bad"; they denounced the worship of false gods and unjust living as the source of suffering and destruction.

Before jumping into the biblical texts, it is prudent to pause and reflect on their approach. *Why exactly do we find it harsh and judgmental?* Is there a way to "hear" their value judgments and condemnations so we can benefit from them?

In 1985, Robert Bellah and four other sociologists launched a discussion of individualism and community in American society with their book, *Habits of the Heart.* It described how we have settled in our public lives for procedural equity with little shared sense of the common good. Bellah and his associates wrote: "We have been afraid to try for a more substantial consensus for fear that the effort may produce unacceptable levels of conflict." [11]

As an example of the difference, Bellah and his colleagues described how at one time in the history of the USA, the corporate form of organization was restricted to those who had demonstrated commitment to a communal purpose serving the public good, including a willingness to view corporate property as belonging to the community, not only the stockholders. Such value judgments are possible only in a society that shares a rough consensus about what is and what is not a "public good." A procedural democracy, on the other hand, avoids that kind of ethical discernment; it permits people to charter corporations for any legal purpose whatsoever.

---

[11]   Bellah et al. *Habits of the Heart: Individualism and Commitment in American Life,* 287.

The Israelite people and the mixed Jewish and Gentile congregations that emerged after Jesus clearly wanted more than procedural equity; *they wanted a good society* based on YHWH's commands, the messages of the prophets and—for those convinced Jesus was the Messiah—his teachings. They understood salvation to be an event that happened in history, not someplace else. Because YHWH loved justice and hated evil, a good society would seek justice and oppose evil.

Moses, the great lawgiver, articulated this worldview: "See, I have set before you today life and prosperity, death and adversity . . . I have set before you life and death, blessings and curses. Choose life so that you and your descendants may live, loving [YHWH] your God, obeying him and holding fast to him; for that means life to you and length of days" (Deut. 30:15–20). Thus, Moses "set before" the Israelite people the command to observe a Sabbath year, when all debts would be forgiven, and a Jubilee year, when all land would return to its original owners.

Throughout Israel's biblical history, the prophets upheld the ethical dimension and denounced wrong-doing. Thus, Amos described the reasons for impending judgment on Israel:

> Because they sell the righteous for silver, and the needy for a pair of sandals, they who trample the head of the poor into the dust of the earth and push the afflicted out of the way; [because] father and son go in to the same girl, so that my holy name is profaned; [because] they lay themselves down beside every altar on garments taken in pledge, in the house of their gods they drink wine bought with [the] fines they imposed. (Amos 2:6–8)

"Woe to him who builds his house by unrighteousness, and his upper rooms by injustice; who makes his neighbors work for nothing, and does not give them their wages," Jeremiah said (Jer. 22:13). But he also proclaimed a way of redemption: "Act with justice and righteousness, and deliver from the hand of the oppressor anyone who has been robbed. Do no wrong or violence to the alien, the orphan and the widow, or shed innocent blood in this place. . . .[Your father] judged the cause of the poor and needy . . . Is not this to know me, says [YHWH]" (Jer. 22:3, 16)?

Within the context of oppression by the Romans and Jewish collaborators, Jesus also proclaimed blessings and curses. "Blessed are you who are poor, for yours is the kingdom of God. Blessed are you who are hungry now, for you will be filled. Blessed are you who weep, for you will laugh . . . But woe to you who are rich, for you have received your consolation. Woe to you who are full now, for you will be hungry. Woe to you who are laughing now, for you will mourn and weep" (Luke 6:20–26).

Similarly, in an early Second Testament text, Paul urged his readers to "abstain from every form of evil" and "hold fast to what is good" (1 Thess. 5:21). "See that none of you repays evil for evil, but always seek to do good to one another and to all" (1 Thess. 5:15).

At times during Israel's history, society was organized as a theocracy with the biblical vision of "good" and "bad" enforced by government. This combination of moral standards, divine sanction and the coercive power of the state is so unattractive that we might avoid entirely any thought of building a good society. At other times, however, the biblical pursuit of a "good society" focused on the authority of culture (not the government) to nurture behaviors that would lead to ethical outcomes.

We encourage readers to engage the Bible with these questions in mind: how can we create a society that *informally* seeks justice, peace and prosperity by celebrating the good and turning away from the bad? Can we imagine a communal politics that is effective by embodying a way of life that is desirable, not by seizing the power of the state? Can we end our fascination with structuring power *over others* and focus instead on nurturing relationships, commitments and values at society's base?

The value judgments found in the Bible can be off-putting because of their authoritative, "god said" framing. Yet we should not let that prevent us from hearing the underlying claim: there is a way of life within our grasp that leads to social justice, peace and prosperity. "For surely I know the plan I have for you, says [YHWH], plans for your welfare and not for harm, to give you a future with hope" (Jer. 29:11). Except perhaps for the writer of **Ecclesiastes**, biblical writers never said it is unimportant how we live because it all will turn out the same in the end. Such a thought simply did not fit their worldview.

The Bible is committed to getting it right, and it does sound judgment.

This brings us to a troubling question: can we pursue a moral vision of society without triggering endless conflict and likely violence? Jesus believed it was possible; although he was committed to peace, he did not dial back his passion for justice and righteousness. Instead, he renounced violence and put his faith in YHWH and the power of self-giving, suffering love. This was Jesus' way of saving the world!

The communities of followers that emerged after his death gave us a glimpse of the positive impact such nonviolent passion can have in the world. Just as Jesus had predicted, his disciples accomplished great things (John 14:12). Yet as they began to make a broader impact on society, the empire violently repressed their movement. Some Jesus followers persisted despite the violence, while others accommodated empire's demands. We will survey texts reflecting this tension in chapter 22.

Reflection and Discussion

1. We construct meaning out of life; this is widely understood to be a uniquely human activity. What we call "god" is part of this meaning-making. The Bible agrees with all of this, but it also insists there is a god, YHWH, who *precedes* human constructions. Before getting into the biblical texts, consider what evidence of such a claim you might find persuasive.

2. Are you more or less interested in getting acquainted with biblical writings now that you know many authors did not assume an afterlife in heaven? Why?

3. Consider how the empire of today impacts your life. Where does it give you privileges and where does it place you at risk? Do you have family members or acquaintances that feel its impact differently? How?

4. Chapter 7 suggests salvation happens within history and that the Bible focuses on how to achieve "a good society." It asks that we consider how this goal might be achieved through the power of culture rather than by seizing the levers of government. Are you supportive or critical of such a stance? Why?

PART II:
The First Testament Writings

From **Genesis** to **Malachi**, the Hebrew Bible (or First Testament) contains 39 books. Many are historical in nature, linked to events that occurred over a 800-year time span that began with the early rivalry between the Northern and Southern kingdoms and concluded with the Greek Empire's occupation of Palestine, desecration of the Jerusalem temple and persecution of religious Jews.

Included as well are stories that go back much further in time, but which cannot be confirmed through sources outside the Bible. These stories are important too; whether history or legend, they shaped Hebrew identity and understandings of their god.

For approximate dates of confirmed historical events, see page 12.

Prior to the development of written language, oral story-telling was the only way to preserve knowledge of events and traditions. After the development of the Hebrew alphabet around 1,000 BCE (the era when King David is said to have lived), literate individuals began using written script to preserve accounts of important events, traditions and stories. This process occurred first among the elite, including those serving the king. Thus, the earliest biblical texts probably date back to sometime in the 10th Century BCE (the 900s).

The process of deciding which written documents should be included in the Bible involved many Jewish leaders, occurred over hundreds of years and concluded during the decades just before and just after the life of Jesus of Nazareth. It was not a tidy process. All along the way, various traditions representing different emphases competed for their versions of events. Editors attempted to reconcile contrasting views, but in some instances achieved consensus only by including different viewpoints. The issue of empire is one example: should the people of YHWH resist, accommodate or pursue its methods and goals?

When trying to understand First Testament texts, it is helpful to know when the final version was assembled and who assembled it. This context gives us important clues about what purpose the text was intended to serve. This is true of any writing, but is particularly true when a text is written long after the events it reports.

For example, among texts written before the destruction of Jerusalem by the Babylonian army in 586 BCE, we see two perspectives that reflect the experiences of the two distinct national states. These two states—the Northern Kingdom (sometimes called Ephraim, sometimes Israel) and the Southern Kingdom (always called Judah)—emerged in Canaan during the tenth century BCE and existed as rivals, even though they worshipped the same god (YHWH), came from similar ethnic stock (Semitic), and shared some of the same oral traditions about their origins. When reading texts written during the era of the kings, it is very helpful to know which of these two states the writer came from.

When we look at the chronological order in which the First Testament books were written in final form, we find it is very different from the order in which these books appear in our Bibles. Nearly all scholars agree on that much. But because these are ancient writings about very ancient events, establishing specific dates is difficult and highly controversial.

Following is a chart describing in chronological order the *approximate* time and likely authorship for each First Testament book. This information is drawn from a variety a sources, most significantly the work of Wes Howard-Brook.[12]

Text	Completion	Author
I Samuel 13—I Kings 10	925 BCE	Scribes in Solomon's court
Exodus	875 BCE	Northern scribes
Obadiah	790 BCE	Southern prophet
Amos	760 BCE	Southern prophet in north
Hosea	730 BCE	Northern prophet
Micah	700 BCE	Rural southern prophet
I Kings 11—2 Kings 20	700 BCE	Southern scribes
Isaiah 1–39	700 BCE	Advisor to kings of Judah
Zephaniah	640 BCE	Prophet in Jerusalem
Nahum	610 BCE	Refugee prophet in south

---

[12]   Howard-Brook, *Come Out, My People: God's Call out of Empire in the Bible and Beyond,* 105.

Deuteronomy, Joshua, Judges, I Samuel 1–11, 2 Kings 21–25

	610 BCE	Southern scribes
Habakkuk	605 BCE	Prophet in Jerusalem
Jeremiah	585 BCE	Prophet in Jerusalem
Lamentations	585 BCE	Prophet in Jerusalem
Ezekiel	570 BCE	Priest in exile in Babylon
Numbers	550 BCE	Scribes in Babylon
Job	550 BCE	Jewish exile in Babylon
Isaiah 40–55	535 BCE	Prophet in Babylon
Haggai	525 BCE	Prophet in Jerusalem
Zechariah 1–8	525 BCE	Prophet in Jerusalem
Leviticus	475 BCE	Scribes in Babylon
Genesis	450 BCE	Scribes in Babylon
Esther	450 BCE	Jewish resident of Persia
Ezra	425 BCE	Scribes in Babylon
Nehemiah	425 BCE	Scribes in Babylon
Malachi	425 BCE	Prophet in Yehud (Judea)
I & 2 Chronicles	425 BCE	Priest or scribe in Jerusalem
Proverbs	400 BCE	Various
Psalms	375 BCE	Various
Isaiah 56–66	375 BCE	Prophet in Yehud (Judea)
Ruth	375 BCE	Prophet in Yehud (Judea)
Jonah	375 BCE	Prophet in Yehud (Judea)
Joel	325 BCE	Prophet in Judea
Song of Solomon	325 BCE	Unknown
Ecclesiastes	250 BCE	Unknown
Zechariah 9–14	175 BCE	Prophet in Judea
Daniel	165 BCE	Prophet in Judea

In chapters 8–12 that follow, we discuss thirteen of the first fourteen books *in the order they appear in the Bible* (we save **Ruth** for later). Thereafter, we will proceed more thematically, collecting texts from across the First Testament that reflect a similar period of time or style. We start with stories about the origins of life on Earth.

Discussion questions related to the chapters of Part II are found on page 88 (after chapter 10); on page 149 (after chapter 13); on page 200 (after chapter 16); and on page 216 (after chapter 18).

8. In the Beginning
Genesis 1–11

The jarring contradictions of life confound us. How can the same life be awful, yet sublime? Is a divine presence part of this? Does it make any difference how we live?

Ancient peoples tried to make sense of this by telling origin stories that explained life's realities and how contradictory aspects somehow fit together. The Israelites were no exception; their origin stories are passed on to us in the first eleven chapters of Genesis.

These stories were written in a form close to what we have today by Israelites living in Babylon under Persian rule. They likely were the great-grandchildren of those who had been exiled from Jerusalem; Babylon and Persia were the places of their birth and where they had lived their entire lives. Thus, the authors of these stories reflected the theology and historical consciousness of Jewish religious leadership at around the mid-point of the First Testament's 800-year literary arc, *not the beginning.*

Several of these stories are similar to stories of the ancient Sumerian civilization, which had once ruled Babylon.   In other respects, the Hebrew stories differ sharply from the origin stories of those who had taken them captive.   For example, violence is not given a role in the creation, governance or well-being of the world.   This simple "no" subverts the most critical of all the imperial claims—that the empire's violence is somehow *necessary* to life and civilization. (For further discussion, see question 5 on page 88.)

A. How did Earth and the heavens come to be? (1:1–2:3)

This is the first of two creation stories; it tells how over the course of six days, YHWH "created the heavens and the earth." On the sixth day, YHWH called upon Earth "to bring forth living creatures of every kind." On the same day, YHWH created "humankind in our image, according to our likeness." And as stated a verse later, "in his image, in the image of [YHWH] he created them, male and female he created them." Then

YHWH said to them, "Be fruitful and multiply. And fill the earth and subdue it, and have dominion over the fish of the sea and over the birds of the air and over every living thing that moves upon the earth."

Several features of the story stand out. YHWH delighted in the creation and repeatedly "saw that it was good." Each creative act built on those that went before, suggesting orderliness, even rationality. Earth is an active agent in the creative process, responding to YHWH's call to "put forth vegetation" and "bring forth living creatures." Humans and animals are vegetarians, without violence among them. There is no conflict, struggle or violence of any kind in the creative process.

Also, the story distinguishes the creation of humankind by two references to it bearing YHWH's "image" and "likeness." *What is YHWH's image in humanity?* The popular view is that it is an immortal soul in each individual, but this idea is not in the text. Instead, two other ways in which humanity is like YHWH are implied: the responsibility to care for ("have dominion over") creation and the generative capacity of being male and female.

B. Who are we as human beings? (2:4–2:25)

This retells the same story, but with a different chronology and an emphasis on the creation of the first man and the first woman.

Before vegetation grew upon Earth, YHWH shaped dust of the ground into a human form and then breathed "the breath of life" into its nostrils. Thus, the earthen figure became a living man. YHWH planted a garden "in Eden" and placed the man there with a mandate "to till it and keep it."

Also in contrast with the first story, this second telling suggests YHWH was not entirely pleased with the initial results: "It is not good that the man should be alone." So YHWH set out to provide suitable helpers and companions for the man. First YHWH made animals and birds out of the ground (just as YHWH had made the man) and brought them to the man for naming. But the man did not find any of them to be a suitable companion.

Next YHWH caused the man to fall into a deep sleep and while he slept, YHWH removed one of his ribs and fashioned it into a woman. This pleased the man who saw the woman as like himself, despite her differences: "This at last is bone of my bones, flesh of my flesh." Thus, the story tells us, a man's desire for woman will cause him to leave his own parents and "cling" to the woman, becoming one flesh with her.

This version of the story clearly reflects a male viewpoint with its emphasis on man finding in union with woman his missing part. It can be read to say that the woman was created to complete the man, but not visa-versa, thus legitimizing hierarchy and male control. This notion is heightened by the way only the man is involved in naming—and thus taking responsibility for—the animals.

YHWH is depicted in this story as determined to address the problem of man's loneliness. As for the disconcerting differences of gender, they are described as sparking attraction and intimacy, not fear, aversion or violence.

C. Why is life so hard? (3:1–3:24)

The man and woman lived in a garden and communicated directly with YHWH, who was nearby. Two special trees stood at the center of the garden (see Gen. 2:9). One bore fruit that when eaten gave eternal life; eating from this tree was permitted. The other bore fruit that when eaten gave knowledge of good and evil; eating from this tree was forbidden.

The story begins with a conversation between the woman and a serpent about this second tree. The woman acknowledged YHWH had instructed her and the man not to eat from it; if they did, they would die. The serpent responded with a half-truth: "You will not die for YHWH knows that when you eat of it your eyes will be opened and you will be like YHWH."

The woman did not say she wanted to be like YHWH. But the fruit on the tree attracted her and *she desired to be wise,* to comprehend life deeply. So though it put her trusting relationship with YHWH at risk, she ate and offered the fruit to the man and he ate.

The text does not claim the fruit failed to deliver knowledge of good and evil. Indeed, it suggests that after eating, the human couple immediately entered a different level of consciousness. They perceived their physical differences to be an embarrassment. They felt guilt about their disobedience and feared meeting YHWH strolling through the garden. They became calculating in their responses; first they hid from YHWH and then, after realizing that would be futile, attempted to deflect responsibility for their actions. With the eating of the fruit, they had become human in the way we are human.

YHWH punished the serpent by cursing it to a life of crawling in the dust and animosity with the woman. YHWH's response to Eve and the man was more ambiguous. Henceforth, the woman's astonishing and god-like capacity to bring new life into the world would be clouded by the painful pangs of childbearing. She would see the man's biological differences as a source of control and intimidation, not only attraction.

The consequences for the man involved a new way of acquiring food: instead of gathering what freely grew on trees and shrubs, he would plant and harvest crops in cultivated soil. But the soil would be resistant, YHWH said, and the change from food gathering to farming would be a very mixed experience. Much toil would be needed and man's efforts would be frustrated by thorns and thistles.

The woman and the man may have experienced these changes as punishments for having eaten the forbidden fruit. But the text doesn't say YHWH viewed it that way, nor does it say their action was evil. And we are left wondering if the woman and man sinned, took a step toward human maturity, or did both. Our puzzlement is heightened by the story's depiction of two trees at the center of the garden, each of which had the power to make humans like YHWH in one respect or another. Eve's interest focused on the one that was off-limits. Perhaps this is how the text conveys a critical aspect of the human condition: we most desire what we cannot have, even when another life-giving alternative is close at hand. And we find it very difficult to accept limits, even beneficial ones.

At any rate, *Eve's short-cut to wisdom changed everything*. It took humanity across a threshold from instinct to calculation. Life became a constant weighing of possibilities embedded in a welter of motives and desires. This did not mean all or even most of the choices were evil, but only that a calculating approach transformed human existence into a divided experience. Writing in the Second Testament, the apostle Paul described this dividedness: "I do not understand my own actions. For I do not do what I want, but I do the very thing I hate . . . I do not do the good I want, but the evil I do not want is what I do" (Rom. 7:15–19).

Did the woman and man die as YHWH had said they would? Not immediately, but eventually. Though YHWH continued to care for them, providing leather clothing to replace the wilted fig leaves, YHWH banished them from the garden because, knowing evil, they might not only choose evil for themselves, but also entrench it as a permanent feature of creation by eating from the tree of life. In an act of mercy, YHWH closed off their path to immortality. "You are dust," YHWH said, "and to dust you shall return."

D. What is the source of evil? (4:1–4:25)

Violence is part of the creation narratives told by many cultures. The victims of this violence are guilty and get what they deserve. This fourth story from **Genesis** follows that general theme, but provides several twists: the victim was innocent and the guilty perpetrator did not get what he deserved.

With the help of the man, Eve gave birth to two sons, Cain and Abel. As adults, Cain grew food in the soil and Abel raised sheep. One day, each gave a portion of what had been produced to YHWH. Cain's offering was nothing special, but Abel's consisted of the firstborn (thus largest) lamb. YHWH was impressed with Abel's offering, but not with Cain's.

Embarrassment and anger filled Cain's heart. YHWH noticed and spoke to Cain, reminding him that it was within his power to offer a gift as special as Abel's. YHWH also warned Cain that if he persisted in offering less than his best, then he risked coming under the control of "sin" that was "lurking at the door." Instead of heeding YHWH's advice, Cain invited Abel to join him in one of the fields. It was a set-up; while there together, Cain killed his brother.

YHWH immediately confronted Cain and asked where Abel was. Cain replied, "I do not know; am I my brother's keeper?" YHWH said: "Your brother's blood is crying out to me from the ground." YHWH banished Cain from the field he had been farming: "When you till the ground, it will no longer yield to you its strength; you will be a fugitive and a wanderer on the earth."

Cain expressed horror at his plight: "I shall be hidden from your face . . . anyone who meets me may kill me." YHWH said that would not happen because whoever killed Cain would bring "sevenfold vengeance" or retribution upon himself. And YHWH marked Cain with a warning to that effect "so that no one who came upon him would kill him."

Cain settled "east of Eden" and away from YHWH's presence. There he started a family and built the first city. The story names descendants from the next five generations. A descendant, Lamech, also killed a man and felt the same horror about potential consequences. He said: "If Cain is avenged sevenfold, truly Lamech seventy-sevenfold."

This is a troubling story that takes us deep into the nature of evil. "Sin" is first mentioned and made manifest in connection with violence— the murder of a brother. Once out of the box, violence threatened to escalate like wild fire and consume many more victims. Cain was likely to be next, but it would not have stopped with him. His death would have produced another round of violence and later in time, the stakes would be even higher.

YHWH heard the cry of Abel's spilt blood; the injustice of that event reached YHWH's ears and YHWH responded. But YHWH did not drive the revenge dynamic; there was no eye-for-an-eye, but instead a candid conversation with the murderer and an attempt to interrupt the cycle of violence with the merciful placement of a warning mark. Yes, the banishment of Cain from his fields can be understood as punishment. Yet it pales when compared with what Cain deserved.

What is the connection between Cain's crime and his building the first city "away from the presence of YHWH" (Gen. 4:16)? Anthropologists have explored this question; they see this story as an account of how escalating violence prompted the ancients to live in settled towns and cities. Protective walls shortened the death spiral by enabling residents to expel high-risk individuals and prevent outsiders from entering. Viewed in this light, the original sin that has plagued human civilization was Cain's violent jealousy, not Eve's desire for wisdom.

E. Is Earth a trustworthy home? (6:5–9:17)

The story of Noah, his ark and the great flood seems on its face to be about the violence of nature. Certainly the power of floods caused ancients to fear, as they do us; this was particularly true where the authors lived, near the rivers of Mesopotamia on low, flat land.

Yet the story is complicated by associating the fearsome power of nature with the violence of humankind. "The earth was filled with violence," the text says. It was so bad that YHWH regretted creating the man and the woman. So, the story tells us, YHWH decided to "blot out" people, animals, creeping things and birds from Earth by bringing a great flood that would destroy "all flesh in which is the breath of life." Thus, the story seems to suggest human violence *caused* nature's fury.

Noah was a righteous man who "walked with YHWH." YHWH told Noah of the impending flood and directed him to make a three-decked ark of very specific dimensions. It was needed, YHWH said, because "I am going to bring a flood of waters on the earth . . . but I will establish my covenant with you."

After Noah, his family and the animals, creeping things and birds of every species alive on Earth had boarded the ark, "the fountains of the great deep burst forth and the windows of the heavens were opened." The rain continued unabated for forty days and forty nights. Flood waters covered Earth, even the highest mountains and everything whose nostrils breathed "the breath of life" died. It took nearly a year for the water to subside. At long last, Noah, his family and the animals, creeping things and birds came out of the ark and on to dry land. Then Noah built an altar and offered to YHWH a sacrifice of "every clean animal and every clean bird."

YHWH was pleased by Noah's act of gratitude and said: "I will never again curse the ground because of humankind, for the inclination of the human heart is evil from youth; nor will I ever again destroy every living creature as I have done. As long as the earth endures, seedtime and harvest, cold and heat, summer and winter, day and night shall not cease." Later in the story, YHWH restated the promise in more limited terms: "never again shall there be a *flood* to destroy the earth." As a sign of this promise, YHWH set the rainbow in the sky.

Along with this reassurance from YHWH came three other changes that suggested violence would not be eliminated by Noah's fresh start. First, the animals, creeping things, birds and fish of the sea began for the first time to fear human beings. Second, human consumption of meat was authorized, thus explaining animals' newfound fear of humans. Third, a principle of proportionality was put in place to control violence: "Whoever shed the blood of a human, by a human shall that person's blood be shed; for in his own image God made humankind." While this may strike us as more severe than the way YHWH dealt with Cain, the more important point is how it restrained the spiral of revenge in which a homicide was avenged first seven-fold, and then seventy-seven fold.

This story does not dispute the cause-and-effect relationship between human violence and nature's storms, nor does it express discomfort with YHWH's use of a flood to purge humanity of evil. Instead, it portrays YHWH as a god who can be trusted to *limit* the impact of nature's destructiveness. Nature's threat remains and many people will die as a result, but some will survive to go on. Because of this "mercy" of YHWH, Earth will never be emptied of all creatures "in which is the breath of life," nor will the seasons and "seedtime and harvest" cease. YHWH had made that promise and sealed it with a bow.

F. How did different cultures come to be? (11:1–11:9)

For a people whose creation story included only one man and one woman, and whose flood story ended with only one family on Earth, the variety of human physical traits, cultures and languages was perplexing. How did such diversity come to be? This story answered those questions.

Once upon a time, all people spoke the same language and lived in the same region of Earth. And they said to one another, "Come, let us build for ourselves a city, and a tower with its top in the heavens, and let us make a name for ourselves; otherwise, we shall be scattered abroad upon the face of the whole earth." And so they started to build a city and completed its tower, a tall ziggurat.

It was a very significant accomplishment. But when YHWH "came down" and paid a visit to the city, YHWH was alarmed: "This is only the beginning of what they will do; nothing that they propose to do will now be impossible for them."

And so YHWH confused their speech so they no longer spoke the same language. And YHWH "scattered them abroad from there over the face of all the earth and they left off building the city." Therefore, the story tells us, "the city was called Babel, because there (YHWH) confused the language of all the earth, and from there scattered them abroad."

The story clearly conveys respect for the human potential to accomplish remarkable feats; even YHWH was impressed by the tower and the emerging city. Although the tower is often interpreted as proof of the human desire to be like YHWH, "the heavens" probably should be understood simply as "the sky." In other words, the builders wanted to construct a really tall tower. Why? Because, the story tells us, *they wanted to accomplish something impressive that would overcome the centrifugal forces of life and hold people together.* That is an admirable purpose, is it not?

Empire-builders and those with an imperial perspective will answer with a hearty "yes!" But to the Israelite people, living under the thumb of empire and feeling its scourge, this story was a great comfort. They did not need to fear the centrifugal dynamics within their communities nor the marginal and scattered character of their lives. YHWH appreciated diversity and applauded the way scattering led to the populating of Earth. YHWH opposed the empire's pretensions and its obsessions with achievement, uniformity and centralization.

The anti-imperial message of the story is clear enough. But the story also reiterates a second message that is very good news: YHWH will prevent evil—which is always present and frequently in charge—*from becoming permanently entrenched.* Just as YHWH denied Eve and Adam eternal life by banishing them from the garden, so God denied Babel eternal dominance by confusing the speech of its residents. It was not that Babel was evil, but it had the knowledge to pursue evil. If it did, YHWH did not want the consequences to be eternal.

9. A Subversive God
Genesis 12—Exodus 15

Beginning with the twelfth chapter of **Genesis** and the first mention of Abram and Sarai, we are told about a particular group of people, the Hebrews. As these stories are told, we also learn more about YHWH, their god.

Nearly 1,400 years passed between the time Abram and Sarai are said to have lived and the time when these stories were written. Texts written earlier than **Genesis** mentioned Abram's name (as well as Isaac's) so we know the Israelites had an oral tradition that included these patriarchs. Imaginative writers, working with that tradition and their own experiences of exile, authored this text.

Who were those authors? They were descendants of prisoners of war who had been forcibly taken into exile. Far from their homes, they voiced despair and a desire for revenge in words recorded in Psalm 137.

By the rivers of Babylon, there we sat down,
    and there we wept, when we remembered Zion.
On the willows we hung our harps, there our captors asked for songs,
    our tormentors asked for mirth, "Sing us the songs of Zion!"
How could we sing the LORD's song in a foreign land?
If we forget you, O Jerusalem,
    let our right hands wither,
    let our tongues cling to the roofs of our mouths;
    if we do not remember you,
    if we do not set Jerusalem above our highest joy.
Remember, O LORD, the day of Jerusalem's fall,
    how they said, "Tear it down! Tear it down!
    down to the foundations!"
O daughter Babylon, you devastator, happy shall those be
    who pay you back what you have done to us!
    Happy shall they be who take your little ones
    and dash them against the rock!

How would their Babylon-born children learn to know YHWH, the god who had called the Hebrew people to be a living witness to a non-imperial way of life? Drawing on ancient oral traditions, manuscripts written before the exile, and their surprising encounter of YHWH "in a foreign land," the authors of **Genesis** wrote to answer that question.

The stories recorded there may surprise us. As we might expect, the authors spoke critically of empire. But they did not reflect the bravado and self-glorification we expect from a proud people who have been humiliated. Instead, they portrayed their ancestors as flawed and YHWH as a god who subverts conventional notions about how the world works.

Many scholars emphasize the editorial work on the book of **Exodus** during the exile in Babylon, near the time **Genesis** was written. Following the work of Howard-Brook,[13] we emphasize that *substantial parts of* **Exodus** *were written 400 years earlier* by scribes who lived in the Northern Kingdom of Israel (Ephraim). It was a time when Ephraim was a vital society, but struggled to resist the Assyrian Empire's encroachment as well as less powerful regional rivals. To clarify its identity and strengthen its resolve, scribes told the heroic story of Moses, the exodus from Egypt and how the people met YHWH at Sinai.

Like **Genesis**, the book of **Exodus** is an imaginative retelling of history that draws on the oral traditions of the Hebrew people. We are convinced some of the Hebrew people had historic roots in Egypt, and the authors may have had access to some Egypt-specific information. Yet the exaggerated way **Exodus** tells the story of the Hebrew departure from Egypt is very different from the self-critical style of **Genesis** and prompts us to wonder what agenda was at work in its writing. To cite one example, the text tells us 600,000 Hebrew men and their families walked out of the empire with their "flocks and herds" plus a large share of Egypt's "jewelry of silver and gold and clothing." Indeed, it says the Hebrews "plundered the Egyptians" before leaving (Ex. 12:35–37).

What were the authors trying to accomplish? As Howard-Brook explains, they wanted to explain why Ephraim had refused to give its loyalty to the "kings" in Jerusalem. By portraying Moses' confrontation with the Pharaoh in epic, YHWH-directed terms, they legitimated

---

[13]   Ibid., 139.

Ephraim's founding leader, Jeroboam, who had led the Northern Kingdom out of the grasp of the empire-infatuated House of David.[14]

When reading **Genesis** and **Exodus**, it is important to recognize the importance of two foundational "covenants" described there. A covenant within these contexts is *a solemn and enduring commitment to a relationship of trust, reliance and responsibility*. Much of the rest of the Bible assumes an understanding of these two covenants, each of which has its literary origin in **Exodus**.

The first entailed the promises of YHWH to give to Abram (later called Abraham) "this land [of Canaan] to possess" (Gen. 15:7), to "be [YHWH] to you and to your offspring after you" (Gen. 17:7), to make of Abram's progeny "a multitude of nations" (Gen. 17:4) and descendants as "countless as the stars" (Gen. 15:5), and to bless all nations though these descendants (Gen. 12:3). Abram's part in the covenant was to "keep" YHWH's covenant (Gen. 17:9), do "righteousness and justice" (Gen. 18:19), and bear a physical reminder of his allegiance to YHWH by shortening the foreskin of his penis (Gen. 17:9–27).

The second covenant entailed an exchange of promises between YHWH and the Hebrew people at the mountain in Sinai where Moses first spoke the words YHWH had given him. YHWH declared the people "a priestly kingdom and a holy nation" who YHWH "bore on eagles' wings." YHWH gave the Israelites the Law of Moses, which would enable them to live in the world as an alternative to empire (Ex. 19:4–6), and promised to provide a home for them in Canaan. In return, the people promised to obey YHWH's commands (Ex. 24:3).

Here then are seven of the conventional notions of authority subverted by the narrative that begins with **Genesis** 12 and continues through **Exodus** 15.

A. The empire is glorious and awesome

In the initial verses of **Genesis** 12, we meet Abram and Sarai, who came from "Ur of the Chaldeans" (Gen. 11:28), an ancient city near the mouth of the Euphrates. But they left that place in the heart of the ancient

---

[14]   Ibid., 100, 138-139.

Babylonian empire of Hammurabi and, in response to the call of YHWH (Gen. 12:1), moved to a backwater called Canaan where they and their servants lived in tents as nomads. There they became acquainted with this new god, later called YHWH, whose unconventional expectations shaped their lives.

By starting in this fashion, the writers proclaimed YHWH to be unimpressed by empire and its grandeur. Who needs it?

Similarly, in the second chapter of **Exodus** we meet Moses, the Hebrew boy adopted by the Pharaoh's daughter and raised in the Pharaoh's court. Moses also turned his back on the opportunities of an empire and lived instead in a backwater, the land of Midian. There in the wilderness he came upon a bush that burned, but was not consumed and he heard the voice of YHWH: "So come, I will send you to Pharaoh to bring my people, the Israelites, out of Egypt" (Ex. 3:10). Moses begged off, citing his various deficiencies, but YHWH persisted. Finally, Moses agreed and moved back to Egypt where he initiated a series of confrontations with the Pharaoh and his advisors.

Even before the story introduces Moses, it tells us of Shiprah and Puah, two Hebrew midwives who disobeyed an order from the Pharaoh to kill the male infants they delivered from Hebrew women. "The midwives feared [YHWH]; they did not do as the king of Egypt had commanded them, but they let the boys live" (Ex. 1:16). When confronted by the Pharaoh for their law-breaking, they explained that because Hebrew women gave birth so quickly, they usually reached the expectant mother's side too late to intervene. The Pharaoh apparently accepted this dubious explanation. Thus, the story portrays YHWH-fearing Hebrew women able to match wits with the great Pharaoh.

Despite their exit from empire, Abram and Sarai found reliance on empire to be a difficult habit to break. Soon after moving to Canaan, they experienced a famine. Accustomed as they were to the empire's way of managing and exploiting crises, they "went down to Egypt" to seek its help. There they immediately encountered an injustice; the Pharaoh conscripted the exotic Sarai into his harem. He thought she was Abram's sister; had the Pharaoh known she was Abram's wife, he probably would have taken her anyway after killing Abram. In any event, the text states that YHWH "afflicted Pharaoh and his house with great plagues because of Sarai" (Gen. 12:17). So the Pharaoh returned Sarai to her husband and expelled them and their household from Egypt. Abram and Sarai then returned to Canaan.

In the story of Abram and his nephew, Lot, the text doesn't deal directly with the empire, but more specifically with the fascination Lot and his family held for empire's methods and ways. Abram and Lot each had large herds of livestock. To avoid strife over access to pasture land, they separated and Lot chose to go east to the plains near the Jordan River, which was "like the land of Egypt" (Gen. 13:10). Though a keeper of flocks, Lot took up residence in Sodom, one of the cities of the Jordan Plain. It was not the empire, but a place occupied by empire wannabees.

Meanwhile, strangers visited Abram and Sarai and spoke about the "outcry" against the wickedness of Sodom and its sister city, Gomorrah. Abram begged YHWH to spare Sodom if fifty, forty, thirty, twenty, or even ten "righteous" people lived there. YHWH replied, "For the sake of ten I will not destroy it" (Gen. 18:32).

But not even ten righteous dwelled there and chapter 19 of **Genesis** tells of the city's final hours. The mindless violence of the men of the city is illustrated by their desire to rape the visitors Lot was hosting. The many references to "the city" throughout the chapter convey the authors' intention that we associate the wanton wickedness of Lot's neighbors with the urban structure of their lives. And when Lot and his family made a miraculous escape from Sodom, Lot's wife "looked back and she became a pillar of salt" (Gen. 19:26). Though Lot escaped, he like his wife remained wistful for the false security of the city. His fascination with empire's ways had made him into a man who could no longer imagine living another way. And so he pled with his rescuers for permission to flee to "a little city" nearby (Gen.19:20–21) where he could again experience a small measure of empire's charms.

Abram's great-grandson, a shepherd boy named Joseph, was sold into slavery by his brothers for twenty pieces of silver (Gen. 37:28). Joseph ended up in Egypt where the captain of the Pharaoh's guard, Potiphar, purchased him. An encounter with Potiphar's wife landed Joseph in prison for a time. Eventually, an ability to interpret dreams brought Joseph to the attention of the Pharaoh, who said "there is no one so discerning and wise" (Gen. 41:36).

Joseph excelled in the ways of empire. After he was appointed chief of staff for the Pharaoh's government, Joseph centralized the storage and distribution of grain. Then, when food became scarce due to crop failure, "all the world came to Joseph in Egypt to buy grain" (Gen. 41:57). When the food shortage continued, Joseph exchanged food for the herds and lands of the Egyptian people. "As for the people, [Pharaoh] made slaves of them from one end of Egypt to the other" (Gen. 47:21).

Joseph's brothers also came to Egypt for food. Through a tense reunion in which revenge hung in the balance, Joseph reconciled with his brothers: "Even though you intended to do harm to me, [YHWH] intended it for good in order to preserve a numerous people" (Gen. 50:20). The brothers brought their father, Jacob, to Egypt and all settled on land east of the Nile River "in the land of Goshen" (Gen. 46:28).

The story of Joseph is told in great detail through the last fifteen chapters of **Genesis**. It offers many lessons, one of which cautions readers against serving the empire: for all of Joseph's success, his efforts were co-opted by the empire and used to enslave Joseph's descendants. As for the vaunted expertise needed to administer an empire, the story suggests it is overblown. Anyone can do it, even an uneducated Hebrew shepherd-boy.

Yet the way the story is told also conveys admiration for the power of Joseph's position, the breadth of his impact on Egypt and the vast number of people who depended upon him for survival. Might YHWH oppose empire because of the character of the people typically in charge? If good people such as Joseph were in charge, wouldn't YHWH support empire? Between the lines, these are the questions we hear the authors asking from their setting as resident Jews within the Persian Empire.

The **Exodus** text, on the other hand, expresses no ambivalence about the empire as it describes Moses' extended confrontation with Egypt's Pharaoh. The Pharaoh responded to Moses' words, "Let my people go" (Ex. 5:1), by increasing their work and cutting back on their support. He called the Hebrews "lazy" when they complained (Ex. 5:17). And so Moses summoned the first of a series of plagues: the waters in the Nile River turned to blood.

Howard-Brook says "the plagues present not a series of arbitrary horrors, but . . . bring to public awareness what life is really like" under empire.[15] The way empires run the world has bad consequences for the quality of the food supply, the balance within nature and the sustainability of natural resources. This is how the first audience understood the plague stories: *a revealing of the empire's hidden costs.* Viewed in this light, we begin to understand how the exodus story served not only to encourage the Northern Kingdom to resist the power grabs of the Assyrian Empire, but also as a warning against mimicking its ways.

But this warning would be successful only if the Hebrew people ended their enchantment with the empire. This is exactly what the story of Moses' confrontations with the Pharaoh was meant to accomplish. Through round after round, it tells of the Pharaoh's agreement to release the people, only then to tell us YHWH had "hardened Pharaoh's heart" so that he withdrew his consent. This is baffling if we try to use the story to describe YHWH. But as a story of disenchantment with and detachment from the empire, the story rings true. The text is very clear in telling us why it includes these Pharaoh stories: so that "[YHWH] may show these signs among [the Egyptians], and that you may tell your children and grandchildren *how I have made fools of the Egyptians*" (Ex. 10:1–2, emphasis added). Rather than regarding the empire's leaders with awe, YHWH wanted the Hebrew people to regard them as fools. Today, as we hear the promises of empire's leaders, might we face a similar choice?

B. Primogeniture rules family life

Primogeniture is a cultural practice entailing the transfer of the father's wealth and status to the oldest son. It is the system by which successful men ensure that the sources of their power are not divided and dispersed. Over time, primogeniture creates a landed aristocracy with special privileges and entrenched powers held by only a few men.

Abraham had eight sons, but "gave all he had to Isaac," his *second* son (Gen. 25:5). This decision is attributed to YHWH, who said: "As for Ishmael, I have heard you; I will bless him and make him fruitful and

---

[15]   Ibid., 146.

exceedingly numerous; he shall be the father of twelve princes and I will make him a great nation. But my covenant I will establish with Isaac" (Gen. 17:20-21).

Isaac and his wife, Rebekah, had twin sons, Esau and Jacob. Isaac intended to bestow his primary blessing on Esau, who was born first. But the boys' mother, Rachel, and Jacob conspired to deceive the elderly Isaac and he inadvertently named Jacob as the primary carrier of his legacy (Gen. 27:1–40). As the story is told, YHWH honored this deception.

Jacob had twelve sons with his two wives and their maid servants. Joseph, the second-to-youngest son, played a much more prominent role in the family than his older brothers. In the distribution of his estate, Jacob gave to Joseph "one portion more than to [his] brothers" (Gen. 48:22).

Joseph married an Egyptian woman and they had two sons, Manasseh and Ephraim.   Near the end of Jacob's life, Joseph brought his two sons to their grandfather for a blessing. To Joseph's disappointment, Jacob's blessing "put Ephraim ahead of Manasseh" (Gen. 48:20).

We see in these stories an insight: YHWH's blessings do not follow conventional patterns of wealth, power and custom. Interestingly, this insight also applies to how the story of the two Israelite nations is told. The northern society—first organized, much larger and the *only* one with an oral tradition that included the patriarchs and Sinai covenant—did not survive. The southern society—second organized, smaller and living on borrowed traditions—endured.

C. Scapegoats make for peace

Scapegoating is a way for a group to release tension and avoid the escalation of violence. But the scapegoat pays a very high price for this. S/he takes on the shame of and blame for the problem and becomes the target for the aggression that enables the group to restore a sense of equilibrium and calm. The story of Hagar tells us that YHWH opposes the scapegoat mechanism and stands with the victim.

Because Sarai was barren and could not conceive a child, she arranged for Abram to take Hagar, her Egyptian slave girl, as "a wife" (Gen. 16:3). Hagar promptly conceived and so irritated Sarai by her fertility that Sarai drove the pregnant young woman out of their camp.

The text tells us an angel found her "by a spring in the wilderness" (Gen. 16:7) and told her to return to the camp, submit to Sarai and bear a son: "You shall call him Ishmael, for [YHWH] has given heed to your affliction" (Gen. 16:11). So Hagar returned and gave birth to Ishmael.

Later, after Sarai (now renamed Sarah) had given birth to Isaac in her old age and the two boys were old enough to play together, tensions rose again: "Cast out this slave woman with her son; for the son of this slave woman shall not inherit along with my son, Isaac," Sarah said (Gen. 21:10). Abraham resisted, but YHWH told him to comply with Sarah's wishes. So Abraham sent his wife and son out into the wilderness again.

This time, Hagar fully expected to watch her son die there. She placed Ishmael under a bush and "lifted up her voice and wept" (Gen. 21:16). The story tells us YHWH heard their cries. And the angel of YHWH again spoke to Hagar, telling her not to be afraid and encouraging her to be strong. "Come, lift up the boy and hold him fast with your hand, for I will make a great nation of him" (Gen. 21:18). And then, the text tells us, YHWH opened Hagar's eyes and she saw a well of water. And so Ishmael's life was saved.

Hagar, the outsider who lacked allies or status, was the ideal target for the hostility produced by the dysfunction in Abraham's and Sarah's relationship. We see the re-enactment of her suffering in our own time as the strong repeatedly shift the blame for their failings onto the weak. Certainly this is a favorite tactic of the empire. Remarkably, the text twice portrays Abraham and Sarah wielding this ugly tactic. Yet YHWH protected Hagar and Ishmael and communicated with this slave-woman in a way that only Abraham had experienced up to that point in the story.

D. YHWH intends possession of the land to be exclusive

YHWH's covenant with Abraham included the promise of land to his descendants. This land stretched "from the river of Egypt to the great river Euphrates" (Gen. 15:18). As noted, Abraham had eight sons. The text tells us YHWH intended for Isaac and his descendants to benefit from the promise of land (Gen. 26:3). Did YHWH intend Isaac's descendants to have exclusive ownership or only some form of shared ownership?

When Sarah died and Abraham needed a piece of land to serve as her final resting place, he certainly did not act as if he had an exclusive claim to any part of the land he had occupied.   Chapter 23 describes his negotiation with the Hittites to buy a parcel for 400 shekels of silver. Chapter 26 recounts Isaac's protracted negotiations with Philistine leaders over water rights; it speaks approvingly of the manner in which Isaac concluded the matter. Both stories reflect the lesson the authors had learned in Babylon: *faithfulness to YHWH did not require geographic segregation.*

YHWH also made the promise of land to Jacob, one of Isaac's sons, as he fled Canaan out of fear of the wrath of his deceived brother, Esau. The context for this promise was an open field where Jacob slept with his head on a rock. In a dream, he saw a ladder ascending from Earth to heaven and YHWH standing at the base, saying:

> The land on which you lie I will give to you and to your offspring; and your offspring will be like the dust of the earth, and you shall spread abroad to the west and to the east and to the north and to the south; and all the families of the earth shall be blessed in you and in your offspring. Know that I am with you and will keep you wherever you go, and will bring you back to this land, for I will not leave you until I have done what I have promised you. (Gen. 28:13–15)

When Jacob awoke, he exclaimed: "How awesome is this place! This is none other than the house of [YHWH], and this is the gate of heaven" (Gen. 28:17).

This story of Jacob and his dream touches two profound aspects of the Israelites' story. One is where YHWH can be worshipped. Earlier biblical texts had insisted only Jerusalem and its temple was an appropriate place, but Jacob's epiphany suggests otherwise.   After all, Jacob was at Bethel, the very place Ephraim's first king, Jeroboam, so controversially designated as a place of worship, the very place that Judah's "good" king Josiah desecrated *so it could never be used for worship again* (2 Kings 23:15–16). This subsequent telling of Jacob's dream served to rehabilitate Bethel and reflected the authors' encounter with YHWH during their exile in Babylon. It demonstrated that YHWH's presence was not limited to the temple in Jerusalem; YHWH could be encountered anywhere.

The story also reiterates YHWH's gift to the Israelites of Canaan as a kind of homeland to which they could always return. How is this promise to be understood? The broader telling of Jacob's story helps answer this question. Jacob, the second-born twin, always wanted to be first and so lived a life of contention and strife. For example, one day Esau returned after working in the field and was "famished." He asked Jacob for a portion of stew Jacob was cooking. Jacob shared the food with his brother, but only after securing Esau's oath that Jacob henceforth would be regarded as the older child and thus entitled to all the rights of primogeniture (Gen. 25:29–34).

This vignette is meant to elicit in the reader strongly negative feelings about Jacob's selfishness and arrogance. But the application of the story to the Israelite and Canaanite claims to the land is usually missed. With regard to the land, the Canaanites were the older brother and the Israelites the selfish and arrogant younger brother. The Canaanites didn't claim to own the land exclusive of the Israelites, but the Israelites made such a claim. They desired to be the "older brother," and once they gained the upper hand, used their power to exclude the Canaanites.

The text tells us how years later, after Jacob had four wives and many children, he prepared to meet his long-estranged brother. During a night of wrestling with the angel of YHWH, Jacob's worldview changed and he repented of his selfishness and arrogance. The next day he met Esau, who approached in the company of 400 men. Jacob greatly feared this encounter, sought to appease Esau with generous gifts and took elaborate precautions to mitigate the carnage he expected to occur if Esau exercised his wrath. But their reunion was not at all what Jacob expected. "Esau ran to meet [Jacob] and embraced him and fell on his neck and kissed him and they wept" (Gen. 33:4). As for the gifts Jacob offered, Esau said, "I have enough, my brother" (Gen. 33:9). Jacob's reply to Esau revealed an astonishing insight: *"Truly, to see your face is like seeing the face of [YHWH]"* (Gen. 33:10, emphasis added).

And so for the first time, Jacob deferred to Esau, saying: "Let my lord pass on ahead of his servant, and I will lead on slowly" (Gen. 33:14).

At long last, Jacob was free of his need to dominate his brother and from the view that YHWH's promise had made him a winner and Esau a loser.

To think of Israelite possession of Canaan as shared is consistent with how we understand YHWH's broader covenant with Abraham. YHWH's blessing benefited Abraham and his descendants, to be sure, but from the very beginning, YHWH intended that blessing to be for "all the families of the earth" (Gen. 12:3). Similarly, YHWH indeed gave the land of Canaan to the Israelite people as a homeland, but from the very beginning intended their possession to be shared with others who lived there. For the writers of **Genesis**, shaped by their experience of exile in Babylon, this is the nature of YHWH's gifts: inclusive, not exclusive.

E. The Israelites are morally superior

As the humiliated victims, the Jewish exiles in Babylon could have sought reassurance by recording stories that demonstrated their superiority to others, including their captors. "We may look like losers," they might have said, "but actually we're morally exceptional."

But that's not how **Genesis** reads. In chapter 20, we read how Abraham again lied about Sarah's identity, telling the Philistine king that she was his sister. In a dream, YHWH revealed *to the king* that Sarah was a married woman. This pagan king confronted Abraham and taught him basic morality: "What have you done to us? . . . You have done things to me that ought not to be done" (Gen. 20:9). Abraham said: "I did it because I thought, 'There is no fear of [YHWH] at all in this place'" (Gen. 20:11). His assumption of moral superiority had led him astray.

Jacob deceived his father and brother. As we saw in the previous section, his brother later became his teacher in the ways of forgiveness and reconciliation.

After Jacob's daughter, Dinah, was raped by a Canaanite man (Shechem), the man's father tried to make things right by proposing the marriage of his son to Dinah and proposing a new spirit of cooperation between their two families. "Make marriages with us; give your daughters to us and take our daughters for yourselves. You shall live with us and the land shall be open to you; live and trade in it, and get property in it" (Gen. 34:9–10). The sons of Jacob "answered Shechem and his father deceitfully" (Gen. 34:13). They arranged for the men of the family to be circumcised and then, during their time of healing, Simeon and Levi killed them all. The Canaanite women and children were taken captive "and made their prey" (Gen. 34:29) and all their property was stolen. Jacob disapproved of this massacre and regretted it until his dying day (Gen. 49:5–7), but failed to act in a timely way to stop the carnage.

Tamar, a Canaanite woman, gave Jacob's son, Judah, a lesson in the how to deal justly with widows. Tamar had been married to Judah's son, but was widowed. Though she appealed to Judah to arrange a second marriage, he neglected to do so. Tamar disguised herself as a prostitute, seduced Judah and conceived by him a child who secured her place in the family that was casting her aside. Judah said, "She is more in the right than I" (Gen. 38:26).

During his years in the wilderness, Moses married Zipporah, the daughter of a Midianite named Jethro who was a priest of another religion. She circumcised their son, Gershom, an act of faithfulness to YHWH that Moses had neglected (Ex. 4:24–26). Later, during the Israelite journey through the wilderness of Sinai, Jethro visited Moses, gave advice that Moses accepted and made offerings to YHWH. "Aaron came with all the elders of Israel to eat bread with Moses' father-in-law in the presence of [YHWH]" (Ex. 18:12). This portrayal of positive Midianite influence is remarkably different from the evil image provided by **Numbers** and **Judges**.

F. YHWH has an appetite for human blood

What do the gods require of mere mortals? The answer varies, depending on the god we are talking about. In general, gods (whether described as deities or as other sources of authority) *demand human commitment*. Nothing demonstrates commitment more convincingly than spilling blood, either one's own or the blood of a loved one.

So what does YHWH require? The twenty-second chapter of **Genesis** addresses this question. Abraham perceived YHWH to tell him to sacrifice his son as an act of worship and commitment. After all, this was what the gods of his Canaanite neighbors expected of them. So Abraham took the boy (**Genesis** says it was Isaac, Islamic scholars suggest it was

Ishmael) and a donkey laden with firewood to a mountain-top. There, Abraham bound his son to an altar piled with wood and drew his knife to kill him as part of a ritual sacrifice to YHWH. But at the last moment, Abraham sensed he should stop. "Do not lay your hand on the boy or do anything to him; for now I know that you fear [YHWH]" (Gen. 22:12).

In contrast to neighboring gods, YHWH apparently does not require child sacrifice. Yet there was enough ambiguity in the story to leave a shadow of a doubt.

That doubt is laid to rest by the story of the Passover. The Passover ritual is described by **Exodus** 12 as a practice instituted by YHWH through Moses just before the Hebrew people left Egypt. In large part it consisted of a meal of preparation for the journey out of empire and into the wilderness where the people would meet YHWH and learn to practice YHWH's ways.

The background for the new ritual was YHWH's intention to "strike down every firstborn in the land of Egypt, both human beings and animals" on the night that the Passover meal was eaten. This horrible event, YHWH said, would be judgment "on all the gods of Egypt" (Ex. 12:12). The Hebrew people avoided this atrocity by placing the blood of a goat or sheep on the doorframes of their houses. Thus, this plague of death passed over their families and flocks.

There is no historical artifact or record confirming that this horrible event ever happened. Nevertheless, it is a prominent part of the exodus story. When read from the perspective of an Egyptian family living at that time and place, it seems to confirm YHWH's bloodlust.

But it was not written for such an audience. Instead, it was written for Israelites who lived many centuries later and knew little about Egyptians. The question they faced was whether to adopt an act of commitment long practiced by their neighbors and encouraged by the encroaching Assyrian Empire: passing their children through the fire and offering them to Moloch, an ancient Canaanite god. Didn't YHWH expect as much? The message of the **Exodus** story was that while other gods required the murder of children, YHWH did not. Instead of the blood of children, YHWH required that the firstborn of each family be "set apart" (Gen. 13:12) for *living* service.

So why does the text attribute the death plague to YHWH? Why not instead attribute it to the Egyptian gods who history tells us did require the shedding of children's blood? Trying to answer that question takes us into the Israelite understanding of the relationship between YHWH and other gods. As discussed in Chapter 1, the Israelite people moved over time from a belief that YHWH was the greatest of many gods to the belief that YHWH was the only god. At the time **Exodus** was written, the authors held the former view. And rather than attribute the death plague to Egypt's lesser gods, the Israelite scribes attributed it to YHWH, the god greater than even the gods of the empire.

Faithful Jews practice the Passover ritual yet today. It remains a witness to the character of YHWH, a god who does not lust after human blood but asks instead for a living commitment.

G. The empire's military is invincible

As previously noted, the people of Ephraim lived in fear of the Assyrian Empire. Its army was without peer and its reputation for ruthless and cruel conquest was enough to make the bravest man cower in fright. When such a power has you in its sights, there are no good choices. There are just various versions of surrender and defeat.

Into the bleakness of this reality, **Exodus** identified another alternative: YHWH will defeat empire for you—not by making you better fighters than they are, but by turning their prowess and pride into liabilities.

When the Pharaoh discovered (how could he not have already known?) that the Hebrews had left their homes and were traveling east toward the Red Sea, he pursued them with his mighty army of horses, chariots, chariot drivers and soldiers.

> As Pharaoh drew near, the Israelites looked back. . . In great fear, the Israelites cried out to YHWH. They said to Moses: "Was it because there were no graves in Egypt that you have taken us away to die in the wilderness? What have you done to us, bringing us out of Egypt? . . . It would have been better for us to serve the Egyptians than to die in the wilderness." (Ex. 14:10–12)

But Moses remained calm and told the people to go forward toward the Red Sea. When they reached its banks, Moses "stretched out his hand over the sea [and] YHWH drove the sea back by a strong east wind all night, and turned the sea into dry land; and the waters were divided" (Ex. 14:21). The people began crossing with the Egyptian chariots closing rapidly behind. But then the Egyptian chariots' wheels sank into the sea bottom and their progress was slowed. When the Hebrews had completed their crossing, Moses again stretched his hand over the sea and the waters returned to their normal depth. Every member of Pharaoh's army that had attempted the crossing drowned; "not one of them remained" (Ex. 14:28). Even the Egyptians realized that [YHWH] had done it (Ex. 14:25).

Apparently the empire's army was not as invincible as it seemed; YHWH made a fool of Pharaoh and his chariots.

Again, apart from the text of **Exodus**, there is no historical artifact or record confirming this event ever happened. To our ears today, it has the sound of a legend whose historicity is beside the point, which is YHWH's commitment to defeat empire and deliver people from bondage. In the poem that completes this narrative, this defeat of empire is called "salvation" (Ex. 15:2).

Living as we do as the empire's citizens, we also lament the fate of Pharaoh's army. We insist our lament is fueled by empathy and maybe it is in part. But it also is fueled by our fascination with empire and its grand accomplishments and unmatched power. What would become of us if empire were to lose its grip? What then would become of the world?

10. Life Beyond the Empire (Part A)
Exodus 16–40, Leviticus, Numbers, Deuteronomy

For those who have no experience trying to live outside the prevailing norms of empire, the texts surveyed in this chapter will seem archaic and irrelevant to the purpose of this book.

But those who have committed time and energy to living out an alternative to the empire's ways know how important it is to be part of a community that shares their commitments, tests and refines their efforts, and makes visible this other way. They are likely to see the relevance of texts that explain how the Jews acquired the stubborn desire and capacity to embody a political alternative.

As we said in chapter 6, empire creates the world's dominant reality. Stepping outside that reality is a stressful and baffling experience that cannot be sustained unless another reality emerges. This other reality must include a different worldview, practices, social expectations and traditions. This is what we see the authors spelling out in the last half of **Exodus** and in the texts of **Leviticus, Numbers** and **Deuteronomy**.

As we noted on page 57, the vision of a non-imperial identity grew out of covenants YHWH made with Abraham in Canaan and later with all the people at Sinai. It is reflected in this text: "You shall be my treasured possession out of all the peoples. Indeed, the whole earth is mine, but you shall be for me a priestly kingdom and a holy nation" (Ex. 19:5–6).

Scribes in the Northern Kingdom of Israel (Ephraim) wrote substantial portions of **Exodus** during the ninth century BCE (see page 56), near the beginning of that society's recorded existence. In addition to a story of how YHWH saved the Hebrew people from the empire and then covenanted directly with them, their text at chapters 20—24 provides the earliest account in the Bible of the Law of Moses.

Leviticus and **Numbers** were likely completed by scribes living in the fifth and sixth centuries BCE respectively. **Numbers** appears to have been completed first and early in the period of exile by authors who wanted their composition to serve as a continuation of **Exodus** and a link to the great literary synthesis achieved during the reign of King Josiah (see page 120). **Leviticus** was written perhaps seventy-five years later and reflects the wisdom acquired through a century of living in Babylon and Persia. The religious practices and subversive ethical teachings it contains were meant to be norms for the relatively new community in and around Jerusalem and, to the extent possible in places where there was no temple, also for the Jewish diaspora.

Scribes from the Southern Kingdom (Judah) wrote the first version of **Deuteronomy,** perhaps late in the ninth century BCE. It was short, probably consisting of only the first three chapters. The version we have today evolved and grew over 250 years; we see references to it in the history of King Jehoshaphat (2 Chron. 17:9); King Hezekiah (2 Kings 18:6, 2 Chron. 31:21); and King Josiah (2 Kings 22 & 23). With the demise of the Northern Kingdom (Ephraim) in 722 BCE, refugee scribes from the north joined the effort and helped enlarge its perspective. More than any other text, it reflects fierce political debates that occurred during the era of Judah's kings.

As we read, it is important to keep in mind the audiences to whom these books were first read. This enables us to focus our attention on the dynamic role these texts played in shaping Jewish life. We then can consider what role (if any) they can play in our lives.

The mistake often made is to focus on the historical accuracy of recounted events. In this case, that leads to a dead-end. The setting for the stories told here is the fifteenth century BCE, hundreds of years before the Hebrew people had an alphabet and the written word. Writing these texts centuries later was clearly an imaginative task. When we further acknowledge the lack of other records or artifacts to confirm the events described here, we must assume significant elements of myth, legend and allegory are included.

Exodus

As chapter 15 ends, the newly liberated Hebrews are three days journey into "the wilderness of Shur" (Ex.15:22) and are badly in need of water. In chapter 16, they have moved further south, into the wilderness of Sin, and are suffering from hunger. Still, they moved south toward the wilderness of Sinai. It was a barren and demanding environment, very different from Egypt where food and drink were ample and near at hand.

As we already have seen with Abram and Moses, the journey from empire to a YHWH-inspired alternative *goes through the wilderness.* We naturally ask why this is so and the text provides several answers.

First, the people remained enchanted with Egypt's ways long after they had left Egypt. Repeatedly, they recalled how much easier life had been in Egypt. They also longed for the entertaining diversion that the pageantry of empire had provided in such abundance. Thus, when Moses left the camp for forty days and nights to receive instructions from YHWH, the people quickly became uneasy and asked for a reassuring image they could incorporate into their burnt offerings and fellowship offerings (Ex. 32:6). Moses' brother, Aaron, provided a golden calf: "Tomorrow shall be a festival to [YHWH]" (Ex. 32:5).

The text never describes the wilderness as an end in itself. The final destination was always Canaan, "a land flowing with milk and honey" (Ex. 33:3). But so long as the Hebrews remained enamored with Egypt, they could not imagine—much less embody—a different way of living. Life in the wilderness purged them of their enchantment. (Regarding liberation from nostalgia for empire, see question 8, page 88.)

Second, in contrast to Egypt, where the people had been unaware of YHWH's presence, in the austerity of the wilderness the presence of YHWH became real. YHWH was present in the midst of all the people, made visible by "the cloud" (Ex.16:10, 19:16, 33:9, 40:34–38) that accompanied their journey. YHWH's instructions to Moses regarding religious rituals emphasized the communal experience of YHWH's presence: "I will meet with the Israelites there [at the altar of sacrifice] . . . they shall know that I am [YHWH] their God" (Ex. 29:43, 45).

Third, life in the wilderness fostered an entirely new understanding of security. In Egypt, a kind of abundance had been achieved through military might and the centralization of power. This system had many victims, but also created an illusion of safety. In the wilderness, there was only enough for today. What about tomorrow?

The stories of manna and of the quails are parables about trusting YHWH to provide enough. Each morning, YHWH frosted the ground with "a fine flaky substance" that could be collected and kept without spoilage for about twelve hours. Each evening, YHWH sent quails that alighted around the camp (Ex. 16:14). When more than a day's supply was collected, it quickly spoiled (except on the sixth day of the week when provision needed to be made for the Sabbath day of rest). But day-to-day, there always was enough new supply to meet people's needs.

The focus of the last half of **Exodus** is the establishment of a covenant between YHWH and the people. The text describes this singular and pivotal event in simple, direct terms: "Moses brought the people out of the camp to meet God. They took their stand at the foot of the mountain" (Ex. 19:17). YHWH descended in a cloud of smoke to the mountaintop (Ex. 19:18) and spoke to Moses within the hearing of all the people (Ex. 19:9). YHWH's words fill chapters 20—23. After Moses had spoken YHWH's covenant terms to the people, they together ratified it in one voice: "All the words that [YHWH] has spoken we will do" (Ex. 24:3). Their commitment was symbolized by burnt offerings prepared by "young men of the people of Israel" (Ex. 24:5). This extraordinary event is portrayed without the trappings of religion or kingly power. Instead, the story tells us, it was YHWH and the people, together in one moment and one place, promising faithfulness one to the other.

As part of this covenanting event, YHWH gave Moses ten concise commandments to govern the life of the people: (1) give allegiance to no god but YHWH; (2) make no idol or other image to honor, and do not honor idols or images made by others; (3) do not use YHWH's name wrongfully; (4) keep the Sabbath day holy; (5) honor your father and mother; (6) do not kill; (7) do not commit adultery; (8) do not steal; (9) do not bear false witness against a neighbor; (10) do not covet a neighbor's wife or his possessions (Ex. 20:1–17).

Each of the first four commandments related to life in empire. Empires demand our allegiance, use imagery to capture our imaginations, use YHWH's name to bolster their own goals and activities, and structure life so that there is no opportunity for rest, assembly and reflection. YHWH's first four commands forbid cooperation with those practices.

Chapters 21–23 describe how the community was to manage slavery; respond to violence, destruction of property and theft; deal with inappropriate sexual relations; and manage economics. Many of these ethical expectations are remarkable in how radically they broke with the ways of empire. Male enslavement was limited to six years; "in the seventh, (the slave) shall go out a free person, without debt" (Ex. 21:2). When lending money to the poor, the taking of interest was prohibited; when taking clothing as security for a debt, the clothing was to be returned by sundown (Ex. 22:25–27). Abuse or oppression of resident aliens was prohibited (Ex. 22:21–24, 23:9) as was the spreading of false reports (Ex. 23:1, 7).

Committing every seventh day to rest is often assumed to be linked to worship. But the text tells us the Sabbath was to be observed "so that your ox and your donkey may have relief, and your homeborn slave and the resident alien may be refreshed" (Ex. 23:12). In other words, the Sabbath requirement ensured that everyone—even the most socially marginal—shared in the blessings of rest from labor. We see this same concern for the equitable sharing of social and economic benefits in the requirement that the land, the vineyards and the orchards be left fallow on the seventh year "so that the poor may eat and what they leave the wild animals may eat" (Ex. 23:10–11).

Criminal conduct was also addressed. Murder with premeditation was punishable by death, but murder without premeditation by banishment (Ex. 21:12-13). Miscarriage caused by fighting was punishable by a fine (Ex. 21:22). Restitution was the primary requirement for a thief or for one whose negligence caused property damage (Ex. 21:28–22:14).

Richard Horsley provides perspective on this story of YHWH meeting the people at the foot of the mountain. The Sinai covenant, Horsley writes, could be compared to "a declaration of independence from imperial kings and their forced labor, since God was now literally the king as well as sole God of Israel. In the covenant commandment, moreover, God demanded just social-economic relations among Israelites *so that no one would gain power to become an imperial-style king.*" [16]

A dozen chapters of **Exodus** describe the Ark of the Covenant and the Tabernacle around the Ark. This moveable shrine served as the

---

[16]   Horsley, *In the Shadow of Empire: Reclaiming the Bible as a History of Faithful Resistance,* 6 (emphasis added).

dwelling place of YHWH as the Hebrew people proceeded on their journey (Ex. 29:42–46; 40:34–38). Why does the text give so much attention to this? In part, it was intended as a rebuke of the grand, cut stone temple described earlier by Solomon's scribes in **1 Kings** 5–8. This rebuke is made explicit in these words of YHWH: "You need make for me only an altar of earth and sacrifice on it your burnt offerings . . . *in every place where I cause my name to be remembered I will come to you and bless you.* But if you make for me an altar of stone, do not build it with hewn stones, for if you use a chisel upon it you profane it" (Ex. 20:25–25).

This is a startling passage; it implies that YHWH is much more than a regional god. Moreover, it delegitimizes the centralization of worship in one place, thus undermining rulers and priests who strengthen their grip on power by joining throne and altar.

The text introduces conflicting descriptions of YHWH that persist throughout the First Testament. One concerns the use of violence to punish sin. After the incident involving the golden calf, Moses claimed the authority of YHWH when he ordered the killing "of your brother, your friend, and your neighbor" by the sword. The sons of Levi "did as Moses commanded and about three thousand of the people fell on that day" (Ex. 32:27-28). While the text stops short of saying YHWH ordered the slaughter, it does clearly state that YHWH sent a plague besides (Ex. 32:35). Yet the text also includes this beautiful description of YHWH: "[A] God merciful and gracious, slow to anger, and abounding in steadfast love and faithfulness, keeping steadfast love for the thousandth generation, forgiving iniquity and transgression and sin" (Ex. 34:6–7).

Remarkably, **Exodus** does not detail special worship-related responsibilities for the Levites. That occurs only in subsequent books of the *Torah* (**Numbers** and the expanded version of **Deuteronomy**).

The way **Exodus** speaks of possessing Canaan is different from what we heard in **Genesis**. It quotes YHWH this way:

> Little by little I will drive them out from before you, until you have increased and possess the land. I will set your borders from the Red Sea to the sea of the Philistines, and from the wilderness to the Euphrates; for I will hand over to you the inhabitants of the

land, and you shall drive them out before you. You shall make no covenant with them and their gods. They shall not live in your land. (Ex. 23:30–33)

In **Exodus**, possession of land is exclusive; the blessing cannot be shared.

Yet nowhere does it suggest that the Israelites will use warfare to gain possession of Canaan. Indeed, throughout **Exodus** the Hebrew term for "holy war" is *never* used in reference to the people of Canaan. Instead, it tells us YHWH will empty the land as they move into it.

I will send my terror in front of you and will throw into confusion all the people against whom you shall come, and I will make all your enemies turn their backs to you. And I will send my [hornet] in front of you, which shall drive out the Hivites, the Canaanites, and the Hittites from before you. (Ex. 23:27–28)

Leviticus

The setting for this text is the same as the last half of **Exodus**: the encampment of the Hebrew people at the base of Mt. Sinai, the place where they remained for a full year. Much of **Leviticus** (the word means "priests' manual") consists of YHWH's detailed instructions to Moses and Aaron about ceremonial rituals. But the text also includes instructions to the entire people on how to become "a priestly kingdom and a holy nation" (Ex. 19:6) and a witness to the world.

The opening chapters describe five different kinds of sacrificial offerings the people were instructed to offer YHWH at the Tabernacle. The burnt offering, the grain offering, and the fellowship offering (chapters 1–3) were voluntary; sin and guilt offerings (chapters 4–5) were mandatory. Often these sacrifices involved spilling the blood of an ox, sheep, goat, dove or pigeon. But a grain offering did not involve the shedding of blood, and if the person making the gift was very poor, the sin offering also was blood-free (Lev. 5:11–13).

The offering of sacrificial gifts created a memorable sensory experience for participants. It was a hands-on activity that often included the transport of an animal or bird to the place of sacrifice. We can imagine the audible complaints of the animals. The smell of roasting meat filled the air (the phrase "pleasing odor" is repeated many times throughout the text). While the altar fire consumed a portion of the gifts, the priests and worshippers ate most of it in a communal meal. All of this happened in a public place for all to see.

This public display of sacrificial giving was meant to be socially and spiritually formative. First, it reminded the Israelites that *ethical accountability* was an intrinsic part of their covenant relationship with YHWH. The covenant involved worship of YHWH, to be sure, but also fellowship with and care for neighbors and the acceptance of responsibility for misdeeds. Second, it brought together worship and justice; we see this in the emphasis on *restitution* along with the guilt offerings (Lev. 5:14–6:7). Third, it provided a public rite for the full *restoration* of wrong-doers to community life. Sins were forgiven and relationships restored. Fourth, it enacted an *egalitarianism* that undermined hierarchy. The sin offering had to be brought by the person for whom it was offered; the offering of well-being had to be brought "with your own hands" (Lev. 7:30). No proxy offerings, in other words, not even by the rich and powerful.

When describing animal sacrifices, the text emphasizes "dashing the blood against all sides of the altar" (Lev. 1:5). This was apparently related to the Israelite understanding of blood: "For the life of the flesh is in the blood, and I have given it to you for making atonement for your lives on the altar; for, as life, it is the blood that makes atonement" (Lev. 17:11). While this suggests life must be given in order for life to be renewed, *it never suggests sacrifice is needed to appease YHWH's anger.* Instead, the text portrays the sacrificial rituals as gifts YHWH gave the Hebrew community so that accountability, restitution, restoration and egalitarianism would be part of its life together.

Our modern sensibilities find any form of blood sacrifice barbarous. But this text was written at a time when gods were assumed to demand the shedding of blood as evidence of commitment. Thus, devout parents would sacrifice their children to appease their gods (see Lev. 18:21 prohibiting this practice). Within such a context, the rituals of commitment required by YHWH take on a different light.

Chapters 11–15 address matters of nutrition, the control and treatment of leprosy, personal hygiene, and purification of those who had become "unclean" because of bodily discharges or the touching of contaminated things. Generally, the consequence for being "unclean" did not involve social shunning, but only the denial of participation in Tabernacle worship and related activities until cleansing had occurred. Of course, even that limited ban was not a small matter.

Chapter 16 introduces the Day of Atonement when the lead priest entered the holy place in the Tabernacle where the Ark rested (later the Temple) and offered a sacrifice for the sins of the people. This annual event was proclaimed as "a statute forever" (Lev. 16:31) and involved everyone in a ritual of self-examination, cleansing and restoration.

The following ten chapters are known as the Holiness Code because of repeated references to ritual and moral purity. Some material repeats what has been covered earlier in the text, but much of it is new.

Chapter 17 begins by prohibiting animal sacrifices at any place other than the gate of the tabernacle where the priests presided. "Anyone . . . who offers a burnt offering or sacrifice and does not bring it to the entrance of the tent of meeting to sacrifice it to [YHWH] shall be cut off from the people" (Lev.17:9). In other words, offering sacrifices to YHWH was not a do-it-yourself activity, but was to be conducted publicly by an authorized priest. This is consistent with the principle of priestly authority ascendant in Judaism in the post-Babylon era, which is when this text was written.

Chapter 18 establishes boundaries related to sexual relations and viewing nakedness, all in order to prevent incest, abuse and rivalry related to the sharing of sexual partners within the household and community.

Chapter 19 authorizes "the poor and the alien" to glean fields, vineyards and orchards. It also prohibits owners from harvesting all of the grain, grapes or fruit (Lev. 19:9–10). It addresses relations with neighbors (including those with whom one has a dispute) with these far-reaching words: "You shall not hate in your heart anyone of your kin; you shall reprove your neighbor, or you shall incur guilt yourself. You shall not take vengeance or bear a grudge against any of your people, but you shall love your neighbor as yourself" (Lev. 19:17–18). Controversially, the text also instructs the people to love aliens as themselves (Lev. 19:34).

Chapter 23 describes six annual festivals that involved all the people and served to order the annual calendar: Passover, the Harvest Festival, the Festival of Weeks, the Festival of Trumpets, the Day of Atonement and the Festival of Booths.

Chapter 25 establishes a way to avoid the entrenchment of wealth by periodically redistributing land ownership. Land was not to be sold "in perpetuity, for the land is mine; with me [YHWH] *you are but aliens and tenants*" (Lev. 25:23, emphasis added). Instead, the purchase and sale of land was to occur within the context of 50-year cycles. "And you shall hallow the fiftieth year and you shall proclaim liberty throughout the land to all its inhabitants. It shall be a jubilee for you: you shall return every one of you, to your property and every one of you to your family" (Lev. 25:10-11). Thus, land price was based on "a certain number of harvests that are being sold" until the next fresh start year (Lev. 25:16). Houses within walled cities could be sold permanently subject to a one-year redemption period. If Levites sold an urban dwelling, however, a right of redemption remained forever.

Chapter 26 describes blessings that follow obedience to YHWH, including "peace in the land . . . you shall lie down and no one shall make you afraid" (Lev. 26:6). It also vividly describes a curse that follows disobedience, one that has much resonance to contemporary residents of the empire: "You shall flee though no one pursues you . . . Your strength shall be spent to no purpose . . . As for those who survive . . . the sound of a driven leaf shall put them to flight" (Lev. 26:17, 20, 36).

Yet even if disobedience persisted, even if the Israelites "perished among the nations" and "the land of your enemies devours you," still **Leviticus** insists YHWH's covenant of faithful mercy would continue. "Yet for all of that, when [you] are in the land of [your] enemies, I will not spurn [you], or abhor [you] so as to destroy [you] utterly and break my covenant with [you]; for I am [YHWH], your God" (Lev. 26:38, 44).

Numbers

This text picks up the narrative early in the second year of the Hebrew journey from Egypt. It begins at Mt. Sinai with a numbering of age-eligible fighting men (603,550); this is described as part of the preparation for the invasion of Canaan and the war against its peoples.

After leaving the encampment at Sinai, the people again complained against Moses: "We remember the fish we used to eat in Egypt . . . the cucumbers, the melons, the leeks, the onions and the garlic; but now our strength is dried up and there is nothing at all but this manna to look at" (Num. 11:5–6). Moses in turn complained to YHWH: "Why have you treated your servant so badly? Why have I not found favor in your sight, that you lay the burden of all this people on me" (Num. 11:11–12)?

So YHWH again provided quails, millions of them, piled deep on the ground on either side of the camp. The people responded by grabbing all of the meat they could, as if by their own efforts their desires would be satisfied. "So the people worked all that day and night and all the next day, gathering the quails. The least anyone gathered was ten homers; and they spread them out for themselves all around the camp" (Num. 11:32). "But while the meat was still between their teeth, before it was consumed, the anger of [YHWH] was kindled against the people and [YHWH] struck the people with a very great plague" (Num. 11:33). The text does not explain the people's error, but recalling the teaching from **Exodus** against pursuing security through the accumulation of material surplus, we take this story to be making the same point.

The huge procession stopped its northward trek at Kadesh Barnea in the wilderness of Paran. From there, Moses sent twelve men into Canaan to "spy out the land" (Num. 13:16). Their report upon returning was sobering: "The people who live in the land are strong, and the towns are fortified and very large" (Num. 13:28, 32). Only two of the spies, Caleb and Joshua, said the people should proceed into Canaan.

The people responded fearfully. "Why is [YHWH] bringing us into this land to fall by the sword? . . . Let us choose a captain, and go back to Egypt" (Num. 14:4). Clearly, the logic of the people remained fixed in the calculus of empire, measuring choices by the metrics of military might. YHWH said to Moses, "How long will this people despise me? And how long will they refuse to believe in me, in spite of all the signs that I have done among them? I will strike them with pestilence and disinherit them, and I will make of you a nation greater and mightier than they" (Num.14:11–12).

Moses interceded and reminded YHWH *that YHWH's reputation was on the line.* "Now if you kill this people all at one time, then the nations who have heard about you will say, 'It is because [YHWH] was not able to bring this people into the land he swore to give them that he has slaughtered them in the wilderness'" (Num. 14:15–16). And so YHWH relented, but only a bit. "Your little ones. . . I will bring in and they shall know the land that you have despised. But as for you, your dead bodies shall fall in the wilderness" (Num. 14:31–32). To ensure only those under the age of twenty entered the land, YHWH decreed forty years of wandering in the wilderness.

From Kadesh the assembly continued north into the wilderness of Zin to Meribah, a place with little water. Again, the people complained bitterly. YHWH told Moses and Aaron to assemble the people before a rock and then "command the rock before their eyes to yield its water" (Num. 20:8). Moses then called them "rebels" and angrily struck the rock with his staff. Water gushed out abundantly, but because Moses struck the rock instead of speaking to it, YHWH said Moses would not enter the land of Canaan either.

Aaron died soon after and was replaced as the chief priest by his son, Eleazar. As the story is told in chapter 20, this occurred at Mt. Hor, a place they reached soon after the incident at Meribah. Later in the text, however, Aaron's death is said to have occurred in the fortieth year "after the Israelites had come out of the land of Egypt" (Num. 33:38).

From Mt. Hor the people trekked east across the head of the Gulf of Aqaba before again turning north toward the lands of Moab and Ammon along the east side of the Dead Sea and the Jordan River. After defeating two chieftains, Sihon and Og, the Israelites "settled in the land of the Amorites" for the remaining time of their forty-year sentence. "They captured its villages and dispossessed the Amorites who were there" (Num. 21:31–32).

The text does not tell us how long the people lived in the lands of Moab and Ammon before crossing into Canaan, but it appears to have been more than thirty-five years. **Numbers** reports no long delays in the journey from Kadesh to Moab, no wandering in circles in the wilderness. Instead, it describes a purposeful trek to a place near their destination.

While living in Moab, Moses ordered a new census in preparation for the formation of the Hebrew militia; 601,730 men of fighting age were identified. Because he knew his time was growing short, Moses "laid hands on [Joshua] and commissioned him, as [YHWH] had directed" to lead the people into Canaan (Num. 27:23). Moses negotiated with the tribes of Gad and Reuben and agreed their settlements in Moab could be permanent. Thus, the Gadites and the Reubenites rebuilt the towns of Moab, fortified them and made the area suitable for raising sheep and cattle (Num. 32:33–38). Moses also prepared the people to enter the land across the River. This entailed a description of the boundaries of the area they claimed and a plan to divide it among the other ten tribes (Num. 34:13–15).

Moses' final preparations included a test-run for his militia: the plundering of the Midianites, a collection of nomadic tribes that lived just east of Aqaba. He assembled a 12,000-man force for this purpose. The Hebrews killed five Midianite kings and every male but "took the women . . . and their little ones captive; and they took all their cattle, their flocks and all their goods as booty" (Num. 31:10). Moses was angry that women had been spared and ordered the killing of every female not a virgin and every male child. He saved 32,000 virgin girls as booty to be divided among the Hebrew men, along with "675,000 sheep, 72,000 oxen and 61,000 donkeys" (Num. 31:33–35).

In summary, **Numbers** offers repellent images of YHWH, Moses and the people. Yes, YHWH gave Moses and Aaron a lovely blessing to share with the people at the end of chapter 6, and the daughters of Zelophehad persuaded Moses to extend property rights to women (Num. 27:1–11), but there is little else that edifies. The people were rebellious and irredeemable. YHWH was capricious, spiteful and violent; only Moses' repeated intercession saved the Israelites from destruction. The text includes virtually no reference to YHWH's covenant with the people, and the requirements of justice are hardly mentioned. The priests and Levites get lots of attention in the text, as do purity regulations, which are tightened via penalties more severe than **Exodus** or **Leviticus** require (Num. 5:1–4, 5:11–31; 9:9–14, 15:32–36).

Numbers was written to fill gaps in the story of the journey from Sinai to Canaan and to legitimate priestly power during the era when Jerusalem was being rebuilt and the area around it resettled. Regrettably, it achieved those purposes in a way that undermines our attraction to YHWH, god of the Hebrews.

Deuteronomy

This last volume of the *Torah* uses three sermons of Moses to tell in summary fashion what is also told in **Exodus, Leviticus** and **Numbers**. The text of **Deuteronomy** is one of the most complex in the Bible. It includes beautiful prose, an expansive covenant and stirring calls to justice. Yet it also demands ethnic cleansing and endorses centralized power via a king. It is helpful to think of it as a document of diplomacy, reflecting many decades of negotiation between the scribes of Judah and the descendants of the scribes of Ephraim. Through the inclusion of contrasting passages, each group gained legitimacy for favored ways of remembering history and describing YHWH's intention for their lives. These passages do not always agree with one another, but the total package reflected Israel's consensus during the final decades of Judah's existence, which was when this text was largely finalized.

Moses' first sermon recounts events of the journey from Mt. Sinai (called Mt. Horeb here) to Canaan. One of the interesting differences between this account and the one in **Numbers** is that this text states the people wandered in the wilderness for thirty-eight years after leaving Kadesh Barnea and before entering the land of Moab east of the Dead Sea (Deut. 2:13–14).

The avoidance of idolatry received particular attention in this first sermon: "For [YHWH] is a devouring fire, a jealous God" (Deut.4:24). Moses warned that the practice of idolatry would lead to the defeat and scattering of Israel. Yet, "because [YHWH] is a merciful God, he will neither abandon you nor destroy you; he will not forget the covenant with your ancestors that he swore to them" (Deut.4:27–31). This is the same expansive covenant we read about in **Leviticus**.

Moses' second sermon begins with the Ten Commandments (Deut. 5:1–21). It includes the *shema*, words of commitment and exhortation that to this day form the core of Jewish morning and evening prayers. "Hear, O Israel: [YHWH] is our God, [YHWH] alone. You shall love [YHWH] with all your heart, and with all your soul, and with all your might" (Deut.6:4–5). Following immediately after the *shema* is practical encouragement:

> Keep these words . . . in your heart. Recite them to your children and talk about them when you are at home and when you are away, when you lie down and when you rise. Bind them as a sign on your hand, fix them as an emblem on your forehead, and write them on the doorposts of your house and on your gates. (Deut. 6:6–9)

A few chapters later, Moses made a similar plea: "So now, O Israel, what does [YHWH] require of you? Only to fear [YHWH], to walk in all his ways, to love him, to serve [YHWH] with all your heart and with all your soul" (Deut. 10:12). Moses followed with ethical guidance: "For [YHWH] . . . is not partial and takes no bribe, who executes justice for the orphan and the widow, and who loves the strangers, providing them food and clothing. You shall also love the stranger, for you were strangers in the land of Egypt" (Deut.10:17–19).

Moses provided much more ethical guidance in chapters 15–24. He began with a startling command: "Every seventh year you shall grant a remission of debts" (Deut. 15:1). Moses rooted this command in what sounds to our ears like an impossible ideal: "There will . . . be no one in need among you . . . if only you will obey [YHWH] by diligently observing this entire commandment" (Deut. 15:4-5). Moreover, the text warns against the tendency to stop lending as the "year of remission" approaches: "Do not be hard-hearted or tight-fisted toward your needy neighbor. You should rather open your hand, willingly lending enough to meet the need, whatever it may be. Be careful that you do not entertain a mean thought, thinking, 'The seventh year . . . is near'" (Deut. 15:7–9).

Moses then followed with other ethical teachings on a wide variety of matters: boundary markers (Deut. 19:14), number of witnesses required for a criminal conviction (Deut. 19:15), the obligation to intervene when a neighbor's ox or sheep strays (Deut. 22:1), the punishment for adultery (Deut. 22:22), the obligation *not* to return escaped slaves (Deut. 23:15–16), a prohibition of the charging of interest on a loan to another Israelite (Deut. 23:19) and the importance of prompt payment of wages (Deut. 24:14–15).

The text insists that after entering Canaan, the Israelites "must utterly destroy" the people living there. "Make no covenant with them and show them no mercy. Do not intermarry with them . . . for that would turn away your children from following me, to serve other gods" (Deut. 7:2–4). "Utterly destroy" refers to holy war. Chapter 20 provides detail on the conduct of war. Moses said "terms of peace" (Deut. 20:10) were to be offered the distant towns at the fringes of Canaan. As for towns in the places where the Israelites intended to live, "you must not let anything that breathes remain alive; you shall annihilate them . . . just as [YHWH] commanded you so that they may not teach you to do all the abhorrent things that they do for their gods, and you thus sin against [YHWH]" (Deut. 20:16–18).

Thus, the text gives us holy war as the norm. **Genesis'** inclusive view is not present here, nor is there any hint of a pilgrimage of nations drawn to YHWH through their fascination with the witness of YHWH's people. Instead, force and violence are presented as the tools of YHWH.

The authors' goal of political centralization is very prominent in the repeated insistence that religious rituals occur "at the place that [YHWH] will choose as a dwelling for his name" (Deut. 16:6). "You shall go there [to the place that YHWH shall choose], bringing your burnt offerings and your sacrifices, your tithes and your donations, your votive gifts, your freewill offerings and the firstlings of your herds and flocks. And you shall eat there in the presence of [YHWH] your God" (Deut. 12:5–7; see also 12:14; 14:23–25; 15:20; 17:8–10; 26:2).

Thus, the Passover could not be practiced in people's homes as it was first observed in Egypt, nor could they offer their sacrifices "in every place where I cause my name to be remembered" as stated in **Exodus** 20:24, but only at the temple in Jerusalem. This marginalized those living a distance from Jerusalem's temple, especially the poor. But it enhanced the authority of the priests who presided in the temple and the king with whom the priests were linked.

The question of a king is specifically addressed in chapter 17. "You may indeed set over you a king whom [YHWH] will choose," said Moses (Deut. 17:15). We can assume the kings of Judah insisted that this language be included.

But some of the scribes in the royal court, including refugee descendants from the defunct North Kingdom, had another agenda: debunking the legends of David and Solomon and their policies of centralizing power in Jerusalem. And so, with an implicit slap at these iconic figures, the text sets limits on how a king may behave: "Even so, [the king] must not acquire many horses for himself . . . and he must not acquire many wives for himself, or his heart will turn away; also, silver and gold he must not acquire in great quantity for himself" (Deut. 17:17). Thus, this text strikes a balance between the admirers of empire and empire's critics.

Moses' third and final sermon is described as "the words of the covenant that [YHWH] commanded Moses to make with the Israelites in the land of Moab" (Deut. 29:1). It included this stirring challenge to all the people: "Surely this commandment that I am commanding you today is not too hard for you, nor is it too far away . . . No, the word is very near to you; it is in your mouth and it is in your heart for you to observe" (Deut. 30:11, 14). In other words, living an alternative to those around you is not impossible; *you can do it!* Going on, Moses said: "See, I have set before you today life and prosperity, death and adversity . . . Choose life so that you and your descendants may live, loving [YHWH], obeying him and holding fast to him; for that means life to you and length of days" (Deut. 30:15, 19–20).

Moses died and was buried east of the Jordan, in the land of Moab. The text includes nothing about a "house of Moses" by which his children would succeed to his authority; instead, the text tells us YHWH had chosen Joshua, someone outside of Moses' family, to lead Israel. But Moses would be remembered; "never since has there arisen a prophet in Israel like Moses, whom [YHWH] knew face to face" (Deut. 34:10).

Reflection and Discussion

5. Empire's legitimacy is rooted in the premise that though violence is regrettable, it is a tragic and necessary aspect of civilization, not only to suppress criminality, but also to give people unity, purpose and justice.   How do the origin stories surveyed in Chapter 8 speak to that premise?

6. **Genesis** portrays the patriarchs as flawed people who had entered into a "covenant" of mutual reliance with YHWH.   They were described by Paul, a Second Testament writer, as men who "believed the promises of YHWH."   Do you think the Creator makes promises to us?   What might such promises be?

7. The stories surveyed in Chapter 9 reveal YHWH to be "subversive."   Does that characterization work for you?   If so, how might such an understanding be applied to contemporary life?

8. The exodus story suggests the Hebrew people experienced liberation only after giving up hope in the Pharaoh and coming to regard him as a fool.   In the wilderness, their transformation as a community happened only as they confronted their own nostalgia for the empire that had enslaved them.   Do these stories connect with our experience within the USA-led empire?

9. Chapter 10 describes the Law of Moses as culture-forming, building within the Hebrew people a capacity to be a social and political alternative to the empire.   Where do you see culture-forming work of this kind going on today?   Does the Law of Moses have continuing relevance to such work?

11. Possessing the Land (or not)
Joshua, Judges, 1 Samuel 1–12

The texts discussed in this chapter tell the story of how the Hebrew people crossed the Jordan River to enter Canaan, gained a foothold in the land, lived there as loosely associated tribes, and then shifted from ad hoc political leadership to a permanent bureaucracy and military led by a king.

Joshua, with its claim that YHWH commanded the Hebrew people to cleanse Canaan of its indigenous population, has served to legitimize atrocities such as the European genocide in the Americas and the expulsion of the Palestinians by modern-day Israel. Yet **Joshua's** claims of ethnic cleansing have not been corroborated by archeology. Some of its stories have been directly contradicted, such as the destruction of the city of Ai. Archeologists report it was destroyed nearly one thousand years before the time **Joshua** suggests.

Archeology has confirmed the emergence in the twelfth century BCE of a culture in the hilly regions of Canaan that had different dietary practices (e.g., no pork), distinct pottery and house-building styles, and the practice of circumcision. It is reasonable to conclude this was the culture of the Hebrews, which **Judges** places in Canaan at about the same time. Apart from such general forms of corroboration, however, we again are reading about events in **Judges** that have not been confirmed through external sources. (For more discussion of these areas of corroboration, see the writings of Norman K. Gottwald[17] and Wes Howard-Brook.[18])

In our view, the three texts surveyed in this chapter were largely written during the time of Judah's King Josiah, late in the seventh century BCE and long after the era they describe. Some of the stories these texts tell may have been harvested from Israel's oral tradition, but historical accuracy was not a key consideration. Instead, the stories explain why the

---

[17]   An essay by Gottwald, "Early Israel as an Anti-Imperial Community," is included in Horsley, *In the Shadow of Empire: Reclaiming the Bible as a History of Faithful Resistance,* 9–24.

[18]   Howard-Brook, 199-211.

Hebrew people organized themselves under kings like other peoples, even though they worshipped a god who called them to be different. This critical piece of Israel's self-understanding is summarized in the first twelve chapters of **1 Samuel**, which is the third text surveyed in this chapter.

Regarding the power of "history" to shape our identities and the choices we make as societies, see also question 10, page 149.

Joshua

As this text begins, two-and-one-half tribes had already settled on lands east of the Jordan. Although they may have occupied the area for nearly four decades, the rest of the people apparently still lived in encampments or other temporary quarters.

Joshua's first action was to send two spies into the walled city of Jericho to assess its strengths and weaknesses. The spies entered the city and then the house of Rahab, a prostitute, who concealed their presence from the local king and helped them escape unharmed. Upon their return, the two spies gave Joshua a confident report.

Joshua then ordered Levites carrying the Ark of the Covenant to lead the people across the Jordan River. As the feet of the Levite priests touched the river's edge, "the waters flowing from above stood still, rising up in a single heap" (Josh. 3:16), and the people crossed over on dry ground. Thus, the story portrays Joshua as the new Moses.

Next, while camped at Gilgal, Joshua ordered the men to be circumcised, a ritual the Israelite people had ignored during their forty-year transition out of Egypt.

There in a vision, Joshua met the "commander of the army of [YHWH]" (Josh. 5:14) a mythic figure who explained that he stood with neither the Israelites nor their adversaries. A puzzled Joshua asked what he should do and YHWH's commander replied, "Remove the sandals from your feet, for the place where you stand is holy" (Josh. 5:15). By its similarity to Moses' wilderness encounter with the burning bush, this story reiterates that Joshua was the new Moses. But it also injects a dissonant note: did YHWH not support all the warring and killing that was about to commence?

By the end of chapter 12, we read that Joshua and his armies had defeated thirty-one Canaanite kings, killed tens of thousands of Canaanites, and razed the cities of Jericho and Ai. "[YHWH] fought for Israel" (Josh. 10:14), the text tells us. In chapters 10 and 11, we read ten references to holy war by which the Israelites killed every man, woman and child. And we read: "So Joshua took the whole land, according to all that [YHWH] had spoken to Moses, and Joshua gave it for an inheritance to Israel according to their tribal allotments. And the land had rest from war" (Josh. 11:23).

But the second half of the book describes matters very differently. It reports YHWH telling Joshua, "Very much of the land still remains to be possessed" (Josh. 13:1). The unpossessed land is described in considerable detail throughout chapter 13 and also at 15:63, 16:10, 17:12 and 17:16. The first chapter of **Judges** continues this litany of failure.

Why this inconsistency about something so important? If taken as an historical account, it may simply reflect the fact that the Israelite people were not numerous enough at the start to hold all of the land they had conquered. More likely, the text reflects a debate between two sets of authors. The first desired a text that described a heroic conquest of Canaan in grand, imperial terms that fit the David-Solomon narrative. The second desired a text that explained the obvious fact that the Israelites lived side-by-side with Canaanite peoples long after Joshua was purported to live, including the authors' time hundreds of years later.

The second half of the book also includes detailed descriptions of the land allocated to each of twelve tribal groups. The tribe of Judah received much of southern Canaan and the tribes of Joseph (Ephraim and Manesseh) much of the central portion.

As noted previously, a few tribes (Rueben, Gad and Manasseh) received allocations east of the Jordan River. When the bulk of the war-making on the west side of the river had ended, warriors from the east returned to their homes. After crossing the Jordan, they built a huge altar as a witness to their commitment to YHWH. When the tribes west of the river heard of this, they viewed it as rebellion against YHWH and the requirement that all sacrifices and ceremonies remain centralized and under control of the Levite priests at Shiloh, where the Tabernacle and Ark of the Covenant rested (Josh. 18:1). Because of the perceived disobedience to the rule of centralization, "the whole assembly of the Israelites gathered at Shiloh, to make war" (Josh. 22:12).

The situation was defused through face-to-face conversations. The leaders of the eastern tribes explained that the Jordan River might be perceived by future generations as YHWH's boundary line and that "in time to come your children might say to our children, 'What have you to do with [YHWH] the God of Israel'" (Josh. 22:24)? After assurances that the altar would not be used for sacrifices, the controversy settled peacefully.

The story highlights a historic power struggle that had contributed much to Israel's division into two kingdoms. Where could religious rituals be conducted? How could those who lived far from the designated place, or who lacked the means to get there, experience YHWH's presence? And if they found some other way to worship YHWH, would that be regarded as idolatry? The answers to these questions had serious political implications. For those who wanted Israel to become a mini-empire in its own right, centralization of worship rituals became a key strategy.

Joshua ended his final sermon with an appeal to the people to "choose this day" which god they would serve. "As for me and my household," said Joshua, "we will serve [YHWH]" (Josh. 24:15). Simple as that sounds, it became a matter clouded by the politics of empire.

Judges

As the story is told in this text, immediately after Joshua died and was buried, "The Israelites did what was evil in the sight of YHWH and worshiped the Baals; and they abandoned [YHWH] . . . they followed other gods . . . so the anger of [YHWH] was kindled against Israel and he gave them over to plunderers . . . and sold them into the power of their enemies" (Judg. 2:11–14).

This prompts obvious questions: why did the people show so little loyalty to their god? Why did they repeatedly need to defend what they had so decisively taken from the Canaanites? Something was amiss. By the end of the text, we learn the authors' explanation: they needed a king.

Along the way, the text describes a tortuous process of reaching consensus in support of a king. The tribe of Judah did as it had been told, driving all the Canaanites out of the land Judah had been given, and the text tells us that "[YHWH] was with Judah" (Judg. 1:19). But the tribes of Benjamin, Manasseh, Ephraim, Zebulun, Asher, Naphtali and Dan did not do as Judah had done. They failed to "drive out the inhabitants" (Judg. 1:21–36), failed to "tear down the altars" of the Canaanites (Judg. 2:2) and lived side-by-side with people who worshipped other gods. Eventually, they began to worship those gods.

In response, the text tells us, YHWH stopped helping the Israelites. "I will no longer drive out before [you] any of the nations that Joshua left when he died." YHWH did this "to test Israel, whether or not they would take care to walk in the way of [YHWH]" (Judg. 2:21–22). And because most of the Hebrew tribes abandoned the effort to *completely* rid their lands of Canaanites, YHWH stopped helping even their partial efforts.

Certainly this explanation worked well at the time **Judges** was written (late seventh century) to show the superiority of the authors' nation and tribe (Judah) and how the tribes making up the other nation (Ephraim) had been disobedient, forsaken by YHWH and destroyed by the Assyrian Empire. Yet it also was rather obviously self-serving.

The text goes on to tell of "judges" raised up by YHWH "to deliver [the Israelites] out of the power of those who plundered them" (Judg. 2:16). This "raising up" was an ad hoc process. Life would go on within usual routines for a time under the authority of local kinship groups. Then, in response to Canaanite raids or intimidation, YHWH would raise up a charismatic leader to mobilize people across tribal lines to respond, usually with violence. The text portrays these crises as learning experiences for the Israelites, precipitated by YHWH as a way to catch their attention, prompt their repentance and regain their exclusive loyalty.

Some judges carried authority across Israel, others did not. The first judge was Othniel (Judg. 3:7); he "judged Israel" for forty years (Judg. 3:10–11) and apparently carried the authority to make decisions on various matters beyond crisis response. A dozen other judges followed, some of whom acted solely as militia leaders.

Deborah, the only woman in the group, was also a "prophetess" who "used to sit under the palm . . . between Ramah and Bethel in the hill country of Ephraim; and the Israelites came up to her for judgment" (Judg. 4:4–5). She appointed a militia leader, Barak; advised him on a strategy to engage a Canaanite king (Sisera); accompanied Barak to the battle field and gave him directions on when and how to carry out the plan of attack. The moment of victory over the Canaanite king was enacted by another woman, Jael, who drove a tent stake through his head while he lay sleeping in her tent. Deborah's victory song featured a third woman, Sisera's mother (Judg. 5:28–30), and pointed jibes at Israelite tribes that did nothing to help the Barak's militia defeat Sisera's forces.

An angel of YHWH recruited Gideon (also known by a Canaanite name, Jerubbaal) to deliver Israel from Midianite rule. He was a farmer, "beating out wheat in the wine press" when the angel of YHWH appeared and said, "[YHWH] is with you, you mighty warrior" (Judg. 6:11–12). Part of what makes Gideon so attractive is that he did not think of himself as a warrior; he was a family man, a bit of a skeptic and a free thinker (Judg. 8:29–32; 6:13). After a sign from the angel, Gideon built two altars to YHWH, sacrificed two bulls on those altars and destroyed an altar of Baal. This angered his neighbors and violated Moses' command to sacrifice to YHWH only with the help of the Levites at prescribed places.

Nevertheless, "the spirit of [YHWH]" was with Gideon and 22,000 men responded to his call to arms (Judg. 7:3). Gideon reduced the militia to 10,000 but YHWH said that still was too many and, through a stream-side drinking exercise, reduced the number to 300. Gideon then proceeded to rout a Midianite army "countless as the sand on the seashore" (Judg. 7:12) with trumpets, clay jars and torches. He and his men shed little blood. It was a physical conflict, to be sure, but not the imperial kind.

Gideon's remarkable victory over the Midianites is Judges' high point of trust in and obedience to YHWH. Ad hoc, charismatic leadership seemed to be working. Yet the story tells us this was not recognized as such by the Israelite people. The tribe of Ephraim "upbraided Gideon violently" for not including Ephraimite fighters (Judg. 8:1–3). Members of the tribe of Gad refused to share bread with him (Judg. 8:4–9); he wasn't the kind of leader they wanted to follow. It was only after Gideon attacked the Midianites in the conventionally violent way (Judg. 8:11) that his star began to rise. Then the Israelites approached him: "Rule over us, you and your son and your grandson also. Gideon declined, saying: "I will not rule over you, and my son will not rule over you; [YHWH] will rule over you" (Judg. 8:22–23).

Gideon's inspiring story ends on two sour notes. To mark his triumphs, Gideon made an ephod from the gold earrings taken from the Midianites. This trophy-like garment became an object of veneration; the text tells us that "all Israel prostituted themselves to it and it became a snare to Gideon and his family" (Judg. 8:27). Secondly, after Gideon died, one of his sons, Abimelech, attempted to become king via a power play that entailed the murder of his many brothers. Abimelech managed to rule as Israel's first king for three years (Judg. 9:22), but met death in the course of his warring with other Israelites when a very strong woman from the walled city of Thebez threw a millstone down on his head "and crushed his skull" (Judg. 9:53). Abimelech's power grab counted for little, but gave rise to a pithy, anti-imperial parable of trees that disparages those who seek power over others (Judg.9:8–15).

After Gideon, the text describes a sharp decline in the moral state of the Israelite people. The last two judges, Jephthah and Samson, are cartoonish figures, caricatures of what Israel apparently had become.

Jephthah, the son of a prostitute and the leader of a pack of wilderness bandits, sought YHWH's favor as he led the eastern tribes into battle against the Ammonites. He vowed: "Whoever comes out of the doors of my house to meet me, when I return victorious, shall be [YHWH's] to be offered up by me as a burnt offering" (Judg. 11:30–31). Jephthah's militia was victorious and the first to greet him at his return home was his only child, a daughter "with timbrels and dancing" (Judg. 11:34). The dangerously muddled Jephthah kept his vow and killed his daughter as a sacrifice to YHWH. Later, the text tells us, his militia killed 42,000 fighters from the tribe of Ephraim because they criticized the way Jephthah's armed campaign had been conducted and insulted Hebrew tribesmen who lived east of the River (Judg. 12:1–7).

Samson is described as a Nazirite committed to ritual purity who ate honey from the carcass of a dead animal, found much pleasure in the company of various Philistine women and exploded in acts of gratuitous violence when "the spirit of [YHWH] rushed upon him" (Judg. 14:19, 15:14). His time as a "judge" of Israel ended in chains in a Philistine temple where he was mocked as a blind trophy of Israel's defeat.

Finally, the text gives us a story that illustrates a corrosive rivalry among Israel's tribes and again portrays the tribe of Judah in a positive light. The inhabitants of Gibeah, a Benjamite town, reenacted the story of Sodom by surrounding a house hosting a Levite guest and his wife from Bethlehem, pounding on its doors and demanding access to the Levite "so that we may have intercourse with him" (Judg. 19:22). The husband gave them his wife instead, who was "wantonly raped . . . all through the night." She was found in the morning, dead on the doorstep (Judg. 19:25–28, 20:5). (The text refers to the woman as "a concubine," which simply means a wife of somewhat lower status.) The Levite cut his dead wife into twelve pieces and sent one to each tribe as a grisly indictment of the tribe of Benjamin. The tribe of Judah led the way in the civil war that followed; supposedly 50,000 Benjamites were killed and 40,000 other Israelites (Judg. 20:19–48).

In the final four chapters, we see repeatedly the phrase "in those days there was no king in Israel" (Judg. 17:6, 18:1, 19:1 21:25). Obviously, the authors of these stories wanted readers to regard an established government led by a king as the solution to Israel's difficulties.

1 Samuel 1–12

Samuel, the surprise son of a woman who was convinced "(YHWH) had closed her womb" (1 Sam. 1:6), is described as Israel's last judge and the key figure in the story of the transition to formal government under the authority of a king. When he was still a small child, his mother Hannah gave him to YHWH (1 Sam. 1:28) as an act of gratitude and commitment. Samuel grew up in the care of the chief priest, Eli, at Shiloh where the Tabernacle and Ark of the Covenant stood. In addition to serving as Israel's judge, Samuel is described as a priest and prophet.

During this era, the Hebrew struggle to possess the land of Canaan focused on the competing claims of the Philistines. Samuel called upon the people to "put away the foreign gods [Baal and Astartes]; direct your heart to [YHWH] and serve him only and he will deliver you." "All of Israel" gathered at Mizpah and responded to Samuel with repentance and fasting. The Philistines attacked "but [YHWH] thundered with a mighty voice . . . threw them into confusion and they were routed before Israel." Samuel marked YHWH's victory by setting up a large stone and naming it "Ebenezer; for he said, 'Thus far [YHWH] has helped us'" (1 Sam. 7:3–12). Years of peace followed. Here again we are given an image of Israel achieving security through a combination of ad hoc leadership, faithfulness and YHWH's miraculous intervention.

Alas, as Samuel aged, it became clear his sons would use their status for personal profit; "they took bribes and perverted justice." With the problem of succession looming, the "elders of Israel" asked Samuel to "appoint for us a king to govern us, like other nations." The request displeased Samuel but YHWH said: "Listen to the voice of the people . . . for they have not rejected you, they have rejected me from being king over them" (1 Sam. 8:3–7).

But first, our text tells us, Samuel warned the people about how a king would behave.

> He will take your sons and appoint them to his chariots and to be his horsemen, and to run before his chariots; and he will appoint for himself commanders of thousands and commanders of fifties, and some to plow his ground and to reap his harvest, and to make his implements of war and the equipment of his chariots. He will take your daughters to be perfumers and cooks and bakers. He will take the best of your fields and vineyards and olive orchards and give them to his courtiers. He will take one-tenth of your grain and of your vineyards and give it to his officers and courtiers. He will take your male and female slaves, and the best of your cattle and donkeys, and put them to work. He will take one tenth of your flocks, and you shall be his slaves. (1 Sam. 8:11–17)

"But the people refused to listen to the voice of Samuel; they said, 'No! We are determined to have a king over us so that we also may be like other nations, and that our king may govern us and go out before us and fight out battles'" (1 Sam. 8:19–20). Our text tells us YHWH told Samuel to listen to the people and "set a king over them" (1 Sam. 8:22). So Samuel began his search.

While on his priestly rounds, Samuel encountered tall and handsome Saul, son of a wealthy Benjamite. Apparently smitten by Saul's appearance, the next morning Samuel anointed Saul with oil, kissed him, and told him, "[YHWH] has anointed you ruler over his people Israel" (1 Sam. 10:1). Later, Samuel summoned the people to Mizpah where he presented Saul as "the one whom [YHWH] has chosen . . . And all the people shouted, 'Long live the king.'" Saul then returned to farming and his detractors asked, "How can this man save us" (1 Sam. 10:24–27)?

An attack by the Ammonites on the eastern tribes of Gad and Reuben provided an opportunity for Saul to prove his worth. The text tells us "the spirit of God came upon Saul in power" and he summoned Israel to join him in battle. Three hundred thousand responded and Saul led them to victory. At Gilgal, Samuel then hosted a *second* ceremony "to renew the kingship" of Saul, now newly credentialed through war (1 Sam.11:14–15).

Our text ends with Samuel's farewell message to the people. He described their desire for a king as "wickedness" (1 Sam. 12:17). Yet he also spoke words of encouragement: "Do not be afraid . . . for [YHWH] will not cast away his people, for his great name's sake, because it has pleased [YHWH] to make you a people for himself" (1 Sam. 12:20–22).

What message would this text have conveyed when the first audience heard it, long after the setting of the story? That submitting to the authority of a king was a choice the ancient Israelites came to reluctantly and only after it became a tragic necessity. That it was not what YHWH desired, and no, it was not ideal, but it was the best Israel could do and it did not cause YHWH to abandon Israel.

It is a rationalization for centralized power and perpetual violence with which we are all too familiar today.

12. Israel Like the Nations
1 & 2 Samuel, 1 & 2 Kings, 1 & 2 Chronicles

This chapter focuses on the four-century era of the Israelite kings. The Hebrew alphabet was developed early in this time period, creating the possibility of texts written in Hebrew. It also was a time when the historical records of neighboring states began to mention the Israelites and their leaders.

The texts surveyed in this chapter describe events and people from the same era in which the authors lived. This contrasts with texts we surveyed in chapters 8–11, all of which portrayed ancient events from many centuries before the authors lived. Thus, in these texts we are closer to what is generally thought of as "history." We can with confidence approximately date the events described in these texts and place them at the beginning of the simple historical timeline we introduced on page 12.

Archeological evidence suggests that during the tenth and ninth centuries BCE, the population and number of settlements in the hill country of Canaan increased significantly. Though not nearly enough to support the huge numbers reported in biblical texts, the population increase corroborates the biblical claim that local structures of government began to emerge during this period. These developments in Canaan occurred at a time when imperial powers such as Egypt were in decline.

Historical artifacts from Assyria and Moab confirm that during the ninth and eighth centuries the Northern Kingdom (sometimes called Ephraim, sometimes called Israel) emerged as a significant nation-state within Canaan. Olive oil production and its control of Mediterranean ports as well as major overland trade routes between Egypt and south Asia made the Northern Kingdom strategically important. Its god, YHWH, is identified on one of these artifacts; found there as well are the names of some of its kings from the Omri dynasty.

Archeological evidence further suggests the Southern Kingdom (Judah) initially was weaker and so small that it did not even register in the accounts of neighboring nations. But during the latter half of the eighth century, multiple attacks on Ephraim by the Assyrian Empire caused many people to flee south. These refugees added to Judah's population and skills and by the time of the reign of King Hezekiah, Judah was "on the map" and began to show up in the official documents of other nations. Jerusalem was enlarged and strengthened during this period; in the seventh century, it became the dominant regional city of Canaan.

All of this seems straight-forward enough. But it does not line up very well with the biblical account, which describes Israel as starting off as one, unified kingdom under King Saul; as having an important capital city in Jerusalem under King David; as becoming a mini-empire under King Solomon; and as splitting into two kingdoms only after Solomon's death. This is a puzzle; the biblical account seems to inflate the importance of David and Solomon and their "kingdom" around Jerusalem. Why?

The key to solving this puzzle is provided by Howard-Brook and his insight into the origins of the book of **Exodus.** As we discussed in chapters 8 and 9, a substantial version of **Exodus** was composed within the northern kingdom in the ninth century BCE (perhaps as early as 875). It described the life of a man named Moses who was born in Egypt and led the Hebrew people out of slavery to the Egyptians. It also described a god named YHWH who first met Moses in a burning bush, made a fool of the Pharaoh, delivered the Hebrew people from certain annihilation at the hand of the Egyptian army, entered into a covenant with the Hebrews at Mt. Sinai and then taught them how to live apart from the empire.

We rarely read **Exodus** and the texts about David and Solomon together. If we were to do so, we likely would assume they describe different times and places. It is only when we realize that they were written very early and at about the same time (perhaps within fifty years of each other) that we begin to notice how differently they describe YHWH and YHWH's relationship to the Hebrew people. And then it dawns on us: *at the very beginning of the Bible's composition, a debate was launched between two very different understandings of this god called YHWH.*

One account said YHWH partnered with kings to enhance imperial power and the other said YHWH made kings look like fools. One said YHWH made eternal promises to kings, but the other said YHWH made eternal promises to common people. One made a big deal of

Jerusalem, its palace and its temple and said YHWH could be worshipped only there. The other said YHWH could be worshipped anywhere.

This all requires more discussion, but it provides helpful context for this chapter's overview of the kings. It helps explain why those with an imperial worldview might have wanted to inflate their own importance. And it helps us see that the historic rivalry between the northern and southern kingdoms was based in part from the start on very different views of YHWH and YHWH's regard for imperial power.

The first text we survey in this chapter (section A. below) begins with the thirteenth chapter of **1 Samuel**, continues all through **2 Samuel** and ends with chapter 10 of **1 Kings**. It was written in the tenth century BCE, *earlier than **Exodus** or any other part of the Bible,* according to Howard-Brook.[19] It tells stories of Saul, David and Solomon set during the eleventh and tenth centuries BCE and claims these kings ruled *all* of the Hebrew people, those in the north and those in the south.

Shockingly, in this long and richly detailed story of three kings, we find no mention of Abraham, Isaac or Jacob; *it is as if they never existed.* We find only four references to Moses; each is incidental and could easily have been added to the text by an editor later. There is no reference to Joshua. There is no reference to a covenant between YHWH and Abraham or between YHWH and the people at Mt. Sinai. Yet we find many detailed references to David's victories, Solomon's wisdom and wealth, and the glory of the temple and palace in Jerusalem. And we find many references to the promise YHWH made to David that a member of his family would always be on Israel's throne. This first written text of the Israelites, in other words, reflects the assumptions of empire.

It is important to ponder what this means (for further discussion of how historical texts impact our lives, see question 11, page 149). The oldest text in the Bible is a collection of larger-than-life tales about kings. These stories conveyed divine approval of a worldview other nations also proclaimed: our king speaks for and is blessed by our god. This was the seminal text to which **Exodus** replied with a very different point of view.

The second set of texts in this chapter (section B. below) was assembled during the era of kings Hezekiah and Josiah, 200–300 years

---

[19]   Ibid., 104-115.

later. This set of texts also has a pro-king bias, but it reflects the influence of refugee scribes from Ephraim (and their descendants) who participated in the writing and editing. These scribes were familiar with **Exodus** and brought into the mix its critique of imperial ways, its references to the covenant YHWH made with Abraham and its story of the covenant YHWH made with Moses and the people at Sinai. This introduced new understandings of YHWH into the story Solomon's scribes had launched and began impacting the way later texts were written.

The third set of texts discussed in this chapter (section C. below) surveys the two volumes of the **Chronicles.** They retell the stories of the kings of Judah, but were written later, after the exile to Babylon. Because of the repetition, our survey of the **Chronicles** is very brief.

The Tel Dan Stele, an Aramean stone slab from the mid-ninth century BCE, confirms that a "House of David" existed. The Mesha Stele from Moab is dated from the same time and also includes a reference to David. Thus, we assume a King David existed, but more as a war-lord than a mighty king. No collaborating reference to King Solomon has been found in the records of other nations; archeological debate about Solomon's reign has focused on excavated structures from the tenth century. Nevertheless, we assume Solomon succeeded David and that his staff wrote the first text, which made David's and Solomon's kingdom seem so much more than it actually was.

Notwithstanding the limited archeological corroboration, David and Solomon maintain a powerful hold on our imaginations to this day. Many Jews and Christians regard the era of David and Solomon as Israel's mature obedience to YHWH's way of living on Earth and a kind of template for the good society YHWH desires.

We are saying the very opposite. We understand the texts of **Exodus** and **Genesis,** the teachings of the prophets and the life and teaching of Jesus to speak *against* the false image of YHWH introduced into the Jewish, Christian and Islamic faiths by the empire-supporting stories of David and Solomon.

A. Saul, David and Solomon (1 Samuel 13–31, 2 Samuel 1–24, and 1 Kings 1–10)

Very early in his tenure as king, Saul is reported to be in trouble. At Gilgal, he mustered a large number of troops from all across Canaan. Then he waited for the chief priest, Samuel, to come and offer sacrifices to YHWH before the battle. By the end of seven days, Samuel still had not arrived and the troops were beginning to "slip away" (1 Sam. 13:8). So Saul presided at the burnt offering. As soon as he had finished, Samuel arrived. He accused Saul of violating "the commandment of [YHWH]" and promptly pronounced harsh judgment: "Now your kingdom will not continue; [YHWH] has appointed a man after his own heart; and [YHWH] has appointed him to be ruler over his people" (1 Sam. 13:13–14).

Only three chapters later (chapter 16), Samuel anoints David as the next king in a private ceremony. David promptly became a public rival of King Saul, even while fighting in Saul's army. Later, David assembled his own militia of discontented and distressed men (1 Sam. 22:2). After Saul died in a battle with the Philistines, the people of Judah gathered at Hebron and seceded from united Israel by anointing David as their king. Seven-and-one-half years later, after a period of rule by Saul's son and continuous war with David and his men, the elders of the other tribes came to Hebron and anointed David as king over the Northern Kingdom, too (2 Sam. 5:3), thus restoring the unity that had existed under Saul. David then captured Jerusalem from the Jebusites and made his capital there.

What commandment did Saul violate? Probably the one that said only priests could preside at the kind of sacrifices Saul offered. But it really does not matter because the point of the story was to get Saul and his sons out of the way and portray David as the founder of the god-approved dynasty.

Chapter 15 also recounts how Saul failed to carry out YHWH's requirement of holy war and genocide. Samuel instructed Saul to "go and attack [king] Amalek, and utterly destroy all that they have; do not spare them, but kill both man and woman, child and infant, ox and sheep, camel and donkey" (1 Sam. 15:3). Saul defeated the Amalekites, a historic foe, but saved the king, the livestock and other valuables. This, we are told, caused YHWH to regret the choice of Saul as king (1 Sam. 15:11).

Samuel himself then carried out YHWH's command by cutting King Agag into pieces in a gruesome sacrificial ritual "before [YHWH] in Gilgal" (1 Sam. 15:33).

Stories of David begin in the sixteenth chapter of **1 Samuel** and fill the remainder of that book and all of **2 Samuel**. David is described as vigorous, brave and strong. He played the lyre superbly, had beautiful eyes, loved women and loved his friend Jonathan even more. His passion for life often led him to break the rules. When that got him in trouble, David's repentance was displayed with great emotion for all to see. David's fecundity seemed boundless and produced many children, loyal defenders and great wealth. And the text tells us that YHWH spoke to David, something YHWH never did to Saul.

David is a singular and commanding figure and reminds us of a Hollywood star. After Samuel anointed him, he rarely sought the guidance of others. Yes, he asked priests for food to eat (1 Sam. 21:3), for a sword to fight with (1 Sam. 21:8), for an ephod to pray with (1 Sam. 23:9, 30:7) and dance in (2 Sam. 6:14). But only once do we see David accepting direction from a messenger of YHWH: near the end of his life, when the prophet Gad told him where to build an altar of repentance (1 Sam. 24:18).

Yes, this text at times portrays David in a negative light.

(a) In 1 Samuel 25, David and his men acted much like a protection racket and used their reputation for violence to extort valuables from Nabal, a wealthy sheep and goat farmer. When Nabal refused to play along, David vowed to kill every man in Nabal's household (1 Sam. 25:22). Nabal's "clever and beautiful wife, Abigail" (1 Sam. 25:3) staved off the violence with a huge amount of food. David piously accepted the gift and then, when Nabal mysteriously died a few days later, took Abigail as his wife.

(b) For sixteen months, David and 600 men worked as mercenaries for the Philistine king, Achish. First from a base in Gath and then from Ziklag, they plundered towns and settlements to the south and west, "leaving neither man nor woman alive, but [taking] away the sheep, the oxen, the donkeys, the camels and the clothing" (1 Sam. 27:9–11). David's leave–no–witnesses approach was successful and he used the wealth gained by his banditry and murdering to buy political support from the elders of Judah (1 Sam. 30:26–30).

(c) After David and his men moved the Ark of the Covenant into Jerusalem, "David offered burnt offerings and offerings of well-being before [YHWH]" (2 Sam. 6:17). The text does not mention any involvement by the Levites in any of this. Furthermore, David danced in the streets wearing only a linen ephod, a garment usually worn by priests. His wife, Michal, scolded him for allowing his nakedness to be seen by the young women and girls. David's responded: "I will make myself yet more contemptible than this" (2 Sam. 6:22)!

(d) David commanded a married woman, Bathsheba, to come to his chamber where he had sex with her. When she became pregnant, David arranged for her soldier–husband to be placed in combat at a place where he would be killed (2 Sam. 11).

(e) David failed to take any disciplinary action against his son, Amnon, who raped David's daughter, Tamar (2 Sam. 13). David's failure led another son, Absalom, to avenge the sexual assault with violence. This in turn led to Absalom's exile for three years and finally his return to Jerusalem to lead a rebellion against his father.

A text that discloses so many negatives about David may strike us as the very opposite of royal propaganda. But the authors of this text were not trying to convince their audience that David was exemplary; that would have been a waste of time, given the proximity in time to David's life and public knowledge that he was "a man of blood" (2 Sam. 16:8). Instead, the authors wanted to establish divine authority and legitimacy for the monarchy, *no matter what sins kings may commit.* Recounting David's many sins was an integral part of this strategy to legitimize the dynasty.

This strategy is confirmed by the number of times the text tells us of the great respect David held for the *office* of king. For all his willingness to break rules, he was scrupulous about honoring Saul. We see this in his playing music for Saul after Saul tried to kill him (1 Sam.

18:10–16); his deferential response to Saul when collecting his reward (Saul's daughter) for killing Goliath (1 Sam. 18:18, 23); his refusal to lay a hand on Saul on two occasions when David could have killed him (1 Sam.24:9–15; 26:22–24); his very public mourning upon the death of Saul (2 Sam.1:11–27); his murder of the man who claimed to have killed Saul *at Saul's request* and then reported the fact to David (2 Sam.1:13–16); his execution of two men who killed Saul's son, who was king of the northern tribes and fighting a civil war with David (2 Sam.4:9–12); and his public show of kindness to Mephibosheth, crippled son of Saul (2 Sam.9:1–13).

Thus, the stories of David tell of a sinful man whose descendants will rule Israel forever. This becomes explicit when the prophet Nathan brought David the message of YHWH, who is reported to have said:

> When your days are fulfilled and you lie down with your ancestors, I will raise up your offspring after you . . . and I will establish the throne of his kingdom forever . . . I will not take my steadfast love from him as I took it from Saul . . . Your house and your kingdom shall be made sure forever. (2 Sam. 7:12–16)

For the Southern Kingdom, which was the source of nearly all First Testament texts, *this promise to David is YHWH's founding covenant with Israel*, not the promise to Abraham to bless the peoples of the earth (Gen. 12:1–2) and not the promise to Moses to make Israel "a priestly kingdom and a holy nation" (Ex. 19:5–6). This is a vital interpretive key.

Next we come to Solomon, son of David and Bathsheba. His story starts with a political struggle with his brother, Adonijah. Through the conspiring of the prophet Nathan and the deception of Bathsheba (1 Kings 1:15–27), David was persuaded to declare Solomon his successor. He ordered the High Priest Zadok and the prophet Nathan to perform an anointing to signify YHWH's appointment (1 Kings 1:33–34).

Solomon began his reign by settling old scores, killing first his brother and rival, Adjonijah (1 Kings 2:13–25), and then David's military commander, Joab, who had supported Adonijah. Solomon's enforcer killed Joab at the altar inside the holiest of places (1 Kings 2:28–35). Solomon then made "a marriage alliance with Pharaoh, king of Egypt; he took Pharaoh's daughter and brought her into the city of David" (1 Kings

3:1). Later, he married princesses of Moab, Ammon, Edom, Sidon and the Hittites (1 Kings 11:1).

The text is extravagant in its praise of Solomon; his wisdom "surpassed the wisdom of all the people of the east, and all the wisdom of Egypt" (1 Kings 4:30). The Queen of Sheba visited Jerusalem "to test [Solomon] with hard questions." Solomon passed with flying colors; the queen was overcome by his wisdom, his palace, his food, the pageantry of his court, and his burnt offerings (1 Kings 10:1–5).

Solomon is further exalted by the story of his humble request to YHWH for wisdom. "Ask what I should give you," YHWH said to Solomon in a dream. Replied Solomon:

> I am only a little child; I do not know how to go out or come in. And your servant is in the midst of the people you have chosen, a great people, so numerous they cannot be numbered or counted. Give your servant therefore an understanding mind to govern your people, able to discern between good and evil. For who can govern this your great people? (1 Kings 3:7–9)

The story of the two prostitutes fighting over a baby (1 Kings 3:16–28) is told to highlight Solomon's wisdom. Howard-Brook views the story as an allegory about which kingdom (Judah or Ephraim) had the rightful authority to rule all of Israel. [20] Unsurprisingly, Solomon concluded Judah was the true "birth mother" and Ephraim the usurper.

Solomon's masterful guidance of the process to build the Jerusalem temple fills three chapters of this text. Chapter 8 then describes the temple's dedication, especially Solomon's speech and prayer. He mentioned David five times in his speech and three times in his prayer and prayed at length about the covenant YHWH made with David to forever keep a descendant on the throne of Israel. Solomon then followed with a blessing of the people and the offering of sacrifices to YHWH. He did it all; the priests are hardly mentioned.

The text also highlights Solomon's administrative skills. He organized Israel into twelve districts (1 Kings 4:7); collected huge amounts

---

[20]   Ibid., 130.

of food from the countryside (1 Kings 4:22–23); entered an agreement with the king of Tyre to provide cedar and cypress timber for the temple and palace in Jerusalem (1 Kings 5:1–12); and conscripted Israelites to fell timber, cut stone and build the temple and palace in Jerusalem (1 Kings 5:13–18). He built "storage cities, the cities for his chariots, the cities for his cavalry and whatever Solomon desired to build" (1 Kings 9:19) and assembled a fleet of ships for import and export (1 Kings 9:26–28). He conscripted resident Canaanites as "slave labor" (1 Kings 9:21).

This is reminiscent of the Pharaohs, yet the text tells us the people were delighted: "Judah and Israel were as numerous as the sand by the sea; they ate and drank and were happy . . . Judah and Israel lived in safety . . . all of them under their vines and fig trees" (1 Kings 4:20, 25).

B. The kings of Ephraim and Judah (1 Kings 11–22; 2 Kings 1–25)

In the very first verse, the authors of this second text begin to pull Solomon off his pedestal.

> King Solomon loved many foreign women . . . Among his wives were seven hundred princesses and three hundred concubines; and his wives turned away his heart . . . Solomon did what was evil in the sight of (YHWH) . . . [He] built a high place for Chemosh, the abomination of Moab, and for Molech, the abomination of the Ammonites, on the mountain east of Jerusalem. He did this for all his foreign wives, who offered incense and sacrificed to their gods. (1 Kings 11:1–8)

A few verses later, Solomon's reputation takes another hit. Representatives of northern and eastern tribes approached his son, Rehoboam, at the place where Rehoboam was to be anointed as the new king. "Your father made our yoke heavy," they said. "Lighten the hard service of your father and his heavy yoke that he placed upon us and we will serve you" (1 Kings 12:3–4). Rehoboam's older advisors counseled him to grant the request, but the younger advisors disagreed. The king followed the young advisors and answered harshly: "My father disciplined you with whips, I will discipline you with scorpions'" (1 Kings 12:11).

So the people replied to Rehoboam: "What share do we have in David? We have no inheritance in the son of Jesse. To your tents, O Israel" (1 Kings 12:16). Thus, ten of Israel's tribes resumed their identity as a separate nation. They made Jeroboam, a former aide to Solomon, their king. Only the tribes of Judah and Benjamin remained loyal to Rehoboam. Israel was never again united and Ephraim and Judah often fought each other in war. Thus, division is cited as one of Solomon's legacies.

A second legacy was fascination with the ways of empire. Though having a king brought with it the injustice, corruption and abuses of power other nations experienced, the Israelites could not imagine an alternative, even when things went very badly. Their affection for the story of Israel's great founding kings precluded it.

Is the worship of Canaanite gods also part of Solomon's legacy?

As we noted above, Solomon is said to have built places for his wives to worship gods other than YHWH. But for the Israelite people, much more common throughout these texts are references to raising "sacred poles" and worshipping at "high places." For example, though Judah had its temple in Jerusalem, its King Rehoboam built "high places, pillars and sacred poles on every high hill and under every green tree" (1 Kings 14:23). Similarly, King Jeroboam of Ephraim built places of worship "on high places" (1 Kings 12:31). By and large, worship at these sites focused on the worship of YHWH, not other gods.

The nub of the problem for the Jerusalem-based scribes who wrote this text was that people were *worshipping YHWH at places outside of Jerusalem's control.* By describing worship at "high places" as something highly offensive to YHWH, these scribes sought to delegitimize such practices. Instead, they hoped to centralize worship in Jerusalem and thereby increase the power and wealth of the city's religious and political elite.

Ephraim is often accused of having begun practicing idol worship via Jeroboam's calves of gold: "Here are your gods, O Israel, who brought you up out of the land of Egypt" (1 Kings 12:28–30). Jeroboam set one in Bethel, at the south edge of Ephraim near Jerusalem, and the other in Dan, at the north edge. But Howard-Brook points out that Jeroboam was not accused of promoting the worship of Canaanite gods. "Rather, he [was] charged with radical liturgical reform. Jeroboam replaced worship practices that supported an imperial social order with new ones designed to be supportive of his alternative vision for YHWH's people."[21]

What about those golden calves? In the holiest place within Jerusalem's temple stood two gold-covered, olive wood cherubim, each fifteen feet tall (1 Kings 6:23–28). No one ever called them idols; they were simply understood to be furnishings that pointed to YHWH's glory. In Jeroboam's liturgical reform, perhaps calves replaced the cherubim with a more agrarian motif.

The heart of the dispute was the powerful unity of religious observance and royal pageantry. Jeroboam knew the loyalty of the people of Ephraim would follow Jerusalem's king it they kept going to Jerusalem's temple to offer sacrifices. So he provided an alternative by which people could worship YHWH in their own country.

Yes, the text bears witness against Jeroboam. The prophet Ahijah, a resident of Ephraim and the one who first encouraged Jeroboam to become Ephraim's king, denounced Jeroboam early in his reign: "But you have done evil . . . and have gone and made for yourself other gods, and cast images, provoking me to anger, and have thrust me behind your back; therefore I will bring evil upon the house of Jeroboam . . . [and] cut off the house of Jeroboam" (1 Kings 14:9–10, 14). This sounds a lot like idol worship. But we also remember this text was written by scribes in Jerusalem. While willing to criticize David and Solomon, they remained committed to the Davidic dynasty. To legitimize its authority, they insisted correct worship of YHWH could occur only in the temple at Jerusalem. As our text puts it, Jerusalem was "the city that [YHWH] had chosen out of all the tribes of Israel to put his name there" (1 Kings 14:21). Everything they wrote about Ephraim conveyed criticism because it rejected this ideology.

Ephraim's kings

In the north, Jeroboam reigned for 22 years, but his son lasted only two years before being deposed and killed. Baasha reigned 24 years, but

---

[21]   Ibid., 158.

again, his son's reign ended in violence after two years. Omri, the early king whose reign is most frequently documented by sources outside the Bible, began a dynasty that ruled forty-four years; it included his son, Ahab, and grandsons Ahaziah and Joram. During this dynasty, Ephraim became strong and prosperous, established extensive trade relations with its neighbors, and began exporting its olive oil and fibers.

King Ahab introduced the worship of Canaanite gods into the life of Ephraim. To cement an alliance with the Phoenicians, he married one of their princesses, Jezebel, and built an altar to the Canaanite god, Baal, in the capital city of Samaria (1 Kings 16:31–32). Shockingly, Ahab sought the blessing of Baal for his reconstruction of Jericho by killing two of his own children as sacrifices and burying their bodies in the footings of important walls. "He laid [Jericho's] foundation at the cost of Abiram, his firstborn, and set its gates at the cost of his youngest son, Segub" (1 Kings 16:34). This conformed to traditional Canaanite religious rituals.

The text also gives a vivid account of Ahab's abuse of power (see paraphrase in the front-piece of this book). He wanted to buy Naboth's vineyard because it was next to the palace, a convenient place for a vegetable garden. Naboth was not selling. So Jezebel conspired with "elders and nobles" who lived with Naboth to proclaim a fast, call people to a meeting, and have "two scoundrels" accuse Naboth of "cursing God and the King" (1 Kings 21:8–16). As the contrived event unfolded, the greedy dynamics of power-pleasing kicked in and people marched Naboth outside the city and stoned him to death. Thus Ahab got his garden.

Rule by the House of Omri ended through the intervention of the prophet Elisha, who sent a young associate to the site of a major battle to anoint Jehu, one of the officers, as king. The young prophet pulled Jehu out of a meeting of military commanders to do the anointing (2 Kings 9:6). When Jehu returned to the meeting, the other officers asked: "Why did that madman come to you?" Jehu replied: "You know the sort and how they babble." But Jehu's colleagues would not relent: "Liar! Come on, tell us!" So Jehu told them he had just been anointed king of Ephraim. "They all took their cloaks and spread them for him on the bare steps; they blew the trumpet and proclaimed, 'Jehu is king'" (2 Kings 9:12–13)!

Jehu proceeded to conspire against King Joram. The climax occurred far from the battle site, near the capital in Samaria, as Jehu's chariot met Joram's chariot beside the vineyard of Naboth. There Jehu "drew his bow with all his strength and shot Joram between the shoulders, so that the arrow pierced his heart." Joram's mother, Jezebel, died when thrown from the window of the royal palace to the road below, where dogs ate much of her flesh (2 Kings 9:24–37). Jehu proceeded to murder all of Ahab's descendants, the priests and prophets of Baal, and all who worshipped Baal (2 Kings 10).

King Jehu ruled for twenty-eight years, often fought with King Hazael of Aram and lost control of Ephraim's eastern regions. The text tells us little about his reign beyond the massive blood-letting with which it began. It does disclose one intriguing tidbit: despite his anointing by the prophet of YHWH and Jehu's obvious "zeal for [YHWH]" (2 Kings 10:16), he did not disturb the golden calves Jeroboam had placed at Bethel and Dan. Again, this suggests an understanding of YHWH-worship that did not preclude the presence of these objects.

Curiously, the text does not tell us that during Jehu's reign, Ephraim became Assyria's vassal (it was never again fully autonomous). The Assyrian Black Obelisk on display in the British Museum depicts Jehu kissing the ground at the emperor's feet. The text of the Obelisk confirms Jehu severed alliances with Judah and Phoenicia as part of the bargain. We assume Jehu took this step because his army was beaten so frequently by King Hazael and Aram's army (2 Kings 10:32–33).

The family dynasty Jehu began ruled Ephraim for 91 years; Jehu's son, Jehoahaz succeeded him and a grandson, Johoash, followed. A great-grandson, Jeroboam II, enjoyed a 41-year reign; he restored lost territory to the north and east (2 Kings 14:25–27) and led Ephraim during its time of greatest prosperity and strongest trade. The dynasty ended in 753 BCE when a political rival assassinated, Zechariah, a son of Jeroboam II.

This launched a violent and unsettled period of five kings in thirty-one years. Only one of the transitions during that period was from a father to a son. Ephraim continued to be a vassal of Assyria throughout this period; over time, the terms and conditions became ever more severe.

During King Menahem's reign, the Assyrian army entered Ephraim as an occupying force and "turned back" only after Menahem transferred to the Assyrian king much wealth raised by taxing the people. During the reign of King Pekah, the Assyrian emperor again entered the land and captured "all the land of Naphtali [in the north] and carried the people captive to Assyria" (2 Kings 15:20–29). Ephraim's final king was Hoshea; during his reign, the Assyrian Empire turned the screws tighter still with more demands for tribute, which Hoshea paid. "But the king of Assyria found treachery in Hoshea; for he had sent a message to King So of Egypt" and discontinued the payments of tribute (2 Kings 17:1–4).

In 725 BCE, Assyria invaded yet again and for three years besieged the fortified capital city. "In the ninth year of Hoshea the king of Assyria captured Samaria; he carried the Israelites away," resettling them in areas known today as eastern Turkey, northern Iraq, northern Iran, Armenia and Azerbaijan. (2 Kings 17:5–6). The city was destroyed. Other peoples were settled in the places the exiles had been (2 Kings 17:24).

How could the people of YHWH have met such a fate? Because, the text tells us, the people had "worshipped other gods and walked in the customs of the nations whom [YHWH] had driven out" (2 Kings 17:7–8). The liturgical reforms of King Jeroboam receive special negative mention, as does the practice of passing children through the fire as sacrifices to other gods (2 Kings 17:9, 17). *Injustice, oppression of the poor and the pursuit of empire are not mentioned*; it is only through the prophets (see chapter 13) that these became significant concerns in the life of Israel.

While it is often assumed that the Assyrian victory ended the Hebrew presence in the central, northern and eastern parts of Canaan, in fact the Assyrian Empire carried into exile only about one-quarter of the population (around 40,000 people). Many fled to surrounding areas, especially Judah, and others remained with the consent of the Assyrians. Thus, the categorical way the text speaks of Ephraim's demise is yet another example of the bias the Judah-based authors held against Ephraim and any political community not led by the House of David and centered in Jerusalem. In fact, a weak and enslaved Israelite political community remained in the north, but we do not read of it again until **Ezra**.

Judah's kings

In the nation to the south, Rehoboam's son, Abijah, reigned for three, war-filled years during which he attacked Ephraim in an effort to reunite Israel. He was followed by his son, Asa, who ruled for forty-one years. Asa opposed mixing the worship of YHWH with worship of other gods. "He put away the male prostitutes out of the land and removed all the idols that his ancestors had made," including an image his mother had made (1 Kings 15:12–13).

Asa's son, Jehoshaphat, succeeded him and governed for twenty-five years in much the same way as his father.   Indeed, he was the first king to follow the Moses' requirement (Deut. 31:10) that every seventh year, the law was to be read aloud for all of Israel (2 Chron. 17:7–9). He also created a network of judges "in all the fortified cities of Judah" to resolve private disputes (2 Chron. 19:5).   Yet he also entered in to a marriage alliance with King Ahab of Ephraim (1 Kings 18:1). And "the high places were not taken away, and the people still sacrificed and offered incense on the high places" (1 Kings 22:43).   Thus, "good king" Jehoshaphat did not require people to come to Jerusalem to worship, nor did his immediate successors. Our text comments negatively about this.

The next king, Jehoram, was married to Athaliah, the daughter of Ephraim's King Ahab. This marriage between members of the reigning royal families of Ephraim and Judah presented the potential of a re-unified Israel. But Jehoram adopted Ahab's policies (2 Kings 8:18) and for this our text gives negative marks. His son and successor, Ahaziah, was killed by Jehu's forces while on a state visit to Ephraim to visit his uncle, the king in the north (2 Kings 9:27).

In retaliation, Queen Athaliah attempted to match Jehu's zeal by extinguishing the Davidic dynasty through the murder of all its members, including her own grandchildren. She nearly succeeded, but the Queen's daughter secreted away one infant child, Joash. The child was kept in hiding for six years while Judah's only female monarch ruled (2 Kings 11:1–3). (She is blamed with restoring sites in Judah for the worship of Canaanite gods.) The House of David was restored to power by the chief priest, Jehoida, who conspired with the temple and palace guards to arrange a coronation of seven-year-old Joash in the temple court. It was a moment of high drama as the Queen entered the temple and confronted the assembled crowd with cries of "Treason! Treason!" (2 Kings 11:14).

The reign of Joash was long, but mixed. He insisted that the priests use part of the money they received in temple assessments for the repair of the temple and when they did not, instituted a system of shared control over funds so the King's staff could monitor balances and pay the tradespeople working to repair the temple (1 Kings 12:9–16). But at the request of local officials, he permitted the restoration of the "sacred poles" at rural worship sites (2 Chron. 24:18). When confronted for this by the prophet Zechariah, Joash ordered him killed by stoning. Late in his reign, Joash paid a large amount of tribute to King Hazael of Aram. His own staff assassinated him in his old age.

Joash's son, Amaziah, aggressively attempted to expand Judah's boundaries, first by making war on neighboring Edom. With that successful campaign under his belt, he turned toward Ephraim and challenged King Jehoash to a fight: "Come, let us look one another in the face" (2 Kings 14:8). Johoash responded with an insult and Amaziah rushed into a battle that resulted in his defeat. The troops of the Northern Kingdom broke down part of Jerusalem's wall and looted the temple and royal treasury. Amaziah was later assassinated, as his father had been.

His 16-year-old son, Uzziah (also called Azariah), succeeded him and enjoyed a long and successful reign of fifty-two years. But he fell afoul of the occasionally enforced rule that a temple priest conduct all sacrifices. "The priest Azariah went in after him with eighty priests of [YHWH] who were men of valor; they withstood King Uzziah and said to him, 'It is not for you, Uzziah, to make offering to [YHWH] but for the priests the descendants of Aaron, who are consecrated to make offering.'" When Uzziah became angry at the priests, "a leprous disease broke out on his forehead" (2 Chron. 26:16–19). Because he had leprosy, his son, Jotham, lived in the palace and conducted royal business. Jotham ruled alone for eight years after his father's death.

The next king in the Davidic succession was Ahaz, son of Jotham. The Assyrian Empire's aggressive foreign policy framed his reign, first in the efforts of neighbors Ephraim and Aram to secure an alliance with Judah so that together, the three nations would be strong enough to withstand Assyria. When King Ahaz refused, Ephraim and Aram prepared to make war on Judah. Ahaz appealed to the empire for protection and as part of the bargain, offered Judah as Assyria's vassal. Assyria agreed; it destroyed Damascus and wiped out the kingdom of Aram and then invaded Ephraim and seized its northern regions. Judah was spared from its immediate neighbors, but paid dearly in tribute and loss of independence to Assyria and will always be remembered for setting in motion the chain of events that led to the destruction of Ephraim, its sister state to the north.

Ahaz was enamored by empire. He met the Assyrian ruler in Damascus and was so taken with an Assyrian altar installed there that he ordered Judah's high priest to replicate it for Jerusalem's temple. He rearranged the temple's furniture "because of the king of Assyria" (2 Kings 16:18). Thus, it is no surprise to read that Ahaz sacrificed his own flesh and blood, making "his son pass through the fire, according to the abominable practices of the nations" (2 Kings 16:3).

Upon Ahaz's death in 715 BCE, his son, Hezekiah, ascended to the throne and the authors of our text finally had a king they liked. One very important reason appears early in Hezekiah's story: "He removed the high places, broke down the pillars, and cut down the sacred pole. He broke in pieces the bronze serpent that Moses had made, for until these days the people . . . had been making offerings to it" (2 Kings 18:4–5). By centralizing worship in Jerusalem, Hezekiah enriched the elite there.

During the final years of Ahaz's reign, Ephraim was extinguished and many residents of that former kingdom fled south to escape exile at the hand of the Assyrians. Their numbers swelled the population of Jerusalem and its environs, and their skills and energy contributed much to the economic output of Judah. Hezekiah addressed the need to integrate refugees by commencing repairs to the temple and reopening it for regular use (it had been closed during his father's reign). According to 2 Chronicles 30, he also re-instituted the practice of the Passover, and called all the people (including residents of the north who had managed to avoid exile) to Jerusalem for the observance. Unsurprisingly, few from the north accepted the invitation. Still, it was a huge and remarkable gathering, a week-long religious revival. "There was great joy in Jerusalem, for since the time of Solomon son of King David of Israel there had been nothing like this in Jerusalem" (2 Chron. 30:26).

Upon the death in 705 BCE of Sargon II, the renowned warrior-emperor of Assyria, many of Assyria's vassals stopped making tribute payments. Hezekiah did the same. He also commenced work to strengthen Jerusalem's walls, stopped up the springs surrounding the city and built a tunnel conduit of 533 meters to bring fresh water into the city. He entered into a security alliance with Egypt. And he hosted emissaries from Babylon and showed them the bounty of his treasure house (2 Kings 20:13).

Toward the mid-point of his twenty-nine-year reign, Hezekiah experienced a life-threatening illness and nearly died. The character of his faith—as expressed in his prayers—is remarkable (2 Kings 20:1–11 and Isaiah 38).

In 701 BCE, the empire struck back, entering Judah under its new king, Sennacherib. The invasion's impact on the Judean countryside was devastating, far worse than the Babylonian invasion a hundred years later. Assyrian records state its army destroyed forty-six cities and took 200,150 captives into exile. Hezekiah sent a message to Sennacherib saying, "I have done wrong; withdraw from me; whatever you impose on me I will bear" (2 Kings 18:14). He also tried to appease Sennacherib by paying a huge tribute of silver, gold and other valuables, stripping the gold from the doors of the temple (2 Kings 18:14–16) in the process. Yet Sennacherib did not relent; his goal was the subjugation of Jerusalem.

Events related to the siege of that city are described in rich detail in chapters 18–19 of **2 Kings**. During the initial stages of the assault, a top Assyrian official ("the Rabshakeh") spoke in Hebrew to Hezekiah's officials, making sure the people also heard and understood the dreadful choice before them. Here is a flavor of his message: "Make your peace with me and come out to me; then every one of you will eat from your own vine and your own fig tree, and drink water from your own cistern . . . Has any of the gods of the nations ever delivered land out of the hand of the king of Assyria? . . . Have they delivered Samaria" (2 Kings 18:31–34)?

The text tells us that Hezekiah consulted with the prophet, Isaiah, who encouraged him to continue resisting. Then, after an interlude when

Assyria finished off the Egyptian and Ethiopian armies, the Rabshakeh renewed his threats. Hezekiah sought YHWH's help; Isaiah assured him that YHWH had heard his prayers. "That very night the angel of (YHWH) set out and struck down 185,000 in the camp of the Assyrians" and Sennacherib withdrew from Jerusalem (2 Kings 19:8–36). Some have speculated the quick exit was due to cholera, which in turn was caused by a lack of fresh spring water outside the city. In any event, Jerusalem endured and the Assyrian withdrawal is remembered as a miraculous victory for Judah.

Sennacherib's Prism, a carved stone touting the emperor, tells a different story. It describes Hezekiah as "a caged bird" and his agreement to again be an Assyrian vassal and pay more tribute as the way the siege ended. It makes no mention of Assyrian loss of life at Jerusalem.

We assume both accounts reflect political spin. Yet the story of Hezekiah's son and successor, Manasseh, gives us a clue that the Assyrian account is probably more accurate. Manasseh became co-regent with his with father in 697 BCE and reigned for fifty-five years. He "did what was evil in the sight of [YHWH], following the abominable practices of the nations . . . [and] made his son pass through the fire." He placed a carved image of the god Asherah *in the temple*; the text says he led the people to do more evil "than the nations had done that [YHWH] destroyed before the people of Israel" (2 Kings 21:1–6, 9).

Why, eleven years before he died, did Hezekiah begin sharing power with his twelve-year-old son? Why did the son Hezekiah empowered govern so differently than the father? We think the answer is obvious: Assyria required it. Manasseh's name appears often in Assyrian records as a vassal of Sennacherib's son, Earshaddon. When he failed to fully cooperate, the Assyrian imprisoned him for a time in Babylon (2 Chron.33:10–11). In addition to making all promised payments of tribute, being a loyal vassal meant hosting Assyrian officials in Judah, showing due respect for Assyrian gods, and organizing local production and international trade in a way that maximized the wealth of the empire and its network of business agents in Judah. What the Assyrian Empire wanted was not to destroy Jerusalem, but make it part of its mechanism for gathering wealth and honoring its gods. It achieved both goals.

The prophets led the opposition to this arrangement, but were brutally suppressed by King Manasseh, who "filled Jerusalem with innocent blood" (2 Kings 24:4).

Manasseh's son, Amon, reigned for only two years before he was assassinated by his servants. Amon's son, Josiah, ascended to the throne at the age of eight and reigned for thirty-one years. Our text says, "Before him there was no king like him, who turned to [YHWH] with all his heart, with all his soul, and with all his might, according to the Law of Moses; nor did any like him arise again" (2 Kings 23:25).

Why did the authors of our text regard Josiah so highly? As a youth, he was highly malleable and we assume some of the authors of our text were powers behind Josiah's throne. Like Hezekiah, Josiah repaired the temple and destroyed all worships sites outside of Jerusalem. Even more than Hezekiah, Josiah pursued centralization of all worship-related activity in Jerusalem. He desecrated "the high places" so they would never be used for worship again. He fired the priests who had led worship at those places and killed many of them (2 Kings 23:5–20). He reinstituted the Passover and required that it be observed in Jerusalem (2 Kings 23:21–23). All of this served to eliminate a level of rural officials, bring more money into the palace and temple treasuries, and empower and enrich Jerusalem's elite.

But there is more: Josiah endeared himself to the writers of our text with his energetic response to the discovery in the temple of "the book of the law" (2 Kings 22:11), which is generally thought to be a version of **Deuteronomy**. Josiah was stricken when he read it and "tore his clothes" (2 Kings 22:11) because it was obvious Judah had not been following the book's commands. He consulted the prophetess Hulda, who told him Judah's days were numbered, but that it would continue beyond Josiah's life. "Because your heart was penitent, and you humbled yourself before [YHWH] . . . I will gather you to your ancestors . . . your eyes shall not see all the disaster that I will bring on this place" (2 Kings 22:16–20).

Josiah read "the book of the law" aloud in the temple in the presence of all the elders of Judah. "The king stood by the pillar and made a covenant before [YHWH] to follow [YHWH], keeping his commandments, his decrees, and his statutes with all his heart and all his soul, to perform the words of the covenant that were written in this book. The people all joined in the covenant" (2 Kings 23:3).

With the discovery of the old manuscript, King Josiah and his advisors saw an opportunity to reunify Israel through a single historical narrative from its earliest origins to the present. For this to happen, they had to find a way to tell Israel's story in a way that reconciled the contradictory perspectives we identified earlier (see pages 100-101).

> Judah's empire-mimicking story of David and Solomon vs.
> > Ephraim's deliverance-from-empire story of Moses;
> Judah's account of YHWH's eternal covenant with David vs.
> > Ephraim's account of YHWH's eternal covenant with the people at Mt. Sinai;
> Judah's YHWH-lives-in-the-temple story vs.
> > Ephraim's YHWH-lives-where-the-faithful-worship story;
> Judah's Jeroboam-delivered-you-into-idol-worship story vs.
> > Ephraim's Jeroboam-delivered-us-from-tyranny story.

Josiah's scribes accomplished this massive synthesis by expanding **Deuteronomy**, by editing the story of the kings to criticize both Solomon and Jeroboam, by elevating Josiah as the new Joshua, and by creating a literary bridge between **Deuteronomy** and the stories of the kings through the composition of texts we know as **Joshua**, **Judges** and the first twelve chapters of **1 Samuel**.[22] Thus, these seven books (**Deuteronomy, Joshua, Judges, 1 & 2 Samuel, 1 & 2 Kings**) hang together in a coherent way.

Through these changes, the Moses of **Exodus** emerged as a huge figure in the books of **Deuteronomy** and **Joshua** and a leader who endorsed Israel having a king. With Moses' endorsement of monarchy safely in the text, Samuel's opposition to a king also could be included. Israel's tradition of local rule was confirmed in **Judges**, but so was its failure to provide security. Judah's version of events prevailed more often than Ephraim's, but elements of both remained, thus creating a text acceptable to the sons of northern refugees who had joined Judah. (For discussion of this approach to these texts, see question 12 on page 149.)

---

[22]   Ibid., 192-197.

A third noteworthy aspect of Josiah's reign was his attempt to absorb the lands of the former Northern Kingdom into Judah. With Assyria's power in decline, Josiah ended Judah's vassal relationship, stopped making tribute payments and began integrating the north into Judah's economy. When the Egyptian Pharaoh Neco led an army up the Mediterranean coast and toward Assyria to help that faltering empire against Babylon, Josiah saw an opportunity to free the region of Egyptian claims as well. Even though Neco had not threatened Judah in any way, Josiah ordered his army to block the movement of the Egyptian army across the northern region. In the battle that followed, Josiah was killed.

As a consequence of Josiah's misjudgment, Judah became a vassal of Egypt. Neco made one of Josiah's sons king but changed his name to Jehoiakim and demanded tribute of silver and gold. Jehoiakim "taxed the land in order to meet Pharaoh's demands" (2 Kings 23:35).

Judah's end was not long in coming. The Chaldean people from Babylon were emerging as the next great power. After defeating Egypt in 605 BCE at Carchemish, the Babylonian army swept through all the lands west of the Mediterranean Sea. To avoid war and save Jerusalem, Jehoiakim pledged his allegiance to King Nebuchadnezzar, paid tribute to him, and permitted Babylon to take some of Judah's most talented young people back to the Babylonian capitol for training. After a Babylonian thrust into Egypt faltered in late 601 BCE, Jehoiakim switched his allegiance back to Egypt. In late 598 BCE, Nebuchadnezzar laid siege to Jerusalem; Jehoiakim died at the start of the siege and his son, Jehoiachin, succeeded him. The Babylonians entered the city after three months and took the king and royal family, as well as 10,000 of the more educated and skilled residents to Babylon. Nebuchadnezzar installed Jehoiakim's younger brother, Zedekiah, as king.

Nearly ten years later, in 587 BCE, Zedekiah rebelled and the second Babylonian siege began. By the end of the eighteen months it lasted, starvation and cannibalism haunted the city. After the wall had been breached, the Babylonians entered, destroyed the city (including its temple) and exiled more of the remaining residents. Babylonian officials ruled the people that remained. The era of the kings ended, as did Judah's hopes for YHWH's miraculous extension of their infatuation with empire.

C. A post-exile history of Judah's kings (1 Chronicles—2 Chronicles)

How would Ephraim's and Judah's histories be told by authors who had seen the collapse of Jerusalem and the House of David, endured catastrophic defeat and exile, and experienced YHWH's presence in a land far from Jerusalem?   We have already worked through three books written by authors with that experience: **Genesis, Leviticus**, and **Numbers**. We found **Genesis** to be a text that avoids chauvinism and often subverts conventional norms of power and authority. **Leviticus** is an intriguing mix of worship rituals, rules for living in community, and radical economics. **Numbers** is a harsh text that puts much emphasis on priests and purity and little on justice or the covenant between YHWH and the Israelites.

In the **Chronicles**, we find a text again proclaiming the greatness of Judah, the House of David and Jerusalem. It is less candid than the version we just finished and more jingoistic. Our survey will be brief.

1 Chronicles

Many of the twenty-nine chapters of this book contain genealogies and lists of people connected with King David.   The authors seemed concerned to connect living and future generations to the elite of the past so that people could glory in their lineage and famous ancestors.

Beginning with chapter 11, the stories of David are retold, often with embellishment. "The fame of David went out into all lands, and [YHWH] brought the fear of him on all nations" (1 Chron. 13:17). The eternal character of YHWH's covenant with David is emphasized; "forever" is used eight times in Chapter 17. The text blames David's unpopular tax census on "Satan" (1 Chron. 21:1).

The most significant difference is the way the text tells of the transition from David to Solomon at the end of David's life. In **1 Kings**, the transition only occurred because Solomon's mother, Bathsheba, and the prophet Nathan conspired to elicit bedridden David's endorsement of Solomon. On the other hand, in chapters 22, 28 and 29 of **1 Chronicles**, David conferred with Solomon on the design of the temple, lined up political support for his reign, gathered resources to support the building, and proclaimed his appointment to the "whole assembly" (1 Chron. 29:1).

Thus, in this text we do not see the destruction of Jerusalem and the humiliation of the House of David as leading to a chastened view of the monarchy and its role in YHWH's work in the world. *Instead, the text exalts Judah's kings even more.* For the authors of this text, the era of kings for the people of YHWH was far from over, even though they were ruled at the moment by the Persian Empire.

2 Chronicles

This book begins with a sanitized view of King Solomon: he was humble, wise, rich, well-connected internationally, devout and (did we say it already?) rich. When he was finished with his prayer to YHWH at the dedication of the temple, as he stood "before the altar of [YHWH] in the presence of the whole assembly of Israel" (2 Chron. 6:12), "fire came down from heaven and consumed the burnt offering and the sacrifices" (2 Chron. 7:1). "The priests could not enter the house of [YHWH] because the glory of [YHWH] filled [YHWH's] house. When all the people of Israel saw the fire come down and the glory of [YHWH] on the temple, they bowed down on the payment with their faces to the ground and worshiped and gave thanks to [YHWH]" (2 Chron.7:2–3). Ah, that Solomon; he could do it all!

His foreign wives are not mentioned (except the Egyptian princess, whom the authors want us to know had a house apart from the palace), nor the places of worship built for them.

Generally, the **Chronicles** tell the stories of Judah's kings in a formulaic manner. Success in war, economics and other endeavors was due to obedience to YHWH. Failure in those endeavors was due to disobedience to YHWH's commands and improper worship.

Ephraim's kings are not mentioned except when necessary to describe the glorious achievements of a king of Judah. For example, Judah's second king, Abijah, was at war much of his three-year reign against Ephraim and its king, Jeroboam. In the most important battle, the army of Judah supposedly killed 500,000 soldiers in Ephraim's army (2 Chron.13:17), an obvious and huge distortion that indicates little concern for accuracy.

13. Speaking Inconvenient Truth
Elijah, Elisha, Obadiah, Amos, Hosea, 1st Isaiah, Micah, Zephaniah, Nahum, Habakkuk, Jeremiah

After living "like other nations" under the authority of kings for perhaps 400 years, the Israelites experienced the destruction of both their nation-states. These failures entailed immense suffering; the people of YHWH became the wretched of the earth. Recognition of this reality prepares us to consider the words of the prophets. Did they offer a viable alternative to the disastrous path of kings?

Walter Brueggemann describes prophecy as "a narrative that summons alternative ways of life."[23] The emphasis is on the present, not the future and yet with profound implications for the future. Israel's prophets looked through the lens of **Exodus** at current events and predicted what the consequences of empire-loving policies would be, often to the dismay of kings who wanted only glowing predictions of success.

One who speaks in this way for YHWH thereby claims enormous clout and that clout is usually perceived as a threat by conventional powers. Thus, the relationships between prophets and kings are typically adversarial. Of course, it is not just kings who are concerned about the potential threat of one who claims to speak for YHWH. Generally, people seek some reliable way of knowing whether the speaker brings a divine message or only pretends to do so. Alas, no reliable method emerged in Israel's history to distinguish imposters from the real thing. One consistent indicator seemed to be that a true prophet's message created risk for him or herself. This screened out many who spoke in YHWH's name for reasons of ego or personal profit, but it still left much uncertainty.

While the First Testament pattern was that only a few individuals filled prophetic roles, the expectation of the later texts (especially **Joel**) was that *many* people would exercise the prophetic gift. This seems to have been Jesus' expectation too; he told his followers they *all* should expect to be "blessed" by persecution for their commitments (Matt. 5:11).

---

[23] Quoted by Richard Beck at experimentaltheology.blogspot.com, Nov. 24, 2014.

In the Hebrew world view, YHWH was known by what YHWH did within the circumstances of life. Every king surrounded himself with insightful men and women, hoping at least one of them also had a prophetic gift to identify where YHWH was active in current events. A few such advisors also are identified in the Bible as prophets. More typically, however, the prophetic perspective was voiced from the margins, calling a society to repentance and change.

Elijah the Tishbite and his assistant and successor, Elisha, are the first Israelite prophets during the era of kings to receive significant attention. Both lived in the Northern Kingdom (Ephraim), probably as part of a company of prophets (2 Kings 4:38). In contrast to their successors who relied on words to bring about change, Elijah and Elisha are portrayed as dramatic action figures exercising supernatural powers to do good and defeat evil. Their sometimes over-the-top activities occurred within the context of Ephraim's frequent wars with neighboring Syria (called Aram in the text) and the Assyrian Empire's over-arching power.

Elijah first appears in the text after he announced the cessation of all rainfall in Ephraim (1 Kings 17:1), thus pushing his nation into years of drought. He was on the run from King Ahab, living in the home of a Canaanite widow in Sidon, northwest of Ephraim.

At some point, "the word of (YHWH) came to Elijah saying, 'Go, present yourself to Ahab; I will send rain on the earth'" (1 Kings 18:1). When they met, the king called Elijah "you troubler of Israel." Elijah returned the accusation: "I have not troubled Israel but you have . . . You have forsaken the commandments of [YHWH] and followed the Baals," which were Canaanite gods (1 Kings 18:17–18). Elijah suggested a kind of contest between himself and the 450 prophets of Baal who received support from the queen. Which god would send fire from heaven to burn the sacrificial offering? Ahab agreed and "all the Israelites" gathered at Mt. Carmel. Fire from above fell only on Elijah's sacrifice, and the prophets of Baal were humiliated and then slaughtered by Elijah.

Today's readers of this story tend to focus on the slaughter of the prophets of Baal and what it tells us about the god Elijah worshipped. But in the setting where it was first told, this story told of the demise of Ephraim's enemies through the defeat of their gods. By portraying

YHWH as energetic and the Baal as inert, the story tried to persuade Israelites to abandon their infatuation with the gods that had apparently blessed the Assyrian Empire with such overwhelming military success.

Immediately after the spectacle on Mt. Carmel, YHWH ended the drought, further validating Elijah's legitimacy as a prophet of the true god.

Oddly enough for a man who had just experienced such dramatic confirmation of his mission, we next see Elijah running for his life, this time from Queen Jezebel, who apparently had avenged the events on Mt. Carmel by killing all of Elijah's fellow prophets. Elijah fled south across neighboring Judah into its southern wilderness. There beneath "a solitary broom tree, he asked that he might die. 'It is enough; now, O [YHWH], take away my life for I am no better than my ancestors'" (1 Kings 19:4).

Instead of death, YHWH provided bread for the journey still ahead, all the way to Mt. Horeb in the Sinai where Elijah experienced a kind of emotional and spiritual crisis. "What are you doing here?" he heard YHWH ask. Elijah reflected on his great zeal for YHWH and lamented how the people of Israel had abandoned their covenant with YHWH. "I alone am left and they are seeking my life, to take it away" (1 Kings 19:10).

In the silence, he heard the voice of YHWH asking him again, "What are you doing here, Elijah" (1 Kings 19:13)? Why was he running in fear from his enemies? At last, Elijah was ready to listen. What Elijah heard changed the subject entirely. YHWH asked him to head toward the wilderness of Syria, hundreds of miles to the northeast, and set in motion a plan that would bring an end to the House of Omri, the dynasty ruling Ephraim. This plan entailed the anointing of a military officer in Damascus as the next king of Aram, and a military officer in Ahab's army as the next king of Ephraim.

Elijah never fully implemented the plan; his successor, Elisha, did that. Yet Elijah got out of his funk and had one more confrontation with King Ahab. It occurred in the vineyard the king had seized after the owner, Naboth, was killed. Elijah confronted Ahab with words from YHWH: "Because you have sold yourself to do what is evil in the sight of [YHWH], I will bring disaster on you; I will consume you" (1 Kings 21:20–21). Ahab died in battle soon after.

Elisha carried out his mentor's final project to end the dynasty of Omri and give Ephraim different leadership. He initially supported Ahab's successor, Joram, by warning him of Aramean troop movements (2 Kings 6:8–12), striking invading soldiers with blindness (2 Kings 6:15–23) and predicting the miraculous delivery of the capital city of Samaria from a terrible Aramean siege (2 Kings 6:24—7:20. But Elisha also healed Naaman, the commander of Aram's army (2 Kings 5:1–19) and prepared "a great feast" (2 Kings 6:23) for captured troops. And he carried out Elijah's unfinished work by going *to Damascus* and anointing Hazael king of Ephraim's foremost enemy, Aram (2 Kings 8:7–15). Next he triggered a *coup d'état* by sending an associate to anoint Jehu king of Ephraim.

During Hazael's reign, Aram's armies seized chunks of Ephraim's territory and (according to Aram's records) killed a king of Ephraim and a king of Judah. The point of all this is clear: the mandate of a prophet of YHWH reflected YHWH's rule over *all* nations, including the anointing of foreign leaders to hold Israel accountable for its sins.

Obadiah

This earliest prophet to score his own book in the Bible lived in Judah and probably in Jerusalem. His text declares a message of coming justice to the people of Edom, a small tribal nation that for many years was a vassal of Judah. The Edomites had descended from Esau, older brother the Hebrew patriarch, Jacob, and lived just across Judah's southeast border. Given their common Semitic origins and Judah's domination, there was much bad blood between the two. Thus, Obadiah's message likely was very popular in Judah. It is not clear why it is part of the biblical collection, except to confirm that early on, Judah had prophets too.

Obadiah condemned Edom for not helping when Jerusalem was attacked and for then "gloating" over Judah's difficulties (Obad. 1:12–14). We cannot be sure whether the attack in question involved the Philistines (when Jehoram was king) or Ephraim (when Amaziah was king); each at one point broke through the city wall and sacked the palace. In any event, Edom would suffer for its failure to help, Obadiah said: "For the day of [YHWH] is near . . . as you have done, it shall be done to you; your deeds shall return on your own head" (Obad. 1:15).

Amos

The speeches of this herdsman from Judah date from Ephraim's time of greatest strength and prosperity, the reign of Jeroboam II. Ephraim was a mini-empire during this period and forced Judah to pay tribute to support the costs of "benefits" Ephraim claimed to bestow on Judah. This may explain why Amos frequently traveled north. He spoke publicly at Bethel, a prominent site for the worship of YHWH within the Northern Kingdom. He directed his message to all of the surrounding nations, including Judah, but spoke primarily to the people of Ephraim.

Amos' criticism of Ephraim focused on marketplace ethics:

> Hear this, you that trample on the needy, and bring to ruin the poor of the land, saying "When will the new moon be over so that we may sell grain; and the Sabbath, so that we may offer wheat for sale? We will make the ephah small and the shekel great, and practice deceit with false balances, buying the poor for silver, and the needy for a pair of sandals, and selling the sweepings of the wheat." (Amos 8:4–6; see also 2:6–7, 5:11–12)

Equally passionate was Amos' criticism of those who knew of the economic injustice, did nothing, *but enjoyed the benefits.*

> Hear this word, you cows of Bashan . . . who oppress the poor, who crush the needy, who say to their husbands, "Bring something to drink." (Amos 4:1)

> Alas for those who lie on beds of ivory, and lounge on their couches, and eat lambs from the flock and calves from the stall; who sing idle songs to the sound of the harp, and like David improvise on instruments of music; who drink wine from bowls and anoint themselves with the finest oils, but are not grieved over the ruin of Joseph. (Amos 6:4–6)

Amos also took aim at those who covered their privilege with a veneer of religious piety: "Come to Bethel and transgress. . . bring your sacrifices every morning, your tithes every three days; bring a thank offering of leavened bread and proclaim freewill offerings, publish them; for so you love to do it" (Amos 4:4–5). He thundered YHWH's disapproval: "I hate, I despise your festivals, and I take no delight in your solemn assemblies . . . Take away from me the noise of your songs; I will not listen to the melody of your harps. But let justice roll down like waters, and righteousness like an ever-flowing stream" (Amos 5:21–24).

The book of **Amos** ends with a vision of a future time of shared prosperity: "They shall rebuild the ruined cities and inhabit them; they shall plant vineyards and drink their wine, and they shall make gardens and eat their fruit" (Amos 9:14). But this would not come to pass by walking the path that began at "Gilgal" with King Saul and continued at "Bethel" (Amos 5:5) with King Jeroboam. Instead, Amos said, the new day of shared prosperity would entail raising up "the booth of David that is fallen and repair its breaches and raise up its ruins and rebuild it as in the days of old" (Amos 9:11).

A booth was a flimsy, temporary shelter constructed by weaving together slender branches from shrubs and trees. It was made when guarding a maturing vineyard, tending a flock of sheep or stopping for a time of rest during a wilderness journey. Each fall as part of the Festival of Booths, the people reenacted this experience of simple, vulnerable living. Obviously, the symbolism of the flimsy booth called into question Israel's emphasis on dynastic kings, extravagant palaces, standing armies and permanent staff. Thus, repairing "the booth of David" suggested restoring the spirit of his leadership before he began pursuing imperial dreams of dominance and control. We sense that Amos imagined an organic kind of leadership emerging from the community and animated by a charismatic spirit.

Hosea

This prophet lived in the Northern Kingdom during a three-decade period when it suffered multiple invasions by the Assyrian army. His text was probably written between the final two invasions. He may have avoided exile by fleeing to Judah before the final collapse in 722 BCE, taking his manuscript with him. His text is one of two (the other being **Exodus)** composed in Ephraim by an author from that nation.

The empire's threat is prominent in the text: "One like a vulture is over the house of [YHWH]" (Hos. 8:1). Hosea viewed the Assyrian threat through the lens of the Sinai covenant, the open-ended exchange of duties and responsibilities described in **Exodus.** The people had demonstrated "no faithfulness or loyalty" to this covenant (Hos. 4:1) and Assyria's threat was the consequence (Hos. 8:1).

To illustrate the unfaithfulness of the people to their covenant with YHWH, Hosea used the story of his own fractured marriage to Gomer, a woman who slept around. Hosea wrote with great emotion about Gomer's repeated betrayals. If she did not stop, "I will strip her naked and expose her as in the day she was born, and make her like a wilderness, and turn her into a parched land, and kill her with thirst" (Hos. 1:3). While Hosea's use of Gomer's promiscuity as an analogy for Ephraim's unfaithfulness to YHWH is fitting and not contrived, his association of YHWH with a husband's violence toward his wife has served to sanctify such behavior and give this text a misogynous message.

Gomer bore three children during the marriage, at least one with a lover. Hosea named the oldest Jezreel after the place north of Samaria where the king's doomed palace was located; Hosea said YHWH would "break the bow of Israel in the valley of Jezreel" (Hos. 1:5). He named the second child Lo-ruhamah, meaning "I will no longer have pity on the house of Israel or forgive them" (Hos. 1:6). He named the third Lo-ammi, "for you are not my people and I am not your god" (Hos. 1:8). "Upon her children I will have no pity because they are children of whoredom . . . For she said, 'I will go after my lovers; they give me my bread and my water, my wool and my flax, my oil and my drink'" (Hos. 1:4–5).

In chapters 4–13, Hosea moved from metaphor to a description of his society's unfaithfulness. Twice (Hos. 4:12, 5:4) he used the phrase "spirit of whoredom" to characterize Ephraim and repeatedly (more than any text but **Ezekiel**) he used the term "whore." What specifically did Hosea have in mind?

In contrast to Amos, who focused on economic exploitation and injustice, Hosea focused on people's lack of understanding of YHWH. There is . . . no knowledge of [YHWH] in the land," he wrote (Hos. 4:1). "My people are destroyed for lack of knowledge" (Hos. 4:6). "Ephraim has become like a dove, silly and without sense" (Hos. 7:11). This ignorance manifested itself especially in the worship of other gods. "My people consult a piece of wood, and their divining rod gives them oracles" (Hos. 4:12); "Ephraim is joined to idols" (Hos. 4:17). It was not that the people did not worship YHWH; *their error was combining YHWH-worship with the worship of other gods.*

Yet "spirit of whoredom" may also suggest something beyond polytheism. Indeed, as we read **Hosea**, we sense it had a lot to do with greed and a desire for wealth and international prestige. "Ephraim is oppressed, crushed in judgment, because he was determined to go after vanity" (Hos. 5:11). The desire for wealth and power prompted Ephraim *to seek out* the embrace of other nations and their ways. "They call upon Egypt, they go to Assyria" (Hos. 7:11). "They have gone up to Assyria, a wild ass wandering along; Ephraim has bargained for lovers" (Hos. 8:9). "They make a treaty with Assyria and oil is carried to Egypt" (Hos. 12:1). Ephraim had become complacent: "Ah, I am rich, I have gained wealth for myself; in all of my gain, no offense has been found in me that would be sin" (Hos. 12:8).

This seeking out of pagan admirers was the "spirit of whoredom" Hosea denounced with yet more sexual imagery. "Though they bargain with nations, I [YHWH] will now gather them up. They shall soon *writhe under the burden of kings and princes*" (Hos. 8:10, emphasis added).

What would a return to faithfulness look like? Not more public piety; "for I desire steadfast love and not sacrifice, the knowledge of [YHWH] rather than burnt offerings" (Hos. 6:6). Not a better king; Hosea dispelled that notion with a caustic reference to the place where Israel's quest to be like other nations had been launched by anointing Saul as the first king (Hos. 9:15). Not the mimicking of mighty nations; "Assyria shall not save us; we will not ride upon horses" (Hos. 14:3).

What then? "Return to your God, hold fast to love and justice and wait continually for your God" (Hos. 12:6). What could that possibly mean? Hosea hinted at an answer very similar to what Amos had offered: "I am [YHWH] your God from the land of Egypt; I will make you live in tents again, as in the days of the appointed festival" (Hos. 12:9). More tents, fewer palaces; this is the vision of **Exodus**.

Hosea was an important figure. Before any other author, he emphasized the Sinai covenant we first read about in **Exodus**, condemned the combining of YHWH-worship with Baal-worship, pointed to the monarchy as a wrong turn, and identified international trade as a danger. With words later quoted in **Isaiah, Jeremiah, Genesis, Romans** and **1 Peter**, Hosea envisioned a community attractive to many, not because of its wealth, but because of the sense of belonging there: "The number of the people of Israel shall be like the sand of the sea, which can be neither measured nor numbered; and in the place where it was said to them, 'You are not my people,' it shall be said to them, 'Children of the living God'" (Hos. 1:9–10).

Notwithstanding Ephraim's demise as a nation-state, Hosea was confident its time of trouble would become "a door of hope" (Hos. 2:15). YHWH's tender love would remain and YHWH's covenant would endure.

> On that day, says [YHWH], you will call me, 'My husband' and no longer will you call me 'My Baal.' . . . I will make for you a covenant on that day with the wild animals, the birds of the air, and the creeping things of the ground; and I will abolish the bow, the sword, and war from the land; and I will make you lie down in safety. I will take you for my wife forever; I will take you for my wife in righteousness and in justice, in steadfast love, and in mercy. I will take you for my wife in faithfulness and you shall know [me]. (Hos. 2:16–20)

1st Isaiah

A writing prophet like Hosea, Isaiah lived in Jerusalem and served as advisor to four kings during his fifty years of service. It is believed he was a member of the royal family in Judah. His writings are found in the first thirty-nine chapters of the book of **Isaiah**.

He lived during years of great tumult. Both Ephraim and Aram attacked and defeated Judah during the time Isaiah advised King Ahaz; Aram took many captives into a Damascus exile (2 Chron. 28:5). Judah was driven by fear to seek protection from the Assyrian Empire, which then turned its wrath on Ephraim and Aram. In the wars that followed during the next ten years, many of Ephraim's people fled to Judah as refugees. Ahaz's son, Hezekiah, tried to end Judah's vassalage to Assyria only to trigger Assyrian retaliation that resulted in the destruction of the cities of Judah outside of Jerusalem and more captive Hebrew exiles than any time before or since. We read Isaiah's lament related to these events in the first nine verses of the book.

Isaiah tried unsuccessfully to dissuade Ahaz from becoming a vassal of and seeking protection from Assyria by predicting the crisis brought on by Ephraim and Aram would pass within a decade. "A young woman is with child and shall bear a son . . . [and] before the child knows how to refuse the evil and choose the good," the two nations threatening Judah would themselves be desolate (Isa. 7:14–15). Forty years later, as Hezekiah tried to free Judah from the bondage to Assyria and the Assyrian army laid siege to Jerusalem, Isaiah had more success persuading Hezekiah not to surrender the city (2 Kings 19:20–34).

At times, Isaiah sounded like previous prophets. For example, he disparaged "many prayers" as the solution for Judah's troubles and instead pointed to ethical transformation: "Wash yourselves; make yourselves clean; remove the evil of your doings from before my eyes, learn to do good; seek justice, rescue the oppressed, defend the orphan, plead for the widow" (Isa. 1:15–17). Like Amos, he denounced those who used their economic power to take advantage of the poor (Isa. 3:14–15) and those who nonchalantly enjoyed the benefits of this advantage (Isa. 5:8–12). Like Hosea, he urged his audience to "wait for [YHWH] . . . and hope in him" (Isa. 8:17). And like Hosea, his understanding of YHWH's purposes reached other nations and peoples. "On this mountain [YHWH] will make for *all* peoples a feast of rich food, a feast of well-aged wines . . . and he will destroy on this mountain the shroud that is cast over all peoples . . . he will swallow up death forever" (Isa. 25:6–7).

He famously articulated what has become the classic definition of twisted ethics: "Ah, you who call evil good and good evil, who put darkness for light and light for darkness, who put bitter for sweet and sweet for bitter" (Isa. 5:20).

More than his predecessors, Isaiah looked into the future. He predicted Jerusalem would be humbled (Isa. 1:21–31) and the royal family would be carried captive to Babylon (Isa. 39:6–7). In scores of texts, he looked ahead to "that day" when "a shoot shall come out from the stump of Jesse" (Isa. 11:1) to reign over Judah and lead the people in obedience to YHWH. On that day, this "root of Jesse shall stand as a signal to the people; the nations shall inquire of him" (Isa. 11:10). That day would be a time of "endless peace for the throne of David and his kingdom" (Isa. 9:7). For Isaiah, YHWH dwelt in Jerusalem, "on Mount Zion" (Isa. 8:18). On that day, Jerusalem would be "redeemed" by the justice of the coming king (Isa.1:27). "The moon will be abashed, and the sun ashamed; for [YHWH] will reign on Mount Zion and in Jerusalem" (Isa. 24:23).

The text of **Isaiah** is best known for compelling images of the peace and justice to come on "that day." Every Christmas, Christians read these stirring texts: 2:2–4; 9:1–7, 11:1–9. Jews read them too, along with similar texts about the return of exiled captives (Isa. 11:11–12), restored unity between Judah and Ephraim (Isa. 11:13), an end to suffering (Isa. 25:7–8), sharing the blessing of YHWH with the entire world (Isa. 27:6) and a relationship of trust and tenderness with YHWH (Isa. 30:19–26). Through beautiful prose and poetry, **Isaiah** paints the messianic vision of a king who "with righteousness will judge the poor, and decide with equity for the meek of the earth." This is a king without violence; his strength is in "the rod his mouth" (Isa. 11:4), the power of his words.

But Isaiah's vision does not take us to Amos' "booth of David," nor to Hosea's tents in the wilderness. For all of his visionary reach, Isaiah remained committed *to the nation state led by a righteous king as YHWH's intention for the world.* We see this in his texts about the coming king (Isa. 9:1–7 and 32:1–8) and in his astonishing use of imperial states as his points of reference: "On that day, Israel will be the third with Egypt and Assyria, a blessing in the midst of the earth, whom [YHWH] has blessed, saying, 'Blessed be Egypt my people, and Assyria the work of my hands, and Israel my heritage'" (Isa. 19:19–25).

To the end, Isaiah remained convinced that with the right king, *YHWH would make the state of Judah as great as Egypt and Assyria!* True to his acculturation as a resident of Jerusalem, a member of its elite and an advisor to its kings, this was the David-and-Solomon worldview in which Isaiah invested his life.

Micah

This contemporary of Isaiah spoke from a small town in the southwest corner of Judah. *His is the only text in the Bible from a southern prophet speaking to Judah from outside the elite environs of Jerusalem.* Whether he first articulated the hope of a coming Messiah is not clear; Isaiah is more often credited. But Micah also saw "that day" approaching: "O Bethlehem . . . from you shall come forth for me one who is to rule in Israel. . . and he shall be the one of peace" (Mic. 5:2–5).

In words also used in the second chapter of **Isaiah**, Micah described YHWH's blessing reaching *all* peoples not by conquest and force of arms, but by the power of attraction. "In days to come the mountain of [YHWH's] house shall be established as the highest of mountains . . . peoples shall stream to it and many nations shall come and say, 'Come, let us go up to the mountain of [YHWH] . . . that he may teach us his ways and that we may walk in his paths'" (Mic. 4:1–2).

Yet Micah was very different from Isaiah. He was rural, obscure and unconnected to royalty. He was highly critical of urban power centers: "What is the transgression of [Ephraim]? Is it not Samaria? And what is the high place of Judah? Is it not Jerusalem" (Mic. 1:5)?

His view of Assyria's invasion of Judah was a third distinction. Isaiah experienced the invasion in the company of King Hezekiah, within the walls of Jerusalem and via the miraculous abandonment of the siege of the city. Micah experienced it in the countryside where the Assyrian army destroyed forty-six cities, killed many, and enslaved and deported 200,000 people, a high percentage of the rural population. From a distance, he saw Jerusalem survive unscathed, but with its king a vassal of the empire, collecting taxes from the country people to support the lavish lifestyle of the royal family and its courtiers plus the Assyrian army and gods.

Micah revealed his stance early in the text as he lamented the destruction of cities and a land nearly emptied of residents (Mic. 1:8–16). He blamed Jerusalem, its rulers and prophets for the Assyrian calamity. Jerusalem housed "the treasures of wickedness" gained by "wicked scales and a bag of dishonest weights. Your wealthy are full of violence, your inhabitants speak lies, with tongues of deceit in their mouths" (Mic. 6:10–

12). The city had "kept the statutes of Omri and all the works of the house of Ahab" (Mic. 6:16), those apostate kings of now-destroyed Ephraim.

Judah's rulers "hate the good and love the evil" (Mic. 3:1–2). We sense Micah included Hezekiah and Isaiah within his indictment.

> Thus says [YHWH] concerning the prophets who lead my people astray, who cry "peace" when they have something to eat, but declare war against those who put nothing into their mouths . . . Hear this you rulers . . . who abhor justice and pervert all equity, who build Zion with blood and Jerusalem with wrong! Its rulers give judgment for a bribe, its priests teach for a price, its prophets give oracles for money; yet they lean upon [YHWH] and say, "Surely [YHWH] is with us! No harm will come upon us." (Mic. 3:5–11)

With Jerusalem's survival of the Assyrian siege still fresh in everyone's memory, Micah made a startling prediction, one that went far beyond Isaiah's: "Zion will be plowed as a field; Jerusalem shall become a heap of ruins, and the mountain of the [temple] a wooded height" (Mic. 3:12).

What did Micah ask the people to do? In general terms, simply this: "He has told you, O mortal, what is good; and what does [YHWH] require of you but to do justice, and to love kindness and to walk humbly with your God" (Mic. 6:8)? How should they organize themselves? Micah spoke of a future leader whose "origin is from old, from ancient days" and who "shall stand and feed his flock in the strength of [YHWH]." (Mic. 5:2–5). This suggests a style of organic leadership with roots going back before the era of kings to a time when YHWH covenanted with the people at Sinai and provided leadership by "Moses, Aaron and Miriam" (Mic. 6:4).

Unlike Isaiah, Micah never referred to David or his royal house; he did not trust that kind of top-down leadership. Then who would protect them when someone attacked? Micah answered: "If the Assyrians come into our land, and tread upon our soil, we will raise against them seven shepherds and eight installed as rulers . . . they shall rescue us from the Assyrians" (Mic. 5:5–6).

His description of the pilgrimage of nations—phrases that also appear in the writings of Isaiah—retains the centrality of the temple in Jerusalem as the dwelling of YHWH. "For out of Zion shall go forth instruction, and the word of [YHWH] from Jerusalem" (Mic. 4:2). This is surprising in a text that generally speaks so negatively of Jerusalem and the temple.

Yet Micah was careful to add an image of the coming day that distinguished it from the **Isaiah** text. After referring to the "many peoples" and "strong nations" that "shall beat their swords into plowshares and their spears into pruning hooks," Micah said "they shall *all* sit under their own vines and under their own fig trees, and no one shall make them afraid" (Mic. 4:4, emphasis added). This is an image of a political community characterized by rural egalitarianism and decentralized power. It may have a temple in Jerusalem, but it has no king.

The image of sitting peacefully under one's own vine and fig tree also is reported to have been used by the Assyrian Rabshakeh when he demanded that Hezekiah surrender Jerusalem to the Assyrian army (2 Kings 18:31). It is surprising to see the same image used by two such different men. Might this have been done by an editor to discredit Micah for his failure to embrace the royal House of David as protector of the Israelite people? This is highly speculative, to be sure.

But it is not speculative to infer fierce disagreement within Judah over how the story of the Assyrian invasion should be told and what shape their political community should take in the future. From where Micah stood, the crisis with Assyria had not ended in YHWH's deliverance, *but in YHWH's judgment.* Thus, he wanted Israel to stop following the political model of other nations; Israel's way of organizing and governing itself should be as distinctive as its god.

Zephaniah

Sixty years later, soon after the long reign of King Manassah and his embrace of the Assyrian Empire, early in the reign of the child-king, Josiah, this prophet wrote from Jerusalem to the people of Judah. As a cousin of the king and a member of Jerusalem's elite, Zephaniah had seen up close the sort of compromises Judah had made under Manassah in order to achieve "peace" with the Assyrian Empire.

Zephaniah articulated this message from YHWH: "The day of [YHWH] is at hand" (Zeph.1:7). "The great day of [YHWH] is near, near and hastening fast; the sound of the day of [YHWH] is bitter . . . that day will be a day of wrath, a day of distress and anguish, a day of ruin and devastation" (Zeph. 1:14–15). He identified the worship of other gods as his particular concern: "I will cut off from this place every remnant of Baal and the name of the idolatrous priests; those who bow down on the roofs to the host of the heavens; those who bow down and swear to [YHWH], *but also swear by [Molech]*" (Zeph. 1:4–5, emphasis added).

Yet Zephaniah also spoke words of hope.

> Wait for me, says [YHWH], for the day when I arise as a witness . . . for in the fire of my passion all the earth shall be consumed. At that time I will change the speech of the people to a pure speech . . . then I will remove from your midst your proudly exultant ones, and you shall no longer be haughty in my holy mountain. For I will leave in the midst of you a people humble and lowly. They shall seek refuge in the name of [YHWH]—the remnant of Israel; they shall do no wrong and utter no lies. (Zeph. 3:8–13)

Zephaniah did not mean Earth would be destroyed, but that it would be *transformed* and *purified* by YHWH's consuming passion. Then the "scattered ones" (Zeph. 3:10) would return; then "you shall not be put to shame" (Zeph. 3:11); then "no one shall make them afraid" (Zeph. 3:13).

During the first dozen years of young Josiah's 31-year reign, Jerusalem's elite class ruled and Josiah was a mere figurehead. Maybe that is why Zephaniah focused on the corruption of those around the king: officials, judges, prophets, priests (Zeph. 3:3–4). Nevertheless, in his vision of the future day of YHWH, Zephaniah did not see the House of David. Instead, he said, YHWH would be "king of Israel" (Zeph. 3:15). In this, Zephaniah's vision was closer to Micah's than to Isaiah's.

Zephaniah's condemnation of idolatry can easily be perceived as *only* a religious message; that is, the people messed up by worshipping more than one god. When properly contextualized, however, Zephaniah's message speaks as clearly to a political reality: gaining the empire's approval *requires* acceptance of the empire's gods. The empire will permit us to continue worshipping YHWH, but it will insist we *also* bow down to gods that require the very opposite of what YHWH requires. In this way, **Zephaniah** reminds us of **Hosea**. Each denounced the accommodation of empire through the worship of multiple gods.

Nahum

Celebrates fall of Nineveh

Before reading this text, it is important to recall the great harm the Assyrian Empire did to Ephraim and Judah. It ended Ephraim's existence as a state and exiled part of its population. Twenty years later, it destroyed the medium-sized cities of Judah and exiled much of the population living outside of Jerusalem. Nahum recalled these events: "Horsemen charging, flashing sword and glittering spear, piles of dead, heaps of corpses, dead bodies without end—they stumble over the bodies" (Nah. 3:3).

Who was Nahum? We can reasonably assume he was a descendant of people who had lived in the Northern Kingdom. He spoke with the passion of one who had heard bitter and gut-wrenching stories of death and exile. And he referred to "Bashan and Carmel," areas in the northern part of Ephraim.

Babylonian forces destroyed Nineveh, the capital of Assyria, in 612 BCE. With Egypt's help, Assyria endured another few years, but its days were numbered. Nahum exulted in the destruction of Nineveh and attributed its astonishing defeat to YHWH. Thus, the book prompts reflection on the nature of this god, YHWH, *who brings devastation to empires once thought to be invincible.*

Nahum articulated his understanding this way: "[YHWH] is slow to anger but great in power and [YHWH] will by no means clear the guilty" (Nah. 1:3). And this: "See, I am against you, says [YHWH], and I will burn your chariots in smoke, and the sword shall devour your young lions; I will cut off your prey from the earth and the voice of your messengers shall be heard no more" (Nah. 2:13). As portrayed by

Nahum, *YHWH is not distant and disinterested, but an engaged partisan,* committed to ending the empire's violence, deceit and oppression: "City of bloodshed, utterly deceitful, full of booty . . . *I am against you,* says [YHWH]" (Nah. 3:1, 5, emphasis added).

It was not only the violence that Nahum highlighted; he also pointed to other aspects of the Assyrian Empire's way of life. Thus, he denounced its "countless debaucheries" (Nah. 3:4) and "merchants more than the stars of the heavens" and "scribes like swarms of locusts" (Nah. 3:16–17). Nineveh's destruction was good news, Nahum insisted: "Celebrate your festivals, O Judah, fulfill your vows, for never again shall the wicked [Assyrians] invade you; they are utterly cut off" (Nah. 1:15).

What about YHWH's mercy? It is not mentioned. Whether Nahum understood YHWH's mercy to encompass the Assyrians, we cannot say. In any event, the time for mercy had passed. The path Assyria had chosen led to the bitter end it had reached. .

Habakkuk

After the untimely death of energetic King Josiah in 609 BCE at the hands of the Egyptian army, Judah became a pawn in the imperial struggle between Egypt and Babylon (the Chaldeans). Over the course of twelve dispiriting years, Judah was Egypt's vassal, then Babylon's, then Egypt's again, then again Babylon's. Habakkuk wrote from Jerusalem early in this era, perhaps around 605 BCE.

His text is less passionate and more philosophical than previous prophets. It is as if he could see where all of this was headed: "the Chaldeans, that fierce and impetuous nation, who march through the breadth of the earth to seize dwellings not their own" (Hab. 1:6), would ultimately rule Judah.

Habakkuk structured his text around hard questions posed to YHWH: "How long shall I cry for help and you will not listen? Or cry to you, 'Violence!' but you will not save" (Hab. 1:2)? Later, Habakkuk asks: "Why do you look on the treacherous, and are silent when the wicked swallow those more righteous than they" (Hab. 1:13)? In a likely reference to the young men taken to Babylon to become eunuchs in the imperial government, he used an analogy to describe Judah's plight: "You have made people like the fish of the sea . . . The enemy brings all of them up with a hook; he drags them out with his net, he gathers them in his seine; so he rejoices and exults . . . Is he then to keep on emptying his net, and destroying nations without mercy" (Hab. 1:14–17)?

YHWH speaks in reply: "Look at the nations and see! Be astonished! Be astounded! For a work is being done in your days that you would not believe if you were told" (Hab. 1:5). In chapter 2, the text offers more from YHWH. "There is a vision for the appointed time . . . it will surely come, it will not delay. Look at the proud! Their spirit is not right in them, but the righteous live by their faith" (Hab.2:3-5). That latter phrase became a favorite of Second Testament writers.

Who were these "proud" ones whose spirit was not right? Habakkuk first pointed an accusing finger at Jerusalem's elite ("alas for you who heap up what is not your own . . . how long will you load yourselves with goods taken in pledge?"), but then he also pointed at Egypt and Babylon ("you have plundered many nations") (Hab. 2:6–8). It appears he viewed the same spirit of domination to animate them all. "The cup [of wrath] in [YHWH's] right hand will come around to you and shame will come upon your glory" (Hab. 2:16). This result was certain, Habakkuk said, because "the earth will be filled with the knowledge of the glory of [YHWH], as the waters cover the sea" (Hab. 2:14).

The text leaves us wishing for details about the astonishing "work" YHWH has promised among the nations, but the only clarity it provides is that YHWH will accomplish it. Habakkuk closes with a hymn of trust.

> I hear and I tremble within; my lips quiver at the sound. Rottenness enters into my bones and my steps tremble beneath me. I wait quietly for the day of calamity to come upon the people who attack us. Though the fig tree does not blossom and no fruit is on the vines, though the produce of the olive fails and the fields yield no food; though the flock is cut off from the fold and there is no herd in the stalls, yet I will rejoice in [YHWH]; I will exult in the God of my salvation. (Hab. 3:16–18)

Jeremiah

Regarded by many as the greatest prophet, Jeremiah completes the roster of Israelite prophets before the destruction of Jerusalem.

Born around 650 BCE as the son of a priest, Jeremiah heard the call of YHWH to be "a prophet to the nations" while still in his early twenties (Jer. 1:5–6). YHWH set before him a huge task: "See, today I appoint you over nations and over kingdoms, to pluck up and to pull down, to destroy and to overthrow, to build and to plant" (Jer. 1:10). YHWH said Jeremiah should expect "the kings of Judah, its princes, its priests and the people to fight against you; but they shall not prevail against you for I am with you . . . I have made you . . . an iron pillar, and a bronze wall against the whole land" (Jer. 1:18–19).

Jeremiah heard YHWH's call in the thirteenth year of King Josiah (626 BCE) while living in Anathoth, a town near Jerusalem. Early in his calling, Jeremiah helped carry out the religious reforms that followed discovery of "the book of the law" (2 Kings 22:3–12). He traveled north of Judah to the former lands of Ephraim urging repentance and inviting the people to participate in Jerusalem's religious festivals (Jer. 3:11–14). He brought the same message to Jerusalem and towns in Judah (Jer. 11:1–8). He was active in the work of composing around "the book of the law" an expanded narrative of seven biblical books combining elements of history, legend, tradition, prophecy and ideology.

Around the time of Josiah's death in 609 BCE, Jeremiah moved to Jerusalem and became a public figure there. He participated in the public lament for Josiah (2 Chron. 35:25). He went to the palace of the new king, Jehoiakim, urged him to "act with justice," and said that if the king would "indeed obey this word," then kings from the House of David would continue to occupy the palace (Jer. 22:1–5).

But soon after, he began to voice open dissent. He criticized the decision of the new king to become a vassal of Egypt (Jer. 2:18, 36). And he stood in the court of the temple and told the crowd, "Thus says [YHWH], 'If you will not listen to me, to walk in my law that I have set before you, and to heed the words of my servants the prophets, whom I send to you urgently, then I will make this house like Shiloh, and I will make this city a curse for all the nations of the earth'" (Jer. 26:1–6). The temple priests and prophets immediately called for his execution because Jeremiah had "prophesied against this city" (Jer. 26:11). He was saved by elders who recalled Micah had prophesied similarly and not been killed.

In light of Jeremiah's participation in Josiah's religious reforms, we expect him to sound some positive notes about Judah's future. Indeed, early in the reign of Johoiakim, it appears Jeremiah did hope for a change in Judah's fortunes. Texts from this period speak conditionally: "if you listen to me . . ." (Jer. 17:24); "turn now and amend your ways" (Jer. 18:11). As Jeremiah prepared to give his famous temple speech, he understood YHWH might "change his mind" if the people would "turn from their evil ways" (Jer. 26:3).

The content of that speech is recorded in chapter 7 of **Jeremiah**. It challenged the false sense of security the people felt because of the miraculous escape of Jerusalem under King Hezekiah 100 years earlier, an escape they attributed to YHWH's residence in Jerusalem's temple.

> Do not trust in these deceptive words: "This is the temple of [YHWH], the temple of [YHWH]." For if you truly amend your ways and your doings, if you truly act justly one with another, if you do not oppress the alien, the orphan and the widow, or shed innocent blood in this place, and if you do not go after other gods to your own hurt, *then* I will dwell with you in this place. (Jer. 7:4–7, emphasis added)

If they failed to amend their ways, Jeremiah said, "the house that is called by my name, in which you trust" would be desolate. "And I will cast you out of my sight, just as I cast out all your kinfolk, all the offspring of Ephraim" (Jer. 7:14–15).

But later Jeremiah's message took on a less open-ended tone. Chapter 19 tells us YHWH told Jeremiah to go to Topheth. Near to Jerusalem, it was the place where child sacrifices had long been offered to Canaanite gods, especially Molech. There, with people gathered around, Jeremiah said the people of Judah had "filled this place with the blood of the innocent, and gone on building the high places of Baal to burn their children in the fire as burnt offerings to Baal" (Jer. 19:4–5). He then broke an earthenware jug and said: "Thus says [YHWH]: 'So will I break this people and this city . . . so it can never be mended'" (Jer. 19:11).

Jerusalem's priests disliked Jeremiah, in part because he de-emphasized the value of sacrifices (Jer. 7:22–23). And when Jeremiah stood in the temple court and repeated his earthenware jar speech, the deputy chief priest had him beaten and locked in stocks. The next day, Jeremiah spoke unequivocally:

> For thus says [YHWH] . . . I will give all of Judah into the hand of the king of Babylon; he shall carry them captive to Babylon and shall kill them with a sword. I will give all the wealth of this city, all its gains, all its prized belongings, and all the treasures of the kings of Judah into the hand of their enemies, who shall plunder them and seize them and carry them to Babylon. (Jer. 20:4–5)

Although released by the temple guards, Jeremiah was barred from the temple grounds (Jer. 36:5). So, during the fourth year of King Jehoiakim, Jeremiah came up with another way of reaching the people with his message. His scribe, Baruch, prepared a scroll of his speeches and read them in the temple court on a day when many people were present (Jer. 36:7). (The first twelve chapters of the book of **Jeremiah** were probably included.) After Baruch had completed the public reading as well as a private reading for royal officials, the scroll was read to Jehoiakim, who promptly cut it in strips and burned it (Jer. 36:23).

It was around this same time (605 BCE) that Babylonian forces defeated Egyptian forces at Carchemish. Jehoiakim thereby became Babylon's vassal. This entailed paying tribute and sending members of the royal family and nobility (including Daniel and his three friends) to serve in the government of Nebuchadnezzar in Babylon.

With these events, Jeremiah believed the die was cast; the people of Judah would not escape judgment at the hands of the Babylonians. *YHWH wanted Babylon to prevail:* "I [YHWH]) will fight against you with outstretched hand and mighty arm" (Jer. 21:5). After Jehoiakim burned the scroll, Jeremiah said Babylonian destruction of Judah was "certain" (Jer. 36:29). In chapter 25, he described this conviction in detail.

As evidence of his sincerity and love for the people of Judah, Jeremiah urged them to surrender. Resistance would be suicide.

This was controversial throughout the latter years of Jehoiakim, as the king switched his allegiance from Egypt to Babylon and back to Egypt again, but became even more so after the Babylonian siege of Jerusalem in 597 BCE The city fell after three months. The victors took the new king, Jeconiah (also known as Jehoiachin), along with 10,000 of Judah's elite (including Ezekiel) captive to Babylon.

But Jerusalem was not destroyed. Babylon installed Zedekiah, a member of the House of David, as king. The temple still stood proudly as the residence of YHWH. So Zedekiah's prophets regrouped and assured him that YHWH would yet deliver Judah from Babylon's grip if only he would stand up to Babylon. Hananiah the prophet said the captivity of the ten thousand exiles would be brief—only two years (Jer. 28:11). Under such circumstances, Jeremiah's counsel to surrender was treason.

Yet Jeremiah persisted with astonishing boldness and energy. When diplomats from nearby small nations (Edom, Moab, Ammon, Tyre and Sidon) came to Jerusalem to consult with Zedekiah, Jeremiah got their attention by fitting himself with a yoke and straps and then urging them to submit to Babylon's yoke (Jer. 27:3). He wrote to the exiles in Babylon, urging them to settle in for a long stay:

> Build houses and live in them; plant gardens and eat the produce. Take wives and have sons and daughters in marriage that they may bear sons and daughters; multiply there and do not decrease. But seek the welfare of the city where I have sent you into exile and pray to [YHWH] on its behalf, for in its welfare you will find your welfare. (Jer. 29:5–7)

He met with King Zedekiah twice in secret, told him that YHWH would "fight against him with an outstretched hand and mighty arm, in anger, in fury and in great wrath" (Jer. 21:5), and urged him to surrender and save the lives of himself and his family (Jer. 37:17–20, 38:14–28). He debated rival prophets who promised peace (Jer. 28:1–17). Throughout, he continued to speak publicly to the people.

Many officials wanted Jeremiah killed. Reluctantly, Zedekiah imprisoned him (Jer. 37:18). Later, royal officials threw Jeremiah into a muddy cistern and left him to die (Jer. 38:6). Ebed-melech, an Ethiopian eunuch on the king's staff, saved Jeremiah's life and kept him in protective detention in the court of the palace guard (Jer. 38:7–13).

Zedekiah felt drawn to Jeremiah's message, but did not have the strength to resist his advisors. And so Zedekiah switched his allegiance to Egypt. Nebuchadnezzar responded with an invasion and siege of Jerusalem that began in 589 BCE. The city withstood the attack for eighteen months; inside the city, people suffered horribly (Lam. 4:4–10). At one point, the Egyptian army drew near and for a few months the Babylonian army withdrew. Early in 587 BCE, Babylonian troops broke through the city's walls. The victors killed Zedekiah's sons in front of him and then they put out the king's eyes. He and other survivors of the Jerusalem siege were taken into exile in Babylon. The number is unclear, but certainly was less than the 10,000 exiled eleven years earlier.

Six months later, Nebuchadnezzar sent another military unit to break down all the city walls, destroy the temple and palace, and burn the houses. While Jerusalem became uninhabitable, other parts of Judah were not so severely affected. Jeremiah was held prisoner for a time, but then released at the order of Nebuchadnezzar. He was given an allowance of food and the choice whether to go with the exiles or stay behind. He chose to stay and went to live with Gedaliah, a Judean (Jer. 40:1–6).

Perhaps three-fourths of the Judah's population remained in the Judean countryside or in neighboring areas. Nebuchadnezzar appointed Gedaliah to be Babylon's governing agent in the region; Gedaliah established Mizpah as his headquarters. The remaining Judean fighters came to meet with Gedaliah who, perhaps upon the advice of Jeremiah, encouraged them to make peace with what had happened:

> Do not be afraid to serve the Chaldeans. Stay in the land and serve the king of Babylon, and it shall go well with you. As for me, I am staying in Mizpah to represent you before the Chaldeans who come to us; but as for the rest of you, gather wine and summer fruits and oil. And store them in your vessels, and live in the towns that you have taken over. (Jer. 40:9–10)

Other Judeans who had fled to neighboring countries also returned and began gathering an abundant harvest.

Soon after, however, a member of the royal family assassinated Gedaliah and took captive his aides and advisors, including Jeremiah. After a short period of intense violence, another militia unit led by Johanan freed the group and the entire assembly fled toward Egypt. At Bethlehem they paused and asked Jeremiah for advice, who told them to stay in Judah. "Do not be afraid of the king of Babylon, . . . for I am with you, to save you and to rescue you from his hand . . . But if you are determined to enter Egypt and so settle there, then the sword that you fear shall overtake you there" (Jer. 42:11–16). But Johanan and his associates did not believe Jeremiah and proceeded to Egypt, taking him with them.

In Egypt, Jeremiah persisted in his opposition to settling there:

> Thus says [YHWH], the God of Israel: "I am determined to bring disaster on you, to bring all Judah to an end. I will take the remnant of Judah who are determined to come to the land of Egypt to settle and they shall perish, everyone; in the land of Egypt they shall fall by the sword and by famine they shall perish from the least to the greatest." (Jer. 44:11–12)

Legend tells us that Jeremiah died in Egypt. Whether his prophecy about the Judeans in Egypt came true is doubtful; 300 years later, in the third century BCE, a large Jewish community flourished in the city of Alexandria.

Jeremiah, a long text covering over forty years, is not presented chronologically. One has to piece together the timeline and Jeremiah's evolving vision. Throughout, it reflects the author's conviction that the Israelites had lost their way: "The harvest is past, the summer is ended, and we are not saved," Jeremiah said. "For the hurt of my poor people I am hurt; I mourn, and dismay has taken hold of me" (Jer. 8:20–21).

So long as the status quo held, Jeremiah felt only gloom about the future. People's illusions related to their exceptionality and YHWH's protection had become part of their worldview; few could escape it. This analysis is implicit in Jeremiah's comments about truth-telling.

> From prophet to priest, everyone deals falsely. They have treated the wound of my people carelessly, saying, "Peace, peace," when there is no peace . . . They are not ashamed; they do not know how to blush. (Jer. 6:13–15)

> They do not speak honestly; [they say] what have I done? (Jer. 8:6)

> They all deceive their neighbors, and no one speaks the truth; *they have taught their tongues to speak lies*; they commit iniquity and are too weary to repent. (Jer. 9:5–6, emphasis added)

As leopards cannot change their spots, so the people were incapable of seeing through the lies (Jer. 13:23, 25).

For Jeremiah, *there was no hope without judgment.* But he was profoundly optimistic about the good that would follow defeat and exile. He was the first prophet to believe the Israelites could thrive as a political community obedient to YHWH while living in a foreign land under the control of the empire. This was astonishing; no one before had suggested people could practice righteous living in a place filled with other gods.

It is clear Jeremiah did not fear living under empire's governing power. Did he then regard empire to be a good thing? When we read his oracle against Babylon in chapters 50—51, we must conclude he did not. And his vigorous denunciation of the decision by some to settle in Egypt only reinforces this conclusion. But he also welcomed the fresh start he saw coming, a new beginning purged of illusions and fictionalized history and energized by lived experience.

> The days are surely coming, says [YHWH], when it shall no longer be said, "As [YHWH] lives who brought the people of Israel up out of Egypt," but "As [YHWH] lives who brought the people of Israel up out of the land of the north and out of all the lands where he had driven them." For I will bring them back to their own land that I gave to their ancestors. (Jer. 16:14–15)

Jeremiah repeatedly referred to his expectation that YHWH would bring the exiles back to Judah (Jer. 16:14–15; 23:3; 29:10–14; 30:1–3;

31:7–14; 32:36–44). In the meantime, he did not fear they would lose their way without the temple and without a leader from the House of David, perhaps because in his view "a new covenant," written by YHWH on the hearts of the people, was near at hand. "No longer shall they teach one another, or say to each other, 'Know (YHWH)' for they shall all know me, from the least of them to the greatest" (Jer. 31:34).

Notwithstanding the shrill tone of his activism, Jeremiah did not oppose Jerusalem, the temple or the House of David. He looked forward to a day when YHWH would "raise up for David a righteous branch [to] reign as king" (Jer. 23:5). Yet he regarded them to be of marginal importance, not essential. *Faithful obedience to the ethical commands of YHWH could be sustained without them.* Defeat and exile would strip away the nonessentials; what remained would blossom and thrive.

Reflection and Discussion

10. Myths, legends and "histories" are powerful despite their lack of historical accuracy. Consider what the Israelites learned about themselves from stories in **Joshua** and **Judges.** How did the self-image people gleaned from those texts serve the purposes of the Jerusalem elite who desired centralization of power and control?

11. The emergence of written language among the Israelites in the tenth century BCE must have seemed magical. Those who mastered it achieved power over others, both by the feat itself and by the way their texts shaped the stories people told one another. Today video plays a similar role. What impact do the stories composed by the empire's scribes have on us? On our worldview?

12. The authors regard biblical materials from **Genesis** 12 though the story of Solomon to reflect facts and legends harvested from oral traditions and imaginatively reshaped with new material into written texts, often with political purposes in mind. What is your reaction to this view? Do you find it disrespectful of the Bible? Consider that we find some modern texts "truthful" or "inspired" even though they are not historically accurate, and that a

sympathetic account of mistakes and failure can teach us more about life than an account of success and victory.

13. The stories of the kings reflect the complexity of governing amid the need for physical security, economic prosperity and justice. One way to read these stories is to search for the kings who got it right and learn from how they did it. Another way is to regard the entire effort as doomed because it used a flawed operating system, one built on centralized power, domination and violence. Which is your view? How does it inform your current political perspective?

14. To which prophet are you most drawn? Why? What political alternative (e.g., social operating system) do you see taking shape in the messages of the prophets? Please describe it.

15. Consider Jeremiah's view that there was no hope until Judah's prevailing worldview, exceptionalism and way of operating utterly collapsed. What is the relationship between judgment and hope in our time?

14. Finding YHWH in Babylon
Ezekiel, Daniel 1–6, 2nd Isaiah, Esther

We have now come full circle, back to the question posed at the start of chapter 9: could the Israelites sing YHWH's song in a foreign land? Or would they disappear as a people, assimilated into the great masses ruled by the Babylonian empire? And if they continued to sing YHWH's song, how would their vision of political community evolve in a place where they had no king, no temple, no national boundaries?

Through our review in previous chapters of three texts written in Babylon—**Genesis, Leviticus, Numbers**—we have learned their distinctive community not only survived, but expressed itself in creative and subversive ways. Next we look at four other books that help explain this surprisingly positive turn of events.

Twenty-five-year-old Ezekiel left Jerusalem as a prisoner in 597 BCE. He was a priest in training and part of the company of 10,000 educated and skilled Judeans who marched north through Aleppo and then southeast along the Euphrates River to their new home. The group of prisoners included Judah's youthful King Jehoiachin. Ezekiel began speaking as a prophet about five years after his arrival in Babylon and continued until his death. He was the author of the text bearing his name.

The first six chapters of **Daniel** tell stories of young Israelite men working as civil servants in the empire during a seventy-year period from their Jerusalem departure in 605 BCE into the era of Persian dominance that began in 539. Written in the apocalyptic style 350–400 years after the events portrayed, it includes elements of history, legend and prophecy.

The unknown author of the sixteen chapters of **2nd Isaiah** (40–55) also wrote from Babylon. Beyond the exceptional quality of the poetry, we know virtually nothing about the writer. S/he wrote at a time when the possibility of return to Canaan existed, perhaps around 535 BCE.

The story of **Esther** is set during the reign of King Xerxes (also known as Ahasuerus), 485—464 BCE. The theology of this text is dubious (it never mentions YHWH) and its historical accuracy doubtful.

Though probably fiction, it reflects an often neglected fact: after King Cyrus of Persia issued his order in 538 BCE giving the Jews (as the exiled Israelites became known in Persia) the option of returning to Canaan, most chose not to return. In Babylon and in Persia, their communities flourished culturally and economically and their religious practices adapted to the absence of a temple and priests by inventing synagogues led by rabbis. The Jewish community in Babylon became the center of rabbinic teaching for at least 1,000 years after the exile. Those who stayed in Babylon and Persia thought of themselves as part of the Jewish diaspora, not as exiles.

These texts reflect dramatic changes in the Jewish understanding of YHWH. See question 16 on page 200 for additional discussion.

Ezekiel

As a prophet of YHWH, Ezekiel focused on healing the trauma of his people. He was convinced the victims of trauma would eventually include not only those exiled with him, but all the survivors of the siege of Jerusalem, and he was mindful of both groups.

He first spoke publicly at a time when sacrifices were still offered daily in the Jerusalem temple. YHWH remained resident there and one could surmise the exiles needed to find a new god who lived in Babylon. Ezekiel addressed this crisis of faith through his vision by the Chebar River: a grand chariot arriving in the northern sky on wheels within wheels bearing two cherubim, the burning coals of sacrificial fires, a great crystal dome, the "thunder of the Almighty" (Ezek.1:24) and "the likeness of the glory of [YHWH]" (Ezek. 1:28).

Later, Ezekiel had a very similar vision of YHWH's presence leaving the temple in Jerusalem (Ezek. 10:1–22) and later still, a third vision of YHWH's presence returning to Jerusalem and a new temple (Ezek. 43:1–3). In an age with very limited publishing and no animation, these visions effectively communicated that the Israelites did not need to seek another god; YHWH could be at more than one place at a time and had travelled with them to Babylon! And if YHWH ruled the skies over mighty Babylon, then YHWH was king of all of Earth.

Ezekiel conducted trauma healing by a method Jeremiah had pioneered with his yoke: enacted messaging. That is, Ezekiel behaved in highly unconventional ways in public places, thereby eliciting within his audience emotional catharsis, reflection and renewal.

After a period of isolation and silence (Ezek. 3:24–26), YHWH instructed Ezekiel to create a small tableau portraying Jerusalem and the siege works and ramps erected against its walls (Ezek. 4:1–4). We can imagine he placed it in the yard outside his dwelling. There, beside that tableau, Ezekiel lay on his left side without turning for a portion of each day for 390 consecutive days. His diet was rough and meagre: a mixture of wheat, barley, lentils, millet and spelt baked over an open fire fueled first by human dung and later by cow dung. Ezekiel limited his water intake as well. Then, he lay for a part of each day for forty consecutive days on his right side without turning (Ezek. 4:9–14).

Next, Ezekiel shaved his head and his beard, removing all of his hair and his masculine appearance with it. One-third of the shaved hair he took into the city and burned in a fire there. One-third he severed into countless tiny bits with a sword. And one-third he scattered to the wind. At YHWH's direction, Ezekiel became a sign of what Judah had become: "You shall be a mockery and a taunt, a warning and a horror, to the nations around you" (Ezek. 5:15).

Later, Ezekiel prepared "an exile's baggage" (Ezek. 12:3) and set it outside his house. At evening when the people were out mingling, he dug through a nearby wall and dragged his baggage through the hole. Then, as darkness fell, he shouldered the baggage and stumbled into the night, his face covered in shame (Ezek. 12:1–16).

Later still, Ezekiel's wife died. The next morning, he dressed, ate and went about his activities as usual. People asked why he was acting this way. Ezekiel explained that Jerusalem's temple would be "profaned" and their sons and daughters killed by the sword. "You shall do as I have done . . . you shall not mourn or weep, but you shall pine away in your iniquities and groan to one another" (Ezek. 24:23).

How did these enacted messages bring healing to the traumatized exiles? Ezekiel's very presence—by its prophetic form—was a measure of YHWH's grace, assuring the people that YHWH was with them in Babylon. YHWH is quoted: "I am sending you (Ezekiel) to them and you shall say to them, 'Thus says [YHWH].' Whether they hear or refuse to hear . . . *they shall know that there has been a prophet among them*" (Ezek. 2:4–5, emphasis added). This did not mean Ezekiel's message would be well-received; in fact, the text tells us YHWH warned Ezekiel that "the house of Israel will not listen to you" (Ezek. 3:7). Yet YHWH told Ezekiel to remain a bizarre spectacle, a sentinel warning the people of what he saw, giving them the chance to "save their life" (Ezek. 3:18). He was "a sign for the house of Israel" (Ezek. 12:6) that YHWH remained their god.

His public displays helped people name and come to grips with the ugliness and brutality they had experienced and that still occurred back in Jerusalem. This enabled them to let go of false hopes that Jerusalem would survive and proceed with necessary grieving. For Ezekiel, the acts of baking his bread on a dung fire and shaving made him unfit for further service as a priest; in effect, these acts renounced his priestly vows and signaled to others that it was time for a decisive moving on. Moreover, his unusual behavior kept the exiles connected emotionally with the second group of exiles still to come, thus facilitating what was likely a difficult reintegration of the two groups.

Ezekiel preached, too. He discredited the lazy and disheartening cynicism reflected in the common saying, "The days are prolonged and every vision comes to nothing" (Ezek. 12:22). Instead, Ezekiel insisted, "The days are near, and [also near] the fulfillment of every vision" (Ezek. 12:23). In other words, *what a great time to be alive*!

As we read this text, it is important to remember that Ezekiel was addressing Judah's elite, those who had exercised power in Jerusalem. Using vivid and sensual images of a female prostitute, he helped this audience come to terms with Jerusalem's sin. That sin, as described in **Ezekiel** 16, was whoring with lustful neighbors: the Egyptians, the Philistines, the Assyrians and the Chaldeans (Babylon). Ezekiel's meaning was political and economic: the animating spirit of the city's elite had been to attract the attention of neighboring powers, acquire their gifts and lustful attention, absorb their powerful thrusts, and acquire their treasures in exchange for what Judah had to offer. In chapter 23, Ezekiel developed this sexual metaphor into a chapter-long tale of two sisters,

Oholah and Oholibah, whose admiration for empire began in Egypt and carried them into liaisons with the Assyrians and Chaldeans.

Ezekiel did not condemn all trade, but rather the elite's infatuation with wealth and power that distorted their values and disrespected the common people of Judah and their YHWH-inspired way of life. "You played the whore with them and still you were not satisfied" (Ezek. 16:28); "you were different from other women in your whoring: no one solicited you to play the whore and you gave payment, while no payment was given to you" (Ezek. 16:34). Ezekiel's point is that in their search for the power and wealth of empire, Jerusalem's elite had lost their moorings; they were "sick in heart" (Ezek. 16:30), like one addicted to sex.

The economic meaning of the sexual imagery is reinforced when Ezekiel compared Jerusalem with her "sisters" Samaria (the destroyed capital of Ephraim) and Sodom (the destroyed city where Lot had lived). Sodom's sin was its "pride, excess food, and prosperous ease [and failure] to aid the poor and needy" (Ezek. 16:49). Jerusalem had been worse, Ezekiel said, so much worse that Sodom was made to appear righteous.

Yet all three cities would be restored; YHWH would do that (Ezek. 16:53–55). And the text quotes YHWH: "I will remember my covenant with you in the days of your youth, and I will establish with you an everlasting covenant . . . and you shall know that I am [YHWH] . . . when I forgive you all that you have done" (Ezek. 16:60–63).

Ezekiel's preaching about consequences and divine punishment showed his concern for his people's spiritual needs. Reflecting their communal mentality, the exiles often said, "The parents have eaten sour grapes and the children's teeth are set on edge" (Ezek. 18:2). YHWH, said Ezekiel, wanted that proverb put to rest. "Know that all lives are mine; the life of the parent as well as the life of the child is mine. It is only the person who sins that shall die" (Ezek. 18:4). "As I live, says [YHWH], I have no pleasure in the death of the wicked, but that the wicked turn from their ways and live; turn back, turn back from your evil ways; for why will you die, O house of Israel" (Ezek. 33:11)? Thus, Ezekiel countered the gloomy fatalism that naturally set in among the people as they reflected on the sins of Jerusalem.

Like Jeremiah, Ezekiel viewed the exile as a fresh start and a second chance.

> As I live, says [YHWH], surely with a mighty hand and an outstretched arm and with wrath poured out, I will be king over you. I will bring you out from the peoples and gather you out of the countries where you are scattered. . . . . and I will bring you into the wilderness of the peoples, and there I will enter into judgment with you face to face. (Ezek. 20:33–35)

And like Jeremiah, Ezekiel thought that YHWH's faithful care would result in a return to the land of Canaan. Then "you shall know that I am [YHWH], when I bring you into the land of Israel, the country that I swore to give to your ancestors" (Ezek. 20:42). "Then they shall settle on their own soil that I gave to my servant Jacob" (Ezek. 28:25–26).

One of the most gentle passages describes YHWH as a shepherd.

> I will rescue them from all the places to which they have been scattered . . . I will bring them out from the peoples and gather them from the countries, and will bring them into their own land . . . . I will seek the lost, and I will bring back the strayed, and I will bind up the injured, and I will strengthen the weak, but the fat and the strong I will destroy. I will feed them with justice . . . I will make with them a covenant of peace. (Ezek. 34:11–16, 25)

Ezekiel expected the House of David to play a leading role in this future: "I will set up over them one shepherd, my servant David . . . and my servant, David, shall be prince among them" (Ezek. 34:23–24). He expected this future to unfold in Canaan; at one point, he reports YHWH speaking directly to the land: "See now, I am for you; I will turn to you and you shall be tilled and sown; and I will multiply your populations, the whole house of Israel, all of it; the towns shall be inhabited and the waste places rebuilt and I will multiply human beings and animals upon it" (Ezek. 36:9–10). In metaphors of dry bones restored to life and broken sticks rejoined, Ezekiel voiced his expectation that Ephraim and Judah would be reunited as one nation under a David-like king (Ezek. 37:1–28).

The restored Israel would feature a new temple, Ezekiel said, separate from the palace and free from royal interference, manipulation and control. His description of this temple began with chapter 40 and filled nearly all of the rest of the book. Quoting YHWH, the text tells us that it will be "the place for the soles of my feet, where I will reside among the people of Israel forever" (Ezek. 43:7–9). From this temple will flow a river of life, the source of Earth's bounty (Ezek. 47:1–12). A restored Jerusalem was only an after-thought for Ezekiel, mentioned at the very end of the book (Ezek. 48:15–35).

These wonders would serve to let the people "know that I am [YHWH]" (Ezek. 37:13). It is a phrase often used by Ezekiel and indicated his deep concern for public witness to surrounding peoples.

> It is not for your sake that I will act, says [YHWH] . . . Be ashamed and dismayed for your ways, O Israel . . . Then the nations that are left all around you shall know that I, [YHWH] have rebuilt the ruined places and replanted that which was desolate. I have spoken and I will do it. (Ezek. 36:32–36)

In summary, Ezekiel's strength was his vision of the present, for the healing of his people. His vision for the future was limited to a new and improved version of the past. As we know, most of the diaspora never returned to Canaan, Ephraim and Judah never came together and a descendant of David never again sat on a throne of Israel. Ezekiel brought healing and renewal to the wounded exiles. But we need to look to others for a vision of political community faithful to YHWH in an era without Davidic kings or Israel-controlled geography.

Daniel 1–6

The first six chapters of this text collect stories about four, young Israelite men who served in the Babylonian government as aides to the king. A proper empire must be expert at dealing with the incredible diversity of its subjects and so needs skilled staff to interpret, translate, host, entertain and advise. When Judah became Babylon's vassal in 605 BCE, King Jehoiakim drafted talented young people to go to Babylon and fill Judah's quota. We can imagine those drafted were not happy to be separated from their community and rendered eunuchs by the empire's surgeons (see Isa. 39:7). Yet they were not common slaves or prisoners. Apart from the surgery, it was not so different from taking a job on Capitol Hill in Washington, D.C.

This setting was a difficult one for the nurturing of an alternative vision of political community. Not only did the Israelite men participate in the exercise of empire's power, they lived in an environment dominated by the gods, images and practices of YHWH's enemies. From the point of view of a devout, YHWH-fearing Israelite, the royal court of Babylon was a bleak and forsaken place.

The first story tells of the young men's training. Daniel (renamed Belteshazzar, which implied a relationship of obedience to a god of Babylon) requested that he and his Israelite colleagues be allowed to follow a vegetarian diet instead of the royal rations. When the "palace master" expressed doubt about such a deviation from protocol, Daniel suggested a ten-day test. The palace master agreed and at the end of ten days found Daniel and his friends "appeared better and fatter" than all the rest (Dan. 1:15). When the class of new recruits had their audience with the king, he was most impressed with the Israelite men and so stationed them in his court. Daniel stayed there until 538 BCE, when he would have been around 75 years old (Dan. 1:21).

Just a year after the food test, Daniel was asked to interpret King Nebuchadnezzar's dream about a great statute with a head of gold, chest and arms of silver, belly and thighs of bronze, legs of iron and feet "partly of iron and partly of clay." In the dream, "a stone was cut out, not by human hands, and it struck the statue on its feet . . . and broke them in pieces. Then the [statue] became like the chaff of summer threshing floors and the wind carried them away" (Dan. 2:33–35). The King's advisors could not explain it.

Daniel and his Israelite colleagues prayed for "mercy from the God of heaven" (Dan. 2:18) and YHWH revealed to Daniel the meaning of the dream. The four metals represented four successive kingdoms, the first being Babylon and the others still to come. The text tells us this interpretation prompted Nebuchadnezzar to prostrate himself before Daniel in worship. The King also affirmed YHWH as "God of gods and

Lord of kings." And he promoted Daniel, making him ruler over the province of Babylon (Dan. 2:46–49).

What is most remarkable in Daniel's interpretation is the stone that broke the fourth kingdom to pieces. It is, the text tells us, an everlasting kingdom. "And in the days of those kings, the God of heaven will set up a kingdom that shall never be destroyed, nor shall this kingdom be left to another people. It shall crush all these kingdoms and bring them to an end, and it shall stand forever" (Dan. 2:44). Apparently, this political force on the far horizon would be something different from the nation-state: not assembled by human effort, powerful enough to dissolve all empires, not owned or possessed by anyone in particular, and resilient enough to endure through the generations.

A second dream story follows in chapter 4; it is told in the voice of Nebuchadnezzar. He dreamed of a mighty tree cut down, leaving a stump and roots in the ground. And he heard a voice from heaven saying: "Let him be bathed with the dew of heaven, and let his lot be with the animals of the field in the grass of the earth" (Dan. 4:15).

Daniel again gave the interpretation. Nebuchadnezzar would be driven from human society "until you have learned that the Most High has sovereignty over the kingdoms of mortals and gives it to whom he will . . . your kingdom shall be re-established for you from the time that you learn that Heaven is sovereign" (Dan. 4:25–26). And so Nebuchadnezzar was humiliated by what apparently was a mental illness; "his hair grew as long as eagles' feathers and his nails became like birds' claws" (Dan. 4:33). After seven years he was restored; his reason returned and he praised the "king of heaven: for all his works are truth and his ways are justice; and he is able to bring low those who walk in pride" (Dan. 4:37).

The text even gives Daniel a role on the very night that conquering Persian forces under Cyrus entered the city of Babylon. In the famous banquet scene that transpired earlier that evening, King Belshazzar saw a hand writing the words "MENE, MENE, TEKEL, PARSIN" on the wall and asked Daniel to tell him their meaning. Daniel explained: "YHWH has numbered the days of your kingdom and brought it to an end; you have been weighed on scales and found wanting; your kingdom is divided and given to the Medes and Persians" (Dan. 5:26–28).

As part of the oral tradition of the exiles, these stories served to build morale and self-confidence. Like the shepherd boy, Joseph, who rose to become prime minister of Egypt, Daniel and his friends could compete with the elite at the center of empire.

More importantly, the stories confirmed YHWH's power to disrupt activity in the throne-rooms of the empire. Babylon controlled everything from Greece to central India, more land than any empire up to that time in history. People assumed this achievement reflected the power of Babylon's gods and the harmony of its rulers with divine purposes. Yet here we have stories of another god, YHWH, disrupting all of that and using Jewish staff as messengers and agents. Then certainly YHWH also was actively present elsewhere in Babylonian society.

The final two stories describe loyalty rituals that Daniel and his friends stoutly resisted. These stories reminded hearers that despite empire's overwhelming power, it did not have the last word. Thus, it made sense to resist, not through intrigue or violence, but by faithful allegiance and open witness to YHWH.

The first of these loyalty stores tells of the refusal of Hananiah, Mishael and Azariah to bow in worship to a golden statue set up by the king. When this came to the king's attention, he had them thrown into a fiery furnace so hot that it killed the guards. Yet the young Israelites were not harmed, a result that prompted the king to make an order prohibiting blasphemy against YHWH (Dan. 3:29).

After the Persian conquest of Babylon in 539 BCE, Daniel found himself in a similar situation. The new leader (described as a king but probably only a provincial governor), Darius the Mede, issued an order that for thirty days, everyone should pray only to him. The text describes this as a trap specially designed to catch Daniel, who knelt before an open window facing Jerusalem three times a day to pray.

Daniel proceeded to pray as usual in violation of the order. His rivals in the new government promptly told Darius of Daniel's contempt for the order and Darius was obliged to punish Daniel by throwing him to the lions. Again, however, the text tells us YHWH acted to save Daniel. Darius responds with a second order "that in all my royal dominion people should tremble and fear before the God of Daniel" (Dan. 6:26).

Because of the exotic context of a palace setting, these stories provided little guidance for the formation of an exilic political community faithful to YHWH. Indeed, the text does not even suggest Daniel and his three colleagues were important people in the Jewish community. They were eunuchs and collaborators, and this diminished their credibility.

But the way these stories describe YHWH's activity, and the way they describe steadfast observance of Jewish practices related to prayer, diet and allegiance, encouraged the first hearers of this text to continue trusting YHWH as their god and taking the risk of saying "no" to empire when it demanded their allegiance. Even though they were not in charge, even though they had no army, their actions still counted, still impacted the empire, still witnessed to the power of YHWH.

2nd Isaiah

Chapters 40—55 of the book of **Isaiah** speak to the new realities of the broader Jewish community in Babylon. Written after King Cyrus famously authorized Jews to return to Canaan for the purpose of rebuilding the temple in Jerusalem, the message of these chapters integrates the catastrophe of Judah's demise, the trauma of exile in Babylon and the astonishing prospect of return to Canaan. This is among the most lyrically beautiful texts of the Bible.

The author began with reassurance: "Comfort, O comfort my people, says your God. Speak tenderly to Jerusalem and cry to her that she has served her term, her penalty is paid" (Isa. 40:1–2). The shameful consequences of attempting to be like the nations are over.

Next, the author anticipated a new beginning, a fresh start launched by a journey through the wilderness to the promised land. S/he imagined the trek toward Canaan in the west: "Make straight in the desert a highway for our God. Every valley shall be lifted up and every mountain be made low; the uneven ground shall become level and the rough places plain. Then the glory of [YHWH] shall be revealed" (Isa. 40:3–4).

Then the text moves to exultation and heart-felt praise. Through a series of rhetorical questions and all the poetic eloquence the author can muster, we read of YHWH's creative power, encompassing care, enduring mercy and far-reaching justice (Isa. 40:12–31). Later, YHWH's singular character is resoundingly confirmed. "I am the first and I am the last; besides me there is no god" (Isa. 44:6). "I am the first, and I am the last. My hand laid the foundation of the earth, and my right hand spread out the heavens" (Isa. 48:13).

Along the way we see it: a vision of the future, a description of what will be different this time from everything the Israelites had attempted before. The text quotes YHWH:

> Here is my servant [Israel], whom I uphold, my chosen, in whom my soul delights; I have put my spirit upon him; he will bring forth *justice* to the nations. He will not cry or lift up his voice, or make it heard in the street . . . he will faithfully bring forth *justice*. He will not grow faint or be crushed until he has established *justice* in the earth. (Isa. 42:1–4, emphasis added)

> I am [YHWH]; I have called you in righteousness, I have taken you by the hand and kept you. I have given you as a covenant to the people, a light to the nations, to open the eyes that are blind, to bring out the prisoners from the dungeon, from the prison those who sit in darkness . . . See, the former things have come to pass, and new things I now declare; before they spring forth, I tell you of them. (Isa. 42:6–9)

With this text, we begin to understand why **2ⁿᵈ Isaiah** overflows with joy and anticipation. The travail of Judah, the destruction of Jerusalem, the exile in Babylon, had brought into being a community with a new understanding of YHWH and a new purpose: justice. We hear it again as YHWH speaks: "Listen to me, my people, and give heed to me, my nation; for a teaching will go out from me, and my *justice* for a light to the peoples. I will bring my deliverance swiftly, my salvation has gone out and my arms will rule the peoples; the coastlands wait for me, and for my arm they hope" (Isa. 51:4–5, emphasis added).

Israel's witness would be strong and useful, like a farm implement: "I will make of you a threshing sledge, sharp, new and having teeth; you shall thresh the mountains and crush them, and you shall make the hills like chaff" (Isa. 41:15). Yet it would be gentle: "a bruised reed [my servant] will not break, a dimly burning wick [my servant] will not quench" (Isa. 42:3).

Indeed, in the vision of **2ⁿᵈ Isaiah**, the suffering of the Jews throughout their encounter with Babylon *would be an integral part of Israel's witness to YHWH's justice.* To make this point, the text gives us the image of a man scarred and disfigured by the travail he has endured and the misery he has experienced. Yet his anguish paradoxically becomes the doorway to deliverance and hope, first for himself and then for others who by his image embrace the irony of finding deliverance and hope through suffering. Thus we see how this text, so important centuries later to distraught disciples trying to make sense of the death of Jesus, was first written to make sense of Judah's travail at the hand of the empire.

> Many [are] astonished at [my servant]—so marred was his appearance, beyond human semblance . . . He was despised and rejected by others; a man of suffering and acquainted with infirmity . . . one from whom others hide their faces, he was despised . . . He was oppressed and he was afflicted . . . By a perversion of justice he was taken away . . . cut off from the land of the living. Yet . . . through [my servant] the will of [YHWH] shall prosper . . . The righteous one, my servant, shall make many righteous, and he shall bear their iniquities. Therefore, I will allot [my servant] a portion with the great. (Isa. 52:14–53:12)

Here is a vision of a political community committed to YHWH, one that reflects the character of YHWH: "You are my witnesses, says [YHWH], and my servant whom I have chosen" (Isa. 43:10). It is not the vision of David and Solomon, not a vision to be as great as Egypt and Assyria. Instead, Israel is summoned by this text to do justice, not just for its elite members, not just for its own citizens, but among the nations and especially for those within the nations who are blind and imprisoned in darkness. "I will give you as a light to the nations, that my salvation may reach to the end of the earth" (Isa. 49:6).

This is a new mission, a new vocation for Israel. It appears only in tiny fragments in the writings from **Deuteronomy** through **Jeremiah**, preoccupied as the authors and editors were by kings and palaces, temples and priests, territory and boundaries, and the burdens of possessing land exclusively, eliminating opposition and holding power. "Do not remember the former things, or consider the things of old. I am about to do a new thing; now it springs forth, do you not perceive it" (Isa. 43:18–19)?

We should not imagine this vision is confined to moralism, as if it merely called upon people to behave better. *Justice* is what YHWH intends for Earth, which is currently under empire's domination. "My purposes shall stand, and I will fulfill my intention . . . I have spoken and I will bring it to pass. I have planned and I will do it" (Isa. 46:10–11).

Yet Israel's new path would be difficult to walk; it required commitment. Justice would be contested; adversaries would be many and YHWH's servants would grow tired. Our text anticipates the blows, the taunts and insults (Isa. 50:6) and reminds readers how at times the path forward would be hard to see (Isa. 50:10). But "[YHWH] helps me; therefore, I have not been disgraced; therefore, I have set my face like flint, and I know that I shall not be put to shame; he who vindicates me is near" (Isa. 50:7). And "[YHWH] has given me the tongue of a teacher, that I may know how to sustain the weary with a word. Morning by morning he wakens my ear to listen as those who are taught" (Isa. 50:4).

And so the author urged the Jews in Babylon to take advantage of King Cyrus' decree: "Go out from Babylon, flee from Chaldea, declare this with a shout of joy, proclaim it, send it forth to the end of the earth" (Isa. 48:20). "Loose the bonds from your neck, O captive daughter . . . your God reigns," not the empires of Persia, Babylon, Assyria or Egypt (Isa. 52:2–7). To those reluctant to accept this bold claim (and yes, there were many), the text ends with words of tenderness and reassurance:

> Ho, everyone who thirsts, come to the waters; and you that have no money, come, buy and eat! Come, buy wine and milk without money and without price. Why do you spend your money for that which is not bread, and your labor for that which does not satisfy? Listen carefully to me, and eat what is good. (Isa. 55:1–2)

> For as the rain and snow come down from heaven, and do not return there until they have watered the earth, making it bring forth and sprout, giving seed to the sower and bread to the eater, so shall

my word be that goes out from my mouth; it shall not return to me empty, but it shall accomplish that which I purpose, and succeed in the thing for which I sent it. For you shall go out in joy and be led back in peace. . . an everlasting sign that shall not be cut off. (Isa. 55:10–13)

Esther

Finally, we get to this novella based on the history of one family that declined the invitation of **2nd Isaiah** and instead moved further east to Persia. Its setting is Susa, one of the four capitals of the Persian Empire, and the court of King Xerxes (Ahasuerus in the text). Susa stood near the modern Iranian city of Shush, a short distance east of its border with Iraq.

It is fitting to turn to the text of **Esther** immediately after **2nd Isaiah** and its focus on "justice" because **Esther** reminds us of the many ways the word is used and its complicated relationship to "the law."

The text begins humorously with the king treated disdainfully by Queen Vashti and the king's advisors afraid the Queen's independence will start a women's liberation movement. So the advisors persuaded the king to issue a decree and send it all across the empire, "from India to Ethiopia" (Esth. 1:1), "declaring that every man should be master of his own house" (Esth. 1:22). In the story, this is the first law.

Next we meet Hadassah, the "fair and beautiful" (Esth. 2:7) niece of Mordecai and the great-granddaughter of one of Jerusalem's elite. Esther was a Jew, a fifth-generation member of the diaspora. She "was taken into the king's palace" (Esth. 2:8), primped and pampered and thus made part of the king's harem. Eventually, Esther presented herself to the king; "he loved her more than all the other women" and chose her to be his new queen (Esth. 2:17). By thus winning the approval of the emperor, Hadassah became Esther, queen of Persia. Through all this, she never disclosed her heritage and she fulfilled to the king's delight the requirements of her role.

Meanwhile, her uncle Mordecai, who had some official capacity as one of the king's staff (Esth. 3:2), uncovered a plot against the king. He promptly told his niece, who in turn informed the king.

Nevertheless, Mordecai angered the king's chief of staff, Haman, by ignoring the king's command that all staff "bow down" and "do obeisance" to Haman (Esth. 3:2–5). For the violation of this expectation (law #2), Haman wanted revenge as noteworthy as he thought himself to be. And so Haman decided to kill all the Jews in the empire. He secured the king's cooperation with this plan of genocide through a rather vague accusation that "a certain people . . . do not keep the king's laws" (Esth. 3:8). Thus, Xerxes issued an edict "giving orders to destroy, to kill, and to annihilate all Jews, young and old, women and children, in one day, the thirteenth day of the twelfth month" (Esth. 3:13). This is law #3.

Mordecai sought his niece's help, saying "Do not think that in the king's palace you will escape any more than all the other Jews. For if you keep silence at such a time as this . . . you and your father's family will perish. Who knows? Perhaps you have come to royal dignity for just such a time as this" (Esth. 4:14). Esther's first reaction was fear; it was against the law to approach the king without being summoned. Death was the punishment for breaking this strict protocol (law #4).

But after the Jews of Susa had fasted and prayed on her behalf (Esth. 4:16), Esther found the courage to approach the king. He received her and wanted to know what she desired. Esther invited the king and his chief of staff, Haman, to a banquet. Everything went swimmingly at the banquet and the king again asked, "What is your request" (Esth. 5:6)? Esther demurred and invited him and his chief of staff to a second banquet where she said she would reveal her petition (Esth. 5:8).

On the day of the second banquet, Haman planned to have Mordecai hanged. But first he prepared to seek the king's consent. Meanwhile, during a sleepless night, the king recalled he had never honored Mordecai for revealing the plot against the king's life. In the morning, the king directed Haman to bestow the empire's honors on Mordecai, thus frustrating Haman's schedule to enact revenge.

Thus, we reach the climactic second banquet, where Queen Esther revealed her ethnic heritage, the law that threatened to annihilate her people, and the role of Haman in orchestrating all this (Esth. 7:3–6). The king promptly ordered Haman hanged on the gallows prepared for Mordecai and appointed Mordecai as chief of staff.

But Esther persisted and again approached the king uninvited: "Let an order be written to revoke the [previous law] devised by Haman . . . which he wrote giving orders to destroy the Jews who are in all the provinces of the king" (Esth. 8:5). Though the previous law could not be revoked (Esth. 8:8), the king agreed to issue a second decree. Following the direction of Mordecai, the king's scribes drafted an edict (law #5) that on the thirteenth day of the twelfth month, all across the empire, "the Jews who were in every city [were allowed to] assemble and defend their lives, to destroy, to kill, and to annihilate any armed force of any people or province that *might* attack them, with their children and woman, and to plunder their goods" (Esth. 8:11, emphasis added). It was a blank check, an authorization for preemptive war against anyone considered to be a threat. In its open-ended and arrogant tone, it is reminiscent of the Authorization for the Use of Military Force law passed by the U.S. Congress three days after 9/11.

"So the Jews struck down all their enemies with the sword, slaughtering, and destroying them, and did as they pleased to those who hated them" (Esth. 9:5). The text tells us the Jews killed 800 in Susa and its citadel and "75,000 of those who hated them" elsewhere in the king's provinces (Esth. 9:16). Mordecai then sent an order to all the Jews across the empire (law #6) "enjoining them that they should keep the fourteenth day of the month . . . and also the fifteenth day of the same month . . . for feasting and gladness" (Esth. 9:21–22). Queen Esther later confirmed Mordecai's directions with her own letter. Today, this is known as the Feast of Purim. It endures as a seductive celebration of how collaboration with empire can be a very useful way to exploit its monopoly on violence and thus transform a little bit of power into a position of privilege.

Six laws: one a lame joke, one ignored, one promising annihilation of the Jews, one broken, one legitimizing preemptive violence, and one leading to a colorful festival still observed for the benefit of children today. Where is justice in all of these laws? In Persia, in Canaan, wherever people answer YHWH's call to form political communities committed to justice, the question begs for an answer.

15. Collaboration with the Empire
Ezra, Haggai, Zechariah 1–8, Nehemiah, Malachi

In 538 BCE, Cyrus issued a decree authorizing the Jews (as they had become known) to return to Canaan to rebuild the temple. The texts we are about to read suggest four distinct groups made the journey over a span of a bit more than ninety years. The first, under the leadership of Sheshbazzar, was tiny and probably returned to Canaan within a year of the decree (Ezra 1:7–11). The second and largest group, numbering 42,360 and under the leadership of Zerubbabel and Jeshua, followed after receiving a report from the first group, perhaps around 533 BCE. Much later, in 458 BCE, Ezra led the third group, numbering around 5,000. The fourth group was again small; Nehemiah led it to Canaan in the year 445 BCE. In total, the returnees numbered around 50,000.

Each group likely made the journey by traveling northwest along the Euphrates River toward Haran, then west toward the ancient city of Aleppo, then southwest through Lebanon to the level land near the Sea, and finally south to Yehud, which is what the Persians called the region of central Canaan. Of course, this is the same route **Genesis** tells us Abram and Sarai took centuries earlier when they left their ancestral homes to follow the call of YHWH. It included passage through a wilderness not unlike the one **Exodus** tells us the Israelites passed through after leaving imperial Egypt many years earlier.

But **Genesis** had not been written yet when the first two groups made their journeys and the acceptance of **Exodus** through the composition of **Joshua** and the expansion of **Deuteronomy** was a relatively recent event (less than one hundred years previous). The parallels so obvious to us may not have been obvious to them.

Nevertheless, we contemporary readers are likely to note how positively the leader of the Persian emperor is described as compared to the Pharaohs, or how differently the journeys through the wilderness—one from Babylon and the other from Egypt—are treated. Indeed, the journey of the largest group of returnees from Babylon is not even mentioned; apparently nothing remarkable happened along the way.

The returnees joined the descendants of the estimated 200,000 Judeans who had remained there after the Babylonian conquest. The experience of those who had never left included elements of Jubilee; that is, with Jerusalem's elite out of the picture, those who stayed behind had reclaimed ancestral lands. Descendants of Israelites who had been part of Ephraim and avoided deportation by the Assyrians also resided in the historic land of Canaan, as did descendants of peoples the Assyrians had transplanted from other places and the descendants of ancient Canaanite peoples. Archeologists suggest the population of the entire area never exceeded one million during this era.

All of these people had one thing in common: the Persian Empire and its appointed governor ruled them and defined the extent of their liberty. Returnees constituted 5–10 percent of this total population. Jerusalem's population was tiny; even after its protective wall was rebuilt during the time of Nehemiah, its population was perhaps only 1,000–2,000 people.

This chapter surveys five texts that relate to life in Yehud during the first 120 years of the resettlement effort. Two of the prophetic books (**Haggai** and **Zechariah**) were written first, around 520 BCE. Nearly one hundred years later, the more broadly historical accounts, **Ezra** and **Nehemiah**, were assembled and the prophetic text of **Malachi** was written.

We start with the text of **Ezra**, which recounts events during an eighty-year period after Cyrus issued his decree. The author (Ezra) was a priest and a scribe. He is sometimes described as the father of Judaism. In addition to the text that bears his name, he is credited with writing the **Chronicles** and contributing significantly to **Leviticus**.

Ezra's chronology soon takes us into **Haggai** and **Zechariah**. Then we return to finish **Ezra** before moving into **Nehemiah**, which originally was part of **Ezra** and overlaps in content and purpose. Some of it was written in the first person by Nehemiah and like **Ezra**, it never quotes YHWH. Nehemiah was a Jewish official of the empire; thus, his identity reminds us of Joseph and Daniel. Yet his story is different because it focuses on his interaction with the Jewish community, not his life in the palace.

Haggai was an elderly prophet who spoke in Jerusalem after a fifteen-year lull in temple reconstruction. His words seem to have been recorded near the time he spoke. Zechariah was a younger prophet and priest who spoke at the same time and place. He likely recorded his words (the first eight chapters of the book) soon after speaking them around 520 BCE. Malachi is thought to have written around 430 BCE, after Jerusalem had been repopulated and Ezra's and Nehemiah's policies established.

In summary, these texts describe how the Jewish returnees again functioned as a political community in Canaan, *but not as a nation-state with a king and control of geographical boundaries.* Required religious practices became the unifying element, enabling the formation of a distinctive culture that focused on faithfulness to YHWH. Important features of this new approach included close collaboration with the Persian Empire and an expanded role for the priests, giving them new authority to shape broader community life beyond the temple courts. Thus, within a narrow sphere permitted by the empire, the society described by these texts had strong elements of theocracy. The reader is encouraged to assess the outcome of this approach by question 17, page 200.

Ezra

The text begins by reminding readers of Jeremiah's prophecy that YHWH would bring the exiles back to Jerusalem and "settle them in safety" (Jer. 32:37).   Surprisingly, it then quotes Cyrus, the Persian emperor, *as YHWH's spokesperson:* "[YHWH], the God of heaven . . . has charged me [Cyrus] to build him a house at Jerusalem in Judah" (Ezra 1:2). Cyrus invited "any of those among you who are of his people" to join in. This is a major departure from the biblical worldview: a pagan emperor speaking for and doing the will of YHWH. We can assume the quoted decree is a document written for Cyrus by his Jewish scribes, evidence that a very close working relationship had been forged.

The Jewish community in Babylon promptly mobilized to support the endeavor with the collection of "silver vessels, with gold, with goods, with animals, and with valuable gifts." Cyrus provided funding too: 5,400 gold and silver vessels. Sheshbazzar, son of the exiled king Jehoiachin (1 Chron. 3:18), functioned as trustee of the valuables (Ezra 1:5–11). He led the first group of returnees and apparently also served as the governor of Yehud, thus carrying the authority of the empire (Ezra 5:14).

Sheshbazzar's nephew (I Chron. 3:19), Zerubbabel, led the second group, which returned to "Jerusalem and Judah, all to their own towns" (Ezra 2:2). The text identifies many of the families who distinguished themselves by making the journey; Solomon's descendants receive special mention (Ezra 2:55–58). The people carried their own valuables on the journey. At some point, the Persian Empire also granted Zerubbabel the powers of governor (Hag. 1:14).

After arriving in the destroyed city, the returnees made freewill offerings "according to their resources" (Ezra 2:68–69) to the rebuilding of the temple. Sheshbazzar and his party are mysteriously absent from the account. Although their arrival and work on the temple foundation is confirmed later in the text (Ezra 5:16), the gold and silver they carried is never mentioned. Was it stolen or misappropriated?

After the people had settled in their towns, Jeshua and his fellow priests called the people back to Jerusalem to build a proper altar "of the God of Israel, to offer burnt offerings on it, as prescribed in the law of Moses." In due time, they celebrated the Festival of Booths and observed all the prescribed sacrifices, morning and evening and "at the new moon" (Ezra 3:1–5). Some of these requirements do not appear in the text of **Deuteronomy** and so we assume they had access to the newly written text of **Numbers**.

Next they commenced laying the foundation for the temple. This entailed ordering cedar logs from Tyre and sending oil as payment for the wood and transport by sea (Ezra 3:7). The workers laid the foundation according to specifications of Cyrus; it was sixty cubits (ninety feet) wide (Ezra 6:3). "All the people" marked the laying of the foundation in the second year of the construction by a celebration led by priests. But many of the older people wept loudly, apparently because the footprint of the structure was modest compared to what had stood before (Ezra 3:8–13).

Events then reached a critical juncture: persons of Israelite background who had lived in the area all of their lives offered their services to the building effort. "We worship your God as you do," they said, "and we have been sacrificing to him ever since the days of King

Esar-haddon of Assyria who brought us here" (Ezra 4:1–2). Zerubbabel and Jeshua declined: "You shall have no part with us in building a house to our God; but we alone will build to [YHWH], the God of Israel, *as King Cyrus of Persia has commanded us*" (Ezra 4:3, emphasis added). The text characterizes persons offering their help as "adversaries" of the returnees, a tip-off that some sort of rivalry existed between the two groups. But most astonishing about this text is that it does not cite YHWH as the authority for this momentous decision but only Cyrus, the emperor. This suggests the empire's authority had become primary, not YHWH's.

Using intimidation, bribes to Persian officials and letters to the reigning Persian king (Ezra 4:4–6), the excluded kinsmen stopped all temple construction for perhaps fifteen years. It is highly likely that this period of delay occurred during the final years of Cyrus' reign (he died in 530 BCE) and during the unstable years of his less revered successors. It is debated whether the account in Ezra 4:7–23 is part of this (in which case "Artaxerxes" was Gaumata, who was king only three months) or occurred much later when the city wall was being built. But the answer to that tangled question does not significantly change the story line.

In 522–520 BCE, many of the conquered peoples under Persian control rebelled. In part, this was due to uncertainty about who would govern after Cyrus' dynasty ended. Darius, a prominent Persian military leader, seized power in late 522 BCE and with the support of the military quelled the revolts. He gradually established control as the new emperor.

Haggai

The empire-wide turmoil of Darius' second year as emperor (520 BCE) created an opportunity to break the stalemate over temple reconstruction. That is when the prophet Haggai stepped forward to speak in Jerusalem (Hag. 1:1). We immediately notice the change in voice: "Thus says [YHWH]: These people say the time has not yet come to rebuild [YHWH's] house. . . Is it time for you yourselves to live in your paneled houses, while this house lies in ruins" (Hag. 1:2–4)? Next Haggai called attention to the general conditions of life in Canaan. "Consider how you have fared. You have sown much and harvested little; you eat, but you never have enough; you drink, but you never have your fill; you clothe yourselves, but no one is warm; and you that earn wages . . . put them into a bag with holes" (Hag. 1:5–6).

The people had found life in Canaan to be very difficult, Haggai said, "because [YHWH's] house lies in ruin, while all of you hurry off to your own houses" (Hag. 1:9). So Haggai told the people to get to work on the temple. "Then Zerubbabel . . . with all the remnant of the people, obeyed the voice of [YHWH] their God and the words of the prophet Haggai" (Hag. 1:12).

During the next three months, as the legality of the renewed building activity remained much in doubt, Haggai kept speaking at the construction site, urging the builders on. "Who is left among you that saw this house in its former glory? How does it look to you now? Is it not in your sight as nothing? Yet take courage, O Zerubbabel, says [YHWH] . . . My spirit abides among you; do not fear . . . I will fill this house with splendor" (Hag. 2:3–7). "Is there any seed left in the barn? Do the vine, the fig tree, the pomegranate, and the olive tree still yield nothing? From this day on I will bless you" (Hag. 2:19). "I have chosen you, says [YHWH]" (Hag. 2:23).

Zechariah 1–8

Toward the end of Haggai's brief time of public engagement, Zechariah picked up the baton and carried it for two years. He described eight visions, some obscure but all encouraging to the builders at the temple reconstruction site. The two clearest visions—the fourth and fifth— affirmed the leadership of the chief priest, Joshua (called "Jeshua" in **Ezra**), and the project administrator, Zerubbabel.

Zechariah said YHWH had cleansed Joshua of his guilt and clothed him "with festal apparel." Moreover, YHWH had promised to give Joshua and his priestly colleagues "a single stone with seven facets . . . [and] engraved inscription" (Zech. 3:4–9). Obviously, the people should follow those with access to such knowledge. After finishing his description of the eight visions, Zechariah again spoke of Joshua and said a crown of silver and gold should be set on his head. "It is he that shall build the temple of (YHWH); he shall bear royal honor and shall sit and rule on his throne" (Zech. 6:9–13). This is an important passage; it indicates that

Zechariah expected the high priest to fill a politically powerful role in the life of Israel, similar in some ways to the role of a king.

What about Zerubbabel, the project administrator?   He was a treasure, Zechariah said, "a lampstand all of gold" who lived "not by might, nor by power, but by [YHWH's] spirit" (Zech. 4:2–6).   In other words, he was a man whose authority did not come from his role, but from how he conducted himself.   Zerubbabel's hand had "laid the foundation of this house; his hands shall also complete it" (Zech. 4:9).

The first vision told of YHWH's return to Jerusalem (even though the temple was not finished) and YHWH's promise that "my cities shall again overflow with prosperity" (Zech. 1:17). The second told of YHWH's protection of "the land of Judah" (Zech. 1:21); the third told of how the city of Jerusalem would again be filled with people (Zech. 2:4).   The sixth described "the whole land" under the rule of law forbidding theft and deceit (Zech. 5:1–4). The seventh told of angelic women who would remove the presence of evil from the land (Zech. 5:5–11); the eighth told of YHWH's sovereignty over Earth (Zech. 6:1–8).

Toward the end of his public role, Zechariah responded to a question asked by a delegation from Bethel: should we continue to "mourn and practice abstinence on the fifth month, as [we] have done for so many years" (Zech. 7:3) as a memorial to the destruction of the temple in the fifth month of 586 BCE?   Zechariah said no, such days were over; the fasting and lamenting had been largely self-centered anyway.   Instead, "render true judgments, show kindness and mercy to one another, do not oppress the widow, the orphan, the alien or the poor; and do not devise evil in your hearts against one another" (Zech. 7:1–10).

Though people resisted this message, Zechariah insisted YHWH was resolute: "Even though it seems impossible to the remnant of these people in these days, should it also seem impossible to me, says [YHWH] of hosts? Thus says [YHWH]: *I will save my people*" (Zech. 8:6–7, emphasis added). And again: "For thus says [YHWH] . . . I have purposed in these days to do good to Jerusalem and to the house of Judah; do not be afraid" (Zech. 8:14–15).   Thus, he encouraged the people to "speak the truth to one another, render in your gates judgments that are true and make for peace" (Zech. 8:16). And celebrate; let your festivals "be seasons of joy and gladness" (Zech. 8:19).

Finally, Zechariah described the future:

> Peoples shall yet come, the inhabitants of many cities; the inhabitants of one city shall go to another saying, "Come, let us go to entreat the favor of [YHWH]" . . . Many peoples and strong nations shall come to seek [YHWH] in Jerusalem, and to entreat the favor of [YHWH] . . . In those days ten men from nations of every language shall take hold of a Jew, grasping his garment and saying, "Let us go with you, for we have heard that God is with you." (Zech. 8:20–23)

In summary, Zechariah envisioned a big tent, a welcoming community where ethical behavior would be the defining feature and a righteous high priest would provide leadership. It was a vision soon put to the test by Ezra and his priestly colleagues.

Ezra

We return to **Ezra** and pick up the narrative in chapter 5 of that text. In response to renewed construction activity at the temple site, the Persian-appointed provincial governor came to Jerusalem to investigate the violation of law. He then sent the new king, Darius, a report of his findings. His report included an extended quote of Zerubbabel's and Jeshua's defense of their activities and their request that King Darius order a search of the royal archives to find the decree from Cyrus (Ezra 5:7–17).

Darius' staff located Cyrus' decree in the archive at Ecbatana, another of the Persian Empire's capitals. And so Darius issued his own decree directing the governor to permit the work to go forward. Moreover, he ordered the governor to pay the construction costs "in full and without delay from the royal revenue" collected by the governor from the people of the province (Ezra 6:7–8). He authorized punishment of anyone who interfered with reconstruction (Ezra 6:11–12). Thus, construction of the temple again became a project of the Persian Empire.

By 515 BCE, the workers completed the temple (Ezra 6:15). Led by the priests and the Levites, the people "celebrated the dedication of this house of God with joy." A month later, the returnees celebrated the Passover; they were joined "by all who had separated themselves from the pollutions of the nations of the land to worship [YHWH]." They followed that with the seven-day festival of unleavened bread. "With joy they celebrated . . . for [YHWH] has made them joyful" (Ezra 6:16–22).

In chapter 7, the setting is again Babylon, *but sixty-seven years later (458 BCE)*. For the first time we meet Ezra, "a scribe skilled in the law of Moses," who has received from King Artaxerxes authority to bring his expertise to the Jewish people in Canaan. The king's written order was a remarkable—even astonishing—document. It said Ezra had been "sent by the king and his seven counselors" to assess the condition of Yehud and Jerusalem by reference to the law of YHWH. It referred to "silver and gold that the king and his counselors [had] freely offered to the God of Israel" and gave Ezra authority to use those resources in the way they thought best. "Whatever else is required for the house of your God . . . you may provide out of the king's treasury" (Ezra 7:14–20).

The order went on to direct Persian administrators in Yehud to fully cooperate with Ezra and authorized a budget for additional costs identified by Ezra. It exempted all priests, Levites, temple singers and doorkeepers, and temple servants from the empire's taxes (Ezra 7:21–24).

Furthermore, it gave Ezra authority to appoint magistrates and judges to apply the Law of Moses in Yehud. "All who will not obey the law of your God and the law of the king, let judgment be strictly executed on them, whether for death or for banishment or for confiscation of their goods or for imprisonment" (Ezra 7:25–26). Thus, Ezra arrived in Jerusalem carrying the executive authority of the emperor and nearly a thousand talents of silver and over a hundred of gold (Ezra 9:26–27).

Ezra's first administrative act called to mind the biblical story in **Joshua** of ethnic cleansing directed against Canaanites. In the rule of Ezra, a version of that story was enacted in real time and directed *against Israelites* who wanted to become part of the new community of returnees. "The people of Israel, the priests and the Levites have not separated themselves from the peoples of the lands . . . They have taken some of their daughters as wives for themselves and for their sons. Thus, the holy seed has mixed itself with the peoples of the lands" (Ezra 9:1–2).

Who were these wives who polluted the holy seed? Given the 75-year period since the first return of Jewish exiles, a number of combinations were in play. Some were daughters of a parent descended from an Ephraimite family; others had a parent of Canaanite descent. Still others had a Persian parent who had married a Jewish returnee as part of a plan to reclaim lost land. Still others had descended from two Judean parents who had not been exiled; after the destruction of the temple, these families had failed to maintain ritual purity. Ezra apparently was appalled by marriages involving women in all of these categories. Yehud was "a land unclean with the pollutions of the peoples of the lands . . . They have filled it end-to-end with their uncleanness" (Ezra 9:11).

Ezra publicly displayed his anguish in front of the temple, "weeping and throwing himself down" (Ezra 10:1). The people knew the die was cast; in Ezra's anger, the law of YHWH and the law of Persia stood arrayed against them. So the "leading priests, the Levites and all Israel" swore "that they would do as he said" (Ezra 10:5). Ezra proceeded to summon all the people to Jerusalem under threat of property forfeiture and a ban from temple worship should they not appear. "All the people" showed up and sat "trembling" in the square in pouring rain waiting for Ezra to re-order their lives. He demanded confession and the people complied. He demanded that they separate themselves "from the peoples of the land and from the foreign wives." That seemed a more complicated matter and the people begged to be released from the square to find shelter from the downpour; let the elders and judges of our town represent us in settling this matter, they said (Ezra 10:8–15).

In the end, all of the men who had married "foreign wives" (Ezra 10:14), about 110 in total (Ezra 10:20–43), "pledged . . . to send away their wives" (Ezra 10:19) "with their children" (Ezra 10:44). Zechariah's vision of a political community led by a priest had indeed come to pass, but it was not a community that welcomed many peoples. Purity of "the holy seed" remained the litmus test, not ethical living. And while this could be construed as a religious test, not a racial one, its practical effect was to equate the Jewish faith with a very narrow definition of Jewish ethnicity.

Recent marriages by male Jewish returnees to Persian women were impacted by Ezra's decree. But given the relatively small number of required divorces, we assume more distant marriages of that sort were not affected, thus retaining their efficacy in renewing land titles for the returning elite and re-establishing their economic privilege.

Nehemiah

The prophetic voices of **2nd Isaiah** and **Zechariah** pointed toward a more inclusive community than what emerged under Ezra's leadership. As we turn our attention to **Nehemiah**, it is appropriate to ask how the prophetic vision got hijacked.

Perhaps we should not be surprised by the turn of events in Jerusalem following Ezra's arrival. From the beginning, only returnees had been allowed to participate in the rebuilding of the temple; long-term residents had been excluded lest they taint the effort. Yet the texts show no parallel concern that the empire's participation might also have a tainting effect. *Was some dynamic other than purity at work to divert YHWH's people in Yehud from the earlier vision of inclusivity?*

Nehemiah served King Artaxerxes as cup-bearer, a cabinet-level position that entailed making sure the King did not drink poisoned wine. In 444 BCE, seventy years after the dedication of the temple and fourteen years after the king empowered Ezra to establish a theocratic society in Jerusalem, it dawned on Nehemiah that the infrastructure of the City was broken down. "The place of my ancestors' graves lies waste, and its gates have been destroyed by fire" (Neh. 2:3). Something about this seems contrived and inauthentic.

Nehemiah asked the king for an order directing the Persian authorities in Yehud to work with him, providing timber for a *"temple fortress* and for the wall of the city and for the house that I shall occupy" (Neh.1:8, emphasis added). The king did as Nehemiah asked. He also sent "officers of the army and cavalry" (Neh. 1:9) along with Nehemiah. Certainly security for the journey was one consideration, but the presence of officers suggests broader military purposes too.

Howard-Brook provides this analysis.

Why would a Persian king sponsor this building project and send a trusted member of his cabinet to oversee it? The answer, despite the superficial ruse of Nehemiah's pious petition, should be clear: reconstruction of Jerusalem was a Persian-sponsored project all along. . . It was Persia's own strategic military needs that led the empire to finance, oversee, and carry out the rebuilding of Jerusalem.[24]

This accounts for the empire's generous support of the return and rebuilding efforts; it was using Jewish religious hopes to further its plan to consolidate power in Yehud. While we are left guessing about tactical aspects of the empire's plan, we can safely assume it included the classic imperial tool of divide and conquer. So long as the Semitic peoples of the area quarreled and fought with one another, the empire would remain solidly in control. We see the reenactment of this tactic in war-ravaged Iraq and the Shia-Sunni conflict.

Upon arriving in Jerusalem, Nehemiah promptly assessed the condition of the wall and organized the rebuilding effort (Neh. 1:11–18). Opponents of the project stepped forward as soon as they became aware of his plan. "When Sanballat the Horonite and Tobiah the Ammonite official and Geshem the Arab heard of it, they mocked and ridiculed us, saying, 'What is this that you are doing? Are you rebelling against the king?'" (Neh. 1:19). Nehemiah's reply conveyed the same tone of exclusivity Zerubbabel and Ezra had voiced earlier: "You have no share or claim or historic right in Jerusalem" (Neh. 1:20).

Later, as the work on the wall progressed, opponents of the project "plotted together to come and fight against Jerusalem and to cause confusion in it" (Neh. 4:8). Information about the plot was passed to Nehemiah, who organized armed guards to deter attack (Neh. 4:16–23).

An even more serious problem was the economic hardship the workers experienced.

Now there was a great outcry of the people and of their wives against their Jewish kin . . . "With our sons and daughters we are

---

[24]   Howard-Brook, 260-261.

many; we must get grain, so that we may eat and stay alive."
There were also those who said, "We are having to pledge our
fields, our vineyards, and our houses in order to get grain during
the famine." And there were those who said, "We are having to
borrow money on our fields and vineyards to pay the king's tax.
Now our flesh is the same as our kindred; our children are the
same as their children; and yet we are forcing our sons and
daughters to be slaves, and some of our daughters have been
ravished; we are powerless, and our fields and vineyards now
belong to others." (Neh. 5:1–5)

This stunning series of complaints pointed to deep structural
injustice. Some of the returnees were making out very well while many
others were becoming debt-slaves. Ownership of the land was sliding
back toward the inequality of former times. The administration of justice
reflected the economic disparity; daughters of poor families were being
raped by sons of wealthy families without accountability or consequences.
This was especially troubling to hear after years of Ezra's leadership.

In anger, Nehemiah assembled the "nobles and officials" and
accused them of charging interest on advances of food and wages and on
delayed payments of taxes. This practice had led to the "selling [of] your
own kin [into debt slavery], who must then be bought back by us." He
went on: "The thing that you are doing is not good. Should you not walk in
the fear of our God, to prevent the taunts of the nations, our enemies"
(Neh. 5:6–9)?

Although not entirely clear, it appears Nehemiah first concern was
that workers' complaints not jeopardize completion of the wall. So
Nehemiah asked the nobles and officials to restore to the workers, "this
very day, their fields, their vineyards, their olive orchards, and their
houses, and the interest on money, grain, wine and oil that you have been
exacting from them." The nobles and officials agreed (Neh. 5:11–12). We
wish the text told us more. Were the problems of rape and unequal justice
addressed? Was the shift in economic policy ongoing or did it end when
the wall was finished? Were debts forgiven? We cannot be sure, but the
wall was finished in fifty-two days (Neh. 6:15). Nehemiah's leadership as
"governor in the land of Judah" had proved decisive (Neh. 5:14).

The text's display of Nehemiah's generosity (Neh. 5:14–19) raises more questions than it answers. It has the sound of a conventional politician bragging about his integrity and magnanimous spirit. Are we really to be impressed by the fact that many ate at Nehemiah's table without cost during the construction of a wall around the empire's citadel?

Soon after the wall's completion, the people gathered at the temple and Ezra read from the recently completed "book of the law of Moses" (Neh. 8:1), probably **Leviticus**. "So they read from the book, from the law of God, with interpretation. They gave the sense, so that the people understood the reading . . . All the people wept when they heard the words of the law" (Neh. 8:8–9), perhaps because in the words of the text they recognized the injustice of their own circumstances. Nehemiah and the other leaders had not expected weeping and so added this instruction: "This day is holy to [YHWH]; do not mourn or weep . . . Go your way, eat the fat and drink sweet wine . . . for the joy of [YHWH] is your strength" (Neh.8: 9–10).

Later that month, the people entered a time of fasting and repentance. "Then those of Israelite descent separated themselves from all foreigners and stood and confessed their sins and the iniquities of their ancestors" (Neh. 9:2). Ezra recounted stories from ancient Hebrew history, apparently reading from **Numbers** and **Genesis**. His prayer described one aspect of their painful situation. "Here we are, slaves to this day—slaves in the land that you gave to our ancestors to enjoy its fruit and its good gifts. Its rich yield goes to the kings whom you have set over us because of our sins; they have power also over our bodies and over our livestock at their pleasure, and we are in great distress" (Neh. 9:36–37).

The event ended with the people entering into a covenant, "a firm agreement in writing, and on that sealed document are inscribed the names of our officials, our Levites and our priests" (Neh. 9:38). The people voiced their oath of agreement. In light of the complaints voiced to Nehemiah a few months earlier, it is important to note the particular promises included in this oath: (1) no intermarriage with "peoples of the land;" (2) no purchase of merchandise or grain on the Sabbath day; (3) no planting of crops or "exaction of debt" in the seventh year; (4) payment of an annual temple tax; (5) provision of wood for the alter fires in the temple; (6) offerings annually of the first fruits of the soil and every tree; (7) offerings of the firstborn of sons and of livestock and of flocks; (8) offerings of "the first of our dough, and our contributions, the fruit of every tree, the wine and the oil, to the priests, to the chambers of the house of our God;" and (9) offering the tithes from the soil to the Levites (Neh. 10:30–37).

Seeing how all but the first three items entail the transfer of valuable items from the people to temple staff, we begin to understand why so many Jews preferred to stay in Babylon and Persia. There the people worshipped YHWH in synagogues under the guidance of a rabbi. In Yehud, within the realm of the reconstructed temple, the priests in collaboration with Persian kings had constructed a system of localized power and narrow economic privilege.

Jerusalem still needed to be populated. Generally, descendants of the returnees received the privilege of living in "the holy city of Jerusalem" (Neh. 11:1), supplemented by the casting of lots among others who were interested. Then the city wall was dedicated (Neh. 12:27–43) and the temple responsibilities assigned (Neh. 12:44–47). The temple staff was large and consisted of many more people than just the priests.

That same day, the temple leaders "read from the book of Moses [Deut. 23:3–5] in the hearing of the people . . . that no Ammonite or Moabite should ever enter the assembly of God. . . When the people heard the law, they separated . . . all those of foreign descent" (Neh. 13:1–3).

In 432 BCE, Nehemiah left Jerusalem briefly to visit the king. Upon his return, he dealt with the problem of temple facilities being used for private gain (Neh. 13:4–9) and encouraged Sabbath observance (Neh. 13:15–22). The text ends with Nehemiah in an encounter with men who had married women of Ashdod, Ammon and Moab. Nehemiah cursed and beat them and pulled out their hair; "thus I cleansed them from everything foreign" (Neh. 13:23–30).

Malachi

Near the time of Nehemiah's return to Jerusalem, Malachi wrote "the word of [YHWH] to Israel" (Mal. 1:1). We do not know who he was or if he spoke publicly. But his message serves as an appropriate post-script to this second attempt to become the people of YHWH in Canaan.

The text is structured around a series of questions, some accusatory, some rhetorical, some sorrowful. The questions create a contentious tone and the feeling of an argument. It is not entirely clear if Malachi was a supporter of Ezra or a critic. But things seem to have turned sour. We hear this in the text's dialogue between YHWH and the people.

"How have you loved us?" the people ask YHWH (Mal. 1:3). "Where is the respect due me . . . O priests who despise my name?" YHWH asks the priests. "How have we despised your name?" the priests reply (Mal. 1:6). So the text continues. YHWH accuses again: "What a weariness this is, you say, and you sniff at me" (Mal. 1:13).

Malachi first aimed YHWH's accusations at the priests. They were not sincere; they did not believe in what they were doing.

> You have turned aside from the way; you have caused many to stumble by your instruction; you have corrupted the covenant of Levi . . . and so I make you despised and abased before all the people inasmuch as you have not kept my ways, but have shown partiality in your instruction. (Mal. 2:8–9)

Malachi then turned to the people and accused them of breaking faith with one another, their relationship to the temple and the wives of their youth (Mal. 2:10–16). "Judah has profaned the sanctuary of [YHWH] . . . and has married the daughter of a foreign god" (Mal. 2:11). "For I hate divorce, says (YHWH), the God of Israel . . . So take heed to yourselves and do not be faithless" (Mal. 2:16).

Was YHWH the figurative "wife" of their youth that the people had betrayed by worshipping other gods? Was Malachi speaking of literal marriages that Ezra had annulled because of his passion for "purity?"? Or was Malachi speaking of other marriages Jewish men had broken because of advantages to be gained by marrying women (including Persians) who worshipped gods other than YHWH? Each reading can be supported.

In our view, the latter reading is most consistent with Malachi's broader characterization of the problem: "You have said, 'It is vain to serve [YHWH]. What do we profit by keeping his command or by going about as mourners before [YHWH]? Now we count the arrogant happy; evildoers not only prosper, but when they put [YHWH] to the test, they escape'" (Mal. 3:15). Thus, it appears the men had twisted Ezra's insistence upon divorce for the sake of purity into a license for casting aside wives who no longer were of child-bearing age and leaving them destitute while marrying younger, "foreign" women.

The people wearied YHWH, asking: "Where is the God of justice" (Mal. 2:17)? Based on what we have seen in the texts of **Ezra** and **Nehemiah**, it seems a fair question. Malachi answered:

> See, I am sending my messenger to prepare the way before me, and the [anointed one] you seek will suddenly come to his temple . . . But who can endure the day of his coming, and who can stand when he appears? For he is like a refiner's fire and like fullers' soap; he will sit as a refiner and purifier of silver . . . until they present offerings to [YHWH] in righteousness. (Mal. 3:1–3)

> Then I will draw near to you for judgment; I will be swift to bear witness against the sorcerers, against the adulterers, against those who swear falsely, against those who oppress the hired workers in their wages, the widow and the orphan, against those who thrust aside the alien and do not fear me. (Mal. 3:5)

Malachi's message reflected deep disappointment with how the fresh start in Yehud had turned out. He focused his criticism on the priests, but did not relieve the people of their responsibility to seek a righteousness rooted in ethics, not ethnicity or ritualistic purity. And he offered a positive vision of what was still to come when "the sun of righteousness shall rise, with healing in its wings. You shall go out leaping like calves from the stall" (Mal. 4:1–3). *On that day, enthusiasm for YHWH would return and right living would be the measure by which people would be judged.* "Then once more you shall *see* the difference between the righteous and the wicked, between one who serves [YHWH] and one who does not" (Mal. 3:18, emphasis added).

16. Beyond State, Tribe or Ritual
3rd Isaiah, Ruth, Jonah, Joel, Zechariah 9–14, Daniel 7–12

The six short, prophetic texts we survey in this chapter bring to a close the First Testament's long conversation about how the Israelite people should structure themselves politically. Before looking at these texts, it is important to assess where the story has taken us thus far.

The first biblical text was a propaganda piece (to put it candidly), most likely prepared by Solomon's scribes and designed to establish the divine legitimacy of the Davidic dynasty. It was followed by a history of the kings in Judah and Ephraim, as well as by various messages from prophets. These texts may give the impression that the Israelites were a distinctive people, but they also describe them as eager for success by copying practices of their neighbors. Thus, Israelite identity was far from settled. This era ended with Jerusalem's destruction.

The story then splintered with most of Israel's elite sent into exile in Babylon, another group (including some of the elite) going to Egypt to live as refugees, and the large majority of common folk staying in Canaan. Thereafter, biblical texts primarily follow the group exiled to Babylon.

Instead of disappearing via assimilation, the exiles reflected on their failures, launched a second settlement effort in what had been Judah, enlarged and reinterpreted their founding stories and myths, generated new and powerful texts, and established religious practices that did not require a priest or a temple. As they lived through these experiences, they formed a distinctive and stable Jewish identity that was strictly monotheistic, followed detailed rituals and a rigorous ethical code, shared vivid written accounts of the patriarchs' lives and YHWH's promises to them, and looked for leadership from priests and rabbis. Though they had no nation-state of their own, they thrived as a political community, not only in Canaan, but also in many other places where their contributions were acknowledged and valued. When we consider this all emerged out of the experience of defeat and exile, it is truly astonishing.

The exiles who returned to Canaan and rebuilt Jerusalem and its temple had no illusions of being a nation state. Yet they aspired to be *a distinctive culture* faithful to and blessed by YHWH. Under the leadership of Ezra, this second attempt focused on ethnic and ritual purity and the authority of priests who presided at religious rituals in the temple. It excluded most of the descendants of Israel who had lived continuously in the land throughout the period of the exile. With regard to the Persian Empire, it worked as a very junior partner to accommodate imperial requirements and benefit from the empire's power, finances and protection. This entailed compromises, but until "that day" of YHWH's triumph somewhere in the future, this was a way to carry on.

With all of this decided (so to speak), other questions remained. Did mixing imperial power with priestly authority pollute the way of YHWH? Would a Jewish culture focused on ethnic and ritualistic purity find a way to welcome others? And most importantly, did this approach result in a good society where justice and righteousness prevailed?

Zechariah left us with the image of a priest crowned with silver and gold; Ezra seemed to embody that priest. But **Malachi** was not impressed with the society that emerged under this approach. Much of the economic and social injustice the Israelites had experienced during the rule by kings reappeared again under priestly leadership. The focus on ethnic and ritualistic purity did not mature in ethical living, but in a preoccupation with privilege, community boundaries and exclusion.

This overview brings us to this final set of historical texts. We start with **3rd Isaiah**, eleven chapters by an unknown author who was a critic of the leadership of Ezra and Nehemiah. It was written as one poetic composition that built on the vision of justice articulated by **2nd Isaiah**.

Next we look at **Ruth**, a short story written during the same era about the survival of a family, and **Jonah**, a parable of salvation for a national enemy. Both consider YHWH's relationship to foreigners and the implications for how the Jewish community defines itself. We do not know the author of either text; both are likely works of fiction.

Joel and **Zechariah 9–14** are prophetic texts that speak of "that day" in the future when YHWH will set the world right. The text of **Daniel 7–12** also fits this genre; it was the last written (around 165 BCE) and reflects events that occurred at the Jerusalem temple during the Seleucid era of the Greek Empire. Each of these three texts reflects the eschatological hope that at the end of history, YHWH's victory would usher in the justice and peace (*shalom*) that had been so long delayed.

These six texts stand in the tradition of **Exodus** and as prophetic critiques of the Second Temple period, a critique Jesus continued. He quoted **3rd Isaiah, Jonah** and **Daniel 7–12** frequently and used imagery from **Ruth** and **Zechariah 9–14** to inspire his own actions. Peter found in **Joel** a way to understand the mysterious events of Pentecost. For additional discussion, see questions 18, 19 and 20 on page 200.

3rd Isaiah

The very first verse declares that ethics is the yardstick by which YHWH measures the world: "Maintain justice and do what is right" (Isa. 56:1). While Ezra and Nehemiah cited imperial decrees as authority for their claims, the writer of **3rd Isaiah** cited YHWH as authority for his.

As we read of a hoped-for community that welcomes "the foreigners" and "the eunuchs" who "hold fast my covenant" and "join themselves to [YHWH]" (Isa. 56:3–6), we begin to suspect that the author is a critic of the approach used by Ezra and Nehemiah. As the text famously puts it, "My house shall be called a house of prayer for all peoples. Thus says [YHWH], *who gathers the outcasts of Israel*" (Isa. 56:7–8, emphasis added).

Ezra and Nehemiah are never mentioned, but the author speaks of blind "sentinels" who ruled the returnee community. They were men "without knowledge," "shepherds with no understanding" who had "all turned to their own way, to their own gain, one and all" (Isa. 56:10–11).

Who was the author? We hear him/her praying in chapter 63: "For you are our father, *though Abraham does not know us and Israel does not acknowledge us* . . . Your holy people took possession for a little while; but now our adversaries have trampled down your sanctuary. We have long been like those whom you do not rule; like those not called by your name" (Isa. 63:16, 19, emphasis added). The author was an outsider to the Jewish community, perhaps one of the Semitic locals who had tried to join that first celebration of the Passover (Ezra 6:21), only to be turned away because of alleged impurity (Ezra 9:2), or perhaps a Jewish eunuch who had resettled in Yehud after imperial service in the Persian court.

Quoting YHWH, the author's critique of empty religious piety fills chapter 58: "Day after day they seek me and delight to know my ways, *as if they were a nation that practiced righteousness*" (Isa. 58:2, emphasis added). The text mocks pious prayers and fasting and then asks:

> Is not this the fast that I choose: to loose the bonds of injustice, to undo the thongs of the yoke, to let the oppressed go free and to break every yoke? Is it not to share your bread with the hungry, and bring the homeless poor into your house; when you see the naked, to cover them, and not to hide yourself from your own kin? (Isa. 58:6–7)

As for the heritage of the patriarchs, it indeed could become a source of strength, but only after the people acted justly (Isa. 58:14).

What does the text mean by justice? In chapter 65, we read an inspiring description of the "new heavens and a new earth" YHWH is "about to create" (Isa. 65:17). It speaks of infant survival, long life, the dignity of productive labor and the end of empire.

> They shall build houses and inhabit them; they shall plant vineyards and eat their fruit. They shall not build and another inhabit; they shall not plant and another eat; for like the days of a tree shall my people be, and my chosen shall long enjoy the work of their hands. They shall not labor in vain, or bear children for calamity . . . They shall not hurt or destroy on all my holy mountain. (Isa. 65:21-25)

But there was nothing about a king in the new Earth, nothing about a Jewish state, and nothing about sanctification via religious ritual. Jerusalem received a mention (Isa. 65:18), but not the temple.

The discussion of righteousness and justice is most prominent in chapter 61 at the very center of the poem. The text speaks first in the voice of the prophet, then in the voice of YHWH and then in the voice of the community responding as one.

[YHWH] has sent me to bring good news to the oppressed, to bind up the brokenhearted, to proclaim liberty to the captives and release to the prisoners, to proclaim the year of [YHWH's] favor, the day of vengeance of our God, to comfort all who mourn . . . They will be called oaks of righteousness, the planting of [YHWH] to display his glory. They shall build up the ancient ruins, they shall raise up the former devastations; they shall repair the ruined cities, the devastations of many generations. (Isa. 61:1– 2, 4)

For I [YHWH] love justice, I hate robbery and wrongdoing; I will faithfully give them their recompense, and I will make an everlasting covenant with them. Their descendants shall be known among the nations, and their offspring among the peoples; all who see them shall acknowledge that they are a people whom [YHWH] has blessed. (Isa. 61:8–9)

I will greatly rejoice in [YHWH]; my whole being shall exult in my God; for he has clothed me with the garments of salvation, he has covered me with the robe of righteousness . . . For as the earth brings forth its shoots, and as a garden causes what is sown in it to spring up, so [YHWH] will cause righteousness and praise to spring up before all the nations. (Isa. 61:10–11)

Chapters 60 and 62 ring this centerpiece with descriptions of how this community of justice will attract other peoples. "Nations shall come to your light, and kings to the brightness of your dawn" (Isa. 60:3). "The nations shall see your vindication, and all the kings your glory" (Isa. 62:2).

Yet as we read this beautiful text, we also encounter images that sound chauvinistic, even imperial.

The abundance of the seas shall be brought to you, the wealth of the nations shall come to you . . . Foreigners shall build up your walls and their kings shall minister to you . . . The nation and kingdom that will not serve you shall perish . . .You shall suck the milk of nations. . . the breasts of kings. (Isa. 60:5, 10, 12, 16)

> Strangers shall stand and feed your flocks, foreigners shall till
> your land and dress your vines. (Isa. 61:5)

The images of subservience are jarring and almost spoil the
inspiring tone of the text by not conveying the kind of "welcome" we
expect. But wait; the author has the empire in mind here. When at last the
nations come seeking instruction in the ways of YHWH, they must leave
some things behind: the arrogance of the imperial worldview and the
hubris of demanding improvements to YHWH's wisdom. Thus, the
subservient images portend an astonishing reversal: mighty nations
seeking instruction in the peculiar ways of the community of YHWH.

This remarkable text ends as it began, with YHWH speaking:

> I am coming to gather all nations and tongues; and they shall come
> and shall see my glory . . . They shall bring all your kindred from
> all the nations as an offering to [YHWH] . . . and I will also take
> some of them as priests and as Levites . . . From new moon to new
> moon, and from Sabbath to Sabbath, all flesh shall come to
> worship me, says [YHWH]. (Isa. 66:18, 20–21, 23)

The new community of justice YHWH will bring into being "shall
be called by a new name that the mouth of [YHWH] will give" (Isa. 62:2).
In biblical texts, a new name often follows a new identity. But this text
does not give us that new name. Perhaps its naming must wait its
emergence in the flesh.

Ruth

With its portrayal of two poor and obscure women who *act* to
improve their lives, this text is unique within the biblical collection and
especially attractive to readers yearning for a critique of Israel's patriarchal
culture. Yet its storyline was shaped mostly by a desire to subvert the
approach taken by Ezra and Nehemiah by providing a positive account of
women who were "unclean" and thus excludable, one by her pagan
identity and the other by her long absence from temple purity rituals.

The story tells of an Israelite couple and their two sons who escape
famine by moving from Judah to the land of Moab, a place known to the

Israelites for its hostility, sexual perversity and idolatry. There the father died. The sons married Moabite women; then the sons also died. Each of the three widows was childless and thus devoid of YHWH's blessing. Facing destitution as an older woman without heirs, Naomi decided to return to Judah. She encouraged her daughters-in-law, Orpah and Ruth, to remain in Moab and remarry; assumedly, Naomi was very aware of the *Torah's* prohibition of a Moabite being admitted "to the assembly of [YHWH]" (Deut. 23:3). But Ruth insisted on accompanying Naomi to Judah: "Where you go, I will go; where you lodge, I will lodge; your people shall be my people and your God my God" (Ruth 1:16).

They arrived in Bethlehem at the start of the barley harvest. Ruth asked Naomi for permission to glean barley in the field of Boaz, "a prominent rich man" (Ruth 2:1) related to Naomi's dead husband. Boaz noticed her, instructed his servants "not to bother her," and told her to help herself to his servants' drinking water. Ruth reported all of this to Naomi.

After the harvest was complete, Naomi instructed Ruth to "wash and anoint yourself, and put on your best clothes and go down to the threshing floor, but do not make yourself known to [Boaz] until he has finished eating and drinking. When he lies down, then go and uncover his feet and lie down, and he will tell you what to do" (Ruth 3:3–4). It was a plan to seduce Boaz and thereby gain marriage; within this context, "feet" referred to Boaz's genitals.

As the contented Boaz lay sleeping against a pile of grain in the pitch darkness, Ruth "came stealthily and uncovered his feet and lay down." Boaz woke at midnight and discovered her. "Who are you?" Ruth identified herself and invited Boaz "to spread your cloak over your servant, for you are next of kin." Boaz responded positively to her presence and described it as an act of "loyalty." But he declined to consummate a sexual relationship because "there is another kinsman more closely related than I." Aware of the astonishing risk Ruth had taken in approaching him. Boaz also reassured her: "Do not be afraid . . . for all the assembly of my people know you are a worthy woman." So Ruth stayed the night, leaving for Naomi's house before morning light (Ruth 3:7–14).

The next morning, Boaz sat at the city gate where legal matters were argued and resolved. When the "other kinsman" happened by, Boaz told him Naomi was selling land owned by her deceased husband. Did he want to buy it, thus keeping it within the family? The other kinsman said, "Yes!" Then with the land, you also will acquire Ruth as your wife, Boaz said, for the purpose of producing an heir to inherit the land. No, the other kinsman replied, I cannot pay for the land now only to give it up later for free. And so Boaz paid Naomi for the land and took Ruth as his wife (Ruth 4:1–13).

Ruth bore a son and Naomi "took the child and laid him on her bosom and became his nurse." The village women named the child Obed and said: "A son has been born to Naomi" and "he shall be to you a restorer of life and a nourisher of your old age." The text ends by telling us that Obed became the grandfather of King David (Ruth 4:13–22).

Ruth recedes in the final verses as Naomi's contentment and security take center stage. Yet Ruth is praised by village women for her loving kindness that brought about such a satisfying result. The Hebrew word for this loving kindness is *chesed;* it is frequently used in the First Testament to describe YHWH. Thus, the text amends the *Torah* by using a foreign woman whose loyalty to Naomi made her willing to break the rules and take great risks to tell us who YHWH is and how we are to live.

Jonah

The concern in this short story is again foreigners, but the context is not the local community as it was in **Ruth**. Instead, this text grapples with a theological issue that emerged with the maturity of Jewish monotheism after the exile to Babylon. If YHWH is also the god of our enemies, then what happens to justice?

Assyria, a violent oppressor of Ephraim and Judah and the source of unspeakable horrors in their conduct of war, serves as the foil for this intense reflection. Its capital city, Nineveh, provides a context for the story to unfold. Jonah, a long-dead prophet from the reign of Jeroboam II of Ephraim, personifies the lead character, which is the extended community of Israel. Jonah's adventures, his attempts to be faithful and his arguments with YHWH reflect the experiences of that broader community.

YHWH told Jonah to go to Nineveh and "cry out against it" because of its wickedness (Jonah 1:2). That sounded like a death sentence to Jonah and so he fled "the presence of [YHWH]" via a ship on the open sea, a place of disorder and chaos. There a storm struck and threatened to break up the ship. While all of the other passengers prayed to their gods, Jonah remained asleep. When he awoke, he did not join the praying and seemed fully resigned to his fate: "Pick me up and throw me into the sea, then the sea will quiet down for you. For I know it is because of me that this great storm has come upon you" (Jonah 1:12). Reluctantly, the sailors did as Jonah had suggested.

Deep beneath the waters, "out of the belly of Sheol," Jonah cried to YHWH for help. To his surprise, YHWH heard his prayer, even in such a god-forsaken place. The analogy is clear; Jonah's descent into the watery depths represented the exile where far from Jerusalem and the temple, the Jews unexpectedly experienced YHWH's presence. Thus, the fish that had swallowed Jonah spit him up on dry land (Jonah 2:10).

YHWH promptly told Jonah again to go to Nineveh "and proclaim to it the message that I tell you." The message was a bit different than what had been first implied: "Forty days more and Nineveh shall be overthrown" (Jonah 3:2–4). The word translated as "overthrown" can also be translated as "transformed;" thus, the text injects an element of ambiguity into what is about to occur. But the people of Nineveh apparently found Jonah's message convincing and so they repented, turning "from their evil ways and from the violence that is in their hands. Who knows? God may relent and change his mind; he may turn from his fierce anger so that we do not perish" (Jonah 3:8–9).

Indeed, after Nineveh was thus transformed by its own repentance, YHWH did change plans (Jonah 3:10) and the city was saved. Notice, however, that nothing is said about how the Assyrians would take responsibility for all the harm they had done to Ephraim and Judah through slaughter, pillaging, economic exploitation and forced deportations.

This was what Jonah had feared: a merciful response from YHWH to a pagan empire whose violence was legendary. "For I knew that you are a gracious God and merciful, slow to anger and abounding in steadfast love [chesed] and ready to relent from punishing" (Jonah 4:2). Justice had been denied, Jonah had played an integral part in this denial and YHWH was behind it all. In despair, Jonah asked YHWH to end his life (Jonah 4:3). He did not want to live in a world without justice, without judgment of the wicked.

The final scene is a flashback and takes us outside the city where Jonah had watched and waited for Nineveh's destruction. There Jonah had been upset by the withering of a plant providing him with shelter from the sun. In response, YHWH had compared Jonah's compassion for the plant with his lack of compassion for the people of Nineveh. "Should I not be concerned about Nineveh, that great city, in which there are more than a 120,000 persons who do not know their right hand from their left, and also many animals" (Jonah 4:11)?

It was a rhetorical question; of course, the people of Nineveh were more important than a bush. And yet Jonah's question remains. If the loving kindness of YHWH is available to all, then are we not left in a world without justice? A world in which murderous empires are no longer held accountable even by YHWH? How can we live in such a world?

This seems like more than enough to ponder, but this provocative text asks yet more of us. Just as YHWH had saved Jonah so he could preach in Nineveh, YHWH had saved Israel from certain extinction in Babylon to bring salvation to the nations, including its enemies. Thus this text also stands as a rebuke of the leadership of Ezra, who turned the riches of YHWH's mercy and the Law of Moses into the private possession of the elite.

Joel

Our text begins with a description of an invasion by locusts and a lament over all that had been lost as a result. The agricultural destruction was sobering and the author interpreted the disaster as an act of YHWH. Joel called for repentance:

> Yet even now, says [YHWH], return to me with all your heart, with fasting, with weeping and with mourning; rend your hearts and not your clothing. Return to [YHWH], your God, for he is gracious and merciful, slow to anger and abounding in steadfast love, and relents from punishing. Who knows whether he will not turn and relent? (Joel 2:12–14)

With this echo of **Jonah,** the text goes on to describe a kind of deliverance: the locusts left, an early rain blessed the Earth, the fig tree and the vine again gave their full yield (Joel 2:18–27).

Then Joel spoke of a future time when the prophetic gift of speaking YHWH's word would be available to all. He quoted YHWH: "Afterward, I will pour out my spirit on *all flesh*; your sons and your daughters shall prophesy, your old men shall dream dreams, and your young men shall see visions. Even on the male and female slaves in those days, I will pour out my spirit" (Joel 2:28–29, emphasis added).

Joel associated this outpouring of YHWH's prophetic spirit with a massive change YHWH would bring to pass. To communicate the magnitude of what was coming, Joel used apocalyptic language: "I will show portents in the heavens and on the earth, blood and fire and columns of smoke. The sun shall be turned to darkness and the moon to blood, before the great and terrible day of [YHWH] comes. Then everyone who calls on the name of [YHWH] shall be saved" (Joel 2:30–32).

Generally, the apocalyptic literary style relies on vivid and often extravagant images to describe "the day of [YHWH]" a great reversal at the end of history when the grip of empire would be broken and YHWH's justice and peace prevail. This style of writing became important within the Jewish community during the 150 years of Greek imperial control that began in 334 BCE. Its details were not meant to be taken literally. Thus, the text's reference to the moon turning to blood was a way to signal deep and far-reaching changes in how the world operates. Slave girls speaking the word of YHWH into current events? That would be earth-shaking.

Significantly, Joel saw no king in Israel's future, only YHWH leading the way.

> [YHWH] roars from Zion, and utters his voice from Jerusalem, and the heavens and the earth shake. But [YHWH] is a refuge for his people, a stronghold for the people of Israel . . . In that day, the mountains shall drip sweet wine, the hills shall flow with milk and all the stream beds of Judah will flow with water" [Joel 3:16, 18].

The narrow and exclusive political community established by Ezra and Nehemiah remained the template for Jewish life through the time of

Jesus and until the destruction of the second temple in 70 BCE.   Thus, though Joel wrote a century after Ezra and Nehemiah, his critique of their approach remained relevant.   And if Joel was right—if YHWH intended to pour out his spirit on all flesh—then a community defined by priestly definitions of purity would have no legitimacy and could not endure.

Zechariah 9–14

Chapters 9–11 of this text describe two important events the author sees in the future of the Jewish community.   The first is a different kind of king, "triumphant and victorious, humble and riding on a donkey, on a colt, the foal of a donkey."   This king will "command peace to the nations," but not by war-making; use of chariots, war horses and battle bows will be ended (Zech. 9:9–10).   The second is that YHWH will reverse the Jewish diaspora. "I will bring them to the land of Gilead and to Lebanon until there is no room for them" (Zech. 10:10).

The other emphasis in these chapters is disappointment with Jewish leadership.   The text refers twice to the failures of "the shepherds" to serve the people.   Chapter 11 appears to describe specific economic exploitation by those leaders.   While there is no reference to the collaboration between these "shepherds" and Persian or Greek imperial overlords, we should not forget that collaboration with empire was an important part of the Jewish political model throughout the era from King Cyrus until the destruction of the second temple in 70 CE.

In chapters 12–14, the phrase "on that day" appears sixteen times, indicating we are reading a text that looks ahead to YHWH's victory at the end of time. The images of the final battle between YHWH and the enemies of "Jerusalem" are apocalyptic; thus, the Mount of Olives is split in two from east to west in the course of the final battle, which ends with YHWH "king over all the earth" (Zech. 14:2–9).

Oddly, the vision of *shalom* at the end of the text seems to hark back to the mistaken notion that proper worship of YHWH can occur only in Jerusalem.   Thus, it states that everyone who survives the final great battle "shall go up year-after-year to worship the King, the Lord of hosts, and to keep the festival of booths."   All who fail to "go up to Jerusalem" will be punished (Zech. 14:16–19).   Perhaps the reference to Jerusalem is metaphorical and means only that the nations will turn humbly to YHWH for understanding (see page 190 and **Isaiah** 60—61). But it also could be understood as nostalgia, a looking-back-to-Sodom, and a failure to grasp the unboundedness of YHWH's mercy in setting the world right.

We noted a similar tension when discussing **3ʳᵈ Isaiah.** We will meet it again later (pages 260-261) in the debate over what Gentile Jesus-followers must do to become full members of the community of YHWH.

Daniel 7–12

An unknown author wrote this apocalyptic text during a time of great crisis for the Jews in and around Jerusalem living under the rule of the Greek Empire. Around 200 BCE, the Seleucid branch of the empire wrested control of the area east of the Mediterranean from the Ptolemy branch. Beginning around 175 BCE, it became the policy of the Seleucids to replace the worship of YHWH with the worship of Greek gods. Imperial officials appointed the high priest, installed a statue of Zeus in the temple, sacrificed pigs on the altar, and outlawed the observance of the Sabbath, the practice of circumcision and the refusal to eat pork.

Many Jews welcomed Hellenization and collaborated with imperial policy. In 167 BCE, one such Hellenized priest ordered a rural priest, Mattathias, to conduct a Hellenistic sacrifice on the temple altar. Mattathias resisted violently and sparked an armed rebellion known as the Maccabean Revolt (167–160 BCE). **Daniel** was written during this era. The author used the stories of how Daniel and his three companions resisted the Babylonian and Persian empires (see page 157) to inspire those who resisted Greek repression. As stated by James Douglass, these writings served as "a primer of Jewish resistance." [25]

Chapter 7 begins with a vision of four terrible beasts representing four empires: Neo-Babylonian (including the Medes), Persian (again including the Medes), Greek and Roman. (Some start the list of four with Assyria and end it with Greece, in part because Rome was a mighty nation but not yet an empire at the time the author wrote this text.) In the vision, the author sees YHWH, "the Ancient of Days" on a courtroom throne

---

[25]   Douglass, *The Nonviolent Coming of God*, 51.

surrounded by flames. "Books were opened," judgment rendered and the last beast "was put to death, and its body destroyed and given over to be burned with fire" (Dan. 7:9–11). Then

> I saw one like a human being coming with the clouds of heaven. He came to the Ancient One and was presented before him. To him was given dominion and glory and kingship, that all peoples, nations and languages should serve him. His dominion is an everlasting dominion that shall never pass away, and his kingship is one that shall never be destroyed. (Dan. 7:13–14)

An angel interpreted the vision, changing the singular "human being" to the plural "holy ones of the Most High" (Dan. 7:18). A few verses later, the text tells us the fourth empire made war against "the holy ones" (Dan. 7:21–22). A summary ends the chapter: "The kingship and dominion and the greatness of the kingdoms under the whole heaven shall be given to *the people of the holy ones* of the Most High; their kingdom shall be an everlasting kingdom and all dominions shall serve and obey them" (Dan. 7:27, emphasis added). This is reminiscent of the political vision described in Dan. 2:44–45 (see page 159).

Douglass emphasizes the "collective meaning" of the "human being" ("Son of Man" in the words of Jesus). And he provides perspective:

> Being given the kingdom of God does not mean . . . that either the book of **Daniel** or the vision of Jesus is beyond history. In Daniel's vision the coming of the human being is not the end of the world. It is the symbolic representation of a new world or a new time, beyond the overwhelming persecution [by empire]. The power of God will respond to the patience of the saints by giving them such a new world, the kingdom of God. [26]

The "holy ones" are portrayed in the vision as recipients of the empire's violence, not as perpetrators of violence. Moreover, they receive the kingdom, they do not take it.

---

[26]   Ibid., 52.

More than any other, this text shaped the worldview of Jesus and his followers. They claimed that through YHWH's deliverance, the power of empire had been broken and an eternal kingdom given to "the holy ones of the Most High." This fifth and final kingdom (Jesus called it "the kingdom of God") was not bestial, ruling by violence; instead, it was humane, ruling through the power of righteous living and justice. Thus the healing of Earth and its residents could begin.

The author of our text described a second vision about conflict between two named empires, Media-Persia and Greece (Dan. 8:20–21), that had already occurred. But the vision went on to include a description of a future, post-Greek empire led by "a king of bold countenance." "By his cunning he shall make deceit prosper under his hand . . . but he shall be broken, and not by human hands" (Dan. 8:23–25).

The text follows with a communal prayer of confession for failing to keep YHWH's commands and listen to the prophets (Dan. 9:6). It is followed by a lengthening of the period of Israel's exile by a factor of seven, from seventy to 490 years (Dan. 9:22–24). Howard-Brook points out that through this revision, "the entire Second Temple period is revealed to be the time of YHWH's punishment."[27]

Chapters 10 and 11 concern the wars between Greek dynasties for control of the region around Jerusalem. The Seleucid king responsible for the worst atrocities against the Jews (Antiochus IV Epiphanes) is described in detail (Dan. 11:21–32). Again, this is history recounted.

The final chapter looks ahead to a time after empire's power has ended. *There is no mention of Jerusalem, a king, a temple or the land.* Instead, the text speaks vaguely of the deliverance of those "found written in the book" and that "many of those who sleep in the dust of the earth shall awake, some to everlasting life and some to shame and everlasting contempt" (Dan. 12:1–2). This is the only reference to "everlasting life" in the First Testament. The text's narrator asks for more details and the reply is noteworthy: "Go your way, Daniel, for [that] is to remain secret until the time of the end. Many shall be purified, cleansed and refined, but the wicked shall continue to act wickedly. None of the wicked shall

---

[27]   Howard-Brook, 353.

understand, but those who are wise shall understand . . . Happy are those who persevere" (Dan. 12:9–12).

The struggle with evil will continue, in other words, right until the end. "But you, go your way and rest; you shall rise for your award at the end of days" (Dan. 12:13).

Reflection and Discussion

16. The god we met in **Genesis** and **Leviticus** reflected the experience and faith of Jews who had been transplanted through exile in Babylon and Persia. It was a god who subverted empire and called people to an alternative way of living. What do **Ezekiel, 2nd Isaiah** and **Daniel** add to the description of this god?

17. The imperial philosophy of Persia included space for conquered peoples to maintain distinct cultural identities so long as they did not try to become autonomous. Through collaboration between the returnees and the empire, this all played out according to plan. What is your assessment of the results?

18. What was most to blame for the narrow vision of Ezra and Nehemiah? The old legends of YHWH endorsing ethnic cleansing? An attitude of entitlement by the elite? The divide-and-conquer tactics of the Persian Empire? Reflect on current examples of these dynamics in our time.

19. "Purity" is a way societies sort out who deserves to enjoy social benefits and to what degree. It operates effectively in many different guises (e.g., religion, ethnicity, culture, pedigree, class). Empires work very effectively to exploit this social reality and thus further fragment and divide people whose oppression by the empire is shared. Where do you see this dynamic at work today?

20. Chapters 61 and 65 of **3rd Isaiah** reflect the highest aspirations of the First Testament writers for political community. What aspects of that vision do you claim for yourself? What is still missing?

17. Living Wisely (Part A)
Ecclesiastes, Job, Song of Solomon, Proverbs

Life is more than political community, more than creating an alternative to the empire's way. Life is also love and loss, success and disappointment and a variety of human relationships. In this chapter and the next, we survey texts that view life through a less political lens.

We will start with **Ecclesiastes**, a text skeptical of visions, strategies and explanations. Its unknown authors likely wrote in the fourth century BCE, early in the era of Greek imperial control.

The text of **Job** describes a righteous man's attempt to make sense of a life suddenly filled with suffering. It was likely written midway through the sixth century BCE, shortly after **Ezekiel,** in reaction to the destruction of Jerusalem and conquest of Judah. The author is unknown.

For those who say we have spoken far too little about love—especially the erotic kind—**Song of Solomon** is the perfect remedy. Its author is unknown; because the text was written early in the fourth century BCE, we know it was not the King Solomon, who died centuries before.

The text of **Proverbs** collects the distilled practical wisdom of the Israelite people over a period of 500 years. The earliest portion dates from the time of Hezekiah (eighth century BCE) and the latest during the early years of Greek rule (fourth century BCE). As a text, it served to build within young men from upper-class Jewish families the character needed for success in leading roles in the community. As a collection of folk wisdom, it focuses on shrewd perception as much as good behavior. Thus, it values not being a fool as much as avoiding immorality.

Ecclesiastes

Generations come and go, but life remains the same; "there is nothing new under the sun" (Eccl. 1:4–9). This is the perspective of the so-called "Teacher" who narrated this text (Eccl. 1:1).

Not only is life going nowhere, "it is an unhappy business that God has given to human beings to be busy with . . . all is vanity and a chasing after wind" (Eccl. 1:13–14). One may imagine this reality can be overcome through the acquisition of wisdom, but that too is "but a chasing after wind. For in much wisdom is much vexation and those who increase knowledge increase sorrow" (Eccl. 1:17–18). Life is not for us to change, in other words. (See question 22 on page 216 for discussion of this view.)

Sensual pleasure, great accomplishments, power, wealth and renown, these too are "vanity and a chasing after the wind" (Eccl. 2:1–11). True, the wise seem more adept at navigating life than the foolish; "yet . . . the same fate befalls all of them. 'What happens to the fool will happen to me also; why then have I been so very wise?'" With time, neither wise nor foolish are remembered; in the days to come "all will have been long forgotten" (Eccl. 2:14–16).

Yes, the writer wanted to believe YHWH would "judge the righteous and the wicked," that YHWH was testing humans to show they were something special. But "the fate of humans and the fate of animals is the same; as one dies, so dies the other. They all have the same breath, and humans have no advantage over animals, for all is vanity. All go to one place; all are from the dust, and all turn to dust again" (Eccl. 3:17–20).

When the Teacher considered economic and political oppression, he "thought the dead, who have already died, more fortunate than the living . . . but better than both is the one who has not yet been, and has not seen the evil deeds that are done under the sun" (Eccl. 4:1–3).

Be careful what you promise YHWH, the Teacher said; "let your words be few . . . [and] when you make a vow to God, do not delay fulfilling it, for he has no pleasure in fools." Similarly, be careful not to dream big "for dreams come with many cares." Accept your lot in life and enjoy your work; "this is the gift of God" (Eccl. 5:1–20).

The Teacher did not believe YHWH blessed obedience and cursed disobedience. "In my vain life I have seen everything; there are righteous people who perish in their righteousness and there are wicked people who prolong their life in their evildoing." Nor did he sense YHWH's call to become part of a political community dedicated to justice. Rather, he urged readers to hedge their bets.

> Do not be too righteous, and do not act too wise; why should you
> destroy yourself? Do not be too wicked, and do not be a fool; why

Buddism – this is called middle way
Native Americas – call "Red Road" or middle way
Indian

should you die before your time? It is good that you should take hold of the one without letting go of the other; for the one who fears God will succeed with both. (Eccl. 7:15–18)

Though the Teacher despaired of making something of life, he offered advice for living.

> Go, eat your bread with enjoyment and drink your wine with a merry heart; for God has long ago approved what you do. Let your garments always be white; do not let oil be lacking on your head. Enjoy life with the wife whom you love, all the days of your vain life that are given you under the sun . . . the race is not to the swift, nor the battle to the strong, nor bread to the wise, nor riches to the intelligent, nor favor to the skillful; but time and chance happen to them all. For no one can anticipate disaster. Like fish taken in a cruel net, and like birds caught in a snare, so mortals are snared at a time of calamity. (Eccl. 9:7–12)

Thus, the Teacher was not a nihilist; he made distinctions and identified better alternatives. "A living dog is better than a dead lion" (Eccl. 9:4). "Two are better than one . . . for if they fall, one will lift up the other . . . and though one might prevail against another, two will withstand one" (Eccl. 4:9–12). So he encouraged his readers to make the best of it; "send out your bread upon the waters" (Eccl. 11:1). And "remember your creator in the days of your youth, before the days of trouble come [when] the silver cord is snapped and the golden bowl is broken . . . and the dust returns to the earth as it was" (Eccl. 12:1–7).

Job

According to the Sinai covenant, obedience to YHWH brought blessings and disobedience brought curses. In most First Testament texts, this understanding of divine justice persists. But the text of **Job** suggests life is more complicated than this. Set as the story of one wealthy and respected man clobbered by life, the text focuses on the "injustice" of suffering when it is inexplicably borne by the righteous.

The author created space for a discussion of divine injustice by an imaginative stage-setter. The heavenly beings (including Satan, the accuser) assembled before YHWH and reported their activities. YHWH bragged about the "blameless and upright" life of Job, a man "who fears God and turns away from evil." Satan challenged Job's sincerity; stop protecting him, Satan said to YHWH, "and he will curse you to your face." YHWH said, "Very well, all that he has is in your power" (Job 1:6–12).

With the withdrawal of YHWH's protection, disaster followed quickly. Job's livestock was stolen, his servants murdered, his sons and daughters killed in a storm, and Job laid low by "loathsome sores from the sole of his foot to the crown of his head" (Job 1:13–2:7).

Job's response illustrates how a righteous but self-absorbed man struggles with YHWH to make sense of his plight. In the end, "YHWH gave Job twice as much as he had before" (Job 42:10). Thus, the author leaves the blessings–and–curses paradigm intact, but deepens its meaning through the extended dialogue. Along the way, the reader receives the opportunity to consider the reality of undeserved suffering, whether experienced individually or collectively as the first audience had through the Babylonian Empire's conquest of Judah and razing of Jerusalem.

Chapters 4–27 are structured around Job's conversations with three friends who came to comfort, counsel and challenge him to identify the reason for his suffering. Chapters 29–31 are a summation of Job's defense against the accusation that his suffering was somehow deserved. Chapters 32–37 record the insights of a younger man who also visited Job. YHWH gives the final speech (chapters 38–41). The final chapter reports Job's humble confession, confirms that Job's three friends had it all wrong and reports details of Job's restoration.

Job began the poetic conversation by cursing the day of his birth: "Let the day perish in which I was born" (Job 3:3). He longed for death and asked why life was given to those "bitter in soul" who "dig for [death] more than for hidden treasure" (Job 3:20–21).

Job's three friends made a variety of arguments over the course of their many speeches. They called into question Job's righteousness, saying his public reputation had masked private and hidden sin. They insisted no mortal could claim to be righteous before YHWH, no matter how uprightly he had lived, and that Job's inability to see this was sin in itself. They accused him of specific wrong-doing. Again and again, they referred to the blessings–and–curses paradigm. And they criticized Job for the candor of his complaints, the startling honesty of his prayers, and his impertinence before YHWH.

While begging YHWH to end his life (Job 6:8–13) and "let me alone" (Job 7:16), Job found the strength to resist his friends' pious counsel. Of course, he said, no mortal is "just before God" (Job 9:2). But does that justify my suffering? "For [YHWH] crushes me with a tempest, and multiplies my wounds without cause; he will not let me get my breath, but fills me with bitterness. If it is a contest of strength, he is the strong one" (Job 9:17–19).

He dismissed his friends' insistence that life is fair: "The tents of the robbers are at peace and those who provoke God are secure" (12:6). At times he seemed to waver, as in these words of anguished prayer: "Make me know my transgression and my sin. Why do you hide your face and count me as your enemy" (Job 13:23–24)? Yet, after self-examination and reflection, he found no sin meriting such suffering: "I hold fast my righteousness, and will not let it go; my heart does not reproach me for any of my days" (Job 27:6). The text tells us that Job examined himself by reference to a long list of sins. Which is it? he asked. "Oh, that I had the indictment written by my adversary" (Job 31:35).

At times, Job spoke words of praise: "I know that my redeemer lives, and that at the last he will stand upon the earth . . . then in my flesh I shall see God" (Job 19:25–26). But generally, he focused on how badly his life had turned out.

Elihu, the younger man, begins speaking in chapter 32. He refused to let Job's complaints frame the conversation. "You say, 'I am clean, without transgression; I am pure, and there is no iniquity in me'" (Job 33:9). That may be true, but so what? Most people experience suffering; some recover and rejoice over the mercy YHWH has shown while others go down to the pit (Job 33:14–30). Why is it so important to explain why Job suffers? How did *that* become the core question? Trying to sort out why one suffers and another does not is futile. The fact of the matter is that all depends on YHWH. "If he should take back his spirit to himself, and gather to himself his breath, all flesh would perish together and all mortals return to dust" (Job 34:14–15).

Next Elihu spoke about justice, something we all say we value. Yet think of the powerful people—kings, princes, nobles, the rich—and how rare it is for any mortal to stand up to them. We stand idly by watching their cruelty and hearing the cry of the poor. It is YHWH who "shatters the mighty without investigation and sets others in their place . . . he overturns them in the night and they are crushed" (Job 34:24). It is YHWH who is just, not us.

And so Elihu sharply criticized Job, who had made his own experience the measure of all things. By such an attitude, Job "adds rebellion to his sin; he claps his hands among us and multiples his words against God" (Job 34:35–37). Besides, what exactly had Job lost by living righteously? How would he have been better off if he had lived a life of sin? His righteousness had been its own reward (Job 35:1–8).

Elihu added one other thought: YHWH "delivers the afflicted by their affliction and opens their ear by adversity." In other words, there is much to be learned during times of suffering, including empathy for the suffering of others (see chapter 24 for the suffering of the poor). But if preoccupied by the unfairness of it all, then concerns of "judgment and justice [will] seize you." So beware; do not let affliction turn you to iniquity (Job 36:15–23).

Finally, we hear the voice of YHWH, who did not mention justice or suffering but *changed the subject* by asking questions that elicited images of nature. "Who shut the sea with doors when it burst out from the womb" (Job 38:8)? "What is the way to the place where the light is distributed" (Job 38:24)? "Is it by your wisdom that the hawk soars and spreads its wing toward the south" (Job 39:26)? "Can you thunder with a voice like [YHWH's]" (Job 40:9)? "Will [the Leviathan] make a covenant with you to be taken as your servant forever" (Job 41:4)?

Job, sitting quietly in dust and ashes, replied: "I have uttered what I did not understand, things too wonderful for me, which I did not know . . . I had heard of you by the hearing of the ear, but now my eye sees you; therefore, I despise myself and repent" (Job 42:3–6). YHWH's last words

Mary Oliver "poem goes to sea, waves back +

upbraided Job's three friends "for you have not spoken of me what is right, *as my servant Job has*" (Job 42:7, emphasis added).

Through the voice of Elihu, **Job** clearly asks us to repent of our preoccupation with ourselves and the injustice we have experienced. Often, this teaching is paired with advice to focus instead on YHWH: "Truly, the fear of [YHWH], that is wisdom; and to depart from evil is understanding" (Job 28:28). Yet YHWH's surprising speech is about the astonishing variety and vitality of creation, all of it loved and cherished by the Creator. Is it telling us that when we reconnect with the wildness and wonder of nature, we, like Job, will find our way to healing? Question 23 on page 216 encourages further discussion of Job's relevance to our time.

Song of Solomon

This short book is distinctive among biblical texts: it never refers to YHWH, the covenant, the Law of Moses or the priests of the temple. It never refers to politics. It is all about love.

The poetry consists of the love-talk between a young woman and a young man caught up in the passionate feelings of sexual desire. Whether their desires have been consummated remains their secret, but the explicitness of their erotic allusions makes us pretty sure they have. Listening in and observing their comings and goings are the female friends of the woman; these friends provide a literary vantage point that explains how it is that we are privy to such intimate exchanges. They also are the audience for the woman's repeated warnings throughout the text: "Do not stir up or awaken love until it is ready" (Song. 2:7, 3:5, 8:4).

Song of Solomon can be read as fantasy; thus, the woman lies on her bed at night, thinking of her lover, imagining herself seeking him out during the night in the city, and then bringing him to her bed: "I held him, and would not let go until I brought him into my mother's house, and into the chamber of her that conceived me" (Song. 3:1–5). She dreams of him arriving on their wedding day with strong and vigorous friends at his side. He is handsome, crowned with "the gladness of his heart" (Song. 3:11).

He delights in the beauty of her body, its smell and taste. "Your lips distill nectar, my bride; honey and milk are under your tongue; the scent of your garments is like the scent of Lebanon. A garden locked is my

. . . bride, a garden locked, a fountain sealed. Your channel is an orchard of pomegranates with all choicest fruit . . . a garden fountain, a well of living water." She replies, "Awake, O north wind, and come, O south wind! Blow upon my garden that its fragrance may be wafted abroad. Let my beloved come to his garden and eat its choicest fruits" (Song. 4:11–16). Whew!

The poetry is lovely. "I am my beloved's and his desire is for me. Come, my beloved, let us go forth into the fields, and lodge in the villages; let us go out early to the vineyards, and see whether the vines have budded, whether the grape blossoms have opened and the pomegranates are in bloom. There I will give you my love" (Song. 7:10–12).

The last chapter includes a stirring stanza about the power of sexual desire:

> Set me as a seal upon your heart, as a seal upon your arm; for love is strong as death, passion as fierce as the grave. Its flashes are the flashes of fire, a raging flame. Many waters cannot quench love, neither can floods drown it. If one offered for love all the wealth of his house, it would be utterly scorned. (Song. 8:6–7)

Proverbs *for upper class Jewish boys in "prep" schools*

The beginning of wisdom is to want it. It starts with humility and the awareness we lack something important. This thought is sometimes expressed religiously: "The fear of [YHWH] is the beginning of knowledge" (Prov. 1:7); "trust in [YHWH] with all your heart, and do not rely on your own insight" (Prov. 3:5). It also is expressed in more secular tones: "The beginning of wisdom is this: get wisdom, and whatever else you get, get insight. Prize her highly, and she will exalt you" (Prov. 3:7–8).

When this humility and desire for wisdom are in place, we are ready to listen to "our father's instruction" and "our mother's teaching" (Prov. 1:8). Moreover, we will find wisdom many places, not only in authority figures. "Wisdom cries out in the street; in the squares she raises her voice. At the busiest corner she cries out; at the entrance of the city gates she speaks" (Prov. 1:20–21). In other words, be alert and be a lifelong learner; there is insight to be gained nearly everywhere. It is "the complacency of fools [that] destroys them" (Prov. 1:32).

Wisdom is different than following the rules and being "good." Wisdom has practical value in life. "She is more precious than jewels" (Prov. 3:15) and adds solid security to one's routines (Prov. 3:21–26); those who miss out on wisdom "injure themselves" (Prov. 8:36). The "path of the wicked" may appear attractive, but "is like a deep darkness; they do not know what they stumble over" (Prov. 4:19). So avoid bad company (Prov. 1:10–19), laziness (Prov. 6:6–11) and adultery with a neighbor's wife (Prov. 6:23–7:27). The warning against adultery illustrates the difference between wisdom and moralism: "a prostitute's fee is only a loaf of bread, but the wife of another stalks a man's life" (Prov. 6:26).

Wisdom is a part of creation; she has been there from the start.

> [YHWH] created me at the beginning of his work, the first of his acts of long ago . . . before the hills I was brought forth, when he had not yet made earth and fields . . . I was daily beside him, like a master worker, and I was daily his delight, rejoicing before him always, rejoicing in his inhabited world and delighting in the human race. (Prov. 8:22–31)

Thus, "whoever finds [wisdom] finds life and obtains favor with [YHWH]" (Prov. 8:35).

Chapter 10 begins the second section. Here, the proverbs tumble out one after the other without obvious connection and without the discussion found in the first section. "A false balance is an abomination to [YHWH] but an accurate weight is his delight. When pride comes, then comes disgrace; but wisdom is with the humble. The integrity of the upright guides them, but the crookedness of the treacherous destroys them" (Prov. 11:1–3).

As compared to the disillusionment of **Ecclesiastes** and the candor of **Job**, **Proverbs** can seem utterly conventional and even Pollyannaish. "No harm happens to the righteous, but the wicked are filled with trouble," it tells us (Prov. 12:21). Really?

Yet there is realism in the way other proverbs describe the nuances of social relationships. "Rash words are like sword thrusts, but the tongue of the wise brings healing" (Prov. 12:18). "By insolence the heedless make strife, but wisdom is with those who take advice" (Prov. 13:10). "A soft answer turns away wrath, but a harsh word stirs up anger" (Prov. 15:1). "Some friends play at friendship but a true friend sticks closer than one's nearest kin" (Prov. 18:24).

Emotional health is addressed. "Anxiety weighs down the human heart, but a good word cheers it up" (Prov. 12:25). "A tranquil mind gives life to the flesh, but passion makes the bones rot" (Prov. 14:30). "A glad heart makes a cheerful countenance, but by sorrow of heart the spirit is broken" (Prov. 15:13).

Family life is a recurrent topic. "Better is a dry morsel with quiet than a house full of feasting with strife" (Prov. 17:1). "A friend loves at all times, and kinsfolk are born to share adversity" (Prov. 17:17). "Discipline your children while there is hope; do not set your heart on their destruction" (Prov. 19:18). "It is better to live in a corner of the housetop than in a house shared with a contentious wife" (Prov. 21:9).

We also see consistent attention to people who are poor. "The field of the poor may yield much food, but it is swept away through injustice" (Prov. 13:23). "Those who oppress the poor insult their Maker, but those who are kind to the needy honor him" (Prov. 14:31). "Whoever is kind to the poor lends to [YHWH], and will be repaid in full" (Prov. 19:17). "Those who are generous are blessed, for they share their bread with the poor" (Prov. 22:9). "Oppressing the poor in order to enrich oneself and giving to the rich will lead only to loss" (Prov. 22:16).

Even the experience of the empire is briefly addressed. "The fear of [YHWH] is life indeed; filled with it one rests secure" (Prov. 19:23). Ponder that next time the media mounts a campaign to make us feel very afraid and very needful of the empire's violent means of protection.

The third section, starting with the seventeenth verse of chapter 22, also covers many topics, but envy is recurring. "Do not desire the ruler's delicacies, for they are deceptive food. Do not wear yourself out to get rich; be wise enough to desist" (Prov. 23:4). "Do not let your heart envy sinners, but always continue in the fear of [YHWH]" (Prov. 23:17).

"Do not fret because of evildoers. Do not envy the wicked; for the evil have no future; the lamp of the wicked will go out" (Prov. 24:19–20).

The fourth considers legal matters. "Partiality in judging is not good" (Prov. 24:23). "One who gives an honest answer gives a kiss upon the lips" (Prov. 24:26). "Do not be a witness against your neighbor without cause, and do not deceive with your lips" (Prov. 24:28).

Chapter 25 begins the fifth section, which dates from the time of Hezekiah. It advises against going quickly to court; "argue your case with your neighbor directly" (Prov. 25:9). It offers advice about enemies that was repeated later by the Apostle Paul: "If your enemies are hungry, give them bread to eat; and if they are thirsty, give them water to drink; for you will heap coals of fire on their heads, and [YHWH] will reward you" (Prov. 25:21–22). It warns against "boasting about tomorrow, for you do not know what a day may bring" (Prov. 27:1). "Iron sharpens iron," it says, "and one person sharpens the wits of another" (Prov. 27:17). And it expresses pessimism about kings: "Many seek the favor of a ruler, but it is from [YHWH] that one gets justice" (Prov. 29:26).

Two appendices end the book. The words of Agur are well known: "give me neither poverty nor riches; feed me with the food that I need, or I shall be full and deny you, and say, 'Who is [YHWH]?' or I shall be poor and steal, and profane the name of my God" (Prov. 30:8–9).

They are followed by words from Lemuel describing "a capable wife." Her husband trusts her, she runs the household while engaging in commerce and real estate, she is skilled with cloth and textiles, "opens her hand to the poor," teaches wisdom to her children and "laughs at the time to come." This may seem exaggerated and even condescending, yet it is a remarkable ending for a collection of folk wisdom in a patriarchal society: "Give her a share in the fruit of her hands, and let her works praise her in the city gates" (Prov. 31:10–31).

18. Despair, Praise, Exultation
Lamentations, Psalms

We end our review of the First Testament with two texts that express the deep and varied emotions of the Israelite people in life and in worship of their god.

Lamentations

This despairing work of poetry recalls the days during and just after the fall of Jerusalem and its destruction by the Babylonian army. It was written by one who did not go into exile, but stayed behind to make the best of things. The prophet Jeremiah was the likely author. YHWH is mentioned but never speaks, having turned away and fallen silent.

The text consists of five laments. Each of the first and last two are twenty-two verses while the center lament contains sixty-six verses.

Two voices speak as we read: a narrator and the city of Jerusalem (Zion) personified by a woman. "She weeps bitterly in the night . . . among all her lovers she has no one to comfort her; all her friends have dealt treacherously with her and they have become her enemies" (Lam. 1:2). The text hints at shameful behavior: "For they have seen her nakedness; she herself groans and turns her face away. Her uncleanness was in her skirts; she took no thought of the future" (Lam. 1:8–9).

The woman speaks: "O [YHWH], look at my affliction, for the enemy has triumphed." She speaks again a few verses later: "[YHWH] has rejected all my warriors in the midst of me; he proclaimed a time against me to crush my young men; has trodden as in a wine press the virgin daughter, Judah. For these things I weep; my eyes flow with tears . . . my children are desolate, for the enemy has prevailed" (Prov. 1:9, 15–16). Briefly, she voices repentance: "[YHWH] is in the right, for I have rebelled against his word . . . I have been very rebellious" (Lam. 1:18, 20).

The narrator voices the unspeakable: YHWH has fought with the Babylonians against Israel. "[YHWH] has become like an enemy; he has destroyed Israel" (Lam. 2:5). Dreadful events of the eighteen-month siege are recalled: starving children, cannibalism, rape and slaughter. "Look, O

[YHWH], and consider! To whom have you done this? Should women eat their offspring, the children they have borne" (Lam. 2:20)?

The woman's voice returns in the third chapter, describing the struggle to survive. She speaks of being pursued and surrounded, fearing the "bear lying in wait for me, a lion in hiding" and being torn to pieces (Lam. 3:7–10). The text attributes all of this to YHWH.

A kind of trust—or is it resignation—remains. In a passage that seems to blend the two voices, we read: "The steadfast love of [YHWH] never ceases, his mercies never come to an end; they are new every morning; great is your faithfulness. '[YHWH] is my portion,' says my soul, 'therefore I will hope in him.'" (Lam. 3:22–24).

The final chapters return to lament. "The tongue of the infant sticks to the roof of its mouth for thirst; the children beg for food but no one gives them anything" (Lam. 4:4). "Why have you forgotten us completely? Why have you forsaken us these many days" (Lam. 5:20)? The text ends with a plea: "Restore us to yourself, O [YHWH], that we may be restored; renew our days as of old unless you have utterly rejected us, and are angry with us beyond measure" (Lam. 5:22).

Psalms

It is helpful to think of the **Psalms** as a hymn book: a collection of favorite songs used in public worship. Each song stands by itself and offers its unique nuances and emphases. Together, the collection stands as a poetic record of the community's life together: its history, its way of speaking about and to YHWH, its heart-felt emotions and its way of integrating those emotions into expressions of faith.

Through regular use, the collection also serves as a catechism, teaching all who join the singing and praying how to reflect on life's experiences and YHWH's presence. To sing them, to pray them is to learn how to speak to YHWH. Much practice over time forms the spirituality of the Jewish faith and its way of engaging life and seeing the world.

Praise and thanksgiving to YHWH are the primary foci of worship and not surprisingly, nearly all psalms reflect these elements. "O magnify [YHWH] with me and let us exalt his name together. I sought [YHWH] and he answered me, and delivered me from all my fears. Look to him and be radiant; so your faces shall never be ashamed" (Ps. 34:3–4).

The psalms are poetic speech. A very common stylistic feature is the addressing of ideas twice consecutively in a parallel fashion, either through synonyms or opposites. Some psalms use an acrostic style by which each line starts with a succeeding letter of the Hebrew alphabet. This pattern is lost in the English text, but accounts for some of the abrupt jumps in imagery and progressions of thought.

Five groups of psalms are presented in the text. Each was assembled over time and used as a unit. Over a period spanning at least 500 years, units were added until the number reached the existing five. It is often assumed the first book was assembled and used in temple worship first while the last book was assembled and used last. But that should not be taken to mean that all psalms within a book fit that pattern, no more than we should assume that a recently published hymn book includes only recently written songs.

The psalms of the first book (1–41) include many that are favored by those who use **Psalms** as a prayer book. Psalm 16 speaks of trust and security, Psalm 22 of deep suffering and Psalm 23 of YHWH's merciful kindness. Psalms 25 and 27 exude confidence in YHWH's guidance through life. Psalms 32 and 38 seek YHWH's forgiveness for sin and Psalms 34 and 40 exult in YHWH's deliverance.

The psalms of the second book (42–72) include other prayer favorites: Psalms 42 and 43 speak to discouragement and depression and Psalm 51 is a beautiful confession and prayer for pardon and restoration. But prayers of petition dominate this section: for judgment on the wicked (53); for personal vindication (54); for vengeance (58); for deliverance from enemies (59, 64, 69 and 70); for national victory (60); and for lifelong protection (70).

Psalms of lament related to the destruction of Jerusalem and exile to Babylon are found primarily in the third book of psalms (73–89). These include recollections of Israel's history and confessions of unfaithfulness to YHWH (77 and 78), a passionate plea for help (79) and a cry of utter despair: "I am counted among those who go down to the Pit . . . like those whom you remember no more" (Ps. 88:4–5). The last psalm in this section recalls the promise claimed by David that his throne had been established by YHWH forever. "But now you have spurned and rejected [David]; you are full of wrath against your anointed . . . [YHWH], where is your steadfast love of old" (Ps. 89:38, 49)?

The psalms that follow in the fourth book (90–106) reflect renewed hope and confidence that YHWH is king and YHWH's purposes will not be denied. "Let the sea roar, and all that fills it; the world and those who live in it. Let the floods clap their hands; let the hills sing together for joy at the presence of [YHWH] for he is coming to judge the earth. He will judge the world and the peoples with equity" (Ps. 98:7–9). This hope and confidence overflows in gratitude in Psalms 103 and 104, each of which begins with the phrase, "Bless (YHWH), O my soul." The last two in this section return to history with a recounting of YHWH's acts of deliverance and confession for the people's many sins. This book ends on the upbeat: YHWH has "remembered his covenant, and showed compassion according to the abundance of his steadfast love" (Ps. 106:45).

The final book (107–150) is difficult to characterize because of its variety. Psalms of triumph begin this section, followed by a long tribute to the law of YHWH (119). Lyrics sung along the road climbing to Jerusalem for festivals come next (120–134). Psalm 139 is a profound reflection on YHWH's presence through the difficult ordeals of life; Psalm 143 a passionate plea for help. Psalm 145 is a lovely recounting of YHWH's goodness and greatness, which Psalm 147 extends to the physical creation and Psalm 148 to all peoples.

Temple worship in Jerusalem was the context for most psalms. Of course, the temple was the center of religious power and it was closely aligned to the rule of kings. Thus, we do not see much criticism in the psalms of priests and kings.

Yet this text includes prophetic perspectives. "[YHWH] loves righteousness and justice; the earth is full of the steadfast love of [YHWH]," but "[YHWH] brings the counsel of the nations to nothing" (Ps. 33:5, 10). Regarding military solutions, we read: "A king is not saved by his great army; a warrior is not delivered by his great strength. The war horse is a vain hope for victory, and by its great might it cannot save" (Ps. 33:16–17). Regarding conspiracies, this: "The nations have sunk in the pit that they made, in the net that they hid has their own foot been caught" (Ps. 9:15). And this confession of the source on one's security: "Some take pride in chariots, and some in horses, but our pride is in the name of [YHWH]" (Ps. 20:7).

Reflection and Discussion

21. Which wisdom text did you like the best? Which the least? Why?

22. The text of **Ecclesiastes** undermines the message of this book with its claim that we are wasting our time when we try to forge a just and sustainable society. What is your response to that view?

23. The text of **Job** struggles to reconcile the unjust suffering of one man with the existence of YHWH. When we substitute the plight of humanity today for Job, we have a text that may speak to the ecological crisis of our time. How would you describe its relevance (if any) for us?

24. Through the zigs and zags of Israel's history, the **Psalms** shaped people's understanding of YHWH and helped them maintain a distinctive and larger sense of social and political purpose. Consider the role that lyrical music plays in your life. Does it shape your faith and the political community you are part of?

PART III:
The Second Testament Writings

From **Matthew** to **The Revelation to John**, the Second Testament contains twenty-seven books. Canaan is again the primary physical setting (called Palestine by the Romans), but the lands of modern Syria, Turkey, Greece, Italy, Cyprus and Crete also appear in the texts. The time span of these writings begins with the birth of Jesus and ends 125 years later. It is particularly important to know whether a particular text was written before or after the First Jewish-Roman War (66–73 CE), especially the destruction of Jerusalem in the summer of 70 CE. It was an event as traumatic for the Jews as the city's first destruction 656 years earlier. For approximate dates of other key events, see the table on page 12.

When we look at the chronological order in which the Second Testament books were written, we again find it was very different from the order in which these books appear in the Bible. Drawing on the work of Marcus Borg [28] (but not following him on **James, Colossians, Philippians** and **2 Timothy**), here chronologically are the texts identified by likely authorship and approximate completion date.

Text	Completion	Author
James	48 CE	James, brother of Jesus
Galatians	49 CE	Paul, the Apostle
1 Thessalonians	52 CE	Paul, the Apostle
1 Corinthians	54 CE	Paul, the Apostle
Philemon	56 CE	Paul, the Apostle
Colossians	56 CE	Paul, the Apostle
2 Corinthians	57 CE	Paul, the Apostle
Romans	57 CE	Paul, the Apostle
Philippians	64 CE	Paul, the Apostle
2 Timothy	65 CE	Paul, the Apostle

---

[28]   Borg, *Evolution of the Word: The New Testament in the Order the Books Were Written*, 31.

Mark's Gospel	70 CE	John Mark, cousin of Barnabas
Ephesians	85 CE	unknown
Matthew's Gospel	87 CE	unknown
Hebrews	88 CE	Priscilla, a Jewish teacher
John's Gospel	90 CE	unknown
Revelation to John	92 CE	John of Patmos
Jude	100 CE	Judas, a relative of Jesus
1, 2, 3 John	100 CE	unknown
Luke's Gospel	104 CE	Luke, a Gentile physician
Acts of the Apostles	105 CE	Luke, a Gentile physician
2 Thessalonians	111 CE	unknown
1 Peter	112 CE	unknown
1 Timothy	115 CE	unknown
Titus	115 CE	unknown
2 Peter	120 CE	unknown

Questions already encountered in the First Testament also will frame our discussion here. (1) What do these texts say (if anything) about the kind of political community people are called to participate in? (2) If an alternative political community is envisioned, what is the glue holding that community together and what is its source of power to impact the world? (3) What do these texts add to our understanding of YHWH?

Discussion questions related to the chapters in Part III are found on pages 246–247 (after chapter 20); on page 267 (after chapter 21); on pages 322–323 (after chapter 23); and on pages 339–340 (after chapter 25).

19. Who is this Man Called Jesus?
Matthew, Mark, Luke

The critical time has come,
the empire of God is at hand;
change your way of thinking and
believe the good news. (Mark 1:15)

With these four cryptic lines Jesus of Nazareth appeared suddenly among the common people of Galilee, according to Mark's gospel.

Matthew and Luke also wrote accounts of the life and teachings of Jesus. The three versions are called the "synoptic" (seeing together) gospels. Their ways of telling the Jesus story are substantially the same and significantly different. A key similarity is that each begins by recalling a prior beginning, the journey out of exile and embrace of YHWH's calling to bring justice to the nations. Thus, each begins with words from Isaiah 40: "Prepare the way of [YHWH], make his paths straight" (Matt. 3:3, Mark 1:3, Luke 3:4).

Matthew portrays Jesus as Israel's Messiah, an anointed leader who takes the experiences and searchings of Israel to a whole new level of challenge to the empire with his kingdom message. Mark shows Jesus engaged in harsh struggles with powers of oppression and ideologies of domination, putting people in touch with their great untapped capacities for life and freedom in God's new empire. Luke shows Jesus on a determined journey toward Jerusalem, where religious and political powers of the old kingdom have united for self-aggrandizement with devastating consequences for the common people.

Each writer gives his understanding of the power struggles that culminated in the execution of Jesus and the belief afterward of a small but vocal community that something of world-changing importance had happened in the Jesus event. The drama of that life from birth to death to apparent resurrection has captured the interest of millions of people for twenty centuries. Why their interest? Why did Jesus die? Did God need the death of Jesus, as so much of Christendom has taught?

A. The harsh reality of empire—Jesus' historical setting

The year before the birth of Jesus, Jewish dissidents from northern Palestine seized a Roman weapons arsenal in the town of Sepphoris, four miles northwest of Nazareth. They used the weapons to join the revolts against Roman rule going on across Palestine after the death of Herod the Great. After entering Sepphoris, clearing it of rebels and killing many residents, the Roman legions burned down the city and sold many survivors into slavery. As part of putting down the broader revolt, they crucified 2,000 Jewish rebels.

A few years later, the city was rebuilt by the new Roman governor, Herod Antipas. People loyal to Rome repopulated the rebuilt city, which included wealthy Jewish landowners with kinship ties to the priests at the temple in Jerusalem. Ownership of land was at the discretion of the Romans, who exacted heavy taxes in return. Much of the working class population of the area labored on their large estates and paid taxes to the Jewish landowners in exchange for the privilege of having work.

Herod Antipas put a similar arrangement into place around the Sea of Galilee. Wealthy Jews purchased fishing rights along the shoreline from the Romans. They then contracted fishing privileges to fishermen for a fee. Only those who paid could fish.

For many of the leadership class in Israel—those who made the expected compromises with the Roman imperial bureaucracy—life was not so bad. They went along to get along, and it worked. The temple in Jerusalem, which Herod the Great had rebuilt and enlarged, served as a key part of the Roman-Jewish power structure. It functioned as a kind of central bank through which much daily trade flowed, and the tax revenue extracted from the people through the temple structure benefited both the Jewish elite and Roman overlords.

It was different for the common people, who seethed with anger toward imperial Rome and its Jewish collaborators. Day and night, they dreamed of deliverance from the oppression of the empire.

B. The empire of God

Into this disputed territory of religious Pharisees and political

Herodians contending for the loyalty of the common people came Jesus, son of a carpenter in Nazareth, announced by a prophet in the wilderness named John the Baptizer. For his efforts to declare that a great new leader was coming to Israel, John was executed by the Roman puppet governor, Herod. Thus Jesus saw his advance man and publicist jailed and beheaded. Not a comforting prospect for his own career.

As for Jesus, what was his message? "The time has come," a moment of crisis and hard choices. Things will not remain as they've been. "The *basilea* of God is at hand, coming here among you" (Mark 1:15). This was familiar language to his listeners; *basilea* was Greek, translatable as "kingdom, kingship, empire, government." It denoted how humans organize society and try to run the world. (The questions on page 246 focus on this aspect of Jesus' message.)

So Jesus started with the familiar in Israel's memory—kingdoms and empires remembered from Egypt, Israel under David and Solomon, Syria, Assyria, Babylon, Persia and the Greeks—and then added the words "of God." That was a startling and portentous modification of kingdom! From there, the rest of his teaching and career was a dramatic process of giving content to that little phrase "of God." The gospels of **Matthew, Mark** and **Luke** tell us how a society of YHWH would function.

Jesus is reported to have said: "My kingdom is not from this world" (John 18:36). He never said his kingdom is not "in" this world (the Greek has a different word for "in"). He intended his way—God's way— of running the world to be very much *in* this world. But with regard to its origin and way of functioning, the kingdom Jesus announced is of God, not of the notions of hierarchy, dominating force and homicidal power that equip the kingdoms and empires from this world.

So the kingdom of God is *in this world but not from it.*

In keeping with this, he taught his disciples to pray: "Your kingdom come, your will be done on earth as it is in heaven" (Matt. 6:10). This leaves no doubt that the kingdom is to be implemented and realized on Earth. It states as well that kingdom means doing the will of God on Earth. The kingdom of God is Jesus' vision of a good society.

In **Matthew's** extended collection of Jesus' teaching called the Sermon on the Mount (Matt. 5–7), Jesus positions himself as a new Moses, defining the practices of a good society with authoritative wisdom and skill. All of this, he says, will be fulfilled, and "he who does these commandments and teaches them shall be called great in the kingdom of heaven" (Matt. 5:17–20). He blesses those "who hunger and thirst to see justice done" and "those who are peacemakers," but also advises them to expect to be persecuted "like the prophets who were before you" (Matt. 5:1–12). It is a clear and bold assertion that he expects his disciples to continue the role of Israel's prophets in the new society that he calls the kingdom of God.

The story portrays Jesus living, teaching and dying with the purpose of demonstrating God's way of running the world, of living in and advocating for a good society. Everybody would have welcomed a man with such a message, right? Yes, unless God's kind of kingdom is very different from the already existing empire, and God's way of running things more than a little in conflict with theirs.

"Love your enemies," the very first imperative spoken by Jesus according to Luke's gospel (Luke 6:27), was not the way Herod ran his kingdom. But according to Jesus, it is the way God intends the world to be run. So, no wonder Jesus once called Herod "that fox" (Luke 13:32). It was not a compliment for being clever, but a slur for being devious and a little bad smelling. Between Jesus and Herod, tension was building—the empires of Caesar and of God were not the same thing. Nevertheless, said Jesus, the empire of God is at hand, coming right among you.

C. The human one

But who, in fact, is this Jesus? A controversial figure, of disputed identity. What gave him the right to question how this society was organized and how things were done?

Stories of Jesus' birth in **Matthew** and **Luke** accent the imperial oppression into which Jesus was born. **Matthew** reports King Herod, puppet of the Roman government, ostensibly wanted to see and "pay him homage" (Matt. 6:8). The wise men disobeyed his instruction to return and report on Jesus' whereabouts, going home instead "another way" (Matt. 2:12). One wonders if people still have dreams that lead them to do civil disobedience.

Luke started his account of Jesus' birth by reporting that the priest Zechariah and his wife Elizabeth were inspired to prophesy the births of children named John and Jesus, saying God would use them to save Israel from its enemies (Luke 1:70). Then Joseph and Mary were forced by Emperor Augustus, along with "all the world" (Luke 2:1) to register for taxation. Their child Jesus was born in circumstances of abject poverty on this onerous taxation trip to satisfy the whims of the empire, and they ended up refugees in Egypt to escape Herod's murderous intent (Matt. 2:13–15). Clearly, Jesus was a child destined to affect Israel's relationship with the kings of this world.

Mark says nothing of Jesus' birth, beginning his account as noted above with the start of his public ministry, when he announced the coming of the empire of God.

Almost immediately, Jesus found himself in serious conflict with Israel's religious leaders over understandings of good and of God.

Mark reports him entering and teaching in a synagogue, where the listeners "were astounded at his teaching, for he taught them as one having authority, and not as the scribes" (Mark 1:22). "Not as the scribes" was a not-too-subtle slight! In the synagogue there was a man with an unclean spirit who cried out: "What have you do with us, Jesus of Nazareth? Have you come to destroy us? I know who you are, the Holy One of God" (Mark 1:24). So in the spirit world, Jesus was identified as a messenger from God, but the common people were left wondering. It appears from this story that the demon(s) (is there one or are there many?) are the voice of the scribal class in the synagogue who feel their authority threatened by Jesus. Hostility brews.

Jesus spent most of his time on the streets and in the homes of common people. He identified himself as a simple human being. In the synoptic gospels he refers to himself as "the son of man" (the human one) seventy-one times, and as "son of God" never (other people and demons called him "son of God," often as an accusation of blasphemy).

Jesus seemed intent on disclosing the character of the true human being who is doing the will of God on earth. He called his acts and teaching "signs" of something bigger, not so much in heaven as on Earth (Matt. 6:10). He seemed quite ordinary, yet he claimed authority to go against all kinds of traditions and announced a new empire. Is this the way a human being trying to be all he can be is supposed to act? What if it is?

We see a trajectory of escalating conflict between Jesus and those presumed to be leaders of Israel in the following sampling of "*son of man*" utterances attributed to Jesus.

After saying to a paralyzed man, "Son, your sins are forgiven," Jesus perceived that some scribes nearby were questioning his authority to do so. In response, Jesus asked, "Which is easier to say, 'Your sins are forgiven,' or 'rise up and walk'" (Mark 2:9)? Well, clearly it is easier to say "your sins are forgiven." Who would know if that changed anything in real time? So Jesus proceeded to say, "So that you may know that the *son of man* has authority on earth to forgive sins, I say to you, rise up and walk," and the man did it (Mark 2:10–11, emphasis added). Mark reports that the observers, not surprisingly, said "We have never seen anything like this" (Mark 2:12). The scribes were not comforted by this event.

In a dispute with some of the Pharisees over rules of Sabbath observance, Jesus said "The Sabbath was made for humankind, and not humankind for the Sabbath, so the *son of man* is lord even of the Sabbath" (Mark 2:27–28, emphasis added). Again, this claim to authority displeased the Pharisees. The tension increased.

Jesus healed a leper, and then told the man to go and show himself to the priest and make the prescribed offering for his cleansing "as a testimony to them" (Mark 1:44; see also 6:11 and 13:9 for other instances of testimony "to" and "against"). Note Jesus' use of the plural, indicating the entire priestly class. This is totally perplexing unless the reader understands that by declaring this leper clean, Jesus had launched a frontal assault on the elitism and privilege of the whole priestly system, which prohibited anyone but priests from dealing with lepers. This explains the opening words of the leper, "If you will, you can make me clean," giving Jesus an out; he did not have to take on that priestly system unless he chose to (Mark 1:40).

So this simple "human one" healed and forgave some individuals, but in the process, in a most ominous way, he angered each of the power players in his religious community: scribes, Pharisees and priests.

Masterful in the use of symbols, Jesus and the writers who tell his story use "bread/loaves" as a symbol of all that is essential to organize and sustain life. So, in a great summary event and passage, Mark reports Jesus' immense frustration with and rebuke of his disciples for failing to understand his project of creating a new political alternative *that included Jews and Gentiles.* First he warned them of the dead-end futility of the two main political options of their time: "Watch out, beware of the yeast of the Pharisees and the yeast of Herod" (Mark 8:15), the Pharisees with their pious isolation from Rome and the Herodians with their opportunistic collaboration with Rome. We do not hear Jesus saying that these leaders were not well meaning, but we do hear him saying that they were wrong. Their ways were not sustainable ways of running the world; their kingdoms were not workable.

Then Jesus reminded his disciples, using highly symbolic numbers, of feeding the Jewish crowd (five thousand fed, twelve loaves left over, Mark 6:30–44) and the Gentile crowd (four thousand fed and seven loaves left over, Mark 8:1–9) with *one loaf*—his loaf. One loaf will feed *both* streams that together will comprise this new community. Only Jesus is offering the bread of life; only Jesus is offering a sustainable political alternative, the empire/kingdom of God. Don't you get it yet? he asks in exasperation (Mark 8:17–21). Do we get it?

In truth, they did not. The disciples who followed Jesus most closely expected great things from him in terms of delivering Israel from Roman oppression. They hoped he would be a mighty warrior king like David. Jesus once asked his disciples who people thought he was, and Peter said, "You are the Messiah—God's anointed one" (Mark 8:29). Jesus immediately ordered them to tell no one. This is puzzling unless you understand that "Messiah" meant conquering warrior in the popular mind. For Jesus, it was worse to be misidentified in this way than to remain an enigma and mystery.

His "bread" was not that of horses and chariots, armies and wars, because the God of his parables, whom he called "Father," was not a god of horses and chariots, armies and wars.

To the great consternation of his disciples, Jesus repeatedly said things like "the *son of man* must suffer at the hands of his opponents, die, and be resurrected" (Mark 10:33–34; Luke 9:44, emphasis added).   And this, he said, must happen in Jerusalem, "for it is impossible that a prophet should perish outside of Jerusalem" (Luke 13:33).   In the face of escalating hostility and life-threatening opposition, Jesus neither runs away nor plans to fight, but goes to Jerusalem, declaring that "the *son of man* came not to be served but to serve, and to give his life a ransom for many" (Matt. 20:28, emphasis added).   This stands in absolute contrast to any program of killing his enemies in order to protect his friends.   This "human one" resisted systems of oppression and those who perpetrated them, but he did it with exorcism, healing and forgiving—it was a nonviolent resistance.

Jesus, calling himself "the human one," did not set out to kill oppressors of the common people, whether Jewish priest or Gentile king, but to unite them all in a new community, a good society.   In his time it seemed a preposterous idea, and even his disciples found Jesus and his way most perplexing. It was simply too far from reality to believe.

D. Teaching a different way

Luke's summary of the teaching of Jesus starts with the words "love your enemies" (Luke 6:27).   His listeners had a long history and many stories of how to deal with enemies, but loving them was not part of their mental furniture.   This was new and radical.

The account in **Matthew** of Jesus' sermon on the mount (Matt. 5:1–7:27) presents Jesus as a new Moses delivering YHWH's words from the mountain top.   Church tradition has utterly failed to do the most obvious thing with these teachings of Jesus; that is, add them to Israel's corpus of revealed truths about how to order society and live the good life and affirm Jesus' own claim that every word of the expanded teaching would be fulfilled.

Jesus said, "Blessed [fulfilled and mature] are those who hunger and thirst to see justice prevail" and "blessed are the peacemakers" (Matt. 5:6, 9).   He affirmed the best of the Israelite tradition where justice and peace kiss each other (Psalm 85:10).

Here Jesus identified with the prophetic tradition of **Isaiah's** servant songs, **Jeremiah** and others, affirming passionate advocacy of justice for the poor and oppressed and at the same time identifying "peace" as the way to achieve that justice. He was on a mission that precluded the use of violence in pursuit of justice. He went on to promise that his followers would suffer and be persecuted like the prophets who had substituted the word for the sword as their method.

He did not, most pointedly, predict his disciples would fight like soldiers and die like heroes of war. He did predict that they could and would share with him and the prophets this vocation of humility and suffering. As "the human one" he presented himself as a model of "common" human behavior, not as a unique, sinless, divine, heaven-sent person in every way different from his lowly listeners.

This fully reflected the message of the book of **Daniel**: the "dominion and glory and kingship . . . that shall never be destroyed" given by God to "one like a human being" would in turn be "given to the saints, the holy ones of the Most High" (Dan. 7:27*). Jesus saw himself as the initiator, not the sole proprietor, of this new reign to be shared by all the faithful.* So he taught that healing and forgiving sins were not his exclusive domain, but the calling of all human beings.

In the process of condemning the First Testament's wars and tantrums of violence by a deafening silence toward those behaviors, Jesus added in his mountain sermon, with no small courage, words which frontally challenged accepted tradition and familiar teachings: "You have heard, but I say..." (Matt. 5:21–48). Jesus was offering a radically new paradigm for running the world. It came to be known as "the way." When Jesus sent seventy of his followers out to proclaim his message, he instructed them: "Whatever house you enter, first say, 'Peace to this house.' And if anyone is there who shares in peace, your peace will rest on that person" (Luke 10:5–6). The way of Jesus was clearly a way of peace. Having added his own teachings, which revised and illuminated the received law, he proceeded to say that "not one letter, not one stroke" (Matt. 5:18) of this enhanced law will pass without fulfillment.

With parables and stories Jesus outlined the main features of this way of God's kingdom. Central to Jesus' way was the displacement of retaliation and punishment with forgiveness as the way to respond to offenses and broken relationships (see question 27, page 246).

Jesus is complaining that people have made the message moved off purpose and source.

Biblical scholar Walter Wink has demonstrated the clear difference between Jesus' active nonviolent resistance to evil and all apathetic and passive responses to evildoing (Matt. 5:38–42). Taking the familiar (and usually misunderstood) words of Jesus "do not resist one who is evil," Wink shows first that the Greek word usually translated "resist" actually means "violently resist" in common usage. Thus, Jesus' real teaching was "do not resist with violence one who is evil." Wink goes on to explain that to "turn the other cheek" was in fact a bold challenge to the aggressor to treat *like an equal* the one he had tried to demean with a slap. In Jewish culture, a slap on the right cheek was delivered with the back of the right hand by one who considered themselves superior to the one slapped. In contrast, a blow on the left cheek was delivered with a fist against one considered an equal. So, turning the other cheek was not servile submission, but nonviolent resistance to oppressive behavior. Wink explains how within that culture giving the second garment and walking the second mile also were ways of challenging oppression.[29]

Jesus told a story of a forgiving father and an unforgiving brother (Luke 15:11–32). The church has, rather misleadingly, called this the parable of the prodigal son. It depicts a father, against all tradition and common sense, welcoming home a rebellious son. An older brother (who from the story's context in **Luke** obviously symbolizes the oppositional Pharisees) is most unhappy about the father's forgiving. One cannot understand the growing conflict between Jesus and the Pharisees without understanding their difference over how to deal with offenses and offenders, including Jesus' teaching of "grace" toward those who are considered outside the pale of salvation.

Christendom has notoriously claimed that Jesus' teaching of forgiveness and welcoming others and enemies is not relevant to national or international affairs, only interpersonal ones. Yet Jesus put the question of forgiveness and inclusion in explicitly "international" or corporate and global perspective when the Pharisees on one occasion asked him for "a sign" (Matt. 12:38). Jesus asserted that the only sign that would be given the Pharisees and "this generation" was the sign of Jonah. **Jonah** tells the story of a prophet who refused God's call to go and preach repentance and

---

[29]   Wink, *Engaging the Powers*, 175–184.

grace to Israel's enemies, the Ninevites (Assyria), a refusal that apparently came to Jesus' mind when he contemplated the attitude of the Pharisees towards his own inclusion of sinners and enemies. One need only read the First Testament books of **Nahum** (see page 139) and **Jonah** (see page 192) in succession to see which side Jesus took on the question of violence or nonviolence toward national enemies. On this subject, Christendom might well ask itself if it wants to continue to take its stand as firmly on **Nahum's** side in the future as it has in the past.

Jesus was asked by a lawyer, "What must I do to inherit eternal life" (Luke 10:25)? The lawyer was clearly concerned, perhaps obsessed, with himself. In the conversation that followed, the lawyer asked "Who is my neighbor?" Jesus replied with the story of the "good Samaritan" who interrupted his journey to care for an injured stranger along the road. The startling (and difficult for the lawyer and probably us) truth of the story is that for Jesus, the important question was not "How can I secure my future?" but "Who is demonstrating genuine love?" So it turns out that the lawyer was forced to declare that the love which Jesus (and *Torah*) expected and commended is shown by a Samaritan, a person considered by pious Jews to be incapable of pleasing God. It was a brilliant contribution to what today is called "interfaith dialogue." For a contemporary reading of Jesus' story, we need only to substitute "Muslim" for "Samaritan."

Jesus' parables of the banquet for the poor, crippled, lame and blind (Luke 14:13–14) and the rich man and Lazarus (Luke 16:19–31) are two of many that voice his passion and compassion for the dispossessed of society. These stories, again, clarify the reason for the grim hostility of the prosperous religious leaders of Israel toward him. To an extent, surely, those leaders did believe that their program was the best for most of the Jews. But it would be culpably naive to presume them above operating that program substantially to their own advantage. Jesus did not refrain from drawing attention to their self-interest when giving his call to compassionate generosity for any who would be his followers.

But surely it looks highly risky and extremely difficult to live in this world by these principles. So Jesus told his parable of the talents (Matt. 25:14–30) in which most of the stewards are afraid to take a risk, but those who take risk are commended as wise.

The parable of the mustard seed (Mark 4:30–32) addresses the inevitable feeling in Jesus' listeners that this empire of God had as much chance of succeeding as a snowball's chance in hell. "To what shall we compare the empire of God?" asks Jesus. How about a mustard seed, which starts as the smallest of seeds, but grows into the greatest of shrubs that provides nests for the birds of the air? Two thousand years later we do not see a full-grown shrub, but we do see more than a small seed.

Finally we notice the parable of the sower and soils (Mark 4:1–20). The message, or secret or mystery, of the empire of God, says Jesus, is understood by some but not all. Surely this is true of any new discovery or information which comes to humankind. Nothing surprising here, but a fundamental and important truth nonetheless.

In sum, the teaching and parables of Jesus illuminate his new, nonviolent way of running the world—the empire of God—but few understood him and even fewer were ready to follow him in trying to live this new way.

E. Confused followers

We have noted above that the disciples failed to understand Jesus' reference to "bread" as a symbol of his program to create a new community of Jew and Gentile. They were perplexed by this man who had captured their imaginations, but baffled their understandings. The idea of maintaining the community of YHWH worshippers they understood very well; they shared that goal with him. Israel had a long history, and in the face of crushing Roman oppression and collaborating Jewish leaders, the disciples along with the dispossessed of Israel desperately longed for a faithful community to continue. But if Jesus was offering a way to make that happen, they could not fathom his way of doing it (see question 28 at page 246 for further discussion).

The synoptic writers return repeatedly to this confusion of the disciples. In Mark 8:32, for example, moments after Peter declares that Jesus is "the Messiah," he is harshly rebuking Jesus! Why? What is this?

It all hinges on the popular expectation of a Messiah who would save Israel from its enemies. Luke's gospel reports the prediction of Zechariah the priest when John the Baptizer was born:

Blessed be the Lord God of Israel, for he has looked favorably on his people and redeemed them. He has raised up a mighty savior for us in the house of his servant David, as he spoke through the mouth of his holy prophets of old, that we would be saved from our enemies and from the hand of all who hate us. (Luke 1:68–71)

The link to the House of David fired popular expectations that this coming deliverer would be mighty in battle, as David had been described. Peter was totally convinced that Jesus the Messiah would lead Israel to success in battle, so of course he rebuked Jesus for saying that he would suffer, be killed and rise again. Suffering and being killed was not victory talk! But Jesus in turn rebuked Peter as the voice of Satan (Mark 8:33). That is strong stuff!

Yet Jesus' words included a cryptic hint that he would "rise again." Israel's First Testament had its stories of Elijah and Elisha restoring the dead to life. That God could do this was no impossibility for the Jewish mind. But something else here did seem impossible. It was that victory over enemies could come from nonviolent suffering.

Jesus was saying that he would accept this way of suffering, but that the suffering, and even death, would not mean defeat. Rather, he would walk this path and come out of it alive and in victory. *So Jesus was not denying he would save Israel from its enemies and establish a kind of empire on earth.* But it would happen by walking a path of forgiveness, compassion and suffering; by doing that, Jesus would reveal the kingdom of God and change the world.

In Mark's story, Jesus predicted his coming torture, execution, death and resurrection on three distinct occasions (8:31; 9:31; 10:34). Immediately following the second of these predictions, the disciples are reported arguing about who of them was the greatest—dramatic evidence that despite Jesus' talk of servanthood and suffering as his way, they were thinking of dominating power and status. Following his third announcement of his way of suffering, they came to him asking for positions of power in his coming kingdom (Mark 10:37), again showing their total failure to understand the way he had chosen for himself.

In Luke's gospel, Jesus constructed a kind of "final exam" to see if his disciples understood his way of nonviolent love (Luke 22:35–38). As tensions built toward the boiling point and a frightening confrontation with Jerusalem authorities loomed, Jesus reviewed the past years with his disciples. He said to them, "When I sent you out without a purse, bag, or sandals, did you lack anything?" They replied, "No, not a thing." (See Luke 10 for their excited report of success upon returning from that mission.) Jesus then said, "But now, the one who has a purse must take it, and likewise a bag   And the one who has no sword must sell his cloak and buy one." They responded, "Look, look, here are two swords." Jesus replied, "It is enough," meaning end of discussion, no more to be said.

Interpreters have asked for centuries why Jesus told his disciples to buy swords. Hadn't his whole teaching been love for enemies and forgiveness as the way to deal with offenses?

But few interpreters have asked the question this brings to mind: why didn't the disciples respond to Jesus by asking *him* what he could possibly mean by the sword instruction or command?   And the answer surely is that they would have asked it if they had really understood that Jesus was committed to nonviolence and expected the same of them.   But they did *not* understand, and so it was immediately clear to Jesus that they had failed the exam. His teaching had fallen on deaf ears.

His followers were confused and ignorant of his most fundamental teaching. They could not imagine how Jesus' way of confronting the power structures with nonviolent resistance was God's will or could possibly succeed.   In particular, they did not understand that he was not proposing to do everything for them, but to do it *through* them and a growing throng of humanity who would adopt his method of overcoming evil with good.

F. Showdown in Jerusalem

In a moment of supreme irony, Jesus said he was not worried about threats from King Herod in Galilee "because it is impossible for a prophet to be killed outside of Jerusalem" (Luke 13:33). He did not fear a threat from the political quarter because it was the religious quarter of his own community that kills the prophets.

And **Matthew, Mark** and **Luke** all portray Jesus as walking with unswerving purpose and determination toward Jerusalem, the center of power for Israel's religious establishment of scribes, Pharisees and priests. There his notion of power as love, forgiveness and reconciliation would confront their notion of power as hierarchy, control and ultimately, if necessary, homicidal coercion. It was a clash of kingdoms, a choice between radically opposed notions of the kind of power necessary to control humans, to run the world, to establish a kingdom, however one chooses to word it.

Jesus staged his entrance to Jerusalem as a dramatic contrast to the style of kings and emperors. Where they would ride into the city on a mighty war horse with lots of snorting and prancing, his mount was just a donkey (Matt. 21:1–11; Mark 11:1–10; Luke 19:28–40). It is very likely that Jesus also staged his entry to contrast with David's centuries earlier, when he entered Jerusalem as a fighting man surrounded by his troops to establish himself as king (2 Samuel 5).

The synoptics each record a succession of conversations or debates between Jesus and the Jerusalem authority classes after his arrival in the city. In one of those conversations, Jesus challenged the scribes' contention that the Messiah would be "the son of David," saying it was impossible for it to be so (Mark 12:35–37). Why was this important to Jesus? Because "son of David" meant a king who ruled by coercion and homicidal might. Jesus was no such king.

Once in Jerusalem, Jesus took his message straight to the center of power, the temple. There he began to drive out those who were selling things and declared, "It is written, 'my house shall be a house of prayer, but you have made it a den of robbers'" (Luke 19:46). This was a frontal assault on the temple authorities, an unforgivable breach of both custom and law. The record says that the authorities turned homicidal, seeking a way to kill him. The conflict between Jesus and the ruling class had escalated to its climax. The Jewish authorities condemned Jesus in their court, then sought the support of the Roman officials by taking Jesus before Pilate and Herod.

Luke traces more of Peter's tortured relationship with Jesus. At one moment, Peter swore he would go with Jesus to prison and to death.

When Jesus was arrested shortly after, one of the disciples, probably Peter, swung a sword to protect Jesus. It was an act of courage for which he could have suffered prison or death in retaliation. But Jesus rebuked him (Luke 22:51). Shortly after that, Peter was lounging in the courtyard. Asked if he was not one of Jesus' friends, he denied three times that he even knew Jesus (Luke 22:54–62). Why? Was Peter a coward? Impossible. He had already shown he was ready for a fight to death. Far more likely is that Peter was appalled, insulted, and disappointed that Jesus had done nothing for his own defense when arrested, leaving Peter alone with his sword. Peter could not stand being identified with this wimp of a man whom he had hoped would save Israel.

Trial scenes followed and the Romans agreed Jesus must be executed. Why? The Jewish and Roman authorities shared in common the deep fear that Jesus (and his message) was eroding their authority to govern with the tools of hierarchy, domination and homicidal violence. Forgiveness, reconciliation and building an inclusive community that excluded no one was not their program, but it was his. Jesus was not willing to turn homicidal over his differences with others, but they were. If people adopted Jesus' way instead of theirs, their legitimacy as rulers would crumble and their power would evaporate. It was that simple and that profoundly true. Jesus was a threat at the deepest possible level to their way of managing humanity and running the world.

Jesus was flogged, executed, and buried under the collusion of religious and political powers that deemed him a threat. Empires still fear active nonviolence more than armies.

Here we add, for the sake of clarity and truth, a note with regard to the role of Jewish authorities (and Roman) in the death of Jesus. It is not necessary to think they were wrong about everything, nor altogether lacking in wisdom, virtue or compassion, to think that they were wrong about one very important thing: the power of love over death, forgiveness over retaliation, and word over sword.

What happened at Jerusalem that weekend was a drama of different emphases in how to participate in the human struggle. On one side was Jesus, saying people are capable of and find their fulfillment in acts of love, forgiveness and generous compassion. On the other side were powers of empire and religion seeking to capitalize on the fact that people also respond to threats, coercion, and the ultimate sanction of homicidal violence. Which understanding of human nature is closer to reality? Which definition of real power is true? Answers to these questions continue to shape the way religious and political organizations seek to channel human behavior and organize society (see question 29 at page 246 for additional discussion).

G. After the tomb, the way forward

Matthew and **Luke** report that on the third day (two days after Jesus was executed) some women went to the tomb where he was buried, found the stone rolled away from the entrance and the tomb empty.

Luke's gospel includes a story of two people (not of the twelve disciples) walking toward Emmaus when a stranger joined them and began talking about Jesus. They did not know who he was until later when they ate together and the stranger took bread, blessed and broke it and gave it to them. At that moment they recognized him as Jesus. Then he vanished, just like that (Luke 24:13–35).

Matthew says that the women who went to the tomb were told by an angel that Jesus had arisen from the dead and they would see him in Galilee. Moments later Jesus met them and repeated the message that his disciples would see him in Galilee.

Mark's gospel ends abruptly at 16:8 in the manuscripts which have been judged most ancient and authentic. Here are the closing words:

> "Do not be alarmed; you are looking for Jesus of Nazareth, who was crucified. He has been raised; he is not here. Look, there is the place they laid him. But go, tell his disciples and Peter that he is going ahead of you to Galilee; there you will see him, just as he told you." So they went out and fled from the tomb, for terror and amazement had seized them; and they said nothing to anyone, for they were afraid. (Mark 16:6–8)

There are significant differences in the stories of the empty tomb and post-resurrection of Jesus. For example, **Matthew** and **Mark** emphasize instructions to the disciples to return to Galilee while **Luke** says nothing about such a return and quotes Jesus as saying. "Stay here in the city" (Luke 24:49). The reader is left to consider what each account may mean and how they relate to each other.

Of course, Galilee was the place where Jesus announced the coming empire/kingdom of God and lived his life of compassionate nonviolence among the common people. Galilee was linked with the experience or awareness that Jesus and his way were not dead (see question 30 at page 246). Thus, the amazing assumption of Matthew's and Mark's gospels is that Jesus' life goes on in the midst of the human struggle of the oppressed in Galilee. In other words, the way Jesus taught and lived the coming of God's reign did not end with his death. It continues in the life and teachings of those who see the truth of his description of the good society. In the life of his followers, Jesus and his way are seen alive and well.

These followers of "the way" had heard in their time of crisis that the empire of God is being formed on Earth, had changed their thinking to accept its new truths, and had both experienced for themselves and shared with others a new way of living as good news indeed (Mark 1:14).

H. The faith of Jesus

Did Jesus expect divine deliverance from death? All three gospel writers recount his anguished prayer in the garden of Gethsemane: "Father, if you are willing, remove this cup from me; yet, not my will but yours be done" (Luke 22:42). His final words on the cross were heart-breaking: "My God, my God, why have you forsaken me" (Matt. 27:46; Mark 15:34)? Jesus seemed on the edge of despair. Yet all three writers agree that he walked through his final week of life with courage and purpose. How do we account for this?

One of the sources of this strength was Jesus' sense of call or vocation. His baptism, performed by the prophet John in the Jordan River, was followed "by a voice from heaven: 'You are my son, the beloved; with you I am well pleased'" (Mark 1:11). Immediately thereafter, Jesus spent forty days and nights in the wilderness, fasting and struggling with questions related to the source and use of political power and how to translate his sense of YHWH's divine calling into public action. At the end of this ordeal, Jesus was "filled with the power of the [divine] Spirit" (Luke 4:14).

He began his public life by teaching in the synagogue near his home in Capernaum and elsewhere around the Sea of Galilee. Then he went to his hometown, Nazareth, and taught in the synagogue there. After reading a text from **Isaiah** on how YHWH's anointed one (the Messiah) would "bring good news to the poor . . . release to the captives and recovery of sight to the blind, to let the oppressed go free, to proclaim the year of the Lord's favor" (Luke 4:18–19), Jesus made this startling claim: "Today, this scripture has been fulfilled in your hearing" (Luke 4:21).

That the prophetic tradition of Israel provided the text by which Jesus defined his mission is significant, but it also is important to see how Jesus' faith was nurtured and supported by that tradition. It grounded him in YHWH's generous mercy, love for righteousness and justice, and determination that *all* people have the opportunity to experience *shalom.*

Jesus often brought healing to people and this served as strong confirmation of YHWH's power in his life. Mark reports the first healings occurred at "the house of Simon and Andrew" there in Capernaum; soon "the whole city was gathered around the door" (Mark 1:29, 33). Stories of Jesus' healing powers spread across the region and into neighboring Syria. "Great crowds followed him from Galilee, the Decapolis, Jerusalem, Judea and from beyond the Jordan" (Matt. 4:24–25).

The experiences of Jesus' disciples as they engaged the public to proclaim the arrival of the empire of God also confirmed that the critical time had arrived. When the seventy Jesus had sent out returned from their travels, they reported to Jesus, "Lord, in your name even the demons submit to us!" Jesus responded with an audible prayer of thanksgiving: "I praise you, Father, Lord of heaven and earth, because you have hidden these things from the wise and intelligent and have revealed them to infants; yes, Father, for such was your gracious will." Then turning to his disciples, Jesus underlined the significance of their experiences: "Blessed are the eyes that see what you see! For I tell you that many prophets and kings desired to see what you see, but did not see it, and to hear what you hear, but did not hear it" (Luke 10:17–24).

That Jesus' courage was rooted in faith in YHWH rather than happy optimism is confirmed when we read Jesus' long and detailed teaching at the temple only two or three days before he was killed. Speaking boldly and in a public place, Jesus clearly predicted that the protracted conflict between Jewish patriots and the Roman Empire would end in disaster. The temple itself would be desecrated and then destroyed. The residents of Jerusalem would experience suffering, "such as has not been from the beginning of the world until now, no and never will be" (Matt. 24:21). After such a shattering calamity, Jesus said, "the sign of the Son of Man"—his sign—would appear and "the tribes of the earth . . . will see the Son of Man coming on the clouds of heaven with power and great glory" (Matt. 24:30).

What is this "sign of the Son of Man" that would be exalted before the nations? It is the love of Jesus in the face of violence. In the words of Anthony Bartlett, this is the elemental "photon of compassion" that has diffused throughout the consciousness of the world. Bartlett calls it "a revolution of incalculable significance" that took "the original 'fiction' of human meaning and made it something wonderfully new, able to bring creation to its intended destiny of peace, life, love."

Since the beginning of time, human meaning has been constructed out of violence, says Bartlett. Without Jesus' death and the way he died, we might never had known that. But now we *do* know. We are aware that the fragility, decay and violence in our world are the products of a flawed meaning-making mechanism that creates never-ending victims. "The key factor producing this awareness [is] the sign of Christ," says Bartlett. "From within the depth of our human experience we are pushed [by the figure of Jesus] to refabricate our universe out of the sign of forgiveness, nonviolence and love."

Will we continue to use violence to make life meaningful? Or will we turn to forgiveness, nonviolence and love? This is the "unavoidable choice" we all now face.[30]

---

[30]   Bartlett, *Virtually Christian*, 114-115.

20. Jesus, One with YHWH
The Gospel of John

The readers of this fourth gospel knew Jesus had been a man, born of a woman. They also knew God had "exalted" Jesus by raising him from the dead and making him divine. That is how Peter is reported to have described what happened (Acts 2:32–33, 5:31) and Paul too (Acts 13:33). Some readers may have been familiar with **Mark,** which hints Jesus became divine in the moments after his baptism, and a few with **Matthew,** which suggests Jesus was divine from the time of conception.

But in **The Gospel of John**, readers encountered an even more mystical account of Jesus' identity: in some unfathomable way, this man they knew as Jesus of Nazareth had been one with YHWH from the very beginning (John 1:10).

Our text begins with an eighteen-verse prologue that takes the reader back to the start of creation when a loving energy brought all things into existence. It calls this energy "Word" and says it is "life" and "light" for all people; "the light shines in the darkness and the darkness [does] not overcome it" (John 1:4–5). Moreover, this loving energy "became flesh and lived among us, and we have seen his glory, the glory as of a father's only son, full of grace and truth" (John 1:14). The text is speaking about Jesus, the man born of Mary in 3 or 4 BCE; he embodied the same loving energy that was there at the very start. Adam was humanity 1.0, Jesus humanity 2.0.

Throughout **John,** we are prompted to reflect on Jesus' identity by his frequent "I am" statements. Jesus is quoted as claiming to be the Messiah (4:26), the bread of life (6:35), living bread (6:51), the light of the world (8:12), alive before Abraham (8:58), the good shepherd (10:11), God's son (10:36), the resurrection and the life (11:25), the way, truth and life (14:6), and the true vine (15:1). Christendom has favored metaphysical renderings of these metaphors, taking them far from the concerns of political community and empire.

Adding to the theological density of our text are the formal titles given to Jesus. "Lamb of God" (John 1:29) can be understood as a reference to Jewish sacrifices, but it also signifies Jesus' nonviolence in the face of hostility. "Christ" (John 4:25) is often thought to indicate divinity, but simply means Messiah, a title describing the human being who would end Israel's political oppression and bring YHWH's peace to the Jews. "Son of Man" (John 1:51) means human one; it was the title from the book of **Daniel** that Jesus claimed for himself. "Son of God" (John 1:34) seems to cinch the case for Jesus' divinity. But then we learn that within Judaism it referred to Israel (Ex. 4:22) and/or its king (Ps. 2:7), and that within the Roman Empire it functioned as a brand-name for its emperors. "Savior of the world" (John 4:42) had similar imperial connotations.

Then there are the frequent references to "eternal life," a phrase commonly thought to refer to heaven and immortality. The phrase is used seventeen times, far more than in any other biblical text. The usual implication is that Jesus could speak authoritatively about such things because he *is* YHWH and came "down" from heaven to become a human being.

Yet such an understanding is misleading. While the author of **John** clearly believed Jesus to be divine, he was careful *not* to flatly equate YHWH and Jesus. Yes, Jesus is quoted as saying, "The Father and I are one" (John 10:30). But he said that as part of a conversation in which he claimed YHWH had "given" him his authority. And yes, Thomas declared "My Lord and my God" upon seeing Jesus in the flesh after crucifixion (John 20:28). But then we learn Thomas' phrase of adoration was demanded by the emperor Domitian during the era the text was written and we are no longer so sure what Thomas meant.

This is a difficult subject, to be sure, much contested within the church during the years *after* the first century. As we read it, the metaphor that best catches the author's understanding of Jesus is the "only Son who is close to the Father's heart" (John 1:18). This conveys an intimacy of communication and unity of purpose between YHWH and Jesus.

We gain insight into the nature of Jesus' divinity from his comments in the temple after a group of Judeans, angered by his claim to be "one" with YHWH, took up stones to kill him "because you, though only a human being, *are making yourself God*" (John 10:33, emphasis added). Jesus defended himself by recalling a First Testament text:

> Is it not written in your law . . . "you are gods" [Psalm 82:6]? If
> those to whom the word of God came were called "gods"—and
> the scripture cannot be annulled—can you say that the one whom
> the Father has sanctified and sent into the world is blaspheming
> because I said, "I am God's Son"? . . . Even though you do not
> believe me, believe the works [I do], so that you may know and
> understand that the Father is in me and I am in the Father. (John
> 10:34–38)

Later, the text quotes the resurrected Jesus speaking to his
disciples: "If you forgive the sins of any, they are forgiven them; if you
retain the sins of any, they are retained" (John 20:23). Forgiving sins is
certainly the work of YHWH, and it was scandalous to the Pharisees that
Jesus forgave sins. Yet here Jesus said his disciples had *this same
authority and power*. Thus, the line between the human and the divine is
not as sharply drawn as we had imagined.

As for the author's frequent references to "eternal life," scholars
have noted it was the author's way of describing the kingdom of God, the
phrase used so often in the synoptic gospels but never here. Thus, "eternal
life" describes "the life of the age to come," [31] a life Jesus embodied
during his short time on Earth, not a life without end in another place.

With all of this as an introduction, we have begun to grasp that
The Gospel of John is an extended theological reflection on Jesus and his
relationship with YHWH. This way of approaching the story of Jesus
required the author to include in his account conversations and stories that
are not documented by the other gospels.

John's gospel was written about twenty years after the destruction
of Jerusalem. Most Jews who accepted Jesus as Messiah did not
participate in the Jewish war of independence and epic defense of
Jerusalem. That decision ripped wide the breach between Jews who
regarded Jesus as the Messiah and those who did not. We see the hostility
expressed from the Christian side in **John's** harsh references to "the Jews."

---

[31]   Borg and Wright, *The Meaning of Jesus*, 199.

The harshness was real and reflected the contempt Christians (both Jews and Gentiles) had experienced from many synagogues during the crisis. Yet **John's** harsh references to "the Jews" may be more accurately translated "the Judeans," meaning those who lived in and around Jerusalem and collaborated with the oppressive temple structure, the empire's bureaucracy and its military forces.

Generally, the author did not feel bound by chronology; for example, the story of Jesus disrupting temple operations is told in chapter 2, even though that event happened at the very end of Jesus' life. The text places Jesus in Jerusalem four times during his adult life instead of once as reported by the synoptic gospels. Astonishing and unforgettable stories such as the raising of Lazarus are told only here. Might they be allegories rather than descriptions of historical events?

Another distinctive is **John's** emphasis on individuals and one-to-one conversation. It provides richly detailed accounts of Jesus' encounters with his mother (2:1–12), Nicodemus (3:1–20), the Samaritan woman (4:1–42), the sick man by the pool of Beth-zatha (5:1–18), the woman caught in the act of adultery (8:1–11), the man born blind (9:1–41), Mary, Martha and Lazarus (11:1–44), Pilate (18:28—19:12), Mary Magdalene (20:1–18), Thomas (20:24–29) and Peter (21:15–23). With our Western worldview, we immediately recognize this as a departure from much of the Bible. Finally, we say, a text that implicitly recognizes me and my importance, and not only the people group I happen to be a part of.

In addition to engaging conversations, the text describes a long teaching Jesus gave his disciples just the day before his arrest. This teaching begins with a description of Jesus washing his disciples' feet (John 13:1–20) and continues over five chapters. Jesus gave his disciples "a new commandment, that you love one another" (John 3:34). He spoke of his departure from them "to prepare a place" (John 14:3) and promised YHWH would send them one he called "the Spirit of truth" (John 14:17), "Advocate" and "Holy Spirit" (John 14:25) to guide them "into all the truth" (John 16:13). He predicted they would be hated; "if they persecuted me, they will persecute you" (John 15:20). Yet he also claimed to "have conquered the world" (John 16:33).

Jesus prayed for his disciples, asking his "Holy Father" to "protect them from the evil one" and "sanctify them in the truth." "As you, Father, are in me and I am in you, may they also be in us, so that the world may believe that you have sent me" (John 17:1–26).

Having said all of this, we at last come to the core purpose of the text: to challenge readers to be "born from above" (John 3:7) and recognize in Jesus the power to accomplish this act of reorientation and resistance. The author stated this purpose at the start: "To all who received [Jesus], who believed in his name, he gave power to become children of God, who were born not of blood or of the will of the flesh or of the will of man, but of God" (John 1:12).

Howard-Brook helps us understand the three birth choices the text asks us to reject.[32] To be "born of blood" is to root one's identity in the power of violence. It was the worldview of Pilate, who voiced empire's arrogance and lack of accountability with the question, "What is truth?" (John 18:38). To be "born of the will of the flesh" is to root one's identity in the conventional wisdom of this world. It was the worldview of Caiaphas, the high priest of the temple, who in an emergency meeting following the raising of Lazarus reached not for the word of YHWH but the *realpolitik* of the scapegoat: "It is better. . . to have one man die for the people than to have the whole nation destroyed" (John 11:50). To be "born of the will of man" is to root one's identity in patriarchy, the social and economic system by which most things got done in the Roman world. It was the worldview of those who ignored insights of the Samarian woman (John 4:1–42), felt contempt for the woman who anointed Jesus' feet with perfume (John 12:1–8) and took pride in dealing with empire by embracing father Caesar as king of the Judeans (John 19:15).

In his conversation with Nicodemus, a leader of the Judean Pharisees, Jesus said more about what being "born from above" entailed (John 3:7). "Just as Moses lifted up the serpent in the wilderness, so must the Son of Man be lifted up" (John 3:14). In other words, for the world to be saved (John 3:17), the innocent must be willing to suffer publicly while trusting YHWH for what happens next. We may recoil in horror at such an unhappy thought, but there it is. This is the "birth from above" Jesus embraced; it is the same birth-from-above Mahatma Gandhi, Dorothy Day,

---

[32]   Howard-Brook, 438.

Martin Luther King and other saints experienced.

It is tempting to view Jesus' suffering on a Roman cross as a once-and-done event that secured a never-ending life in heaven for all individuals who give their assent to the right list of beliefs.   That interpretation has been extracted often from this text, but only by ignoring the story in the very center: Jesus' confrontation with death in the raising of his friend, Lazarus, from the grave.

Out of fear of the authorities, Jesus and his disciples journeyed east of the Jordan where news of Lazarus' illness reached them.   The disciples argued against going to help Lazarus; it was simply too dangerous and they were afraid.   But they failed to dissuade Jesus, and Thomas exclaimed, "Let us also go [to Bethany], that we may die with [Lazarus]" (John 11:16).

When Jesus arrived at the grieving household, Lazarus' sister upbraided him for not arriving sooner.   "If you had been here, my brother would not have died" (John 11:21).   Jesus replied: "I am the resurrection and the life. Those who believe in me, even though they die, will live, and everyone who lives and believes in me will never die" (John 11:26). Jesus's words seemed to scramble the conventional meanings of life and death.   What did he mean?

Jesus then proceeded to the grave site, taking in all of the rituals of grief put into place as an accommodation of death.   Something about the entire production caused him to weep (John 11:35).   Over the objections of the mourners, Jesus requested the removal of the stone covering the mouth of the burial cave.   Then "he cried in a loud voice, 'Lazarus, come out!'" And to those standing by, "Unbind him and let him go" (John 11:28–44).

John Dear helps us grasp the meaning of the story.   Lazarus represents us, all of humanity.   We all are stricken, as good as dead within a culture that has surrendered to violence and the threat of violence as if they are forces of nature, like gravity or Earth's rotation.   The stench surrounds us, but we are disabled by fear. The best we can do is assuage the horror by our tears, pious speeches and fastidious attention to the rituals of dying.

Amid this despair, Jesus' call to Lazarus is an invitation to all of us to new life here and now, a life from above, a life unfettered by fear and unbound by the trappings of death. In this new life, we stop cooperating with empire's violence, patriarchy and other false authorities of the world; *instead we experience eternal life.* Not necessarily individual existence that never ends but the individual experience of *living now the very life of YHWH.* In **John's** theology, this was the great reversal launched by Messiah Jesus.[33]

With this story in mind, we can hear anew the words of Jesus.

> Truly I tell you, anyone who hears my word and believes him who sent me has eternal life, and does not come under judgment but has passed from death to life. Truly I tell you, the hour is coming, *and is now here,* when the dead will hear the voice of the Son of God, and those who hear will live. (John 5:24–25, emphasis added)

> The thief comes only to steal and kill and destroy; I came that [you] may have life, and have it abundantly. (John 10:10)

Near the end of this text, its purpose is stated this way: "These are written so that you may come to believe that Jesus is the Messiah, the Son of God, and through believing you may have life in his name" (John 20:31). That ties it all together. And it points to the alternative political community that emerged in Jesus' name and carried on his saving work.

Though we are weary of the stench of death, we have been hesitant to commit ourselves to Jesus' new community because we have been afraid and dazzled by promises of a free pass to heaven if we will just embrace the religion built around his name. But now we see how that kind of eternal life—a clock that never stops ticking, an immortal existence with YHWH—can easily become a vanity and a conceit. And that the "eternal life" Jesus spoke of can instead be the life *of* YHWH, the life *of* his Son, the life *of* confronting nonviolently all that steals and kills and destroys, the life *of* abundance. Jesus invited us to a life in which we, like his first disciples, *will name and forgive sin.* For such a challenging life, we will need a political community that follows his ways.

Standing before Pilate, Jesus said: "My kingdom is not *from* this

---

[33]   Dear, *Lazarus, Come Forth*, 48-61.

world. If my kingdom were *from* this world, my followers would be fighting to keep me from being handed over to the (Judeans). But as it is, my kingdom is not *from* here" (John 18:36, emphasis added). His authority and power did not rely on the techniques Rome had mastered: deception, fear and violence. Yet it claimed the same terrain, the same time in human history, the same populace.

"It is finished," Jesus said just before he died (John 19:30). Something powerful was unleashed as he hung there. But would it be stronger than empire? Or would Jesus' claim to "have conquered the world" (John 16:33) prove to be merely another hollow boast of a fallen hero?

Reflection and Discussion

25. Do you agree that Jesus intended "the kingdom of God" to describe a new understanding of power, new use of power and new way to run the world?

26. How did Jesus, calling himself "the human one/son of man," position himself in relation to common and dispossessed people on the one hand, and those who held power in the religious and political structures on the other? How would similar positioning look today in the society where you live?

27. What practices for living the new ways of the kingdom/empire of God are described in the parables of Jesus?

28. How would you explain the fact that the disciples of Jesus are portrayed as repeatedly failing to understand his message? As you reflect on this question, consider as well your contemporary situation and the reasons people resist messages similar to the one Jesus offered. Note that we will return to this question later (question 34).

29. Do you agree with the authors' assertion that Jesus emphasized an aspect of human nature that the empire preferred to ignore (see page 234)? Can you cite examples today where Jesus' emphasis is reflected in social norms, structures and ways of conducting activities?

30. What do you think of Matthew's and Mark's promise that, after his death and burial, Jesus will be seen in Galilee? What is the historical and symbolical significance of Galilee in Jesus' life?

31. What is the difference between an emphasis on having faith *in* Jesus and adopting the faith *of* Jesus as one's own?

32. In chapter 20, the authors start from the premise that Jesus was human and then discuss the sense in which Jesus also was divine. What is your response to this way of thinking about Jesus' identity? Did Jesus seem to think that other humans could be divine in the sense that he was?

33. Being "born from above" is the pathway to "eternal life;" that is the core of John's message. Compare John's use of the phrase "eternal life" with its use in conventional Christianity. What differences and similarities do you see?

21. A New Political Community
Acts of the Apostles

As we have seen in the previous two chapters, the life and message of Jesus followed the arc of the First Testament's story: the world is saved through the formation of a community that embodies a nonviolent but assertive alternative to empire. Jesus called this community "the kingdom of God." **Acts** provides a partial history of this community during the years following Jesus' crucifixion (from 30 CE–62 CE).

Borg notes that "when **Acts** was written, 'the parting of ways' between Judaism and early Christianity was more than well under way—it had happened." This is clear from "the way **Acts** characterizes Paul's opposition as 'the Jews' and the 'synagogue.' They are virtually generic terms."[34]   Following Borg, we take the view that this text was finalized and published early in the second century, using the earlier writings of an author named Luke, who also wrote the gospel known by his name. In three of Paul's letters, a co-worker (and physician) named "Luke" is mentioned. We think this Luke authored the original text, but likely died before the work was published. Others then edited the version we have.

The author began his history with a brief description of a forty-day period when the resurrected Jesus appeared often to his eleven surviving disciples (called "apostles" in the text), speaking to them "about the kingdom of God" (Acts 1:3). Time spent in Galilee is not mentioned. Instead, Jesus "ordered them not to leave Jerusalem but to wait there" (Acts 1:4). On their final occasion together, the disciples remained eager to talk about the restoration of a Jewish national state. Jesus changed the subject: "You will receive power when the Holy Spirit has come upon you; and you will be my witnesses in Jerusalem, in all Judea and Samaria, and to the ends of the earth." And then "a cloud took [Jesus] out of their sight" (Acts 1:6–11).

The text provides remarkably little information about Jesus' withdrawal from sight. Perhaps Luke did not perceive much to be needed;

---

[34]   Borg, 426.

the resurrected Jesus was no longer visible but his messianic spirit had been promptly embodied in a community of followers. So Luke emphasized how Jesus' disciples lived in Jerusalem and embraced a vocation to proclaim to people near and far that a new day had dawned. In other words, they did not become a band of rural rebels trying to regain control of ancestral lands, but an urban collective announcing to one and all a new social system and a new way of making the world work.

Of course, the era in which Luke wrote had a comprehensive social system (patriarchy) and widely accepted way of making the world work (the Roman Empire). But in Luke's view, Jesus had been on a collision course with those authority structures from the start. Luke had made that clear in his account of Mary's pregnancy and Jesus' birth. It snubbed patriarchy by never naming the father of her child (Luke 1:26–38) and by featuring Mary's efforts to cope with the scandal of her pregnancy via unaccompanied travel to visit Elizabeth (Luke 1:39–45). It tweaked empire by highlighting Mary's politically subversive vision of YHWH's work in the world (Luke 1:46–55) and by borrowing words from empire's vocabulary to describe Jesus' birth: good news, Savior, peace on earth.

In **Acts**, Luke continued the story he had begun in his gospel.

A. Pentecost

The initial setting of our text is Jerusalem, where the apostles and their companions (women included) gathered to mark the Festival of Weeks (called Pentecost in Greek). While together,

> suddenly from heaven there came a sound like the rush of a violent wind, and it filled the entire house where they were sitting. Divided tongues, as of fire, appeared among them and a tongue rested on each of them. All of them were filled with the Holy Spirit and began to speak other languages, as the Spirit gave them ability. (Acts 2:2–4)

Outside the house, members of the Jewish diaspora "from every nation under heaven" heard speech in their native languages. The text identifies a dozen of the languages spoken. "All were amazed and perplexed, saying . . .'What does this mean'" (Acts 2:1–12)?

Peter, ever the first to speak, explained to the curious crowd what had just occurred: the fulfillment of a prophetic description of "the last days" (Acts 2:17) when YHWH's animating Spirit would overflow. Notice that Peter did not claim this was the Spirit's first appearance, nor did he make an effort to explain the miraculous nature of the event. Instead, Peter emphasized its *abundance* and how it *crossed social boundaries.* Male and female, old and young, apostles and servants had all been blessed by the same astonishing experience. Peter went on to quote apocalyptic references to "the sun [turning] to darkness and the moon to blood" (Acts 2:20). This was his way of saying world-changing events were occurring.

And then he spoke of Jesus, "a man attested to you by God with deeds of power, wonders and signs that God did." You killed him, Peter said, "but God raised him up, having freed him from death because it was impossible for him to be held in its power" (Acts 2:24). It was this resurrected Jesus who had "poured out this [Spirit] that you both see and hear" (Acts 2:33). "Therefore, let the entire house of Israel know with certainty that God has made [Jesus] both Lord and Messiah" (Acts 2:36). Those that heard Peter's words "were cut to the heart" and asked, "What should we do?" Peter answered, "Repent and be baptized . . . so that your sins may be forgiven, and you will receive the gift of the Holy Spirit" (Acts 2:37–38). That day, about 3,000 people became Jesus-followers.

Though Peter thought something historic had just occurred, signaling a heightened presence of YHWH among the people, he said nothing about David's throne, the land of Israel or the temple.

As reported by **Acts**, Pentecost's "wind" and "tongues" occurred in a private setting among people already persuaded by Jesus, much like the resurrection and ascension. Those two events had not resulted in any publicly visible social change. But with the din of multi-lingual voices and Peter's sermon to the crowd, the story turned from the private and miraculous to something very public and verifiable. This turning defined the character of the community that emerged from Pentecost. It functioned out in public places for all to see, engaging in politically charged activities that clearly communicated the conviction that in Jesus, the world had changed.

B. Forming, storming and norming

Many of those 3,000 Jews probably went back to their own countries after the Festival of Weeks ended, carrying their stories and new-found convictions with them and defining the new community as an international movement from the get-go. But some resided in Jerusalem and they added strength and vitality to the group led by Peter there.

Like any other new group, the Jesus-followers in Jerusalem went through the classic stages of formation and development. They selected a new twelfth apostle, Mathias, to replace Judas (Acts 1:12–26) and provide leadership. They confirmed their core values, committing time to "teaching and fellowship, to the breaking of bread and the prayers" (Acts 2:42). They instituted key practices: sharing property, selling possessions and distributing the proceeds to those in need. They established routines that supported their mission, such as public gatherings at the temple and meetings in private homes for shared meals (Acts 2:44–46).

The economic sharing was remarkable. The text reports: "There was not a needy person among them, for as many as owned lands or houses sold them and brought the proceeds of what was sold. They laid it at the apostles' feet and it was distributed to each as any had need" (Acts 4:34–35). Curiously, the text does not provide a rationale for this practice; it assumes readers understand this is how the world works, now that the Messiah has come.

The storms of conflict came along too. As we can imagine, many needy people joined a movement that assumed the world worked on the principle of abundance rather than scarcity. The apostles could not keep up with the work and apparently helped first those with whom they were most familiar. Thus, they neglected the widows of Hellenist background, meaning Jews who had lived in places dominated by Greek culture and language. This led to complaints. The problem was addressed by adding individuals of Hellenistic background to leadership (Acts 6:1–7).

An instance that ended unhappily involved Ananias and Sapphira, a married couple who owned land, joined the new community and decided to sell a property and commit the proceeds to the common purse. But they held divided intentions, wanting to retain some proceeds for private use while also receiving public credit for giving it all. When they acted on these divided intentions by misrepresenting the amount of the proceeds, Peter confronted them with their deception. Both were stricken and died (Acts 5:1–11). Evidently, transparency was a core value of the new community; deception was anathema.

Miraculous healings occurred as well, apparently in great number (Acts 5:12–16). The healing of a crippled beggar at a gate to the temple attracted much public attention because the beggar was well known. Peter used the occasion to give a second impromptu sermon. Speaking to the crowd that had gathered to gawk at the healed cripple, Peter spoke of Jesus as the fulfillment of the First Testament story that started with YHWH's covenant with Abraham, ran through Moses and his promise of a great prophet to come, and included "all the prophets . . . from Samuel and those after him [who] predicted these days" (Acts 3:24). Again, Peter said nothing about King David, the land of Israel or the temple.

And Peter voiced this appeal to the crowd, which tells us much about his expectations for the future:

> Repent, therefore, and turn to God so that your sins may be wiped out, so that times of refreshing may come from the presence of [YHWH] and that he may send the Messiah appointed for you, that is, Jesus, who must remain in heaven until the time of universal restoration that God announced long ago through his holy prophets. (Acts 3:19–21)

C. Harassment and scattering

Peter's speech ended with his arrest by the temple guards, apparently because Peter had caused a public disturbance. The next day, the high priest and other officials of the temple bureaucracy convened a public hearing to inquire into the activities of the Jesus movement.

Peter again spoke of "[Messiah] Jesus of Nazareth whom you crucified [and] God raised from the dead" (Acts 4:10). He spoke boldly: "There is salvation in no one else, for there is no other name under heaven given among mortals by which we must be saved" (Acts 4:12). "Salvation" was a political term; it was what *Pax Romana* claimed to bestow on the people. Peter said no, it comes from Messiah Jesus.

Beside Peter as he spoke stood the healed cripple, living proof that a miracle had occurred. The temple authorities assessed their position and found it surprisingly weak. And so they simply ordered Peter to stop talking about Jesus, to which Peter replied: "We cannot keep from speaking about what we have seen and heard" (Acts 4:20). The high priest threatened further punishment and then released them.

The incident served to bolster the new community. After gathering to debrief and pray, "they were all filled with the Holy Spirit and spoke the word of God with boldness" (Acts 4:31).

So the high priest carried through with his threats and "arrested the apostles and put them in the public prison" (Acts 5:18). But apparently the guards included sympathizers of the new community for during the night, the doors were unlocked and the apostles walked out of jail and returned to the temple court where they began teaching at daybreak.

Arrested a third time and again arraigned, Peter defended himself with these words: "We must obey God rather than any human authority." He then proceeded to speak of how God, by raising Jesus from death, had "exalted" Jesus "as leader and savior" (Acts 5:29–31).

Some among the temple leaders wanted to kill the apostles and put an end to such talk. They were dissuaded by one of their number, a famous teacher known as Gamaliel, who said that if the apostles were not doing the work of YHWH, they would soon self-destruct. So the high priest had the apostles flogged and then ordered them again to stop speaking about Jesus. The apostles again ignored the order and continued teaching every day in the temple, proclaiming Jesus to be the Messiah (Acts 5:33–42).

Opponents next targeted Stephen, one of the men appointed earlier to help manage food distribution. They accused Stephen of blasphemy uttered during a debate at a local synagogue and managed to have him arrested and brought before the temple council. There Stephen spoke at length about Israel's history. After speaking of Solomon, the building of the temple, and how YHWH "does not dwell in houses made with human hands," Stephen made an accusation: "Which of the prophets did your ancestors not persecute? They killed those who foretold the coming of the Righteous One, and now you have become his betrayers and murderers"

(Acts 7:48, 53). Then he raised his eyes and said, "Look, I see the heavens opened and the Son of Man standing at the right hand of God" (Acts 7:56). This so angered the temple council and its sycophants that they carried Stephen out of the city and stoned him.

The murder of Stephen uncorked more harassment and violence. Saul, a member of the Jewish diaspora, a Pharisee, a student of Gamaliel and a participant in the stoning of Stephen, led a group of officially–authorized vigilantes who "entered house after house, dragging off both men and women . . . to prison" (Acts 8:3). Although the apostles apparently enjoyed a measure of immunity, other members of the new community fled Jerusalem in fear to places we know today as Lebanon, Cyprus, Syria and Turkey. There they continued to proclaim, mainly to Jews but occasionally to Gentiles too, that the Messiah had come and the direction of history changed.

D. Saul of Tarsus

Saul acted as an agent of the high priest, authorized to purge synagogues of Jesus-followers. On his way to Damascus for that purpose, a flash of light surrounded him and he heard a voice saying, "Saul, Saul, why do you persecute me?" Saul replied, "Who are you, Lord?" The voice answered, "I am Jesus" (Acts 9:1–5). Though Saul's eyes were open, he saw nothing. His companions led him to Damascus where for three days he fasted and prayed.

Meanwhile, a Jesus–follower named Ananias felt summoned by YHWH to the house where Saul was staying. Ananias feared Saul and was reluctant to go near him, but went nevertheless.

> He laid his hands on Saul and said, "Brother Saul, the Lord Jesus who appeared to you on your way here has sent me so that you may regain your sight and be filled with the Holy Spirit." Immediately something like scales fell from his eyes, and his sight was restored. Then he got up and was baptized and after taking some food, he regained his strength. (Acts 9:17–19)

This story is usually told in a way that emphasizes the event along the road to Damascus, but the text tells us Saul remained blind and without understanding until his enemy addressed him as "Brother Saul" and laid hands of blessing on his body. That was his moment of conversion.

Saul immediately began talking about Jesus in Damascus synagogues. "He is the Son of God," Saul said, borrowing the commonly-used phrase describing the Roman emperor (Acts 9:20). What's more, Saul said Jesus was the Messiah (Acts 9:22). Saul's turn-about prompted former colleagues to hatch a murder plot. But an informer let Saul know of the plan, and so he left in the dark of night by slipping over the city wall in a basket (Acts 9:23–25). From there, he went to Arabia for a time before returning again to Damascus, where he apparently joined Ananias in the local synagogue. This period in Saul's life lasted three years (Galatians 1:18).

Saul then returned to Jerusalem, intending to join the Jesus-followers there (Acts 9:26). A respected Jew, Barnabas, introduced him to a still-skeptical Peter and to James, the leader of the Jerusalem assembly (Galatians 1:18–19). The introduction went well enough, but most Jesus-followers were afraid to meet with him. When Saul began to attract attention in the city by publicly engaging people about Jesus, Peter and James stepped in, escorting him out of the city and sending him to Tarsus along the southern coast of present-day Turkey, where he apparently had family (Acts 9:30).

Sometime around 40 CE, Barnabas was put in charge of the synagogue of Jesus-followers in Antioch of Syria (currently Antakya in southern Turkey). Barnabas invited Saul to join the group as a teacher. There, the word "Christian" was first used to describe Jesus-followers (Acts 11:26). Though still a reform effort within Judaism rather than a separate religion, the strength of the movement had earned it a name of its own. It also attracted interest among Gentiles living in the area.

E. Gentile converts and the Jerusalem council

Chapter 8 of the text attributes the scattering of Jesus-followers to Jewish persecution, but it appears imperial persecution also played a role. King Herod Agrippa, the childhood friend of Emperor Claudius and the empire's vassal king of Palestine, put James the disciple to death by the sword. Herod Agrippa also imprisoned Peter (Acts 12:1–5).

The scattering of the Jesus-followers caused the movement to spread among people who aspired to live as Jews, but had been denied that opportunity. The text provides two accounts of this involving a man named Philip. First he healed and preached in Samaria, "proclaiming the good news about the kingdom of God and the name of [Messiah] Jesus" (Acts 8:12). A local magician, Simon, was convinced and baptized; thereafter, he "stayed constantly with Philip," apparently captivated by Philip's miraculous healing powers.

The apostles heard of Philip's work and sent Peter and John to provide guidance to the group around Philip. Peter and John "prayed for them that they might receive the Holy Spirit," which occurred when they "laid their hands on them" (Acts 8:15–17). Whether this again entailed speaking in foreign languages is not clear, but whatever manifestation of the Spirit occurred, it impressed Simon, who offered the apostles money if they would teach him how to summon the same power. Peter replied: "May your silver perish with you, because you thought you could obtain God's gift with money" (Acts 8:20–24).

The second story occurred on the road to Gaza where Philip encountered a YHWH-fearing Gentile and eunuch who held a high position in the Ethiopian royal court. The man had been reading from **Isaiah** about one "like a sheep . . . led to the slaughter" (Isaiah 53:7) and asked Philip who the text referred to. Philip answered by proclaiming "the good news about Jesus" (Acts 8:35). Upon coming to some water, the man asked to be baptized and Philip agreed.

This story obviously suggests Jesus and the kingdom he had proclaimed were attractive to many kinds of people, not only ethnic Jews. But it also signifies the arrival of the Messianic age in which **Isaiah** had said YHWH would give eunuchs, flawed sexually as they were, "an everlasting name that shall not be cut off" (Isaiah 56:5).

The story of Peter and Cornelius illustrates how unsettling the broad appeal of Jesus could be. Cornelius was a Gentile and an officer in the Roman army where he commanded a battalion of soldiers that— because of its proximity to Jerusalem—may have been involved in the execution of Jesus. Cornelius was not a convert to Judaism but "a devout man who feared God . . . [and] gave alms generously to the people and prayed constantly to God" (Acts 10:2). Probably, he attended synagogue and was well-versed in Jewish teaching.

The text tells us that through coordinated visions, YHWH spoke to Cornelius and Peter, prompting Cornelius to seek a meeting and Peter to set aside his normal refusal to fraternize with Gentiles. The meeting occurred in Cornelius' house, where a group of his friends had assembled. Peter spoke first about YHWH, the god who "shows no partiality but in every nation anyone who fears him and does what is right is acceptable to him." He then spoke of Messiah Jesus bringing "peace" and called him "Lord of all," aiming both quotes directly at an imperial ideology that boasted of the "peace of Rome" and applied the title "Lord" to its emperors. Peter implied that even Caesar was now accountable to this new standard: "[Jesus] commanded us . . . to testify that he is the one ordained by God as judge of the living and the dead" (Acts 10:34–42).

"While Peter was still speaking, the Holy Spirit fell upon all who heard the word" prompting them to speak in tongues. The Jews in the gathering were astonished that Gentiles had been affirmed by YHWH in this way. Peter said, "Can anyone withhold the water for baptizing these people who have received the Holy Spirit just as we have?" And so they proceeded with baptism (Acts 10:44–48).

Meanwhile, around 45 CE in Antioch of Syria, the synagogue of Jesus-followers had grown strong enough to send two of its members, Barnabas and Saul, on a preaching campaign to Cyprus and then into Galatia (central Turkey). On such a journey, they expected often to engage Gentile audiences. What message would Barnabas and Saul give them about becoming part of this new Jewish movement?

This was a potentially huge issue and before proceeding with the preaching campaign, the group in Antioch sent Paul and Barnabas to Jerusalem to deliver a sum of money for the needs of the Jesus-followers there (Acts 11:30) and to consult with James, Peter and John, the acknowledged leaders of the movement. In private conversations during the visit, Paul and Barnabas asked whether circumcision would be required of the Gentiles who became Jesus-followers. As recounted by Paul, the Jerusalem leaders made no such requirement, "but gave to Barnabas and me the right hand of fellowship. They asked only one thing, that we remember the poor" and continue to collect money for their needs (Galatians 2:9–10).

Empowered by the blessing of the Jerusalem leaders, Barnabas and Saul sailed to Cyprus, where they spoke in synagogues all across the island. When they reached Paphos on the western shore, they engaged the Roman governor, who accepted their message and became a Jesus-follower (Acts 13:4–12).

After sailing north to Perga and traveling overland to the region of Galatia, they again visited synagogues. As a scholar and former student of Gamaliel, Saul (now going by the name Paul) routinely received invitations to speak. The text records in detail his remarks at Antioch. After speaking about Jewish history, Paul explained that though the residents of Jerusalem and their leaders asked the Romans to kill Jesus, "what God promised to our ancestors he has fulfilled for us, their children, by raising Jesus" (Acts 13:32–33). The message was well received and Paul was invited to speak again the next Sabbath.

When that day arrived, nearly the entire city turned out, including Gentiles. Local Jewish leaders felt uncomfortable with the enthusiasm of the Gentiles and so contradicted what the two men said. In response, Barnabas and Paul withdrew from the synagogue and directed their message to the Gentile audiences. Many became Jesus-followers. Thus, when some time later the city's leaders expelled Barnabas and Paul, they left behind a largely Gentile assembly (Acts 13:48–52).

In each of the cities of Galatia they visited next (Iconium, Lystra, Derbe), a similar pattern unfolded. Barnabas and Paul began preaching in the synagogues, encountered interest but also serious opposition, turned to mainly Gentile audiences who were eager for their message, and then found themselves part of a city-wide uproar in which "some sided with the Jews and some with the apostles" (Acts 14:4). The conflict in Lystra was so intense that some residents nearly stoned Paul to death.

It is easy to understand the divided Jewish response. For 1,000 years the Jewish way of faithfulness to YHWH had entailed a clear separation from Gentiles. However attractive the message of Jesus as Messiah might have been to Jews, the enthusiasm of the Gentiles at least suggested that devout Jews should keep their distance. Yes, the prophets had spoken of the pilgrimage of the nations to the mountain of YHWH, but wasn't it odd for devout Jews and pagans to embrace enthusiastically the same man as savior of the world?

Moreover, as pointed out by Crossan, a sizable share of the first Gentile Jesus-followers may have been "YHWH-fearing Gentiles" already associated with Jewish life through synagogue attendance and support. Though not full converts, they worshipped YHWH and had accepted some Jewish practices, such as Sabbath observance. They were attracted to a message like Paul's that offered full membership in a community committed to the Messiah without compliance with requirements such as circumcision. In the reshuffling that occurred in Galatia following Paul's preaching, synagogues lost these supportive Gentiles and their resources. [35]

After Derbe, Barnabas and Paul retraced their steps, stopping in the places they had visited previously to appoint leaders for each new community and "encourage them to continue in the faith, saying: 'It is through many persecutions that we must enter the kingdom of God.'" (Acts 14:22–23). Then they sailed to Antioch of Syria, perhaps in 49 CE.

Judaism had a long tradition of missionary activity and long-established practices by which a convert entered into relationship with a local synagogue, either as a circumcised proselyte or a YHWH–fearing Gentile. Prior to this first preaching campaign, those long-established practices usually had been used to integrate Gentile Jesus-followers into synagogue life. But the situation in Galatia was unprecedented: new assemblies made up *primarily* of Gentiles and estranged from nearby synagogues. This required new forms of guidance and oversight, and men from Jerusalem stepped forward to help by visiting the new assemblies. Despite the careful discussions Barnabas and Paul had initiated before starting their preaching campaign, these leaders from Jerusalem required the male Gentile converts in Galatia to be circumcised (Acts 15:1).

Paul and Barnabas objected strenuously to this requirement (Acts 15:2) and the resulting controversy became so intense that a meeting of apostles and elders convened in Jerusalem around 50 CE. Peter spoke of his experiences in which YHWH "gave [Gentiles] the Holy Spirit, just as he did to us, and in cleansing their hearts by faith he has made no

---

[35]   Crossan, 157-158.

distinction between them and us" (Acts 15:8–9). Barnabas and Paul told of similar experiences.

Then James, brother of Jesus and leader of the Jerusalem apostles, spoke. He noted how Peter had described YHWH acting "to take from among [the Gentiles] a people for his name" (Acts 15:14). He recalled the words of the prophet Amos, who looked ahead to "that day" (Amos 9:11) when YHWH would "rebuild the dwelling of David, which has fallen; from its ruins I will rebuild it, and I will set it up so that all other peoples may seek (YHWH), even all the Gentiles over whom my name has been called" (Acts 15:16–17). And he said, "I have reached the decision that we should not trouble those Gentiles who are turning to God" (Acts 15:19).

Our text quotes the decision of the so-called Jerusalem Council, which was conveyed to the new communities via letter. "It has seemed good to the Holy Spirit and to us to impose on you no further burden than these essentials: that you abstain from idols and from blood and from what is strangled and from fornication. If you keep from these, you will do well. Farewell" (Acts 15:28–29). The Gentiles received the letter joyfully (Acts 15:31). While it included conditions, it freed them from the obligation of meeting circumcision requirements and opened the way for them to freely participate with Jewish followers of Jesus in shaping the character and identity of their communities.

If circumcision, the very sign that evidenced Abraham's covenant with YHWH (Genesis 17:10) was no longer required, *why attach such importance to old rules about food?* Howard-Brook provides perspective on this pivotal decision that yielded such a puzzling list of prohibitions. The four items retained all are linked to "practices that mark inclusion within imperial society." By prohibiting them, the Council conveyed its insistence that "people imbedded in imperial behavior must withdraw in order to become 'brothers and sisters' in the way of Jesus." [36]

The reference to fornication can be particularly difficult for us to understand because we think of it exclusively in terms of sexual morality. The term used in the original text (*porneia*) referred to prostitution, which occurred in various settings, but prominently in connection with temples,

---

[36]   Howard-Brook, 432.

festivals and events that entailed worship of deceased emperors or one of the other gods of Roman–Greco culture. Such settings also entailed eating food that had been offered to and blessed by an idol. This included meat—a food not widely available for daily meals—from animals killed by strangulation. Such settings also invariably entailed celebration of the living emperor and thanksgiving for the peace empire had provided. The Council insisted Gentile Jesus-followers make a break with all of this by discontinuing practices that suggested allegiance to empire.

"Fornication" is often used metaphorically in the Bible to describe efforts to gain status and wealth *by giving oneself to powerful men for their pleasure.* **Hosea** and **Ezekiel** used the image of a whore to make this analogy; **Jeremiah** used the image of a donkey in heat. By its reference to fornication, the Council also meant this sort of covetous, suck-up behavior. Though such conduct might be the norm among pagan peoples (as well as among unrighteous Jews), to become full members of Jesus-following synagogues, it had to be left behind.

F. Turning the world upside down

The decision of the Jerusalem Council removed what had been the primary barrier to expansion of the new community among Gentiles. Thereafter, the message of the kingdom of God as a political community following the way of Jesus could be appropriately contextualized without needing to resemble exactly the Jewish expression of it.

Chapters 16 through 20 of our text describe two preaching campaigns Paul completed from 50–58 CE. Twice more he spent time with the communities he and Barnabas had launched in the region of Galatia. He also began new communities of Jesus-followers in the provinces of Asia, Macedonia and Achaia (the first in modern-day Turkey, the other two in modern-day Greece) and then returned to work with them again a few years later.

As in his travels with Barnabas, on these additional campaigns Paul usually began in a new city by attending Sabbath services in the local synagogue and engaging the people there. If no synagogue was present, Paul sought out individual Jews or Gentiles who were YHWH-fearing and acquainted with Jewish teaching. Thus, in Philippi in the province of

Macedonia, Paul's initial contact was with a group of women who gathered near a river for prayer. Lydia, a Gentile, "worshiper of God" (Acts 16:14) and textile merchant, joined the conversation and then asked to be baptized as a sign of her allegiance to Jesus. She hosted Paul and opened her home to the community of Jesus-followers that formed in Philippi.

Wherever he went, Paul's experience included conflict. Thessalonica, also in the region of Macedonia, is an example. Paul spoke in the synagogue, "explaining and proving that it was necessary for the Messiah to suffer and to rise from the dead, and saying, 'This is the Messiah, Jesus whom I am proclaiming to you'" (Acts 17:3). Some Jews were convinced, but the response from "devout Greeks and not a few of the leading women" was more broadly positive (Acts 17:4). This led to controversy and civil disturbances provoked by those seeking to undermine the attractiveness of Paul's message. These civil disturbances led to the involvement of civil authorities who had the responsibility to keep the peace.

Paul's opponents accused him of "turning the world upside down" by "acting contrary to the decrees of the emperor, saying that there is another king named Jesus" (Acts 17:6–7). Local officials took such accusations seriously because they suggested sedition against the empire.

At Corinth, in the region of Achaia, Paul stayed with a Jewish couple, Aquila and Priscilla, and engaged in his craft of tent-making. Every Sabbath he attended synagogue and testified there "that the Messiah was Jesus" (Acts 18:5). When it became clear that his message had been rejected, Paul moved his teaching to the home of Justus, a Gentile and "worshiper of God" who lived *next door* to the synagogue (Acts 18:7). He carried on there in direct competition with the synagogue for eighteen months. This situation also ended up before the civil authorities, this time a high–profile hearing before Gallio, the governor of Achaia, where Paul was accused of "persuading people to worship God in ways that are contrary to the law" (Acts 18:13). Gallio brushed aside the accusation, but the very fact that he was involved showed that Paul's teaching had ignited a high–stakes political controversy.

At Ephesus, in the region of Asia Minor, Paul arrived at a time when about a dozen members of the local synagogue already had become Jesus-followers. Paul "laid his hands on them, the Holy Spirit came upon them, and they spoke in tongues and prophesied" (Acts 19:6). Paul attended synagogue for three months, "arguing persuasively about the kingdom of God" (Acts 19:8). When he sensed the majority had turned against his message, he and the Jesus-followers left the synagogue and Paul "argued daily in the lecture hall of Tyranus. This continued for two years so that all the residents of Asia [Minor], both Jews and Greeks, heard the word of [YHWH]" (Acts 19:9–10).

Ephesus was home to the Temple of Artemis, a Greek goddess also known as Diana. The temple was one of the seven wonders of the ancient world, superior (according to the ancient compiler of the list) to the others. It was 450 feet long, 225 feet wide and surrounded by 127 columns gilded by gold and silver. The interior was adorned by sculpture and paintings by famous artists. Throughout the last half of the first century, the Temple of Artemis increasingly became entwined with the imperial cult and veneration of the emperor.

During the time that Paul was "arguing daily" at the civic lecture hall, the artisans who made knock-offs of the goddess and sold them to visitors experienced a significant drop in sales. One of them, a silversmith named Demetrius, organized the artisans to oppose Paul.

> Men, you know that we get our wealth from this business. You also see and hear not only in Ephesus but in almost the whole of Asia [Minor] this Paul has persuaded and drawn away a considerable number of people by saying that gods made with hands are not gods. And there is danger not only that this trade of ours may come into disrepute but also that the temple of the great goddess Artemis will be scorned, and she will be deprived of her majesty that brought all of Asia [Minor] and the world to worship her. (Acts 19:25–27)

Much controversy and confusion followed, climaxing in a confrontation at the lecture hall that went on for hours at near-riot pitch. Apparently some of the blame focused on the Jews, perhaps because of Paul's earlier association with the synagogue. The incident ended without further violence, and Paul soon left the city (Acts 19:28–41).

For modern readers, these stories prompt a question: was not Paul responsible for a significant portion of the conflict he so frequently encountered? As a follower of the Prince of Peace, why didn't he proceed in a more conciliatory manner?

But such a critique fails to take into account an important aspect of the context: because it believed Jesus was Lord, the new community was *unavoidably in a posture of conflict* vis-à-vis those who were loyal to the empire's worldview and methods. Recognition of this reality was part of the decision of the Jerusalem Council. It appears again in the story of Paul in Philippi, where he was dragged into court and accused of "disturbing our city . . . and advocating customs *that are not lawful for us as Romans to observe*" (Acts 16:20–21, emphasis added). The magistrate had Paul flogged and imprisoned; he understood that Paul was asking Romans citizens to transfer their loyalty from the emperor to Jesus. A modern parallel would be a Christian youth ministry that instructed young believers not to say the Pledge of Allegiance in their schools or sing the national anthem.

Paul's subversion of the authority of the goddess Artemis is yet another example. It may appear Paul made only a religious argument, yet it set in motion changes that had deep economic and political implications. The silver artisans recognized this and responded with political counter-moves. A contemporary analogy would be a religious campaign to delegitimize US military spending by revealing the deceptive nature of the rationale that supports it. Many Americans would prefer continued deception to the job losses that would occur if defense and security contracting dried up.

Paul assumed he would encounter conflict because he had committed himself to a lord other than Caesar. Whether or not he relished it misses the point. *Conflict with the empire was a given when you followed Jesus,* who had revealed the way YHWH intended for life on Earth to be lived. It could not be avoided through finesse or conflict resolution skills; in the nonviolent way of Jesus, it had to be engaged.

G. Preaching to the empire

Upon returning to Jerusalem after his third preaching campaign, Paul visited the leaders and reported "one-by-one the things that God had done among the Gentiles through his ministry." James and the elders rejoiced at the report, but voiced concern about Paul's reputation. Many Jewish Jesus-followers were zealous for the law, they said, and had been angered by reports that "you teach all the Jews living among the Gentiles to forsake Moses, and that you tell them not to circumcise their children or observe the customs. What then is to be done" (Acts 21:19–22)?

The elders answered their own question. They asked Paul to go through a Jewish rite of purification to demonstrate his faithful observance of the Jewish law. Paul agreed. So Paul shaved his head and along with other men began a seven-day purification ritual at the temple. Near the end of the seven days, Jews from Asia (Minor) recognized him and "stirred up the whole crowd. They seized him, shouting . . . 'This is the man who is teaching everyone everywhere against our people, our law and this place; more than that, he has actually brought Greeks into the temple and defiled this holy place'" (Acts 21:27–28). The people in the temple court seized Paul and began beating him. Roman soldiers arrived, rescued Paul from his attackers, bound him and then took him away. The mob continued to press in on Paul so fiercely that the soldiers had to carry Paul on their shoulders to protect him.

Just before Paul was brought into the barracks, he spoke in Greek to the commander. "I am a Jew, from Tarsus in Cilicia, a citizen of an important city; I beg you, let me speak to the people" (Acts 21:39). Having just been rescued from probable death, Paul now offered extended impromptu remarks to the angry crowd: "Brothers and fathers, listen to the defense that I now make before you" (Acts 22:1).

During the final seven chapters of our text, Paul was in the empire's custody, first in Jerusalem, then in the Roman garrison at Caesarea and finally in Rome. The conditions of his confinement apparently were not severe, and he continued writing and communicating with his extensive network.

His accusers said he was "an agitator among all the Jews throughout the world and a ringleader of the sect of the Nazarenes [who] tried to profane the temple" (Acts 24:5–6). Paul was examined by the chief priest and temple council, by two Roman governors (Felix and Festus), and by King Herod Agrippa II. From all accounts, he relished the opportunity to speak to Roman officials about Jesus. He was consistently respectful. He insisted he had done nothing to profane the temple or Jewish law and repeatedly spoke of the resurrection of the dead, which he said was the root of his dispute with temple leaders. He was careful not to trigger a charge of sedition; thus, in his statements to officials he used the word "Lord" to refer to Jesus only once (Acts 26:15) and never referred to "the son of God."

Yet the way Paul spoke of YHWH's purpose in sending him to preach to the Gentiles implied that the way of Jesus was an alternative to the empire's: "I [YHWH] am sending you to open [the Gentiles'] eyes so that they may turn from darkness to light and from the power of Satan to God" (Acts 26:17–18). In reply, Festus exclaimed: "You are out of your mind" (Acts 26:24). How could a sane person call the way of Jesus an alternative to *Pax Romana?*

When Festus suggested moving Paul's trial to Jerusalem, Paul appealed to the emperor, thereby taking the matter out of the governor's hands (Acts 25:10). Two things motivated Paul's appeal: fear of what awaited him if he were tried in the hostile setting of Jerusalem, and eagerness to travel to Rome where he could speak face-to-face with Jews and curious Gentiles living there. His resort to the empire's legal system for protection could be characterized as a lack of trust in YHWH's promises. Yet the text reveals no hint of defensiveness about this.

In 60 CE, Paul was transported under guard to Rome, surviving a shipwreck along the way. There Paul lived under house arrest and was able to confer freely with local Jewish leaders. Our text does not tell us how Paul's story ended. Instead, it finishes with these words: "[Paul] lived there two whole years at his own expense and welcomed all who came to him, proclaiming the kingdom of God and teaching about the Lord Jesus [Messiah] with all boldness and without hindrance" (Acts 28:30).

Given that **Acts** was published perhaps forty years after the Roman Empire executed Paul, why doesn't it report this fact? Borg suggests such an ending would have "undermined" the author's effort to portray Christians as unthreatening "to the imperial way of ordering the world." Although **Acts** reports how Jesus' followers turned the world upside down and occasionally got into trouble with Roman authorities, the final text—published during an era when imperial persecution had intensified—was careful not to push this theme too far. [37]

This explains why **Acts** often portrays "the Jews" as the primary opponent of the Jesus-movement and the empire as the fair-minded upholder of the law. We see positive references to the empire most clearly in the apology of the Philippian magistrate (Acts 16:35–39), the refusal of the Roman governor in Corinth to bring charges against Paul (Acts 18:12–17), the helpful actions of the Roman tribune in Jerusalem (Acts 21:31—22:29), and the generous confinement arrangements it made for Paul after taking him into protective custody in Jerusalem. The stories of the empire's harsh jailing of Paul while he lived in Ephesus (see page 282 below) and its execution of Paul are omitted entirely.

Reflection and Discussion

34. In chapter 19 and question 28, we discussed how Jesus' disciples failed to grasp Jesus' message. How do you account for the change we see in **Acts**? Why do Jesus-followers now get it?

35. What do you make of the very public style of the Jesus movement? Did this reflect missionary zeal, an attempt to undermine the Roman Empire, both, or something else?

36. What was glue holding the Jesus movement together? Can that glue serve us today in forming an alternative to empire, or is there something analogous that could serve that purpose?

37. What was the source of the movement's social/political power?

38. How would you characterize the way **Acts** describes the Roman Empire and its officials? What parallels (if any) does it offer to the way you relate to the USA-led empire and its officials today?

---

[37]   Borg, 491.

22. Life Beyond the Empire (Part B)

Galatians, Thessalonians, Corinthians, Philemon, Colossians, Romans, Philippians, Timothy, Ephesians, Hebrews, Jude, John, Peter, Titus

Though in a sustained confrontation with the Roman Empire, the new communities of Jesus-followers did not commit time and energy to overturning it. Instead, as Howard-Brook tells us by a quote from Dorothy Day, they began to "build a new civilization within the shell of the old." [38]

As the practices and rituals required by the *Torah* shaped Jewish life after the Babylonian exile, so the texts discussed in this chapter shaped the Jewish-Gentile communities of Jesus-followers. In each context, the desired outcome was a corporate body that bore public witness to YHWH and stood before the nations as an alternative to empire.

This shaping dynamic was particularly important for Gentiles who previously had not been part of a synagogue and tradition that stood some distance from the norms and expectations of prevailing powers. As part of their embrace of Jesus and his way, these Gentiles had stepped away from participation in the rituals of empire and severed important social and economic linkages. Now they needed a new network of support and the opportunity to grow into habits of counter-culture living.

Many of the texts surveyed in this chapter are letters. Even more than the other biblical texts, letters are context-specific. Thus, we should be cautious about applying them too broadly; perhaps what we read was written because of particular dynamics within a very specific context.

A. Paul's letters

Before any of the gospels had been written, the Apostle Paul wrote at least seven letters (we say nine) to Jesus-followers in communities he had helped start. These letters, written over a period of fifteen years, will be introduced next *in the order written.* Because Paul wrote before anyone except James and expressed himself in theological terms, his impact on Christianity has been greater than any other author.

---

[38]   Howard-Brook, 433.

The word translated "church" in these texts is *"ekklesia"* in the language in which Paul wrote. He used it to refer to regular meetings of Jesus-followers, whether these occurred as a synagogue or as a group apart from the synagogue. In the context of Paul's time, *ekklesia* referred to a civic gathering or citizen assembly; the word had a political, not religious, connotation. *The fact that Paul chose a political term to refer to groups of Jesus-followers tells us he expected them to be a public presence.* In line with Paul's usage, we use "assembly" rather than "church" when referring to the first century groups.

Before we survey Paul's letters, it is important to introduce briefly his worldview and theology, including his positive view of human capacity and his analysis of how structures of deception had blocked expression of that capacity. "What can be known about God is plain" and has been "understood and seen," he said (Rom. 1:19–20), but also has been distorted by false worship and an imperial worldview (Rom. 1:21–23). With its vision thus obscured, humanity had traded a righteous and just path for a road to destruction, the so-called wrath of YHWH (Rom. 1:18; 3:4; 3:9–18; 6:15–16). Yet Paul did not regard destruction to be humanity's certain fate; in his view, the life and death of Jesus of Nazareth (Rom. 5:10) were singular historical events that had broken the bondage to deception and opened a new opportunity for humanity to embrace the promises of YHWH. This made a new world possible in which people would freely choose a righteous and just path.

Thus, for Paul the human predicament is defined by idolatry and deceptive worldviews, not "original sin." As Howard-Brook explains Paul, "It is because of this 'exchange of the truth about God for the lie' [Rom. 1:25] that the creation itself has been 'in bondage' to empire" and made subject to decay.[39] When discussing deliverance from empire's deceit, Paul meant individuals at last living out their longings for *shalom;* he also meant "creation itself . . . set free" (Rom. 8:21).

Also by way of introduction to these letters, it is important to briefly describe a key aspect of the cultural environment in the eastern Roman provinces (Cyprus, Pamphylia, Galatia, Lycia, Asia, Bithynia-Pontus, Macedonia and Achaia) where these assemblies were located.

---

[39]   Ibid., 459.

These historically Greek provinces had a long tradition of emperor worship going back to the era of Alexander the Great. Starting with Julius Caesar, Roman leaders opposed official deification of a *living* ruler as a contradiction of Rome's republican ideology. However, Nero bucked that tradition by encouraging unofficial emperor worship *during* his reign.

In addition to a temple or shrine dedicated to explicit religious rituals, many eastern cities hosted a calendar of activities (processions, feasts, festivals, athletic competitions, arts events, guild meetings, civic gatherings) where participants would venerate the emperor as the source of public values such as health, safety, unity, productivity and prosperity. Local elites organized these events. A city unified in its enthusiasm for the emperor, as evidenced by broad and enthusiastic public participation in activities honoring him as the source of life and peace, thereby demonstrated qualities that merited imperial visits, appointments, building projects and financial subsidies. Thus, emperor worship was woven into the fabric of community spirit and economic well–being.

No one forced people to participate in the imperial cult, but it was noticed if one did not join in. There might be many reasons for one's absence, such as illness or laziness. But when a Jesus–follower failed to participate, it often was viewed in political terms as an act of dissent and a challenge to the legitimacy of the emperor's rule.

Galatians

Soon after Paul's and Barnabas' preaching campaign in the province of Galatia, Jewish Christians from Jerusalem visited the new assemblies to guide the converts in the way of Jesus, which in their view included circumcision of Gentile men and compliance with other Jewish conversion requirements (see Acts 15:1 and pages 259–261).

This angered Paul and he wrote this letter in 49 CE to the assemblies of Galatia, scolding them for "so quickly deserting the one who called you in the grace of [Messiah]" (Gal. 1:6). A year or so later, the Jerusalem Council confirmed the position Paul took in this letter and it became the official teaching of the movement. But at the time Paul wrote, he was a relatively junior member of the leadership and unsure if his opinions would be affirmed.

At the beginning of his letter, Paul identified Jesus as Messiah ("Christ") whom YHWH had raised "from the dead" (Gal.1:1). Paul further described Jesus as the one "who gave himself for our sins to set us free from the present evil age" (Gal.1:4). Jesus' purpose, the reason he gave his life, was thus rooted in *liberation from existing structures and powers* of this world.

Next, Paul used very strong language, accusing those who demanded compliance with Jewish conversion practices as "perverting the gospel of [Messiah]" (Gal. 1:7). Let those who preach this be accursed, he said at two points in the letter (Gal. 1:8–9); at another point, he stated he wished they "would castrate themselves" (Gal. 5:21)!

Paul addressed the heart of his concern in a passage that has become a Christian classic. A person is justified (i.e., made righteous) in YHWH's eyes, Paul wrote, not by following the requirements of the Jewish law, but by faith in the promises of YHWH. We understand this "faith" to be *"the faith of Jesus"* (2:16; 3:22, emphasis added), the *"faith of the Son of God"* (2:20, emphasis added). [40] Jesus accepted the defeat and humiliation of a Roman cross because he trusted YHWH's promise to bring new life out of his death. Even as he faced execution, Jesus remained convinced that compassion, forgiveness and nonviolent resistance would save the world, not domination, vengeance and bloodshed. *This is the faith of Jesus* (see pages 236-237 above). It is the faith to which Paul called the Galatians, a faith that would cause YHWH to regard them as righteous, whether they were Jews or Gentiles.

"You foolish Galatians! Who has bewitched you?" Paul asked rhetorically (Gal. 3:1). Did you see evidence of YHWH's spirit in your communities because you embraced the faith of Jesus or because you followed the rules of Jewish conversion? Certainly those rules have value, Paul wrote; he described them as a kind of teacher or disciplinarian. "But now that faith has come, we are no longer subject to a disciplinarian, for in [Messiah] Jesus you are all children of God through faith . . . There is no longer Jew or Greek, there is no longer slave or free, there is no longer male or female; for all of you are one in [Messiah] Jesus" (Gal. 3:25–28).

---

[40] Harink, *Paul among the Postliberals*, 40-45.

Before the first vestiges of Judaism had emerged, Abram had believed YHWH's promises "and it was reckoned to him as righteousness" (Gal. 3:6). Paul even claimed ancient Abram had learned of "the gospel," the good news of liberation declared by Messiah Jesus. How could this be? Because, Paul said, Abram understood that the promises of YHWH included *everyone* (Gal. 3:8), even pagan peoples "enslaved to beings that by nature are not gods" (Gal. 4:8).

Were the recipients of Paul's letter as upset as he was by the requirement that they follow the traditional rules for entering Judaism? Evidently not; it appears they had complied with the requirements of the Jerusalem leaders. Yet Paul was irate over their betrayal of the cause. What was that betrayal?   Paul explained it concisely: "Neither circumcision nor uncircumcision is anything; but a new creation is everything" (Gal. 6:15). This new creation, this new political community of Jews and Gentiles who believed the promises of YHWH and saw Jesus—not Caesar—as the one saving the world, would never amount to anything if the Gentiles had to *become* Jews in order to participate.

Paul refused to let that happen. He coined a slogan: "For freedom [Messiah] has set us free." And he begged them not to "submit again to a yoke of slavery" (Gal. 5:1).

Then Paul turned to ethical guidance rooted in Jewish tradition, but now transformed as the freely given service of people who know history has turned a sharp corner and Earth has entered its long-awaited restoration. "Become slaves to one another," Paul said, and "love your neighbors as yourself" (Gal. 5:13–14). "Bear one another's burdens and in this way fulfill the law of [Messiah]" (Gal. 6:2). "Whenever we have an opportunity, let us work for the good of all, especially for those of the family of faith" (Gal. 6:10).   And seek "the fruit of the Spirit: love, joy, peace, patience, kindness, generosity, faithfulness, gentleness and self-control. There is no law against such things" (Gal. 5:22).

Questions of empire do not appear explicitly in this letter, but it is saturated with political concerns. Old divisions that served to divide-and-conquer were being rebuilt in Galatian assemblies, divisions that would prevent the new communities of Jesus-followers from becoming a potent alternative to empire. Paul would not stand for it: "From now on, let no one make trouble for me" (Gal. 6:17)!

1 Thessalonians

During his second preaching campaign, Paul and two traveling companions spent a month in the Greek city of Thessalonica, located at the northern tip of the Aegean Sea and capital of the Roman province of Macedonia. Opponents of Paul's message recruited a band of ruffians to organize an angry mob to threaten civil disorder. The situation was so threatening that Paul slipped out of the city at night (Acts 17:6–8) and went on to Athens.

From there he dispatched an assistant, Timothy, to visit the assembly in Thessalonica. Later, Timothy rejoined Paul in Corinth and gave an upbeat report (1 Thess. 3:6). Paul then wrote this letter. The first half recalls his visit and compliments the Thessalonians on their exemplary conduct. "For in spite of persecution you received the word with joy inspired by the Holy Spirit" (1 Thess. 1:6).

In chapter 4, Paul began addressing future concerns: "We ask and urge you in the Lord Jesus that, as you learned from us how you ought to live and to please [YHWH] (as, in fact, you are doing), you should do so more and more" (1 Thess. 4:1). Paul mentioned sexual self-control as an area that needed attention and his concern "that no one wrong or exploit a brother or sister in this matter" (1 Thess. 4:5).

The final concern Paul addressed was anxiety Timothy had reported about the death of some individuals. Had they missed out on "the coming of the Lord" (1 Thess. 4:15)? Don't worry, Paul wrote; when "the Lord himself . . . will descend from heaven, the dead in Christ will rise first . . . to meet the Lord in the air" (1 Thess. 4:16–17). Paul's imagery drew from imperial rituals enacted by enthusiastic city residents who would meet a returning emperor and escort him into a city. His reference to "the archangel's call and the sound of God's trumpet" was apocalyptic, signifying the great reversal that will occur at the end of time. His purpose was reassurance: "We will be with the Lord forever" (1 Thess. 4:16–17).

This begs the question: when will that final "day of the Lord" (1 Thess. 5:2) occur? They won't see it coming, Paul said; it "will come like a thief in the night . . . then sudden destruction will come upon them, as labor pains come upon a pregnant woman, and there will be no escape." And who are "they?" Those that say, "There is peace and security" (1 Thess. 5:3). This clear and unambiguous reference to the Roman Empire's "peace and security" propaganda speaks volumes about Paul's view of empire as the source of deceit and confusion.

Thus, Paul's reassurance was framed by his subversive political analysis. The members of the assembly had nothing to fear; they were "children of the light . . . destined not for wrath but for obtaining salvation through our Lord Jesus [Messiah] who died for us, so that whether we are awake or asleep, we may live with him" (1 Thess. 5:5–10). Those who put their faith in empire, on the other hand, had much to fear; disaster awaited, like a thief in the night.

Then Paul returned to practical ethics that would keep the community honest and build its resilience. In contrast to the hierarchical Roman world, where leading men were responsible for setting the community's moral tone, Paul addressed all of the assembly's members with his ethical challenge.

> Be at peace among yourselves . . . admonish the idlers, encourage the faint-hearted, help the weak, be patient with all of them. See that none of you repays evil for evil, but always seek to do good to one another and to all. Rejoice always, pray without ceasing, give thanks in all circumstances . . . Do not despise the words of prophets, but test everything; hold fast to what is good; abstain from every form of evil. (1 Thess. 5:12–22)

The assembly, this alternative to empire, belonged to its members. Each person carried a share of responsibility for making it strong.

1 Corinthians

Corinth was an ancient Greek city rebuilt by Julius Caesar around 44 BCE and repopulated with retired soldiers, freed slaves and Rome's urban poor. It was a busy commercial hub where some men made fortunes. These factors combined to form an opportunistic, hypercompetitive and coarse culture that fostered moral laxity, harshness toward the poor and weak social bonds. Above all, it valued making money.

Paul lived there eighteen months toward the end of his second campaign (Acts 18:1–17). He promptly followed his stay with two letters. The first was lost but is referred to at 5:9 in our text. The second, which credits the former leader of the synagogue in Corinth as co-author, is our text. Paul likely wrote it in Ephesus in 54 CE, very early in his third preaching campaign.

The assembly in Corinth included some leading Jews and wealthy Gentiles who had formerly been associated with the synagogue, but mostly consisted of lower class Gentiles. "Not many were powerful, not many were of noble birth" (1 Cor. 1:26). There is no hint of strife between Jews and Gentiles; Paul addressed the entire group as if the distinction no longer mattered (1 Cor. 10:20; 12:2). But the letter implies the assembly contained much dissension driven by economic disparities, hierarchical assumptions and Corinth's corrosive culture.

More than in other letters, Paul's expectations for the future (his eschatology) shows through in this text. In the death and resurrection of Jesus, Paul saw convincing evidence that YHWH had *interrupted* human history to move Earth and its residents in another direction. The era in which one empire or another held the world in awe was over; the long-awaited manifestations of YHWH's righteousness and justice had become compellingly visible. As Howard-Brook puts the matter via a quote from Neil Elliot, "If one crucified by Rome had been vindicated by God— vindicated by being raised from the dead already—then the 'time given to Rome' was at hand [and] the changing of the ages was at hand." [41]

This worldview is a key to understanding Paul's writing about problem behaviors. At first reading, Paul may appear to be a moralist, preoccupied by right and wrong and the maintenance of behavior that would please YHWH. *But that is a misreading of Paul.* He believed history had turned a corner; the radically different kingdom of YHWH had begun. In myriad ways, the assemblies announced this change and functioned as living signs of the new way to run the world. Those who joined this mission were like athletes in training. "Run in such a way that

---

[41]   Howard-Brook, 453.

you may win," Paul wrote. "Athletes exercise self-control in all things; they do it to receive a perishable wreath, but *we an imperishable one"* (1 Cor. 9:24–25, emphasis added). This "imperishable" reward is the salvation of Earth. (See question 39, page 322, for further discussion.)

Thus, in his reply to wealthy men who regarded the pleasures of prostitutes like the pleasures of a good meal, Paul focused on their lack of fitness for the rigors of "the kingdom of God" (1 Cor. 6:10). These men thought the Jesus-movement was all about their personal liberation; thus, they bragged about how "all things are lawful" (1 Cor. 6:12). You are free enough, said Paul, but that is not the point. *It's not about you; it's about the global transformation Jesus began!* How is your body engaged in *that* cause? Do you imagine our unity with Messiah Jesus is a now-and-then thing? Many have suffered to bring this transformation to birth; "therefore, glorify God in your body" (1 Cor. 6:20).

Paul began the letter with an extended discussion of the cliquishness within the assembly. "Be united with the same mind and the same purpose," Paul wrote (1 Cor. 1:10). He gently shamed his readers for their egotism and divisive attitudes. But he also flattered them by reframing the matter as a discussion of wisdom, a heady subject. Implicitly, Paul asked: who understands how the world works? Who understands how to flourish in life? Paul answered with the scandalous phrase, "[Messiah] crucified." For both Jews and Gentiles, this crucified Messiah is "the power of God and the wisdom of God" (1 Cor. 1:23–24), explaining how the world works.

We may regard this as religious talk, but that would be a mistake; Paul was speaking politically. When describing those who were embarrassed by a crucified Messiah, Paul was critiquing Corinth's elite: the wise, the powerful, those of noble birth (1 Cor. 1:26–28). When he boldly proclaimed "Jesus crucified" (1 Cor. 2:2), he was reframing the empire's most powerful weapon of repression as part of the transforming justice of YHWH. When he referred to "the rulers of this age" who "crucified the Lord of glory" and "are doomed to perish," Paul clearly meant the leaders of the Roman Empire (1 Cor. 2:6–8). He also had the empire in mind when he spoke later in this text about how at the return of

Jesus to Earth, he would destroy "every ruler and every authority and power" (1 Cor. 15:24).

In contrast to imperial ideology, Paul called readers to the "mind of Jesus" (1 Cor. 2:16), which freed them from petty rivalries and self-promotion. He skewered their preoccupation with status and challenged their association of upward mobility with the wisdom of YHWH.

> Already you have all you want! Already you have become rich! Quite apart from us, you have become kings! . . . We are weak, but you are strong. You are held in honor, but we in disrepute. To the present hour we are hungry and thirsty, we are homeless, and we grow weary from the work of our own hands. When reviled, we bless; when persecuted, we endure; when slandered, we speak kindly. We have become like the rubbish of the world, the dregs of all things, to this very day. (1 Cor. 4:8–13)

Beginning in chapter 5, Paul addressed issues that had arisen in the prior exchange of letters. Sexual immorality was the first. Paul asked the Corinthians to discipline a member who was living with his father's wife and to disassociate themselves from a member of their community "who is sexually immoral or greedy, or is an idolater, reviler, drunkard, or robber. Do not even eat with such a one" (1 Cor. 5:11). God will judge those outside the community, Paul said; you must maintain discipline within.

Next, Paul scolded members who had taken other members to court. Why weren't they handling such matters internally? "Do you not know that the saints will judge the world? And if the world is to be judged by you, are you incompetent to try trivial cases" (1 Cor. 6:2)? Acting as if the empire's courts were a higher authority needed to resolve disputes between members of the assembly was itself a "defeat." "Why not rather be wronged? Why not rather be defrauded" (1 Cor. 6:7)?

Context is an important element here; only those with wealth had access to the courts of Corinth and they routinely prevailed against the poor. Thus, a second concern for Paul was the way use of the legal system drove a wedge between the wealthier and poorer members.

He also expressed concern about the impact economic disparities had on community gatherings. Usually these occurred in larger homes of wealthier households and involved a meal. Regrettably, these mealtimes reflected the status differences of Corinthian society. Paul wrote: "When the time comes to eat, each of you goes ahead with your own supper, and one goes hungry and another becomes drunk . . . Do you show contempt for the church of God and humiliate those who have nothing?" He then outlined proper procedure: break bread *together,* then eat the meal, then *share* the cup (1 Cor. 11:21–25).

Van Steenwyk describes how in Paul's view, this way of eating and drinking together was a "revolutionary sacrament. It isn't magical—by eating bread and wine we don't simply become like Jesus. Rather, it is a place where we can reimagine our shared humanity in such a way that we can then go forth and infect the world with healing and liberation." [42]

With regard to marriage, Paul encouraged husbands and wives to freely give each other "conjugal rights" and spoke of each having such rights, first the wife and then the husband (1 Cor. 7:3–5). But he encouraged the single not to marry unless "they are not practicing self-control" or were "aflame with passion" (1 Cor. 7:9). His reluctance to encourage marriage was based on his reading of the times. "I mean, brothers and sisters, the appointed time has grown short . . . for the present form of this world is passing away" (1 Cor. 7:29–31).

Probably for the same reason, Paul urged readers not to make great efforts to change their stations in life. "Let each of you lead the life that the Lord has assigned, to which God has called you . . . Were you a slave when called? Do not be concerned about it . . . In whatever condition you were called, brothers and sisters, there remain with God" (1 Cor. 7:17–24).

Clearly, women played an active part in the assemblies, including public prayer and prophecy (1 Cor. 11:5, 13). This was commonplace in assemblies under Paul's leadership and is evidenced by the many female names in the lists of people commended at the end of some of Paul's letters (see Rom. 16, 1 Cor. 16, Col. 4). Paul did insist on retaining one gender distinctive—the head covering—when women spoke in such fashion (1 Cor. 11:2–10). Crossan notes that culturally, the veil signified marriage and unavailability. The problem was that married women *who had taken vows of celibacy* were speaking publicly while unveiled, thus

---

[42]   Van Steenwyk, 173.

signifying their vows. This was causing confusion because to the uninformed, it signaled their availability as romantic partners. [43]

As for the text's teaching that "woman should be silent in the churches" (1 Cor. 14:34–36), the inconsistency with what Paul wrote elsewhere is too great to reconcile. We conclude these three verses were not from Paul, but were added later by an editor.

Though Paul was convinced the moral authority of the empire had been radically undermined by the cross of Jesus, he also knew its grip on humanity would be extended if people continued to conform to its dehumanizing norms. Thus, Paul engaged those norms, subverted their power and made them into something new. For example, he asked readers to think of themselves as "the body of [Messiah] and individually members of it" (1 Cor. 12:27). Within Greek stoicism, "body" was a term often used to promote social harmony, especially by encouraging oppressed groups to accept their lot in life. Thus, the image served the powerful. Paul reframed the metaphor to promote an egalitarian ethos.

> To each is given the manifestation of the Spirit for the common good. (1 Cor. 12:7)

> But God has so arranged the body, giving the greater honor to the inferior member, that there may be no dissension within the body, but the members may have the same care for one another. If one member suffers, all suffer together with it; if one member is honored, all rejoice together with it. (1 Cor. 12:24–26)

John Fairfield deepens our understanding of this passage. When Paul told the assembly in Corinth that they were the body of Messiah (1 Cor. 12:27), he was going beyond metaphor. "Messiah is a role, it is Jesus' mantle that is taken by the church incarnating God's spirit." The assembly was now the Messiah, not because Jesus was dead, but because the assembly *embodied in history the same spirit embodied in Jesus,* the same trust in YHWH's promises, the same understanding of purpose, the same commitment to resisting evil by engaging enemies. When Paul

---

[43]   Crossan, 182-183.

spoke about being "in Christ" (see Rom. 6:3–4, 1 Cor. 12:12–13, 2 Cor. 5:17), Fairfield says, "I take Paul to mean we are part of the Messiah." [44]

Paul follows in chapter 13 with his lovely paean to *agape* love. It ends with these words: "Now faith, hope and love abide, these three; and the greatest of these is love" (1 Cor. 13:13).

Paul's long discussion of eating meat offered to idols (chapters 8—10) often is viewed as an application of the rule of love. In contrast, Richard Horsley focuses our attention on the political context of temple banquets and urban festivals (1 Cor. 8:10, 10:21). These events, sponsored by leading individuals and organizations, paid homage to the empire and its ideology, much as meetings in our time and place include the Pledge of Allegiance, presentation of an honor guard, and offering of prayers for military personnel. In Paul's time, such events also invariably included food (especially meat) that had been offered to and blessed by the gods. For the poor, such events were the only place to gain access to meat.

How did this become an issue in Corinth? Jesus-followers knew the religious rituals of the imperial cult were rubbish (1 Cor. 8:1–6). Yet social and economic success required participation in group events and activities where such rituals were an integral part. Thus, with a wink or a roll of the eyes, Jesus-followers in Corinth joined in.

In private settings, Paul told his readers they could continue to follow their consciences, keeping in mind how their actions may affect other believers (1 Cor. 10:23–33). But Paul told them *to stop participating in the public festivals and banquets.* "I do not want you to be partners with demons. You cannot drink the cup of the Lord and the cup of demons. You cannot partake of the table of the Lord and the table of demons" (1 Cor. 10:20–22). It is one of Paul's strongest and clearest instructions.

Again, Paul's way of seeing faith, righteousness and politics as a unity drove his approach. Horsley explains:

> For Paul the sharing of "food offered to idols" was not an issue of ethics, but of the integrity and survival of his assemblies as an alternative society. In 8:1–13, Paul clearly criticized the enlightened Corinthians' ethic of individual liberty. But that was

---

[44]   Fairfield, *The Healer Messiah,* 43-44.

only the first step . . . in the struggle of the new movement to maintain discipline and attain its goal . . . His principal concern was for the integrity and solidarity of the alternative society he was attempting to build up over against the networks of power relations by which the imperial society was organized. [45]

Chapter 15 is Paul's rousing affirmation that YHWH had raised Jesus from the dead and would at some future time likewise raise from death "those who belong to [Messiah]" (1 Cor. 15:23). It is the earliest surviving account of Jesus' resurrection and strongly influenced the subsequent accounts we find in the gospels. Furthermore, though the most specific and detailed explanation of resurrection found in the Bible, it is rare to find a christianity today that fully teaches this text.

Paul did not hold the modern view that death is the doorway into eternal bliss; instead, he regarded death as a present enemy that would be destroyed only at the very end of history (1 Cor. 15:26). Only resurrection would finally relieve the sting of death (1 Cor. 15:54).

But "how are the dead raised? With what kind of body do they come" (1 Cor. 15:35)? Paul tackled those mind-bending questions with an analogy to a plant that emerges from a seed after it has been planted in the ground. "What is sown is perishable, what is raised is imperishable," he said (1 Cor. 15:42). Unsurprisingly, his description of the "spiritual body" (1 Cor. 15:44) of the resurrected is difficult to comprehend. Bishop N. T. Wright provides some help: "Paul is not asking whether the resurrection state is physical or nonphysical; that is our late-modern question. His question is, rather, what sort of physicality is it? It is, he says, a *transformed* physicality, with new properties and attributes, but still concrete and physical." [46]

Paul's commitment to a linear timeframe is clear. He said the resurrection of the dead would occur at the time of Jesus' "coming" to Earth (1 Cor. 15:23). "When this perishable body puts on imperishability, and this mortal body puts on immortality, *then* the saying that is written will be fulfilled . . . 'Where, O death, is your sting?'" (1 Cor. 15:54–55,

---

[45]   Horsley, *1ˢᵗ Corinthians*, 146.

[46]   Borg and Wright, 120.

emphasis added). Thus, Paul did not speak of eternal life as a qualitative aspect of the present. Paul wrote: "If the dead are not raised, let us eat and drink for tomorrow we die" (1 Cor. 15:32); "If for this life only we have hoped in [Messiah], we are of all people most to be pitied" (1 Cor. 15:19). One cannot imagine such words by the author of **The Gospel of John**.

Decisively, Paul "believed in Jesus" when he became convinced that YHWH had "declared" him the Messiah and "Son of God" by raising him from the dead (Rom. 1:4). This vindication of Jesus awaits all who follow Jesus' way, Paul believed. And so he concluded with a stirring challenge to "be steadfast, immovable, always excelling in the work of [YHWH], because you know that in [YHWH] *your labor is not in vain*" (1 Cor. 15:58, emphasis added). This may be the key to understanding Paul's eschatology. Earth was *not* passing away, nor the individuals who belonged to Jesus, nor the communal impact of each individual's righteous deeds. YHWH is saving all of this for the great consummation of the new era now already begun in Messiah Jesus.

Philemon

For three years during Paul's third preaching campaign, he lived in and around Ephesus, an important city on the western shore of modern Turkey (see Acts 19). During this time, Paul endured an ordeal in which he was "so utterly, unbearably crushed that [he] despaired of life itself." As he put it in a letter to the assembly in Corinth, "We felt that we had received the sentence of death" (2 Cor. 1:8–9). This ordeal included a period of harsh confinement. No text describes Paul's arrest, but it likely was related to the unrest in Ephesus following Paul's debunking of the goddess Artemis and the consequent loss of revenue at the temple named in her honor (Acts 19:23—20:3; see page 263 above).

During his time in jail (and perhaps in 55 CE), Paul became acquainted with Onesimus, a man from Colossae, an inland city 100 miles east of Ephesus. In his letter, Paul referred to Onesimus as a slave (Phlm. 1:16) and most scholars take this literally. We assume Onesimus had run away from his master, not permanently so as to merit the death penalty under Roman law, but temporarily.

Paul much appreciated Onesimus, wrote of him affectionately (Phlm. 1:10–13) and gently suggested to those receiving the letter that they regard Onesimus "no longer as a slave but [as] a beloved brother . . . both in the flesh and in the Lord." Paul then applied a bit of pressure: "So if you consider me your partner, *welcome him as you would welcome me.* If he has wronged you in anything, charge that to my account" (Phlm. 1:16–18, emphasis added).

We do not have a response to Paul's request, but we do have a reference to Onesimus in the letter Paul wrote soon after to the **Colossians,** where Onesimus is described as "the faithful and beloved brother, who is one of you" (Col. 4:9) and who will convey Paul's report. Thus, it is assumed that Onesimus' slavery ended as Paul had inferred it should.

This text is an important reference for analyzing Paul's attitude toward slavery as an institution. Some see little criticism in Paul's remarks, only a request for a favor on behalf of one man whom Paul had come to appreciate. Others see in Paul's rhetorical shift from "slave" to "beloved brother" a powerful subversion of the entire structure of slavery.

Colossians

Colossae sat along the highway connecting Ephesus with Syrian cities at the headwaters of the Euphrates River. It was the smallest city to which Paul sent a letter. Paul must have passed through it a year or two prior to writing, but he did not stop and did not help start its assembly. In 60-61 CE, an earthquake destroyed much of the city and it was not rebuilt.

Not long after writing **Philemon,** Paul—with the help of his assistant, Timothy—wrote this second letter from a prison somewhere in the province of Asia (western Turkey). The Colossian assembly was relatively new and most members had never met Paul (Col. 2:1).

Early in his letter, Paul made an assertion with strong anti-imperial overtones: "(YHWH) has rescued us from the power of darkness and transferred us into the Kingdom of his beloved Son, in whom we have redemption, the forgiveness of sin" (Col. 1:13–14). It was the Roman philosopher Cicero who had called the empire "the light of the world" and the Roman Empire that called Nero "the son of god" after he was named emperor in 54 CE, the adopted son of the deceased Emperor Claudius, whom the Roman Senate had declared to be divine. So Paul was using imperial rhetoric while speaking about Jesus of Nazareth.

Paul proceeded to write a hymn of praise to Jesus as the alternative to Nero.

> He is the image of the invisible God, the firstborn of *all* creation . . . *All* things have been created through him and for him . . . and in him *all* things hold together . . . in him *all* the fullness of God was pleased to dwell, and through him God was pleased to reconcile to himself *all* things, whether on earth or in heaven, by making peace through the blood of the cross. (Col. 1:15–20, emphasis added)

The scope of what Paul included in the "peace" of Jesus is remarkable. It includes not just a few righteous followers, but *all* of creation.

Of course, this is empire-talk; Paul was combining comprehensive claims with the promise of peace. Keesmaat and Walsh call the hymn "seditious." "It [explains] who rules the world, where the world has come from and where it is going, where wisdom ultimately is to be found, and even which community of people hold the promise and destiny of the world in its hearts and lives." [47]

Tired as we are of christendom's claims of superiority, Paul's rhetoric may strike us as an imperialism of another sort. If so, how would that imperial order be described? Paul called it a mystery, the key to which "is [Messiah] himself, in whom are hidden all the treasures of wisdom and knowledge" (Col. 2:2–3). Not an ideology or system of control to save the world, *but wisdom embodied in one person.*

Going further into chapter 2, Paul issued a warning: "See that no one takes you captive through philosophy and empty deceit, according to human tradition, according to the elemental spirits of the universe, and not according to [Messiah]" (Col. 2:8). The point of view Paul warned against claimed there was ample space for Jesus within the empire's pantheon of gods, thus avoiding the need for either/or choices. In response, Paul did not emphasize the exclusivity of Jesus but rather his completeness: "For in him the whole *fullness* of deity dwells bodily, and you have come to

---

[47]   Keesmaat and Walsh, 98-99.

fullness in him, *who is the head of every ruler and authority"* (Col. 2:10, emphasis added).

Paul implied he recognized other authorities. But they must find their purpose and direction in Jesus, not in their power to dominate and control. Whatever authority they may have had been set aside; God nailed it to the cross. "(YHWH) disarmed the rulers and authorities and made a public spectacle of them, triumphing over them *in it"* (Col. 2:15, emphasis added). Thus, Jesus and his suffering define this empire of which Paul is an emissary. It is not a new religion or a new ideology, but a new politics, one that rules the world by way of compassion and the suffering of the cross.

Going on, Paul wrote dismissively about religious "regulations." "These have indeed an appearance of wisdom in promoting self-imposed piety, humility and severe treatment of the body, but they are of no value in checking self-indulgence" (Col. 2:23). Paul emphasized a self-disciplined life, but only as part of preparation for the mission of Messiah Jesus, not to meet some standard of morality or achieve some exalted spiritual state. Paul's surprisingly dismissive attitude does help us understand why critics of Jesus-followers often accused them of being atheists, and thus a threat to the order of broader society.

He then shifted to a positive vein. "So if you have been raised with [Messiah], seek the things that are above, where [Messiah] is seated on the right hand of God. Set your minds on things that are above, not on things that are on earth, for you have died, and your life is hidden with [Messiah] in God" (Col. 3:1–3). Many find Paul's distinction between the "earthly" and the "above" confusing. This confusion also arises in Paul's other texts where he distinguishes between "flesh" and "spirit" and seems to reject the body. In all cases, Paul was making a distinction between the old era of entrenched injustice and imperial violence and the new era of the kingdom of God. Keesmaat and Walsh expand on this.

> When Paul says "put to death whatever in you is earthly," he is not counseling otherworldliness. Rather, he is saying: "Abandon the false allegiances, the pretentious sovereignties, that have held you captive. Secede from the unholy unions of power and money, genius and war, outer space and inner vacuity, that distort your

lives." Put to death what is earthly means put to death the remaining vestiges of an imperial imagination and praxis that still have a grip on your lives. Put all of this to death before it kills you. [48]

This entails a disciplined way of living. Seceding from empire and making justice through the power of compassion, forgiveness and nonviolent resistance is not a walk in the park. So put aside all that distracts you or keeps you dependent on empire's way of running the world: "fornication, impurity, passion, evil desire, greed" (Col. 3:5). Stop lying to one another, "seeing that you have stripped off the old self with its practices" (Col. 3:9).

Instead, set your mind on the new way Jesus has begun. In this new way, "there is no longer Greek and Jew, circumcised and uncircumcised, barbarian, Scythian, slave and free; but [Messiah] is all and in all" (Col. 3:11). So "clothe yourself with compassion, kindness, humility, meekness, and patience; bear with one another and if anyone has a complaint against another, forgive each other, just as the Lord has forgiven you. Above all, clothe yourself with love, which binds everything together in perfect harmony" (Col. 3:12–14). "Do everything in the name of the Lord Jesus" (Col. 3:17), not the Lord Caesar. "And let the peace of [Messiah] rule in your hearts" (Col. 3:15), not the peace of Rome.

Paul followed with advice for household management. Two verses concern wives and husbands, two concern children and parents, and five slaves and masters. Paul's approach conveyed respectfulness and balance; he consistently spoke directly to the one whose duty he was describing.

Yet these verses sound more conventional than other things Paul had written, especially when he addresses slaves. In **Philemon**, Paul subverted the structure of slavery with his emphasis on brotherhood. Here that emphasis is missing, as is the resounding refrain Paul had written just a few verses earlier—how in Messiah Jesus, there is no slave or free (Col. 3:11).

Where did this leave the Colossian assembly? They needed to figure out how Paul's formula differed from the conventional one. After

---

[48]   Ibid., 160.

all, this kind of formulaic advice was not original with Paul; it had long served within Greek culture and law to maintain clear lines of authority in the household and thus bolster stability within broader society.

Briefly, Paul's advice included several novel features: reciprocal obligations, thus bringing a new degree of balance to each dyad; treating each individual as a moral agent in his/her own right with a duty before God; public accountability within the assembly for what had heretofore been regarded as a private matter for the man of the household to decide; and an underlying teaching subversive to hierarchy—that each member of the assembly is a slave of the Lord Jesus (Col. 4:1).

"Remember my chains," Paul wrote in closing (Col. 4:18). Never be ashamed of suffering.

2 Corinthians

During his three-year stay in Ephesus, Paul travelled to Corinth on a visit not recorded in **Acts** to work on matters addressed in a previous letter (see pages 274-282). It was a short and "painful" visit (2 Cor. 2:1) that ended with an angry confrontation, perhaps about Paul's trustworthiness as courier of funds given for poor assemblies, or perhaps about Paul's refusal to accept financial support from the assembly in Corinth for his personal needs. Paul then returned to Ephesus.

There followed three more letters. The first is lost, though it is referred to (2 Cor. 7:7–16). It apparently was very stern, but resulted in some improvement in the relationship. The next is included as the first nine chapters of this biblical text and was written from Macedonia as Paul made his way toward Corinth for another visit; it reflected Paul's perception that the relationship was on the mend. The last letter begins with chapter 10 and continues to the end of this biblical text; it also was written from Macedonia, not more than a month or two later, and reflects another new stress in the relationship. Throughout, the reader can sense that the conflict with the assembly in Corinth had wounded Paul deeply.

Early in our text, Paul referred to affliction, a word he used seven times. He mentioned Jesus' abundant sufferings (2 Cor. 1:5) as well as the threatened "sentence of death" from authorities in Asia that he had lived through (2 Cor. 1:8–10), thus reminding readers how much was at stake.

He explained why he had not returned earlier to Corinth as promised (2 Cor. 1:12—2:4). He referred to the "punishment" the assembly had meted out, perhaps to the person who had sparked the prior confrontation. It was "enough" and forgiveness was now in order. "Anyone whom you forgive, I forgive" (2 Cor. 2:10), thus affirming the authority and responsibility of the assembly in Corinth.

The text hints at prior accusations and Paul sounds defensive. He tried to strike a philosophical tone: "Since it is by God's mercy that we are engaged in this ministry, we do not lose heart" (2 Cor. 4:1). He used an image of "treasure in clay jars" to describe the gospel of Messiah Jesus embodied by flawed persons such as himself. "We are afflicted in every way, but not crushed; perplexed but not driven to despair; persecuted but not forsaken; struck down, but not destroyed; always carrying in the body the death of Jesus, so that the life of Jesus may also be made visible in our bodies" (2 Cor. 4:8–10). Though Paul never wanted a disembodied existence (see 2 Cor. 5:4), he sometimes wished for an easier life.

Paul's most soaring rhetoric accompanied his brief description of their common purpose. "In [Messiah], God was reconciling the world to himself, not counting their trespasses against them, and entrusting the message of reconciliation to us. So we are ambassadors for [Messiah], since God is making his appeal through us" (2 Cor. 5:19–20). Thus, "in [Messiah], there is a new creation; everything old has passed away; see, everything has become new" (2 Cor. 5:17). This is Paul's plea for reconciliation.

In chapters 8 and 9, Paul made a delicate appeal for donations in support of "the ministry to the saints" in Jerusalem. "God loves a cheerful giver," Paul wrote (2 Cor. 9:7). "I do not mean that there should be relief for others and pressure on you, but it is a question of a fair balance between your present abundance and their need, so that their abundance may be for your need, in order that there may be a fair balance" (2 Cor. 8:13–14).

We should not gloss over the significance of these collections, which entailed mainly Gentile Jesus-followers in Macedonia and Achaia gathering funds for people in Palestine who they had never met and who were culturally very different from themselves. Certainly this was evidence that a new, trans-national community was forming out of shared allegiance to Jesus. For those steeped in First Testament texts, it also marked the fulfillment of the vision from **Isaiah**. "Nations shall come to your light . . . the wealth of the nations shall come to you" (Isaiah 60:3, 5).

Chapter 10 begins with a portion of Paul's last letter to the assembly in Corinth. The previous letter had been delivered and the courier had returned to report that Paul's leadership was again under attack by new rivals. Paul referred sarcastically to these newly ascendant leaders in Corinth as "super-apostles" (2 Cor.11:5), but he also seemed stung by the report and referred repeatedly to his own "weaknesses" in comparison (2 Cor. 11:30–12:10). He asserted that "whenever I am weak, then I am strong" (2 Cor. 12:10) and recalled that Jesus too had been regarded as weak. "If I come again, I will not be lenient, since you desire proof that [Messiah] is speaking in me. He is not weak in dealing with you, but is powerful in you . . . For we are weak in him, but in dealing with you we will live with him by the power of God" (2 Cor. 13:3–4).

We have no report about Paul's third visit to Corinth, but apparently it went well. He stayed three months (Acts 20:3), was given a sum of money to carry back to Jerusalem (Rom. 15:26), and had time to write his letter to the assembly in Rome before retracing his steps back through Macedonia and making his final trip to Jerusalem.

Romans

Paul wrote this letter from Corinth during his third visit there. He sent it to a mixed audience of Jewish and Gentile Jesus-followers in Rome, a place he wanted to visit on his way west to Spain. Indeed, as Paul hoped the assemblies in Rome would sponsor him on a preaching campaign to the far-west, this letter can be understood as a kind of grant proposal in which Paul seeks to show that he merits financial support from the assembly in Rome (Rom. 15:23–24).

Because Paul had not visited Rome, his letter did not focus on specific problems. Instead, Paul focused on his worldview and theology, as noted in our introduction to Paul's letters (see page 269). Yet long sections of the letter speak sympathetically to Jewish concerns, thus implying that within Rome's assemblies, those concerns were not being adequately respected by Gentile believers. While these sections of Paul's letter affirmed the value of the Jewish tradition, Paul also reframed that tradition within the bigger and broader context of YHWH's intention to save the Gentiles and the entire cosmos.

Early in this text, Paul made a declaration. "I am not ashamed of the gospel; it is the power of God for salvation to everyone who has faith, to the Jew first and also to the Greek. For in it the righteousness of God is revealed through faith for faith; as it is written, 'The one who is righteous will live by faith'" (Rom.1:17).

In Paul's time and place, "gospel" referred to the ascension of a new emperor. It had a common political meaning. When Paul linked it to Jesus, he was making a political claim: *this man is the world's Lord and Savior.* N.T. Wright suggests we think of Paul "not simply in terms of a traveling evangelist offering people a new religious experience, but as an ambassador for a king-in-waiting, establishing cells of people loyal to this new king, and ordering their lives according to his story, his symbols, and his praxis, and their minds according to his truth." His preaching "was a direct summons to abandon other allegiances and give total loyalty to this Jesus," [49] this new Lord and Savior, who "is the power of God."

"Salvation" was another of the empire's terms; it was used to describe what Emperor Nero provided the people under his control. What did "salvation" mean to Paul? Certainly it included a future resurrection from the dead, but it also included release from the bondage of empire's deceptions and the renewal of human institutions and Earth itself. Often, we assume salvation means a *perfect* world, one we know has not arrived. But in Paul's worldview, it was YHWH's *interruption* of human history in Jesus that was decisive and "saving". Jesus embodied YHWH's justice and created *a clear image of the world set right* so people could clearly recognize YHWH's justice and embrace it as their own.

Paul called his readers to have the same faith Jesus had, the same confidence that YHWH is saving the world through human compassion, forgiveness and nonviolent resistance, not through Caesar's way of domination, vengeance and bloodshed. This is the faith that "justifies" (Rom. 3:26). To buttress this claim and illustrate how Gentiles could have

---

[49]   Wright, *Paul and Politics,* 161-162.

this faith, Paul told the story of Abram, the uncircumcised Chaldean who "believed God, and it was reckoned to him as righteousness" (Rom. 4:3).

Paul highly valued Jewish teaching and never advised Jews to ignore the Law of Moses or abandon their distinctive ways, but he regarded what YHWH had done in Messiah Jesus to be decisive for Jews (as well as Gentiles) because it had changed the direction of the world. "Just as by the one man's disobedience the many were made sinners, so by the one man's obedience the many will be made righteous" (Rom. 5:19). Individual merit had nothing to do with the impact that Jesus' "obedience" was having on the direction of history; it was a game-changer, whether one was a righteous Jew or an unrighteous Gentile, because it was so compelling.

In chapters 6—8, Paul reflected on the difficulty of living out this new reality inaugurated by Messiah Jesus amid the opposing and often hostile claims of empire. His language was dramatic; he described baptism as being "buried with [Jesus] into death" (Rom. 6:4), insisted we all are slaves of the one we obey, "either of sin, which leads to death, or of obedience, which leads to righteousness" (Rom. 6:16). He confessed divided feelings about the choices he encountered (Rom. 7:15), but also offered reassurance about the tenacity of "the love of God in [Messiah] Jesus our Lord" (Rom. 8:38–39).

In chapters 9—11, Paul struggled to make sense of the fact that most Jews did not accept Jesus as the justice of YHWH. He consoled himself with the thought that "the gifts and calling of God are irrevocable" and so "all Israel will be saved" (Rom. 11:26, 29). In part, he expected this to happen through the envy Jews would feel over "the riches for the world" produced by Gentiles who had become part of the justice of God (Rom. 11:11–14).

In chapters 12—15, Paul turned to ethical transformation, the kinetic energy Jesus had set loose in the world. It entailed "the renewing of your minds" (Rom. 12:2), membership in a community he called "the body" (Rom. 12:3–5), and a flipping of the usual fear-and-scarcity-driven approach to life. "Let love be genuine, hate what is evil, hold fast to what is good, love one another with mutual affection, outdo one another in showing honor" (Rom. 12:9–10). "Contribute to the needs of the saints;

extend hospitality to strangers. Bless those who persecute you, bless and do not curse them" (Rom. 12:13–14). "Do not repay anyone evil for evil, but take thought for what is noble in the sight of all. If it is possible, so far as it depends on you, live peaceably with all" (Rom. 12:17–18). "Do not be overcome by evil, but overcome evil with good" (Rom. 12:21).

Were we not acquainted with Paul's many run-ins with civil authorities, we could easily be misled by his words in chapter 13 about "being subject to" government. Certainly he gave governing authorities much more credit than they deserved when he wrote, "for rulers are not a terror to good conduct, but to bad" (Rom. 13:3).

To be fair, the challenge Paul took on in this passage is difficult: how to "overcome evil with good" when the evil is entrenched in the ideology, imagery and morality-fueled propaganda of the empire. Yet in several other letters **(1 Thessalonians, 1 Corinthians, Colossians, Philippians),** Paul was not hesitant to teach that the empire embodied death and idolatry and stood as the great obstacle to YHWH's intention for the world.

Apparently, here Paul had practical concerns in mind. Only a few years earlier, during the reign of Emperor Claudius, many Jews had been expelled from Rome due to controversy and social unrest related to claims about the identity of Jesus of Nazareth. Since then, Jews had been allowed to return, but Paul may have wanted to avoid any risk of attracting imperial scrutiny, at least not until he became acquainted with local dynamics.

Also, we need to keep in mind that Paul wrote this soon after spending time in prison, perhaps for the capital crime of sedition (2 Cor. 1:8–10). Given this fact and given his reputation as an activist, perhaps he felt the need to express himself cautiously, especially if he wanted to win financial support for his preaching campaign to Spain.

Paul believed that with the life of Jesus, a new day had dawned (Rom. 13:11–12). In this new day, love should guide the assemblies in Rome. All of the commandments "are summed up in this word: 'love your neighbor as yourself'" (Rom. 13:8–10).

Yet he also recognized how the cultural and religious differences between Jewish and Gentile believers in Rome's assemblies were sparking disputes about what faithfulness to the way of Jesus entailed. So Paul encouraged his readers to be generous with one another, keeping in mind the purpose for which "[Messiah] died and lived again" (Rom. 14:9). "Welcome those who are weak in faith, but not for the purpose of quarreling over opinions" (Rom. 14:1). "Resolve never to put a stumbling block or hindrance in the way of another" (Rom. 14:13). "Pursue what makes for peace and mutual up-building" (Rom. 14:19).

Douglas Harink puts this all into perspective.

> Paul hoped that the social space of the Jewish communities and synagogues in Rome would become a space of cultural harmony . . . . This would have amounted to a clear and profound testimony in the very heart of the imperial capital that the one God of Israel . . . was creating . . . a startlingly new cultural-social-political order—a counter-empire—through which his glory would be revealed among the nations. [50]

All this fulfilled the prophetic promise of an alternative to empire: "The root of Jesse shall come, the one who rises to rule the Gentiles; in him the Gentiles shall hope" (Rom. 15:12, quoting Isa. 11:10). Jesus, the embodiment of Israel's prophetic call for organic leadership, had become the hope of *all* the nations. Jesus, not Caesar, was saving the world.

Philippians

While imprisoned under imperial guard awaiting sentencing on charges of a capital crime, Paul wrote from Rome to the assembly in Philippi, a mainly Gentile group he started in 50 CE on his second preaching campaign (Acts 16). The city had a unique history and status. It had been a major project of the first emperor, Caesar Augustus (also known as Octavian), who rebuilt it, settled it with Roman soldiers he had defeated in a civil war and granted it colony status. Philippi residents were unusually devoted to the emperor as "lord and savior," as evidenced by the very active imperial cult in the city. Because of its devotion and colony status, Philippi's leaders had special access to the empire and its resources.

---

[50]   Harink, 225.

Two references tell us Paul's prison was in Rome: through his conversations with guards, "the whole imperial guard" (Phil. 1:13) had become acquainted with the gospel of Messiah Jesus; and Jesus-followers from within Nero's "household" (Phil. 4:21) sent greetings to the Philippi assembly. We know Paul had been charged with a capital crime because his life hung in the balance (Phil. 1:19–22). We know Paul felt isolated (Phil. 1:15–18; 2:20–21) and that he was suffering (Phil. 1:17; 1:29; 3:10). This group of factors distinguishes this imprisonment from prior ones.

What brought about this arrest may never be known. We assume Roman authorities had released Paul from house arrest in 62 CE because his accusers back in Jerusalem had not pursued their charges against him (Acts 28:21). He then began a fourth preaching campaign during which he visited assemblies in Crete (Titus 1:5) and in the province of Asia (1 Tim. 1:3).   Sometime during this fourth campaign, Paul was rearrested, probably in Troas (2 Tim. 4:13) and probably on a charge of sedition for comments he made related to the practices of the imperial cult. Because Paul was a Roman citizen, he was sent to Rome for trial and sentencing.

Given the grave threat Paul was under when he wrote this letter, it offers a unique opportunity to examine Paul's view of the tension between allegiance to Jesus as Lord of Earth and allegiance to Nero as Lord of the Roman Empire.

Of course, Paul wrote this letter under the eyes of prison guards to a group of people who also may have been under surveillance. Insofar as Paul addressed the tension between allegiance to Jesus or Caesar, we should expect his counsel to be less than explicit.

Yet Paul spoke clearly enough: "Our citizenship is in heaven, and it is from there that we are expecting a Savior, the Lord [Messiah] Jesus" (Phil. 3:20). Wright provides perspective: "These are Caesar-titles. The whole verse says: Jesus is Lord, and Caesar isn't. Caesar's empire, of which Philippi is a colonial outpost, is the parody; Jesus' empire, of which the Philippian church is a colonial outpost, is the reality." [51]

The reference to heaven can confuse us, given the commonly-held view that religious folks hope to fly away someday. Wright clears this up:

---

[51]   Wright, 173.

The point of having "citizenship in heaven" . . . is not that one might eventually go home to the mother city; Rome established colonies precisely because of overcrowding in the capital, and the desire to spread Roman civilization in the rest of the empire. The point was that, if things were getting difficult in one's colonial setting, the emperor would come *from* the mother city to rescue and liberate his loyal subjects, transforming their situation from danger to safety. [52]

Does this emphasis fit the rest of the letter? Yes, says Wright; "this is a coded message of subversive intrigue." [53] He points to the tip-off Paul gave readers: "To write the same things to you is not troublesome to me, and for you it is a safeguard" (Phil. 3:1).

The heart of this letter is Paul's famous plea to "let the same mind be in you that was in [Messiah] Jesus, who though he was in the form of God, did not regard equality with God as something to be exploited, but emptied himself, taking the form of a slave" (Phil. 2:5–7). The "mind of Jesus," in other words, does not cling to privileges to which one is entitled, but for the sake of a larger purpose willingly gives them up and accepts even a demotion. Jesus did this on the cross; it is the path YHWH exalted in the resurrection (Phil. 2:9). It is what has given Jesus "the name that is above every name, so that . . . every knee should bend . . . and every tongue should confess that (Messiah) Jesus is Lord" (Phil. 2:9–11).

Paul recounted how he had walked that same path. "If anyone else has reason to be confident in the flesh [i.e., by conventional standards], *I have more*" (Phil. 3:4–6, emphasis added). Indeed, his credentials as a Jew and scholar were impeccable. Yet, Paul wrote, for the sake of the one who he followed, "I have suffered the loss of all things, and I regard them as rubbish" (Phil. 3:8). This is not a righteousness of my own, Paul wrote, but a righteousness received "through *the faith of [Messiah] Jesus*" (Phil. 3:9, emphasis added).

When the assembly in Philippi read Paul's plea to "join in imitating me" (Phil. 3:17), they knew they were being asked to follow the

---

[52]   Ibid., 173-174.
[53]   Ibid., 175.

path already walked by Jesus and Paul: not clinging to the privileges and opportunities to which they were entitled as residents of the emperor's favorite city, but accepting the loss of status certain to follow the refusal to participate in the imperial cult. Paul described this attitude as *humility* (Phil. 2:3, 8); he did not mean self-abasement, but the *willingness to experience loss* because of confidence in YHWH and the way of Jesus.

Paul was aware that voices within the Jesus movement said such suffering was unnecessary; he called such persons "enemies of the cross" (Phil. 3:18) and shed tears over them while sharply criticizing their lack of vision and preoccupation with short-term concerns. "Their end is destruction; their god is the belly; and their glory is in their shame; their minds are set on earthly things" (Phil. 3:19). To their shame, they had turned the gospel into a personal benefit that fit snugly into empire's methods and ways. (See question 40, page 322, on the role of suffering.)

Scattered across the letter are Paul's encouragements not to be intimidated (Phil. 1:28), hold fast (Phil. 1:16; 3:16), stand firm (Phil. 4:1), and keep on (Phil. 4:9). He offered no formula for success; instead, the assembly in Philippi would have to "work out your own salvation with fear and trembling" (Phil. 2:12). Given the unavoidable confrontation of their faith with the empire, much depended on their acting wisely. Yet Paul did not sound afraid: "It is God who is at work in you, enabling you both to will and to work for his good pleasure" (Phil. 2:13).

With his call for disciplined resistance, what specifically did Paul want the assembly in Philippi to do? Wright explains:

> Paul is warning them not to compromise their allegiance to Jesus, and to be prepared, by refusing to take part in cultic and other activities, to follow their Messiah along the path of suffering, knowing that Jesus, the one true Lord, was the Savior who would rescue them and give them the only glory worth possessing. [54]

Paul ended with personal comments to two female co-workers (Phil. 4:2–3) and appreciation to the assembly in Philippi for its financial support over the years (Phil. 4:15–18). He sounded an upbeat tone:

---

[54]   Ibid., 179.

> Rejoice in the Lord always; again, I say, rejoice. Let your gentleness be known to everyone. The Lord is near. Do not worry about anything, but in everything by prayer and supplication with thanksgiving let your requests be made known to God. And the peace of God . . . will guard your hearts and your minds in [Messiah] Jesus. (Phil. 4:4–7)

2 Timothy

The setting of this letter is the same as **Philippians**: a prison in Rome. Paul wrote his long-time associate, Timothy, who was in Ephesus giving oversight to the assembly there. The two men had worked together for fifteen years. Although Paul was perhaps twenty-five years older than Timothy and clearly his mentor, the two were close friends. As we would expect in a farewell letter to a trusted colleague, Paul spoke warmly and seasoned his letter with personal memories. Paul also said he "longs to see" Timothy (2 Tim. 1:4) and asked him "to do your best to come to me soon" (2 Tim. 4:9). Paul even assigned Tychicus to carry out Timothy's duties in Ephesus (2 Tim. 4:12).

Paul was executed not long after writing this text; it was something he expected to happen. He wrote:

> As for me, I am already being poured out as a libation, and the time for my departure has come. I have fought the good fight, I have finished the race, I have kept the faith. From now on there is reserved for me the crown of righteousness, which the Lord, the righteous judge, will give me on that day. (2 Tim. 4:6–8)

One feature of this letter that is very similar to other letters of Paul is the clear teaching that the way of Jesus entails suffering. He asked Timothy to "join with me in suffering for the gospel" (2 Tim. 1:8), to "share in suffering like a good soldier" (2 Tim. 2:3), avoid entanglements "in everyday affairs" (2 Tim. 2:4) and "endure suffering" (2 Tim. 4:5). Paul even found it necessary to say to his trusted friend, "*All* who want to live a godly life in [Messiah] Jesus will be persecuted" (2 Tim. 3:12, emphasis added).

Paul asked Timothy "not to be ashamed, then, of the testimony about our Lord or of me as a prisoner" (2 Tim. 1:8), an obvious reference to the fact that Jesus had *not* been delivered from the cross nor Paul from his cell on death row. "I am not ashamed," Paul wrote, "for I know the one in whom I have put my trust, and I am sure that he is able to guard until 'that day' what I have entrusted to him" (2 Tim. 1:12). A bit later, Paul returned to this theme: "If we have died with him we will also live with him; if we endure, we will also reign with him" (2 Tim. 2:11–12).

The letter makes no obvious reference to the choice between allegiance to the way of Jesus and allegiance to the ways of empire. Yet in Paul's description of a "counterfeit faith" (2 Tim. 3:8) that "holds to the outward form of godliness but [denies] its power" (2 Tim. 3:5), such a choice is assumed. We know this from the obscure (at least for prison censors) example Paul cited of persons who mouth a desire to understand the truth but lack sincerity: "Jannes and Jambres," (2 Tim. 3:8), two spiritually sophisticated miracle workers *who served the empire* during the time of Moses. Avoid such people, Paul said.

A sizable chunk of the text consists of Paul's advice to Timothy as leader of the assembly in Ephesus. For example, Paul repeatedly warned of empty talk and what we might call the seminar approach to faith. "Avoid wrangling over words" (2 Tim. 2:14) and "profane chatter" (2 Tim. 2:16); "have nothing to do with stupid and senseless controversies" (2 Tim. 2:23). Avoid those "who are always being instructed and can never arrive at a knowledge of the truth" (2 Tim. 3:7), who with "itching ears" "accumulate for themselves teachers to suit their desires" (2 Tim. 4:3).

And he urged Timothy to remain assertive: "Proclaim the message; be persistent *whether the time is favorable or unfavorable*; convince, rebuke, and encourage with the utmost patience in teaching" (2 Tim. 4:2, emphasis added). Difficult times are coming; "as for you . . . carry out your ministry fully" (2 Tim. 4:5). You are well prepared, Paul said (2 Tim. 3:14–17). Paul ended by sending greetings to old friends, a second plea for Timothy to "do your best to come before winter," and these words of blessing: "Grace be with you" (2 Tim. 4:19–22).

B. Other encyclicals, sermons and letters

The emphasis on embodying a political alternative to empire slowly recedes in the texts we survey next. To a degree, this simply reflects another set of authors who highlighted different facets of the gospel than Paul did. But more significantly, this shift reflects changes in the Jesus movement in response to a series of significant events.

In 70 CE, Roman troops destroyed Jerusalem and Herod's magnificent temple. This was a traumatic event that heightened the tensions between Jesus-following and traditional Jews. In separate executions around 65–66 CE, the empire under the rule of Nero killed Paul and Peter and, over a period of several years, violently persecuted Jesus–followers in Rome. After Nero's death in 68 CE, the situation eased and the lull lasted two decades. But starting in 89 CE, empire-wide persecution became severe under Emperor Domitian. After Domitian's death in 96 CE, the intensity receded, but persecution continued through the reign of Trajan during the first two decades of the second century.

These events changed the Jesus movement; the biblical texts written after 70 CE gradually reflect ever-greater concern for good order, prudence and moderation. Rarely do these later texts use language that assumes the confrontation with empire that Paul perceived to be unavoidable because of what YHWH had done in Jesus.

Again, we survey these texts in the order they were written.

Ephesians

About twenty years after Paul's death, during a time of relative quiet in the relationship between the assemblies and the Roman Empire, one of his disciples wrote this text for Gentile Jesus-followers who lived across the Greek provinces. The earliest copies did not refer to Ephesus at all; thus, this text apparently functioned as a circulating encyclical.

We conclude Paul did not write it because the text does not include the kind of contextual detail commonly found in Paul's letters and the style is distinctly different from Paul's.

During the first century, it was not uncommon for authors to attribute writings to venerable teachers and thus give them credit as the source of the contents. This was not regarded as deceitful. The assemblies that first read this text and the church fathers who later compiled the Second Testament concluded it truly reflected Paul's teaching and accepted it into the inspired collection.

Ephesians is about the broader church as a new social and political entity and where it fits into the cosmos, the entire creation.   As a more philosophical text, **Ephesians** uses language in a way that may leave the reader less engaged. In addition, the content is more general in nature because the author was writing to dozens of assemblies. Certainly its style is less edgy and energetic than Paul's. It speaks once of the author's suffering (Eph. 3:13) *but never of readers suffering.* It frequently uses terms that distance the new life in Jesus from the nitty-gritty of Earth: "inheritance," "mystery" and "the heavenly places."

To clarify, "heavenly places" means those aspects of life *on Earth* where the kingdom Jesus inaugurated holds sway. Thus, an assembly faithful to the suffering witness of Messiah Jesus is a heavenly place, as is a prison cell where forgiveness and fellowship have replaced bitterness and strife. Or a workplace where cooperation and profit-sharing have replaced rivalry and greed.

By "inheritance," the author means the enduring benefits of life lived the Jesus-way; it is what Paul meant when he said that "in the Lord your labor is not in vain" (1 Cor. 15:58).

By "mystery," the author means "the plan hidden for ages in God" (Eph. 3:1–9). It answers the question that has bedeviled countless rulers through the ages: how can people divided by long-standing injustice and hostility live together without strife and violence?

This introduction brings us to the heart of **Ephesians:** salvation as reconciliation and peace. "Now in [Messiah] Jesus you who once were far off have been brought near by the blood of [Messiah]. For he is our peace; in his flesh he has made [Jews and Gentiles] into one and has broken down the dividing wall, that is, the hostility between us" (Eph. 2:13–14). The text goes on:

> He came and proclaimed peace to you who were far off and peace
> to those who were near . . . So then you are no longer strangers
> and aliens, but you are citizens with the saints and also members

of the household of God, built upon the foundation of the apostles and prophets, with [Messiah] Jesus as the cornerstone. (Eph. 2:17–20)

Reconciliation of Jews and Gentiles in the assemblies of Jesus; that is the *reality* the author wants "the rulers and authorities" (Eph. 3:10) to see. It is the new political phenomenon that subverts and delegitimizes those who insist domination and violence are *necessary* for justice and peace to prevail.

All of this recalls prophetic texts that looked forward to "that day" when YHWH's servant would end strife among the nations. As Gerhard Lohfink sees it, our text describes the pilgrimage of nations using a "different terminology against a completely different horizon of thought. The people of God grow into society . . . through the fascination which it exerts. The church is then quite simply the *efficacious sign* of the presence of God's salvation in the world." [55]

Walter Wink explains why the author emphasized that "the rulers and authorities" become aware of "the wisdom of God" (Eph. 3:10) made visible in the way of Jesus. "The goal is not only our becoming free *from* the Powers . . . but *freeing* the Powers; not only reconciling people to God despite the Powers, but reconciling the Powers to God."[56] Our text attributes this transformation to the vindication of Jesus, whom YHWH

raised from the dead and seated at his right hand in the heavenly places, far above all rule and authority and power and dominion, and above every name that is named, not only in this age but also in the age to come. And [YHWH] has put all things under his feet and made him the head over all things for the church, which is his body, the fullness of him who fills all in all. (Eph. 1:20–23)

Ephesians also reprises key theological themes from Paul's letters: the richness of God's mercy, the greatness of YHWH's love, and how salvation depends entirely on YHWH's initiative in the first place, not our merit (Eph. 2:4–5, 8–9). We all were "children of wrath," out text

---

[55]   Lohfink, *Jesus and Community,* 145-146.
[56]   Wink, 319.

says, bearing the emotional and economic scars passed one generation to the next, "following the course of the world, following the ruler of the power of the air" in our efforts to settle old scores and get our share, ruled by passions and desires that never brought us any closer to our goals. But God has "made us alive together with [Messiah] . . . and raised us up with him . . . to be renewed in the spirit of [our] minds" (Eph. 2:2–6; 4:17–24).

Like **Colossians,** this text speaks to the often contentious relationships of wives and husbands, children and parents, slaves and masters (Eph. 5:21–6:9). The discussion is prefaced by a leveling principle: "be subject to one another out of reverence to [Messiah]" (Eph. 5:21). The instruction to husbands goes on for eight verses and is quite demanding. In general, what we said in previous commentary related to **Colossians** (see pages 286–287) applies here as well.

The final section is an inspirational call to "be strong in the Lord and in the strength of his power" (Eph. 6:10). It is a bracing statement to people engaged in a demanding confrontation: "Our struggle is not against enemies of blood and flesh, but against the rulers, against the authorities, against the cosmic powers of this present darkness, against the spiritual forces of evil in the heavenly places. Therefore, take up the whole armor of God, so that you may be able to withstand" (Eph. 6:12–13). Upon inspection, we find the military metaphors are entirely defensive in function. As John H. Yoder puts it, "The church does not attack the Powers; this [Messiah] has done. The church concentrates upon not being seduced by them." [57]

This section adds a key insight: powerful structures and institutions are animated by spiritual forces that we dare not ignore. Wink calls these forces "the interiority of earthly institutions" and cites as an example the spirit of greed that animates Western capitalism. What motivates the host of junior and senior managers in that system "is almost irrelevant. They need not be greedy for profit at all; *the system is greedy on their behalf.*" Moreover, "it is not just that people are making choices about how they will behave in the economic system; the system is also making choices about who will remain viable in the system." [58] Thus, "the

---

[57]   Yoder, *The Politics of Jesus,* 150.

[58]   Wink, 77-79.

church's peculiar calling is to discern and engage both the structure and the spirituality of oppressive institutions." [59]

The tone of **Ephesians** is more restrained than the letters of Paul, with less emphasis on public proclamations and displays. Perhaps this is as additional reason why it is a favorite within western Christianity. The shift in tone suggests an evolving understanding of core purposes. Lohfink states: "For the author of **Ephesians,** the striking point is that missionary preaching of the gospel to the Gentiles no longer figures *as a current task.* The church is *the result,* but no longer the *bearer of mission.*" [60] Yoder makes a similar point: "The very existence of the church is its primary task. It is in itself a proclamation to the powers from whose dominion the church has begun to be liberated." [61]

Hebrews

A few years later, an educated teacher wrote to Jewish Jesus-followers living in Italy (Heb. 13:24). The author of this skillfully composed text has long been a mystery. We think it was Priscilla, wife of Aquila. Although her initial residence seems to have been Rome (Acts 18:2), she also lived with her husband in Corinth and Ephesus and worked with Paul at all three locations. Paul praised her and usually placed her name ahead of her husband's (Rom. 16:3). She taught Apollos early in his ministry (Acts 18:26). The very fact that mystery surrounds the authorship of **Hebrews** suggests that controversy attached itself to the author. Priscilla's gender may have been the source.

Chronologically, **Hebrews** was written 18-20 years after the destruction of Jerusalem and Herod's magnificent temple. Traditional Jews viewed these events as catastrophic, but Jesus-following Jews viewed them as evidence of the new era Jesus had inaugurated. This difference drove people apart and extinguished the practice of Jesus-believing Jews and traditional Jews maintaining close relationships and united synagogue worship. It also caused many Jews to end their membership in separate Christian assemblies. Indeed, this is the problem that caused **Hebrews** to

---

[59]   Ibid., 84.
[60]   Lofink, 145.
[61]   Yoder, 150.

be written: Jews denouncing their prior allegiance to Jesus (Heb. 2:1–4; 6:4–9; 10:19–31).

Priscilla responded to this problem in religious terms, trying to show how commitment to Jesus fit within Judaism and resulted in a new-and-improved Judaism.

> Long ago God spoke to our ancestors in many and various ways by the prophets, but in these last days he has spoken to us by a Son, whom he appointed heir of all things, through whom he also created the worlds. He is the reflection of God's glory and the exact imprint of God's very being, and he sustains all things by his powerful word. (Heb. 1:1–3)

As we have seen, the Jewish faith tradition spoke of its spiritual leaders first as kings, later as prophets, and still later (during the period after the Babylonian exile) as priests. It spoke of faithfulness to YHWH as obedience, justice and sacrifice. **Hebrews** emphasizes Jesus as priest and sacrifice, thereby implying that these were the elements of Judaism where many Jews most often found Jesus' credentials deficient.

In reading First Testament texts, we have seen how suffering and affliction are often described as pathways toward repentance, cleansing and renewal. Following that theme, our text states: "It was fitting that God, for whom and through whom all things exist, in bringing many children to glory, should make the pioneer of their salvation perfect through sufferings" (Heb. 2:10). In this human experience of suffering, Jesus became "like his brothers and sisters in every respect, so that he might be a merciful and faithful high priest in the service of God, to make a sacrifice of atonement for the sins of the people" (Heb. 2:17).

The text also refers to Sabbath rest, one of the most visible Jewish ways to witness to YHWH. The full experience of this rest had always eluded the Jews; neither Moses nor Joshua succeeded in leading their followers there (Heb. 3:18; 4:8) and Priscilla reminded readers that this incompleteness continued. "So then, a Sabbath rest still remains for the people of God . . . let us therefore make every effort to enter that rest" (Heb. 4:9, 11).

Chapters 5—10 portray Jesus as a high priest, one who "has been tested as we are, yet without sin" (Heb. 4:15). Although described as the Son of God, he "learned obedience through what he suffered; and having been made perfect, he became the source of eternal salvation for all who obey him" (Heb. 5:8–9). "Unlike the other high priests, he has no need to offer sacrifices day after day, first for his own sins, and then for those of the people; this he did once for all when he offered himself [on the cross]" (Heb. 7:27). The text refers repeatedly to the rituals of Jewish sacrifices, but the setting is always the tabernacle in the wilderness, *never* the temple in Jerusalem. For the loss of that temple, the text offers no lament.

Chapter 8 takes a brief detour to assert that while Jesus more than meets all of the qualifications for a traditional high priest, he "has now obtained a more excellent ministry . . . mediator of a better covenant, which has been enacted through better promises" (Heb. 8:6). This is the "new covenant" described in **Jeremiah** 31:31–34, a covenant written in the minds and hearts of the people that YHWH will be their god and they shall be YHWH's people (Heb. 8:10). "And they shall not teach one another or say to each other, 'Know the Lord,' for they shall all know me, from the least of them to the greatest" (Heb. 8:11). But then the text brings this "new covenant" within traditional discourse and insists this new way could be inaugurated only in the same way as the old way: by the shedding of blood. For "without the shedding of blood there is no forgiveness of sin" (Heb. 9:22).

Next the text brings us briefly to a message of the prophets: YHWH does not desire sacrifices and offerings, but only a willing spirit ready to do justice (Heb. 10:1–18). The section ends with an appeal to "hold fast to the confession of our hope without wavering" (Heb. 10:23).

Chapter 11 shifts the focus from sin and sacrifice to the promises of YHWH. Priscilla names First Testament heroes ("a cloud of witnesses," see Heb. 12:1) who believed those promises. Jesus is the last named:

> the pioneer and perfecter of our faith, who for the joy that was set before him endured the cross, disregarding its shame, and has taken his seat at the right hand of the throne of God. Consider him who endured such hostility against himself from sinners, so that you may not grow weary or lose heart. (Heb. 12:2–3)

In the last eighty verses, using both present and future verb tenses, Priscilla referred to "city" again and again. Abraham "looked forward to the city . . . whose architect and builder is God" (Heb. 11:10); YHWH "has prepared a city" for those who died in faith without receiving what God had promised (Heb. 11:13, 16); "you have come to Mount Zion and to the city of the living God, the heavenly Jerusalem" (Heb. 12:22); "for we have no lasting city, but we are looking for the city that is to come" (Heb. 13:14). This was her acknowledgement that Jerusalem, long regarded as YHWH's place of primary residence, had been destroyed.

The text encourages practical virtues: giving thanks, mutual love, hospitality to strangers, visiting prisoners, honoring marriage, living free of the love of money, sharing with others, and obeying the leaders of one's assembly (Heb. 12:28). It ends this way: "Now may the God of peace, who brought back from the dead our Lord Jesus . . . make you complete in everything good . . . through [Messiah] Jesus, to whom be the glory forever and ever" (Heb. 13:20–21).

Jude

Jude was the "brother of James" (Jude 1:1), who was the leader of the first century assemblies in Jerusalem and a brother of Jesus. Thus, the author is often described as a brother of Jesus.

However, the text speaks of "the faith . . . entrusted to the saints" (Jude 1:3) and exhorts readers to "remember the predictions of the apostles" (Jude 1:17), thus suggesting time has passed since the deaths of Jesus' contemporaries. We conclude the author is likely to have been a member of the next generation and wrote this text around 100 CE, not long after the reign of Emperor Domitian and his persecution of Christians.

It is styled as a warning against traveling teachers "who pervert the grace of our God into licentiousness and deny our only Master and Lord, [Messiah] Jesus" (Jude 1:4). Apparently, these teachers taught the loving and merciful character of the divine presence had revealed the material aspect of earthly life to be a mirage; it did not count for much when viewed in the light of the spiritual hope promised in Jesus.

Devaluing earthly existence in this way was a way to rationalize the suffering Jesus' followers had endured during Domitian's reign.

In response, the author recalls First Testament stories in which YHWH showed great mercy, only to turn later toward harsh judgment because people were unfaithful. In other words, *YHWH responds to human behavior on Earth.* This insistence on locating YHWH's actions squarely within human history is fully consistent with traditional Jewish teaching.

The tone is combative, sharply distinguishing true and false teaching and asking readers to "contend for the faith" (Jude 1:3). We may be suspicious of such either-or thinking, yet the text itself opposes a philosophical dualism that separates YHWH from history. Instead, it calls readers to the nitty-gritty work of building on Earth the new community Jesus had launched: "Have mercy on some who are wavering; save others by snatching them out of the fire; and have mercy on still others with fear, hating even the tunic defiled by their bodies" (Jude 1:22).

1, 2, 3 John

First circulated to local assemblies early in the second century, **1 John** was a sermon that responded at greater length than **Jude** to the influence of Gnosticism. **2 John** and **3 John** were private letters sent by the same author to "the elder lady" and "Gaius" respectively; they concern practical matters related to interactions with gnostic teachers. The author probably was the same man who wrote the **Gospel of John.**

Gnosticism was not a full-blown philosophy; instead, it was (and is) a way of thinking about good and evil. This way of thinking separates soul from body, essence from matter and creator from creation, thus relieving the tension between good and evil and "explaining" suffering.

The gnostic mindset shows itself as an approach to life. The most common gnostic path assumes earthly life is a dream experienced as real for a brief time, but then giving way in physical death to the true reality with the divine being. For those following such a path, wise living may entail an ascetic life of complete devotion to one's god. Or it may entail a life of hedonistic pleasure-seeking and violence until "real" existence begins. Each of these very different ways of living can be reconciled with the "knowledge" of a beautiful, spiritual reality in another realm. The knowledge of this other reality is often said to be available only to those initiated through special teaching, heightened sensitivities or mysterious rituals and spiritual experiences.

Another life path reflecting the gnostic attitude resolves the tension between good and evil by coercively *imposing* good. Examples include Hernan Cortes' conquering Christianity, Woodrow Wilson's militant democratic idealism, and Vladimir Lenin's missionary Marxism.

The specific gnostic teaching at issue in these texts is Docetism, which taught YHWH had walked on Earth in the form of Jesus of Nazareth, but had only appeared to be human. Thus, the resurrected Christ reigning in heaven was real, but not the bloodied Jesus on a cross.

In response to these grand philosophical debates, our text disarmingly says it offers nothing new (1 John 2:7). Instead, it simply insists *earthly experiences* (what we hear, what we see, what we touch, what we do) *are important.* Sin is harmful and must be addressed. Love is strong and must be practiced. The commands of YHWH are beneficial and must be followed. It is a down-to-earth teaching.

Like the **Gospel of John,** the text speaks of "eternal life" not as chronological time *but as the life of Messiah Jesus*: "This life was revealed, and we have seen it and testify to it, and declare to you the eternal life that was with the Father and *was revealed to us*" (1 John 1:2, emphasis added). "The darkness is passing away and the true light is *already shining*" (1 John 2:8, emphasis added). "Beloved, we are God's children *now*" (1 John 3:2, emphasis added). "This is the testimony: *God gave us eternal life*, and this life is in his Son. Whoever has the Son *has life*" (1 John 5:11–12, emphasis added).

Again, the way Jesus lived is important; you "*ought to walk just as he walked*" (1 John 2:6, emphasis added). Living ethically is important; "everyone who does what is right is righteous, just as he is righteous" (1 John 3:7). Loving one another is important, not only in "word or speech, *but in truth and action*" (1 John 3:18, emphasis added). Each assertion refutes the gnostic practice of using high-sounding religious rhetoric to denigrate or avoid the importance of day-to-day living on Earth.

The love described by the text is practical; it "casts out fear" (1 John 4:18). "Those who say, 'I love God,' and hate their brothers and sisters are liars; for those who do not love a brother or sister whom they have seen, cannot love God whom they have not seen" (1 John 4:19–20).

In response to the claim that Jesus only appeared to be human, our text states: "By this you know the Spirit of God: every spirit that confesses that [Messiah] Jesus has come in the flesh is from God, and every spirit that does not confess Jesus is not from God" (1 John 4:2–3).

Implicitly, these words insist that Earth and human history are the setting for YHWH's salvation and that the way of Jesus is the pathway to that salvation. It is not metaphysics and mysterious transactions in another realm that will save us; *it is the life Jesus lived on Earth.* "This is the victory that conquers the world" (1 John 5:4).

2 Thessalonians

In chapter 21, we noted three *public* events that signaled to believers that the flow of history had been interrupted, that the world had turned a corner and had begun moving toward the empire of God. The first occurred in Jerusalem on Pentecost when young and old, female and male, slave and free all experienced a manifestation of God's spirit. The second was a new community meeting in and around the temple with a commitment to justice that entailed the sharing of financial assets. Within a few years, similar communities sprang up in Samaria and Syria, then in Cyprus, the provinces of Greece and Italy. The third marvel brought Jews and Gentiles together in united communities, which accepted leadership from women, viewed slaves and slave-owners as brothers, supported one another financially across huge distances, and improbably perceived themselves to be a political alternative to the Roman Empire.

Occurring over a space of only twenty to twenty-five years, these events fueled powerful expectations within the Jesus movement that history was rapidly approaching a tipping point. The repressive violence of Domitian was understood to be the empire's last-ditch effort to save itself, thus heightening the sense that the time was rapidly approaching when Jesus would appear again on Earth, summon the righteous from their graves, and put the *fullness* of YHWH's empire into place.

This is the background for this second letter to the assembly in Thessalonica, written early in the second century. The great persecutor, Domitian, was gone, but harassment continued under his successor, Trajan, and in some places violent persecution, too.

First, our text confirms that YHWH was putting the world right. "It is indeed just of God to repay with affliction those who afflict you, and to give relief to the afflicted" (2 Thess. 1:7). It goes on to promise "vengeance" and "eternal destruction" for "those who do not know God and those who do not obey the gospel of our Lord Jesus" (2 Thess. 1:8–9). "Vengeance" and "destruction" are often assumed to mean YHWH will use violence against enemies. The text does not support that view; it sees "separation from the presence of [YHWH]" (2 Thess. 1:9) as the just end of those who hate justice. Instead of resurrection at the end of history, the unrighteous will simply perish.

Second, our text asks readers to ease off expectations of imminent divine deliverance from the struggle they are in.

> We beg you, brothers and sisters, not to be quickly shaken in mind or alarmed . . . to the effect that the day of the Lord is already here. Let no one deceive you in any way, for that day will not come unless the rebellion comes first and the lawless one is revealed, the one . . . whom the Lord Jesus will destroy *with the breath of his mouth*. (2 Thess. 2:2–3, 8, emphasis added)

The identity of this "lawless one" is vague, but it is strongly associated with deception, delusion and falsehood (2 Thess. 2:9–12). *Telling the truth will bring about his downfall.*

"So then, brothers and sisters, stand firm and hold fast to the traditions that you were taught" (2 Thess. 2:15). This may take a while, in other words, but the transformation has begun. "The Lord is faithful; he will strengthen you and guard you from the evil one" (2 Thess. 3:3). So get to work and avoid idleness; "brothers and sisters, do not be weary in doing what is right" (2 Thess. 3:6–13). Also avoid those who ignore this sort of practical, down-to-earth teaching; "do not regard them as enemies, but warn them as believers" (2 Thess. 3:15).

1 Peter

The author of this text wrote in Peter's name to Jesus-followers who lived in the Roman provinces of modern day Turkey, including Bithynia-Pontus (1 Pet. 1:1). They lived under threat of arrest, imprisonment and execution by the empire because they bore "the name of [the Messiah]" (1 Pet. 4:14). Here is the passage that frames this text: "Beloved, do not be surprised at the fiery ordeal that is taking place among you to test you . . . but rejoice insofar as you are sharing [Messiah's] sufferings" (1 Pet. 4:12–15).

In 112 CE, about when this text was written, Pliny the Younger, the Roman governor of the province of Bithynia-Pontus, wrote Emperor Trajan for instructions on how to deal with Jesus-followers.

> I interrogated [them] as to whether they were Christians; those who confessed I interrogated a second and a third time, threatening them with punishment; *those who persisted I ordered executed.* For I had no doubt that, whatever the nature of their creed, stubbornness and inflexible obstinacy surely deserve to be punished. There were others possessed of the same folly; but because they were Roman citizens, I signed an order for them to be transferred to Rome.

> Soon accusations spread, as usually happens, because of the proceedings going on, and several incidents occurred. An anonymous document was published containing the names of many persons. Those who denied that they were or had been Christians, when they invoked the gods in words dictated by me, offered prayer with incense and wine to your image, which I had ordered to be brought for this purpose together with statues of the gods, and moreover cursed Christ—none of which those who are really Christians, it is said, can be forced to do—these I thought should be discharged. Others named by the informer declared that they were Christians, but then denied it, asserting that they had been but had ceased to be, some three years before, others many

years, some as much as twenty-five years. They all worshipped your image and the statues of the gods, and cursed Christ.

But what about those who recanted? This was where Pliny needed direction. In his response, Emperor Trajan affirmed Pliny's practices.

You observed proper procedure, my dear Pliny, in sifting the cases of those who had been denounced to you as Christians. For it is not possible to lay down any general rule to serve as a kind of fixed standard. They are not to be sought out; if they are denounced and proved guilty, they are to be punished, with this reservation, that whoever denies that he is a Christian and really proves it—that is, by worshiping our gods—even though he was under suspicion in the past, shall obtain pardon through repentance. But anonymously posted accusations ought to have no place in any prosecution. For this is both a dangerous kind of precedent and out of keeping with the spirit of our age. [62]

How should Jesus-followers live under such a policy? Our text attempts to answer this question. The author addressed his readers as "exiles" and "aliens living in "exile" (1 Pet. 1:1, 1:17, 2:11). He reminded them of "a living hope—the resurrected Jesus" (1 Pet. 1:3) and "a salvation ready to be revealed in the last time" (1 Pet. 1:5). He assured them they "have been born anew, not of perishable but of imperishable seed, through the living and enduring word of God" (1 Pet. 1:23). He told them they fulfilled the vision from **Exodus** of a new political community:

You are a chosen race, a royal priesthood, a holy nation, God's own people in order that you may proclaim the mighty acts of him who called you out of darkness into his marvelous light. Once you were not a people, but now you are God's people; once you had not received mercy, but now you have received mercy. (1 Pet. 2:9–10)

---

[62]   *Internet Medieval Source Book,* Fordham University, 1996 (emphasis added).

He told them "the end of all things is near; therefore be serious and discipline yourselves" (1 Pet. 4:7). "Above all," he said, "maintain constant love for one another" (1 Pet. 4:8).

And he told them they must conform to prevailing norms. "*Accept* the authority of every human institution, whether of the emperor as supreme, or of governors, as sent by him to punish those who do wrong and to praise those who do right . . . Fear God. Honor the emperor" (1 Pet. 2:13–14, 17, emphasis added). "Slaves, *accept* the authority of your masters with all deference, not only those who are kind and gentle but also those who are harsh . . . For to this you have been called, because [Messiah] also suffered for you, leaving you an example, so that you should follow in his steps" (1 Pet. 2:18, 21, emphasis added). "Wives, in the same way, *accept* the authority of your husbands, so that even if some of them do not obey the word, they may be won over without a word by their wives' conduct" (1 Pet. 3:1, emphasis added).

The author of this text recognized these efforts to conform to existing political, economic and cultural norms would not be enough; Jesus-followers would still be arrested. It simply was too easy for an envious neighbor, an offended patriot in the imperial cult, or a disgruntled former member of an assembly to file an accusation with the authorities that so-and-so "bore the name of Jesus." Arrest would soon follow.

And so the author told readers to prepare themselves for questioning:

> Do not fear what they fear, and do not be intimidated . . . always be ready to make your defense to anyone who demands from you an accounting for the hope that is within you; yet do it with gentleness and reverence. Keep your conscience clear, so that when you are maligned, those who abuse you for your good conduct in [Messiah] will be put to shame. (1 Pet. 3:15–16)

The strategy was plain: keep your nose clean and avoid calling attention to yourself. If you find yourself interrogated and your life hangs on every word you say, do not give them any reason to put you to death other than your faith in Jesus.

Repeatedly the text recalls Jesus' suffering (1 Pet. 1:11; 2:21–24; 3:18; 4:1; 4:13). Repeatedly, far more than any other text in the Second Testament, it refers to the suffering of those who follow Jesus. "If any of you suffers as a Christian, do not consider it a disgrace, but glorify God because you bear this name . . . Therefore, let those suffering in accordance with God's will entrust themselves to a faithful Creator, while continuing to do good" (1 Pet. 4:16, 19).

This text elicits strongly mixed feelings. It reflects what Paul preached: Jesus-followers are the new political community that the First Testament anticipated. It recognizes the empire as the great enemy of YHWH; we know this by the closing greeting from "your sister church in Babylon" (1 Pet. 5:15), a reference to Rome first used by the author of **Revelation**. It shows no shame over suffering for the empire of YHWH. Yet it also calls assemblies to "accept" injustice, using Jesus' death as an example.

We are left to ponder this text written under duress and then compare it with the two that follow (see question 42 at page 323).

1 Timothy

Though **1 Timothy** says it was written by Paul after his fourth preaching campaign, the content and literary style suggest to us that it was written by someone else in Paul's name around 115 CE, about fifty years after Paul's death.

The text is styled as instructions to Timothy, who gave oversight to assemblies in and around Ephesus. It speaks of qualifications for the "office" of bishop (1 Tim. 3:1–7), outlines qualifications of deacons (1 Tim. 3:8–13) and refers to a "council of elders" (1 Tim. 4:14), thus implying the assemblies had developed a formal structure in their various locations. It offers advice to Timothy: "train yourself in godliness" (1 Tim. 4:7), emphasize "the public reading of scripture" (1 Tim. 4:13), and speak to people in a way that reflect their age and gender (1 Tim. 5:1–2). It goes into detail about the administration of the widows' financial fund (1 Tim. 5:3–16); describes how to support and discipline "elders" who "rule" over assemblies (1 Tim. 5:17–22); and suggests a little wine as an aid to good health (1 Tim. 5:23).

It speaks of "the faith" as a collection of settled beliefs, something Paul never did. "Certain persons have suffered shipwreck in *the faith*;" they have been "turned over to Satan so that they may learn" (1 Tim. 1:19–20, emphasis added). Gnostic attitudes threatened *"the faith,"* as evidenced by those who "forbid marriage and demand abstinence from foods" (1 Tim. 4:1–3, emphasis added); they should be reminded that "everything created by God is good . . . provided it is received with thanksgiving" (1 Tim. 4:3–5). "The love of money" is a cause for error; "in their eagerness to be rich some have wandered away from *the faith* and pierced themselves" (1 Tim. 6:10, emphasis added).

In contrast to Paul's writings, which constantly engaged and challenged wider society and its authority structures, the text reflects a desire for the assemblies to find favor with the status quo by conforming to and propping up the existing social and political order.

The author urged prayers for the "kings and all who are in high positions" (1 Tim. 2:2). He detailed rules for women's dress to ensure modesty (1 Tim. 2:9–10), set down a rule for women to "learn in silence with full submission," forbid women from teaching men (1 Tim. 2:11–12), and implicitly excluded women from leadership positions (1 Tim. 3:1–13). Slaves were commanded to "regard their masters as worthy of all honor *so that the name of God and the teaching may not be blasphemed."* The slave who shared a commitment to Jesus with his or her master was not to form any expectations of a changed relationship; *"rather, they must serve them all the more, since those who benefit by their service are believers and beloved"* (1 Tim. 6:1–2, emphasis added).

Thus the gospel of Jesus, which in Paul's letters subverted structures of oppression, is portrayed in this text as a reason *not* to upset the power of the strong over the weak.

The text does not mention suffering for the faith. This factor, when added to those noted above, suggests a strategy of accommodation toward empire and a departure from the gospel of Messiah Jesus.

Titus

This letter to Titus is similar to **1 Timothy.** It claims to have been written by Paul after putting Titus in charge of the assemblies in Crete

(Titus 1:5). But its tone suggests a later period of time when the Jesus movement had adjusted to imperial hostility by carefully conforming to prevailing norms. Consider this general instruction: "Remind [members of the assemblies] to be subject to rulers and authorities, to be obedient, to be ready for every good work, to speak evil of no one, to avoid quarreling, to be gentle and to show every courtesy to everyone" (Titus 3:1–2). The text does not mention suffering for the faith of Jesus.

As in **1 Timothy**, the author told slaves to "be submissive" and "give satisfaction in every respect," thus making "the doctrine of God our Savior" attractive to the powerful. "[Slaves] are not to talk back, not to pilfer, but to show complete and perfect fidelity, so that in everything they may be an ornament to the doctrine of God our Savior" (Titus 2:9–10).

The text instructs Titus on the practical teaching he should provide for older men and younger men, older women and younger women. It is striking that women are told to love their husbands and be submissive to them, while men are given no instructions regarding their wives (Titus 2:1-8). Jews receive harsh criticism as "rebellious people, idle talkers and deceivers . . . they must be silenced" (Titus 1:10–11). This text was frequently cited later in church history as authority for cutting off all fellowship with Jews, and still later, for requiring Jewish conversion to a version of Christianity under penalty of death.

Like **1 Timothy**, this text directs Titus to appoint "elders" and outlines qualifications for a man to be "bishop" (Titus 1:5–9). The requirement that he have been married "only once" has been understood to imply a teaching against polygamy.

In contrast to **1 John**, the author speaks of "eternal life" as a future hope (Titus 1:2), not present reality. In contrast to Paul, who described the promises of YHWH as revealed in the life of Jesus and in the community of his followers, the author pushed the reality of the great day of YHWH off into the future. "For the grace of God has appeared, bringing salvation to all, training us to renounce impiety and worldly passions, and in the present age to live lives that are self-controlled, upright and godly while we wait for the blessed hope and the manifestation of the glory of our great God and Savior" (Titus 2:13).

What sort of salvation had Jesus brought? For Paul, it immediately began subverting deceitful structures of power, reconciling enemies and creating a new political community. But in this text, tangible salvation is entirely a future hope for which readers are to prepare by living quiet and accommodating lives. As for the empire, one should go along to get along.

2 Peter

Around 120 CE, an unknown author writing in Peter's name circulated this sermon to assemblies of Jesus-followers. The text includes many references to **Jude**, quotes from the synoptic gospels and refers to the writings of Paul. It is commonly regarded as the last written First Testament text.

It speaks harshly of "false teachers" (2 Pet. 2:1) who claim to follow Jesus, but have returned to their former ways of living. They are like the dog that "turns back to its own vomit" or the pig that "is washed only to wallow in the mud" (2 Pet. 2:22). As in **Jude** and the letters of **John**, the text opposes making the faith of Messiah Jesus into a kind of knowledge rather than a way of life. "They promise [their listeners] freedom, but they themselves are slaves of corruption; for people are slaves to whatever masters them" (2 Pet. 2:19).

The second focus of the sermon is the doubt readers were experiencing due to the delayed arrival of "the day of the Lord" (2 Pet. 3:10). The time when justice and peace would prevail had been anticipated by First Testament prophets and boldly claimed by Jesus to have arrived. As interpreted by Paul, the new creation begun in Jesus had indeed shifted the trajectory for human history toward justice and peace, but the *fullness* of that new creation awaited Jesus' return to Earth. Now, ninety years after Jesus' death, the voices of the scoffers were gaining traction: "Where is the promise of his coming" (2 Pet. 3:4)?

In reply, the author said that "with the Lord . . . a thousand years are like one day." In other words, not much time had yet passed since Jesus had faded from eyesight. Also, the author asserted "the Lord is not slow about his promise . . . but is patient with you, not wanting any to perish, but all to come to repentance." Quoting **1 Thessalonians**, he said the day of YHWH would come unexpectedly, "like a thief." To adjust their expectations, the author urged godly living, "waiting for and hastening the coming of the day of God" (2 Pet. 3:8–11). "Regard the patience of our Lord as salvation" (2 Pet. 3:15).

The text speaks of Earth's future in an unusual way.

> The present heavens and earth have been reserved for fire, being kept until the day of judgment and destruction of the godless. (2 Pet. 3:7)

> Then the heavens will pass away with a loud noise, and the elements will be dissolved with fire, and the earth and everything that is done on it will be disclosed. (2 Pet. 3:10)

> In accordance with his promise, we wait for a new heavens and a new earth, where righteousness is at home. (2 Pet. 3:13)

"Reserved for fire" and "kept" for the day of disclosure suggest the author expected creation to be purified and restored, much as Paul expected it to be transformed and "set free" (Rom. 8:18–22). Certainly the author of our text did not expect YHWH to *destroy* Earth; that word is used only in connection with "the godless" (2 Pet.3:7).

23. Living Wisely (Part B)
The Letter of James

The authorship, historical setting and date of this letter are all disputed items, so the reader is left to decide what is most convincing in these regards.

Our judgment, however, is that the themes and strong vocabulary of the letter suggest a date in the late 40s CE, before the writings of Paul. James, the brother of Jesus and reputed by many scholars to be the author, was murdered by stoning in 61 or 62 CE, making a later date impossible. We assume he wrote from Jerusalem for Jewish synagogue audiences.

The letter's rare mention of Jesus has puzzled readers. About that we can only suggest that its advocacy of Jesus' way of peacemaking and nonviolence without his name stands in marked contrast to the common use of Jesus' name in our time without his way of peacemaking and nonviolence. Borg's comment is important to note: "James echoes more sayings of Jesus than any document in the New Testament other than the gospels themselves. Its fiery passion reflects the passion of Jesus himself."[63]

Readers of **James** have long been impressed with strong language in the letter: severe testing, the need for endurance, passion for justice and the poor, intense anger, the dangers of hypocrisy, inflammatory speech, references to adultery and murder and the calls for action/work, not faith alone.[64] All of this may have been a response to the internal dynamics of a local assembly, but that assumes a very unusual assembly and either limited interaction or deliberate bypassing of engagement with the world. Yet the letter warns against yielding to the ways/thought patterns of the world (Jas. 1:27, 4:4), so apparently the voice of the world was being heard loud and clear in these communities.

During and after the reign of Emperor Caligula, violent resistance to

---

[63]   Borg, 196.

[64]   Reiher, "Violent Language—A Clue to the Historical Occasion of James" *Evangelical Quarterly*, 2013.

the empire's occupation and oppression in Palestine became an increasingly attractive option for Jewish (and no doubt Jewish-Christian) partisans, especially those who lacked the resources to grease the palms of Roman officials. Freedom fighters called zealots led this movement. From 46–48 CE, an open revolt led by two zealot brothers, Jacob and Simon, flared in Galilee. The Jewish Jesus-followers addressed by James lived among "the twelve tribes of the Dispersion" (Jas. 1:1). Is it likely that these Christians were unaffected by or disinterested in the struggles for justice, which so passionately engaged the Jews in their time, and indeed the violent Maccabees 160 years before Jesus?

James began: "My brothers, whenever you face *trials* of any kind, consider it nothing but joy, because you know that the *testing* of your faith produces endurance" (Jas. 1:2, emphasis added). Followers of Jesus knew well the story of his testing in the wilderness around questions of power and how he would use it. Now, they were being tested around similar questions, and James advocated *"endurance,"* which may be translated "steadfast resistance."

But what was his readers' *test?* James said that *wisdom* is available from YHWH. He said, "Ask [for wisdom] in faith, never doubting, for the one who doubts is like a "wave of the sea, driven" (Jas. 1:5–11). He names the lifting of the poor and bringing low of the rich as a truth of *wisdom.* Zealots saw this social upset as implementation of *justice.* But, James warned, "Do not be *deceived"* (Jas. 1:16, emphasis added) by zealous calls for violence to create *justice.* Anger and violence don't create *justice.*

James frequently used a word translated either as "justice" or "righteousness" (Jas. 2:21, 23, 25; 3:18; 5:6). The *testing* and *deception* likely have to do with what does in fact accomplish *justice/righteousness.* Zealots held that violent behavior, including killing selected enemies, furthered the cause of justice. But James counseled *patient endurance and* steadfast resistance of the devil (Jas. 4:7), a nonviolent method of pursuing justice. And he said, "The anger of man does not work the *justice* of God" (Jas. 1:20, emphasis added).

Interestingly, James exhibited his own anger in the letter. He was not counseling unemotional stoicism toward the world's suffering, but the discernment of how to channel anger at injustice. For that he offered the wisdom from God, which shows how to choose between the violent and nonviolent options. This does not come easily; it takes strong faith and it is easy to be deceived.

At the climactic center of his letter James affirmed peace as the way to justice. "A harvest of righteousness [justice] is sown in peace for those who make peace" (Jas. 3:18). In contrast to the message of those who say that justice is the prior condition of peace, James argued that justice is the result of peace(ful) advocacy, the steadfast endurance of faithful works based on YHWH's wisdom (see question 43 at page 323).

With the struggles for liberation from empire and for justice between rich and poor in mind, along with the central issue of what kind of power should be used in that struggle according to the wisdom of YHWH, the progression of thought in the letter of James becomes clear.

"Be doers of the word, and not hearers only" (Jas. 1:22) and related advocacy for "works" becomes counsel not only to pray for and believe in the establishment of YHWH's justice (which zealots would have dismissed as idle dreaming), but to act: "Religion that is pure and undefiled before God, the Father, is this: to care for orphans and widows in their distress, and to keep oneself unstained by the world" (Jas. 1:27). Do not tell the poor to be warmed and filled on their own, do something. But do not accept the zealots' counsel to take up violent means to impose justice/righteousness and change the balance of power between the rich and the poor; that is the wisdom of the world.

Favoritism toward the rich (Jas. 2:1–13) seems unlikely in a community with a passion to do justice for the poor until one thinks about real church communities, in which there are competing viewpoints. On the one hand, there are voices calling for radical action to lift the poor. On the other hand, there are voices saying, "We need the rich and their money to fund the life of this community."

Who is right? Factions arguing in a church inevitably choose their favorite law to be obeyed and most awful sin to be avoided. One could think of the homosexuality debate in the church today. In the assemblies James addressed, maybe it was the rich stressing that adultery was an awful sin, and the poor stressing that oppression of the poor was an awful sin. James said, "Keep the whole picture in mind."

Speech is important. Flaming rhetoric from worldly zealots can be believed, even adopted, by Jesus-followers. But God's way/wisdom is "first pure [consistent, not double-minded], then peaceable, gentle, willing to yield, full of mercy and good fruits, without a trace of partiality or hypocrisy" (Jas. 3:17; 4:8).

The rant on the rich—"Come now, you rich people, weep and wail for the miseries that are coming to you" (Jas. 5:1)—may have had in mind the rich of the world more than the rich in the assemblies. This would explain James' stark statement about the high cost of nonviolent advocacy for the poor: "You [the rich of the world] have condemned and murdered the righteous one, who does not resist you" (Jas. 5:6).

At the end of the letter (Jas. 5:7–11), we again see the emphasis on steadfast resistance with which the letter began. And James assured his readers: "The prayer of the righteous [just] is powerful and effective" (Jas. 5:16), reminding them of the character of true power.

Reflection and Discussion

39. Paul was convinced that Jesus had changed the direction of history. The empire had been exposed as deceptive, violent and unjust and had thus been defeated; a new way of running the world had begun. For this bold claim to be accepted, Paul knew evidence was required. What evidence did he cite, and what evidence did he challenge the assemblies to produce?

40. Consider the role of suffering in Paul's worldview and leadership; consider it as well in the lives of other movement leaders. How would you describe its impact and significance?

41. What is the difference between a social movement and a social organization? Over the course of the texts surveyed in chapter 22, we see the Jesus-following community shifting from a movement based structure to an organizational structure. Compare the way a movement approaches questions of purpose (why it exists), leadership, membership (who is inside the movement and who is not) and self-discipline with the way an organization approaches those questions. Where do you see religious communities functioning as social movements today?

42. Except for the book of **Revelation,** texts written after 90 CE sound less like resistance literature. Of course, this shift coincides with Domitian's empire-wide persecution of Christians. How do you characterize this shift: betrayal, adaptation or something else? What is your reaction to the authors' view that **1 Timothy** and **Titus** were "a departure from the gospel of Messiah Jesus" (see page 315)?

43. **James** speaks of wisdom as resistance without violence. As you think of efforts to create an alternative to the empire today, what forms of resistance need to be celebrated? Emphasized more? Emphasized less? Where is **James'** teaching about violence most relevant?

24. Steadfast Resistance & Faithful Witness
The Revelation to John

A. The author's central message and style

During the intensely hostile reign of Emperor Domitian, John the Revelator asked the churches and disciples of his times: "How are you doing, living this nonviolent, simple life of Jesus in an empire organized around greed and violence? Can you withstand the pressure?" These are the questions which frame the entire book of **Revelation** and must inform our reading of it.

Revelation is "big picture" writing, composed of a series of dramatic scenes with stimulation for eyes, ears, nose and the emotions. John was an artist—musician, painter, story teller, poet—not a logical rationalist. He did not have the vehicle of Technicolor movies or HD television to convey his truth, so he used what was available to him, and did it with great skill and effect.

To avoid one of the most common and destructive mistakes interpreters of this text have made over the years, let us first set aside our Western obsession with linear sequence and timeline development and read the book as it was written, as a big stack or bowlful of dramatic, largely simultaneous, imaginative scenes describing not some future series of events, but the very difficult life of the Christian assemblies to whom John wrote.

Second, observe that the big picture is composed of small elements, starting with words. To say the obvious, it is important to pay attention to words and their meanings in **Revelation**, but especially words which are repeated throughout the writing, because repetition is one of John's key techniques. As with scenes, so with words; the impact of their repetition makes a cumulative impact on the reader. "Where did I see this before?" is a good mental attitude for the reader.

Third, assume that which is most likely: John wrote for his contemporaries, first of all. He wrote to tell them how to think about and respond to what they were experiencing as a minority, alternative community in the midst of an empire of social and political forces which pressed its agenda hard, sometimes with clever seduction and other times with vicious persecution.[65]

Revelation is, by its own account, a prophetic book by a prophet. But the word "prophecy" has misled many people and many of our readers may assume this text is about future events or can be safely ignored because it has long since been proven mistaken about future events. Both assumptions are wrong. The first is wrong because the book is primarily about John's and his readers' present, not about the distant future. The second is wrong in supposing that Christians today can ignore the book at no loss to themselves.

The book does say one profoundly important thing about the future: *good is sustainable while evil is not.* This is profoundly significant because it assures mere mortals like you and me that no good deed goes unrewarded, and that the enterprise of unbridled greed, organized fraud, and homicidal state violence will ultimately fail, abjectly and absolutely. Surely we need to hear that message today. Who among us is awake to what is going on in our world but does not need assurances that good is overcoming evil and will surely prevail in the end?

At the outset, we will help ourselves greatly to understand John's message if we permit him, like ourselves, to know less than everything about everything. That is, we must allow him to get some things more right than others, some things really right and others wrong.

For example, John knew less, or at least said less than he should have, about the power of love to transform lives and situations. And in his enthusiasm to assure us that evil will not triumph in the end, he portrayed God's hand as destroying evildoers rather than, as he might have, showing evildoers reaping the inevitable consequences of their actions and God working through Jesus in humans to transform people in ways that begin to strangle evil itself—in Paul's words, overcoming evil with good. So let us try to get beyond expecting perfection of John and get on with seeing the great good he does offer.

As a prophet hearing a word from God, John speaks to the situation of immense struggle in which he and the assemblies to which he

---

[65] Richard, *Apocalypse: A People's Commentary on Revelation*, 3-5.

wrote found themselves. His readers had already seen many of their brothers and sisters die at the hands of imperial and financial powers. They were greatly tempted to give up the struggle and join the powers of commerce, consumption, and imperial force—to just go along to get along.

John describes grim scenes, scenes of pain, suffering, blood, destruction. *They are all about the consequences of the way the empire runs the world.* The message is very simple: bad behavior has bad consequences. There is a philosophical and theological question here, to be sure: does YHWH plan, instigate and deliver all of the consequences of bad behavior (is YHWH the great punisher)? Or is there some distance between the immediate hand of YHWH and the inevitable consequences of bad behavior/sin? If there were an easy answer to this, you would already know it. What we can say with confidence is that two thousand years ago John put less distance between YHWH's intervening hand and consequences that are inevitable than we are inclined to do today.

In summary, John brings his call to relentless persistence (i.e., patient endurance, steadfast resistance—several translations are equally possible) into the sights, sounds and smells of the epic drama he portrays with apocalyptic rhetoric: overflowing cauldrons, mighty winds, torrential rain and hail, fire and light and medicinal trees and life. He does all of this to encourage readers to continue walking in the ways of goodness and community and peace to which they had committed themselves in their new communities now called "churches."

B. The author's introduction (chapter 1)

"God made the revelation of Jesus Christ known by sending it to his servant John, who *witnessed* to the word of God and to the *witness* of Jesus Christ" (Rev. 1:1–2, emphasis added). Here John repeats twice the key word of the whole poetic script—*witness*—and also states the critical conceptual doublet, "word of God and witness of Jesus," a play on words by which he unites the old and new, familiar and unfamiliar, for his Jewish and Gentile readers. This doublet is repeated at critical moments throughout the book, and concludes with a striking reversal in the order of the concepts: "*the witness of Jesus and the word of God*" (Rev. 20:4, emphasis added).

John wrote his message for followers of Jesus (called "servants" in Rev. 1:1), but more specifically "to the seven churches that are in Asia: Grace to you and peace from him who is and who was and who is to come . . . and from Jesus Christ, the faithful witness, the firstborn of the dead, and the ruler of the kings of the earth" (Rev. 1:4).

That is the tip-off: in this text, we are reading about what is powerful, what rules the world, what will endure and set the world right. Not just the world of my lost job or your lost retirement savings, although those things matter, but our world of war, of economic exploitation and inequality, of mindless destruction of the environment on which life itself depends, of air and water and food and shelter. The large themes of the First and Second Testaments, and of Jesus' teaching, are also the major themes of **Revelation** (see questions 44-47 at pages 339-340)

Now let us put ourselves for a moment in the shoes of John's contemporaries in the seven churches to which he wrote. Under the iron heel of the Roman Empire and blandishments of pagan religions, they were saying: "This is a hard life. What are we supposed to do with it? On the one hand, they're telling us that we can have a good life if we buy and sell lots of their stuff (see chapter 17 of **Revelation**). On the other hand they're saying they'll kill us if we don't fit in like good patriots." Sound familiar? It is the carrot and the stick, the method of the empire.

But the empire is dying, John reminded his readers; its end is within view. In the face of this earth-shaking change, John quoted "one like the Son of Man" (Rev. 1:13) who says: "Do not be afraid; I am the first and the last and the living one" (Rev. 1:17–18). Jesus has shown another way to run the world; it is a kingdom of life. John's message is that this way will endure.

As noted above, John introduced Jesus as "the faithful witness, the firstborn from the dead, and the ruler of kings on earth." What is meant by this term "witness" (Greek, *martus*, martyr)? To bear witness, as in a court, is to give a fair and faithful account of what one has seen and experienced. So Jesus, as one sent by YHWH to represent the fullness of YHWH's intention for humanity, gave a faithful witness to that intention.

C. Messages to the seven churches (chapters 2–3)

John addressed seven churches (a symbolic number) in his great poem. This grounds the book thoroughly within history. Churches were new socio-political communities formed by individuals who had changed their thinking (repented) and moved their loyalty from the death ways of the Roman Empire to the life ways of Jesus' empire/kingdom.

Each church is a lampstand, a source of light for a dark world. Above, beyond, or over each church is a star, which represents the corporate spirit, collective understandings, unique identity and spiritual/cosmic character and mission of that specific church.

John heard Jesus address the star of each church with critique and encouragement tailored to its unique mission and behavior. We notice John began each message by restating one specific attribute of the Son of Man figure in the vision, so the message was specific to the character and needs of that church. Every message ends with the phrase "to everyone who conquers." **Revelation** is a book about struggle and the possibility of success.

Each message identifies specific "works" or behaviors to which believers are called, and which implement a "faithful witness" in the world. These "works" include "patient endurance" (Rev. 1:9; 2:2,19; 3:10); "testing/discerning" (Rev. 2:2); "faithfulness" (Rev. 2:10); "faithful witness" (Rev. 1:5; 2:13); "keeping my word" (Rev. 3:8); "holding fast" (Rev. 2:13, 25; 3:11); "service" (Rev. 2:19); "remembering" (Rev. 2:5; 3:3); "waking and watching" (Rev. 3:2–3); "being passionate and earnest" (Rev. 3:15, 19); and "repent"—change your thinking, your mind (Rev. 2:5, 16, 21; 3:3, 19; see refusal to repent at 16:9, 11). All of these works define a non-imperial way of running the world. They are the ethical lifestyle of the new communities. It is for the encouragement of these life-giving, world-changing behaviors that the entire writing is devoted.

In our time, what should we expect of the church? We should expect what John expected of the seven churches: wise critique and strong encouragement, using the standard of "patient endurance" or steadfast resistance (Rev. 1:9; 2:2, 19; 3:10), which is the "work" (Rev. 2:2, 19, 23; 3:1–2, 8, 15) by which the churches and saints make their "faithful witness" (Rev. 1:5) to the way/kingship of Jesus in this world. *It must not escape us that the churches are judged by their "works"*: "I know your works," the angel says time after time (a major theme of the Bible, see for example Eph. 2:10).

We must inevitably ask: Is my church, is your church, giving us guidance and nurture in making a faithful witness to the "faithfulness of Jesus" (Rev. 1:5; 14:12)? Jesus maintained faith in YHWH and YHWH's way of tending creation, loving enemies and dismantling oppression right to the cross. Are we doing this?

Is the church of our time helping us to see through the lies the corporations and government are telling us with their media mouthpieces, each playing the role of the beast that arises out of the earth (see Rev. 13:11–18)? Or is it avoiding confrontation with deception, such as Monsanto's lies about caring for Earth and sustainable agriculture?

Is the church of our time renewing for us the vision of the triumph of the way of nonviolence, the Lamb's way? Do we believe that those who currently control Earth will be judged and found wanting, or do we expect the empire to prevail and save us? And at the same time, do we believe those nations will finally be transformed by the life symbolized in the leaves of trees that grow by the river of the water of life (Rev. 21:24—22:2)? Is the church's worship helping us live worshipful lives engaged in restorative justice and active peacemaking, lives that demonstrate the deception of the empire's war against terrorism?

Is our church showing us **Revelation's** celebration of the Creator, which is inseparable from celebration of the wisdom of creation? Does it understand how the way this world works sustainably is built into its genetic and relational reality? Which means no technology that violates the fundamental laws of nature's infinite inter-connectedness, no economy that is based on mindless extraction of irreplaceable resources from Earth's finite store, and no ethic that denies the priority of generosity over greed in the fundamental expression of human nature, is sustainable?

The future lies with those who know and live as if YHWH knew what s/he was making in the billions of years of this earth's history. The church, with good help from Jesus speaking in the book of **Revelation**, could help us know this.

D. Lion or Lamb? (chapters 4–5)

When we look at history, we are looking at a great struggle to manage the unpredictability, complexity and injustice of life. Who is defining the terms of engagement in this ongoing struggle and with what kind of power are they doing it? The book of **Revelation** is obsessed with this question, and uses two key animal images to illustrate it.

John imagined a little scroll that held the secret of history, but that scroll was sealed (locked) and there was the question of who could open it. So first a voice said in John's ear, "The Lion of the Tribe of Judah, the root of David has conquered—he can open the scroll" (Rev. 5:5). So it appears that history is run by the dominating, violent power of great men (kings). This Lion will do the job. This is the expectation created by what John heard with his ear.

But then to John's eyes appeared a Lamb that looked like it had been slaughtered, and next all the angelic choirs and animals and saints of heaven and earth were singing that this Lamb is the one who can open the scroll of history, and to this Lamb is given all power and wisdom and honor and wealth and glory and blessing (Rev. 5:6–13). Oh! That's a reversal! *The Lamb has replaced the Lion.* John never mentions a lion again with reference to anything good; the Lamb takes over the story. So history, after all, is not run by violence! And this, despite all superficial appearances to the contrary, becomes the underlying truth of **Revelation**.[66]

E. The Lamb opens the seven seals (chapters 6–7)

Next in John's imaginative account, the Lamb begins to open the seal(s) of history and we see what is going on in our world. In rapid succession, four horsemen appear as four seals are opened: a rider on a white horse is able to conquer, one on a red horse takes away peace and makes war with a sword, one on a black horse manages the economy and one on a pale green horse wields the power of death. Another seal opens and souls appear of those who "had been slaughtered for the word of God

---

[66]   Hays & Alkier, *Revelation and the Politics of Apocalyptic Interpretation,* 69-83.

and the witness they had given" (Rev. 5:9; notice the word/witness doublet). They are given white robes (remember the white horse?) and told that they will be vindicated when the suffering of their fellow servants, brothers and sisters is complete. Here John honestly names the very real human longing to know *that suffering in the cause of good is not the same as defeat.*

This scenario of struggle moves to the opening of the sixth seal, revealing the disaster about to befall the kings and magnates, the generals and the rich and powerful when the Lamb assumes his power.

After this, John saw "a great multitude that no one could count, from every nation, from all tribes and peoples and languages, standing before the throne and before the Lamb, robed in white," singing "salvation belongs to our God and the Lamb" (Rev. 7:9–10). This vast crowd is the seven churches and all like them who have conquered in this great struggle, and *they did it by sharing the witness of the Lamb to YHWH's way of running the world.*

F. Seven trumpets: the world refuses to repent (chapters 8–11)

Finally, the seventh seal opens and the story spirals back, starting again to reveal another layer of this great struggle of history in which the seven churches are heroically engaged. This time the symbol of trumpets, seven of them, is used to assault the reader's ears with sounds of the horrific consequences of humanity's violence to the tender ecology of the earth. People are seeing the destruction of their environment and cultures, but in spite of this great woe, they do not repent and turn toward YHWH's way of running the world revealed by the Lamb (Rev. 9:20–21). All of this is clearly a reprise of the plagues on Egypt and the refusal of the empire to repent (Ex. 1—15).

However, the sixth trumpet discloses not only woe, but also witness. Chapter 10:1—11:14 says that for centuries already, the world has received a witness to YHWH's way through the prophets. A little scroll, eaten by John, again symbolizes truth written and revealed; the two bold and strong witnesses represent the universal discipleship vocation of speaking YHWH's truth to the world. These two witnesses are assaulted and assailed by the inhabitants of the earth (to "witness" is a great struggle!), but in the end they are victorious, lifted up to heaven (Rev. 11:7–13). It is a scene to encourage the hearts of Jesus' followers in making their faithful witness. Here John used symbols from **Zechariah** 4.

Then the seventh angel blows his trumpet. The drama is intensifying! Now "the kingdom of this world has become the kingdom of our Lord and of his Messiah" (Rev. 11:15). It is the time "for judging the dead, for rewarding your servants, the prophets and saints and all who fear your name, both small and great, and for destroying those who destroy the earth" (Rev. 11:18). One could hardly imagine a more emphatic statement of the consequences of environmental degradation; those who destroy Earth are destroyed.

G. The steadfast resistance of the saints is tested (chapters 12–14)

Next, in order to heighten the drama, John shifted from earthly events to scenes of mighty struggle in heaven. A woman giving birth to a son appears—symbols of life in a world hostile to life and bent on dealing death and destruction. A great dragon called both "Devil" and "Satan" makes war in heaven against Michael and his angels. The dragon is thrown down to Earth where he makes war on the woman and all of her children "who keep the commandments of God and hold the witness of Jesus" (Rev. 12:17, notice the doublet again).

Then great beasts arise from the earth and from the sea. They represent the powers of homicidal, idolatrous and deceitful imperial institutions. Their power seems to be inescapable and overwhelming. But then a countervailing power appears; it is "the Lamb, standing on Mt Zion! And with him were one hundred and forty-four thousand who had his name written on their foreheads" (Rev. 14:1). These have been redeemed from humankind and they "follow the Lamb." The beasts have not conquered them!

Angels appear in the heavens, proclaiming an eternal gospel to all, announcing that the empire, "Babylon the great," is fallen (Rev. 14:8) and that those who worship the beast will drink the wine of YHWH's wrath. All of this, the reader is told, "is a call for the endurance [steadfast resistance] of the saints, those who keep the commandments of God and hold fast to the faith of Jesus" (Rev. 14:12, the doublet again). John's obsessive concern was always the life of this community, which is living as an alternative to empire.

H. Seven plagues call for repentance (chapters 15–18)

Finally in the heavens appear seven angels with seven plagues. The stack of scenes grows even higher and more dramatic! These angels hold and pour out bowls of the wrath of YHWH. They come out of "the temple of the tent of witness" in heaven (Rev. 15:5). The drama here, the struggle, is the world's struggle to choose between the witness of the prophets and angels, which comes from heaven, and the enticements and threats of the beasts, representing earthly empires.

Repeatedly, the emptying of bowls of destruction is followed by the words "but they did not repent" (Rev. 16:9, 11). The world/humanity is largely choosing the enticements and threats of empire. In chapters 15–18, John described, with a series of overlapping and diverse scenes, the ultimate defeat of evil and triumph of good. As he described it, it looks like a process which goes on for a long time, but not forever; that is as specific as the book of **Revelation** gets about the climax of history as we know it. Included in chapter 18 is a graphic description of human greed and commerce under the symbol of Babylon, culminating in great mourning over the end of commerce in a multitude of items including "cattle and sheep, horses and chariots, slaves—and human lives" (Rev. 18:13). All of this goes down to defeat.

It takes little imagination to see today's realities of fossil fuel-dependent global trade and carbon-generated global warming in these scenes. Instructive analogies suggest themselves.

I. God's victory: a new heaven and new earth (chapters 19–22)

Victory celebration follows in "what seemed to be the loud voice of a great multitude in heaven, saying, 'Hallelujah! Salvation and glory and power to our God, for his judgments are true and just'" (Rev. 19:1–2).

John imagined a great marriage supper, where the Lamb is the groom, and the bride "has made herself ready," clothed in "fine linen, bright and pure—for the fine linen is the righteous deeds of the saints"

(Rev. 19:7–9).   And so the church is united with the one who has shown it the way to live an alternative life of nonviolence in the midst of violent empire.

Beginning with 19:11 and continuing into chapter 21, seven paragraphs depict a progressive defeat of evil.   Each begins with the words, "then I saw."   First a rider on a white horse, who appears and defeats evil with "the sword from his mouth;" his name is "the Word of God."   There is language of violence and images of blood, but from the names of the rider, "Faithful and True," (Rev. 19:11) to the "wordness" of his sword to his "shepherding" of the nations, the rider is depicted as nonviolent, fully consonant with the Galilean Jesus we met in the gospel accounts and Paul's letters.

The second paragraph describes "an angel standing in the sun" summoning the birds of the air to "the great supper of God" to clean up the decay of death (Rev. 19:17–18).

The third portrays the kings, captains, the mighty, horses and riders and the beast and the false prophet thrown into the lake of fire that burns with sulfur (Rev. 19:19).   The fourth describes "an angel coming down from heaven" seizing the dragon, binding him and throwing him into the pit, which is locked and sealed over him for a thousand years "so that he would deceive the nations no more" (Rev. 20:1–3).

The fifth paragraph portrays those who were "beheaded for their testimony to Jesus and to the word of God" (the first time this couplet is in this order, putting Jesus first!) given sovereignty to reign with Messiah Jesus for a thousand years (Rev. 20:4).   Here in the middle of the process through which evil is defeated is a foretaste of victory for the faithful.   In other words, the victory does not wait until *all* evil has been *finally* defeated.   *The church now, within history, lives in this time of evil's partial, and promise of ultimate, defeat.*

The sixth portrays Death itself and Hades, and anyone whose name is not found written in the book of life, thrown into the lake of fire, thus breaking evil's power (Rev. 20:11–15).   Here as throughout, it is important to remember we are reading John's imaginative account, his word-pictures meant to help assemblies understand the very difficult experiences of their lives.   Crass literalism is not good interpretation.

The stage is now set for the coming of the new heaven and new earth, which is described in the seventh paragraph starting at 21:1. Here we defer mainly to the reader's spirit and imagination, letting the text speak for itself, but offering just a few notes.

(a) The culmination of all is not in another world, but "the new Jerusalem comes down out of heaven" (Rev. 21:2) to Earth.

(b) The river of the water of life and the trees it waters "are for the healing of the nations" (Rev. 22:2) as well as a renewed and nurturing Earth (Rev. 21:6, 26). In some sense, empire(s) are not only defeated, but transformed and healed!

(c) Jesus, the faithful witness, reassures John, saying: "Surely I am coming soon." John responded, "Amen [so be it], come Lord Jesus" and ended his text by sharing this grace of Jesus' presence "with all the saints" (Rev. 22:20–21). This "coming" in the book of **Revelation** is the constant irruption of the Jesus-way of life in the life of his disciples. This "soon" is the present world in which their steadfast resistance to imperial oppression is their faithful witness. This grace is here and now.

The whole message of **Revelation** is in the prophetic tradition of Israel. The choices between life and death, truth and falsehood, love and hate, nurture and destruction, compassion and vengeance, which Israel's prophets at their best always presented, are the matrix of human living. The choices people make have real consequences. The stewardship of Earth and life is the human vocation. Do it well.

25. So What?
The authors' concluding words

One conclusion we reach after all of this is that YHWH, god of the Israelites, is not a human construct made of mulberry wood or wishful thinking. Yes, some of what is said about YHWH is just that, but we cannot ignore at least two of the surprises we see in the biblical story: the Jews singing YHWH's song in a strange land after their defeat and exile, and Jesus of Nazareth, a life and legacy unimaginable until it happened.

These make the biblical story worth every minute we've given it.

An alternative political community

Our focus in reading the Bible has been the long effort by worshippers of YHWH to form a political community whose way of organizing and running the world is different from empire's way.

We have learned how efforts to become a nation like Assyria or Egypt—and then later to collaborate with the Persian Empire—distorted the Israelites' understanding of YHWH and enmeshed them in systems of injustice and oppression. And we have learned how the prophets' partial visions of another way flowered in the teachings of Jesus, who taught not a new religion, but a new politics.

This new politics does not seek to gain control of the levers of government. Instead, it creates a community committed to the justice described by **Isaiah** and the generous mercy of a god who "makes his sun rise on the evil and on the good, and sends rain on the righteous and the unrighteous" (Matt. 5:45). It pays as much attention to means as to ends, and thus lives with the conviction that the world will be saved by compassion, forgiveness and nonviolent resistance, not by domination, vengeance and bloodshed.

Yes, this community seeks to be powerful, not only kind and loving. It is comfortable with the language of power, but it is convinced that the way empires understand and use power is destroying Earth and its inhabitants. So it seeks a different kind of power, the power of people acting in myriad contexts out of a shared faith, worldview and commitment.

As people are drawn to its wisdom, this community becomes a subculture, one that "lives faithfully by the permanent things." [67] It understands life to be a gift and justice to be our shared calling. It acts quietly, like yeast mixed into flour (Luke 13:21), but also stands in the public square like Peter or Paul claiming to have found in Jesus of Nazareth another way to run the world. It regards people first as producers (rather than consumers) with the capacity to "tend their own vines and fig trees" (Micah 4:4).

A different understanding of power

The faith of Messiah Jesus is that the vulnerable confrontation of injustice moves the world toward healing.[68] It sees in compassion, forgiveness and suffering a power that awakens the spirit of YHWH in people, subverting and eventually disarming the most oppressive forces. Though it believes the promises of YHWH, it also expects loss and suffering. Thus, it is fiercely resistant *and* nonviolent.

It is a banquet to which all prepared to celebrate are invited, where divisions nurtured by empire are dissolved and the hostilities of the ages overcome. It is multi-voiced and decentralized, yet unabashed in claiming authority to discipline itself and judge the world.

We do not claim that this political community—this subculture, this kingdom—excludes all vestiges of government. We understand government to be a helpful structure created to serve limited purposes within the requirements of justice and public accountability.

But an empire is unwilling to be so constrained. An empire exalts itself, establishes its own secret purposes, resists accountability to anyone or anything, thrives through deception and violence, co-opts or suppresses all alternatives and delivers us into the hands of death. Efforts to seize control of such a beast, as it is called in **Revelation**, do not fit within the

---

[67]   Dreher, *Crunchy Cons: The New Conservative Counterculture and Its Return to Roots,* 227.
[68]   Fairfield, 109-130.

political purposes envisioned by the prophets, articulated by Jesus of Nazareth and manifested in the assemblies of early Jesus-followers.

Solidarity and group-mindedness

The modern social movements led by Eugene Debs, Mahatma Gandhi, Martin Luther King, Lech Walesa, Nelson Mandela and Aung San Suu Kyi have much to teach us about the sources and expressions of nonviolent power seeking broadly–based justice.   The writings of nineteenth century supporters of producing over consuming, proprietorship over wage dependence and community over class, all described compellingly by Christopher Lasch,[69] are a rich resource.   Contemporary writers such as Arundhati Roy, Naomi Klein, Cornel West, Greg Boyd and Shane Claiborne can help us.

Scattered around the world are congregations of Christians, Jews or Muslims whose sacred texts sound the call to embody a just alternative to empire. If they answer that call through the means embodied by Jesus and not through the methods of empire, such congregations can become vital nodes of a global network of spiritual liberation, public engagement and resistance to evil. Practitioner networks, such as those focusing on community food security or local energy sustainability, also can answer this call, though likely in a less religious way.

In part, the point of mentioning these possibilities is to emphasize the importance of forming the habits of solidarity and group-mindedness. So long as we remain isolated from one another, an alternative political community will remain beyond our grasp.

Seceding from the empire

Formation of communities capable of articulating political alternatives will entail repentance, maybe even time in the wilderness, to slough off our infatuation with empire and its pathologies.

The signs of such are all around and creating something different will not be easy. Though national political leaders repeatedly deceive us, we continue giving them the benefit of the doubt. Though the market is

---

[69]   Lasch, *The True and Only Heaven: Progress and its Critics,* 203-225.

rigged to deliver huge rewards to the economic elite, we continue to regard the market as sacrosanct. Though our consumption of a disproportionate share of the world's resources obviously depends on the empire's use of overwhelming violence and coercion, we continue to nonchalantly enjoy the benefits. Though partisan labels, ethnic and sexual identities, and the distinctions of gender, class and celebrity serve the purposes of empire by dividing and distracting us, they remain our cherished badges of selfhood. Though professional and career norms sap our courage and dull our dissent, we continue to give them top priority.

Repentance, nurturing relationships within groups that are embracing another politics, learning from those who have embodied an alternative to empire, and practicing the power of vulnerable confrontation: these are the experiences that will sustain us on the path to a just, compassionate and nonviolent alternative.

Increasingly in the years ahead, we expect those who are walking this path will feel a new urgency to bind themselves together in physical communities that live day-to-day in a sustainable, non-imperial way. It will be the witness of such communities that makes alternatives to empire visible again. It is there that the surprising presence of YHWH will again be known, demanding justice, reconciling enemies and restoring Earth.

Reflection and Discussion

44. "Pain, suffering, blood, destruction—all consequences of the way the empire runs the world" (page 326). What costs are you or people you know experiencing because of the way the empire runs the world? If you know no one experiencing costs, where can you find accounts of people with such experiences?

45. Re-read the second half of Section C in chapter 24 (page 329), which asks pointed questions about churches today. If you are part of a congregation, how does it measure up? Are you part of any other group you can measure in this fashion?

46. Conversation about the future of humankind often has had a pointless quality because it is so speculative. Yet John the

Revelator does speak of the future in his text and insists that the way of Jesus is the key to Earth's survival. In our time, as the carbon load of the atmosphere increases, scenarios about humankind's future on Earth have taken on empirical weight. Do you find it important to make decisions *now* based on Earth's future prospects? How does the way of Jesus fit into that?

47. **Revelation** suggests that most people do not change their minds (repent) about the empire until it has been vanquished by its consequences. But some do "make themselves ready" for the vindication of the way of Jesus (page 333). What might "making ready" mean in our time?

48. Where do you see political community in our time that lives out the biblical vision traced by this book? Describe what you see that prompts you to make this association.

49. What can you do to secede from the empire and strengthen a community you identified in your response to question 48?

PART IV:
Praying Biblical Texts

Spoken prayer is a form of human communication with God. Written words fail to reveal the mystery of prayer. Yet we gain insight through its practice, which is at once poetic, self-disclosing and spiritually evocative. Starting such a practice can be difficult; voicing biblical prayers can help.

Moses' prayer of blessing (Numbers 6: 24–26)

"The LORD bless you and keep you; the LORD make his face to shine upon you and be gracious to you; the LORD lift up his countenance upon you and give you peace."

Moses' prayer at the alter when bringing his offering (Deuteronomy 26:5–15)

"A wandering Aramean was my ancestor; he went down into Egypt and lived there as an alien, few in number, and there he became a great nation, mighty and prosperous. When the Egyptians treated us harshly and afflicted us by imposing hard labor on us, we cried to the LORD, the God of our ancestors; the LORD heard our voice and saw our affliction, our toil, and our oppression. The LORD brought us out of Egypt with a mighty hand and an outstretched arm, with a terrifying display of power, and with signs and wonders; and he brought us into this place and gave us this land, a land flowing with milk and honey.

"So now I bring the first of the fruit of the ground that you, O LORD, have given me."

Hannah's prayer of gratitude after her time of barrenness ended (1 Samuel 2:1–8)

"My heart exults in the LORD; my strength is exalted in my God. My mouth derides my enemies, because I rejoice in my victory. There is no Holy One like the LORD, no one besides you; there is no Rock like our God.

"Talk no more so very proudly, let not arrogance come from your mouth; for the LORD is a God of knowledge, and by him actions are weighed. The bows of the mighty are broken, but the feeble gird on strength. Those who were full have hired themselves out for bread, but those who were hungry are fat with spoil. The barren has borne seven, but she who has many children is forlorn. The LORD kills and brings to life; he brings down to Sheol and raises up. The LORD makes poor and makes rich; he brings low, he also exalts. He raises up the poor from the dust; he lifts the needy from the ash heap, to make them sit with princes and inherit a seat with honor.

"For the pillars of the earth are the LORD's, and on them he has set the world."

David's prayer for justice (Psalm 10:1–3, 12–14; 17–18)

"Why, O LORD, do you stand far off? Why do you hide yourself in times of trouble? In arrogance the wicked persecute the poor—let them be caught in the schemes they have devised. For the wicked boast of the desires of their heart, those greedy for gain curse and renounce the LORD.

"Rise up, O LORD; O God, lift up your hand; do not forget the oppressed. Why do the wicked renounce God, and say in their hearts, 'You will not call us to account?' But you do see! Indeed you note trouble and grief, that you may take it into your hands; the helpless commit themselves to you; you have been the helper of the orphan.

"O LORD, you will hear the desire of the meek; you will strengthen their heart, you will incline your ear to do justice for the orphan and the oppressed, so that those from earth may strike terror no more."

David's prayer for forgiveness (Psalm 51:1–12)

"Have mercy on my, O God, according to your steadfast love; according to your abundant mercy, blot out my transgressions. Wash me thoroughly from my iniquity and cleanse me from my sin. For I know my transgressions, and my sin is ever before me. Against you, you alone, have I sinned, and done what is evil in your sight, so that you are justified in your sentence and blameless when you pass judgment.

"You desire truth in the inward being; therefore teach me wisdom in my secret heart. Purge me with hyssop and I shall be clean; wash me and I shall be whiter than snow. Let me hear joy and gladness; let the bones that you have crushed rejoice. Hide your face from my sins and blot out all my iniquities. Create in me a clean heart, O God, and put a new and upright spirit within me. Do not cast me away from your presence and do not take your holy spirit from me. Restore to me the joy of my salvation and sustain in me a willing spirit."

David's prayer for help in time of trouble (Psalm 86:1–7)

"Incline your ear, O LORD, and answer me, for I am poor and needy. Preserve my life, for I am devoted to you. You are my God; be gracious to me, O LORD, for to you do I cry all day long. Gladden the soul of your servant, for to you, O LORD, I lift up my soul. For you, O LORD, are good and forgiving, abounding in steadfast love to all who call on you. Give ear, O LORD, to my prayer; listen to my cry of supplication. In the day of my trouble I call on you for you will answer me."

Prayer for guidance (Psalm 119:33-40, author unknown)

"Teach me, O LORD, the way of your statutes, and I will observe it to the end. Give me understanding, that I may keep your law and observe it with my whole heart. Lead me in the path of your commandments, for I delight in it. Turn my heart to your decrees, and not to selfish gain. Turn my eyes from looking at vanities; give me life in your ways. Confirm to your servant your promise, which is for those who fear you. Turn away the disgrace that I dread, for your ordinances are good. See, I have longed for your precepts; in your righteousness give me life."

Isaiah's prayer after a mystical experience (Isaiah 6:5, 8)

"Woe is me! I am lost, for I am a man of unclean lips and I live among a people of unclean lips; yet my eyes have seen the King, the LORD of hosts . . . Here am I; send me!"

Hezekiah's prayer for recovery from a life-threatening illness
(Isaiah 38:14–19)

"Like a swallow or a crane, I clamor, I moan like a dove. My eyes are weary with looking upward. O Lord, I am oppressed; be my security! But what can I say? For [you have] spoken to me, and [you yourself have] done it. All my sleep has fled because of the bitterness of my soul.

"O Lord, by these things people live, and in all these is the life of my spirit. Oh, restore me to health and make me live! Surely it was for my welfare that I had great bitterness; but you have held back my life from the pit of destruction, for you have cast all my sins behind your back. For Sheol cannot thank you, death cannot praise you; those who go down to the pit cannot hope for your faithfulness. The living, the living, they thank you, as I do this day."

Jeremiah's prayer when discouraged by his opponents
(Jeremiah 17:14–18)

"Heal me, O LORD, and I shall be healed; save me, and I shall be saved; for you are my praise.

"See how they say to me, 'Where is the word of the LORD? Let it come!' But I have not run away from being a shepherd in your service, nor have I desired the fatal day. You know what came from my lips; it was before your face.

"Do not become a terror to me; you are my refuge in the day of disaster. Let my persecutors be shamed, but do not let me be shamed; let them be dismayed, but do not let me be dismayed; bring on them the day of disaster; destroy them with double destruction!"

Jesus' prayer that he taught his disciples (Matthew 6:9–13)

"Our Father in heaven, hallowed be your name. Your kingdom come, your will be done, on earth as it is in heaven. Give us this day our daily bread. And forgive us our debts, as we also have forgiven our debtors. And do not bring us to the time of trial, but rescue us from the evil one."

Jesus' prayer as he anticipated arrest (Matthew 26:39)

"My Father, if it is possible, let this cup pass from me; yet not what I want but what you want."

Jesus' prayer on the cross (Mark 15:34)

"My God, my God, why have you forsaken me?"

Mary's prayer after her cousin, Elizabeth, blessed her pregnancy (Luke 1:46–53)

"My soul magnifies the Lord, and my spirit rejoices in God my Savior, for he has looked with favor on the lowliness of this servant. Surely, from now on all generations will call me blessed; for the Mighty One has done great things for me and holy is his name. His mercy is for those who fear him from generation to generation. He has shown strength with his arm; he has scattered the proud in the thoughts of their hearts. He has brought down the powerful from their thrones and lifted up the lowly; he has filled the hungry with good things and sent the rich away empty."

Tax collector's prayer in the temple (Luke 18:13)

"God, be merciful to me a sinner!"

Jesus' prayer on the cross (Luke 23:34)

"Father, forgive them for they do not know what they are doing."

Prayer of Jesus' followers after Peter's and John's release from prison (Acts 4:29–30)

"And now, Lord, look at their threats and grant to your servants boldness to speak your word with all boldness while you stretch out your hand to heal, and signs and wonder are performed through the name of your holy servant, Jesus."

Prayer for the assemblies of Jesus
(Ephesians 3:16–21, author unknown)

"I pray that, according to the riches of [YHWH's] glory, he may grant that you may be strengthened in your inner being with power through his Spirit, and that [the Messiah] may dwell in your hearts through faith, as you are being rooted and grounded in love. I pray that you may have the power to comprehend, with all the saints, what is the breadth and length and height and depth, and to know the love of [the Messiah] that surpasses knowledge, so that you may be filled with all the fullness of God.

"Now to him who by the power at work within us is able to accomplish abundantly far more than all we can ask or imagine, to him be glory in the church and in [Messiah] Jesus to all generations, forever and ever. Amen."

Pricilla's prayer of blessing (Hebrews 13:20–21)

"Now may the God of peace, who brought back from the dead our Lord Jesus . . . make you complete in everything good so that you may do his will, working among us that which is pleasing in his sight, through [Messiah] Jesus, to whom be glory forever and ever. Amen."

John's prayer of saints around YHWH's throne (Revelation 11:17–18

"We give you thanks, Lord God Almighty, who are and who were, for you have taken your great power and begun to reign. The nations raged, but your wrath has come, and the time for judging the dead, for rewarding your servants, the prophets and saints and all who fear your name, both small and great."

Bibliography

Bartlett, Anthony W. *Virtually Christian: How Christ Changes Human Meaning and Makes Creation New.* O-Books, 2011.

Bellah, Robert N., et al. *Habits of the Heart: Individualism and Commitment in American Life.* Harper and Row, 1985.

Borg, Marcus. *Evolution of the Word: The New Testament in the Order the Books Were Written.* HarperOne, 2012.

Borg, Marcus and N.T. Wright. *The Meaning of Jesus.* HarperOne, 2007.

Crossan, John Dominic. *God and Empire: Jesus Against Rome, Then and Now.* HarperOne, 2008.

Dear, John. *Lazarus Come Forth.* Orbis Books, 2011.

Douglass, James W. *The Nonviolent Coming of God.* Orbis Books, 1991.

Dreher, Rod. *Crunchy Cons: The New Conservative Counterculture and Its Return to Roots.* Three Rivers Press, 2006.

Fairfield, John. *The Healer Messiah: Turning Enemies into Trustworthy Opponents.* Self-published at www.rruuaacchh.org, 2014.

Harink, Douglas. *Paul among the Postliberals.* Brazos Press, 2003.

Hays, Richard B. and Stefan Alkier, eds. *Revelation and the Politics of Apocalyptic Interpretation.* Baylor University Press, 2013.

Holy Bible New Revised Standard Version. Zondervan, 1989.

Horsley, Richard A. "The Bible and Empires" and "Conclusion." In *In the Shadow of Empire: Reclaiming the Bible as a History of Faithful Resistance,* edited by Richard A. Horsley, 1–8, 177-182. Westminster John Knox Press, 2008.

Horsley, Richard A. *1ˢᵗ Corinthians.* Abingdon Press, 1998.

Howard-Brook, Wes. *"Come Out, My People!" God's Call Out of Empire in the Bible and Beyond.* Orbis Books, 2010.

Kleesmat, Sylvia C. and Brian J. Walsh. *Colossians Remixed: Subverting the Empire.* Inter-Varsity Press, 2004.

Lasch, Christopher. *The True and Only Heaven: Progress and its Critics.* Norton, 1991.

Lohfink, Gerhard. *Jesus and Community.* Fortress Press, 1984.

Myers, Ched. *Binding the Strong Man: A Political Reading of Mark's Story of Jesus.* Orbis Books, 1988.

Reiher, Jim. "Violent Language—a Clue to the Historical Occasion of James." *Evangelical Quarterly.* Vol. LXXXV No. 3. July 2013.

Richard, Pablo. *Apocalypse: A People's Commentary on Revelation.* Orbis, 1995.

Van Steenwyk, Mark. *The Unkingdom of God.* IVP Books, 2013.

Wink, Walter. *Engaging the Powers: Discernment and Resistance in a World of Domination.* Fortress Press, 1992.

Wright, N.T. "Paul's Gospel and Caesar's Empire." In *Paul and Politics: Ekklesia, Israel, Imperium, Interpretation,* edited by Richard A. Horsley,160–183. Trinity International Press, 2000.

Yoder, John Howard. *Politics of Jesus.* Wm. B. Eerdmans, 1972.

Made in the USA
Middletown, DE
08 June 2015